THE ECONOMICS OF WOMEN, MEN, AND WORK

THE ECONOMICS OF WOMEN, MEN, AND WORK

FRANCINE D. BLAU
University of Illinois
 at Urbana-Champaign
Champaign, Illinois

MARIANNE A. FERBER
University of Illinois
 at Urbana-Champaign
Urbana, Illinois

PRENTICE-HALL, Englewood Cliffs, New Jersey 07632

Library of Congress Cataloging-in-Publication Data

BLAU, FRANCINE D.
   The economics of women, men, and work.

   Bibliography: p.
   Includes index.
   1. Women—United States—Economic conditions.
2. Women—United States—Social conditions.   3. Women—
Employment—United States.   4. Housewives—United States.
5. Sexual division of labor—United States.   I. Ferber,
Marianne A., date.   II. Title.
HQ1426.B62 1986   305.3 '0973   85-30746
ISBN 0-13-233719-3
ISBN 0-13-233701-0 (pbk.)

Editorial/production supervision and
   interior design: Janis Oppelt
Cover design: Joe Curcio
Manufacturing buyer: Ed O'Dougherty

Printed in the United States of America
10 9 8 7 6 5 4 3 2 1

ISBN 0-13-233719-3   01
ISBN 0-13-233701-0 {PBK}

Prentice-Hall International (UK) Limited, *London*
Prentice-Hall of Australia Pty. Limited, *Sydney*
Prentice-Hall Canada Inc., *Toronto*
Prentice-Hall Hispanoamericana, S.A., *Mexico*
Prentice-Hall of India Private Limited, *New Delhi*
Prentice-Hall of Japan, Inc., *Tokyo*
Prentice-Hall of Southeast Asia Pte. Ltd., *Singapore*
Editora Prentice-Hall do Brasil, Ltda., *Rio de Janeiro*
Whitehall Books Limited, *Wellington, New Zealand*

For

Larry Kahn
Daniel Blau Kahn
Lisa Blau Kahn

and

Bob Ferber
Don Ferber
Ellen Ferber Rogalin

With love

CONTENTS

Chapter 4
THE ALLOCATION OF TIME BETWEEN
THE HOUSEHOLD AND THE LABOR MARKET   67

Chapter 9
DIFFERENCES IN JOBLESSNESS: DISCOURAGEMENT, FRICTIONAL AND STRUCTURAL UNEMPLOYMENT

Chapter 10
SEX DIFFERENCES IN OTHER COUNTRIES: WHAT CAN WE LEARN FROM INTERNATIONAL COMPARISONS?

PREFACE

This book was written to fill the need for a text that would acquaint students with the findings of recent research on women, men, and work in the labor market and in the household. It is written at a level that should both utilize and enhance students' knowledge of economic concepts and analysis but do so in terms intelligible to those not versed in advanced theory. Even though we assume a knowledge of introductory economics on the part of the reader, an interested and determined individual wanting to learn more about the economic status of women as compared to men could benefit considerably from the material offered here.

The text, used in its entirety, is primarily intended for courses specifically concerned with the economic status of women. We think, however, that this book could be used to good advantage in interdisciplinary women's studies courses, as well as introductory level courses in economic problems. Selected readings would also make a useful supplement to round out a general labor economics course. Lastly, it contains enough information about publications in the field to be of use as a reference work for those not familiar with this rapidly growing body of literature.

Since we have both taught a course on women in the labor market for some time, we believe that the book has benefited from the experience and insights we have gained from our students. We are grateful for their patience and interest while we were developing our ideas. We are also particularly indebted to a rather large and diverse group of colleagues, from a number of disciplines, whose comments were often voluminous and always extremely valuable:

Orley C. Ashenfelter, Princeton University
Nancy S. Barrett, American University
Andrea H. Beller, University of Illinois, Urbana-Champaign
Lourdes Beneria, Rutgers University
Barbara R. Bergmann, University of Maryland
Charles C. Brown, University of Michigan, Ann Arbor
Clair Brown, University of California, Berkeley
Glen G. Cain, University of Wisconsin
Greg J. Duncan, University of Michigan
Paula England, University of Texas, Dallas
Belton M. Fleisher, Ohio State University
Daniel S. Hamermesh, Michigan State University
Joan A. Huber, Ohio State University
Joan R. Kahn, University of North Carolina, Chapel Hill

Lawrence M. Kahn, University of Illinois, Urbana-Champaign
Mark R. Killingsworth, Rutgers University
Shelly J. Lundberg, University of Washington, Seattle
Julie A. Matthaei, Wellesley College
Barbara B. Reagan, Southern Methodist University
Barbara F. Reskin, University of Illinois, Urbana-Champaign
Patricia A. Roos, State University of New York, Stony Brook
Steven H. Sandell, National Commission for Employment Policy
Myra H. Strober, Stanford University
Louise A. Tilly, New School for Social Research
Donald J. Treiman, University of California, Los Angeles
H. F. (Bill) Williamson, University of Illinois, Urbana-Champaign.

Without their help, this book would have had many more deficiencies. For these, as well as for all opinions expressed, we, of course, take complete responsibility.

This list of acknowledgments would be incomplete if we did not also thank Janet L. Norwood, Commissioner of Labor Statistics, for supplying us with unpublished data, and Laura Mayer and Denise Dorigo, the research assistants who helped us track down sources and references. We wish to express particular gratitude to Hope Cook, the very tolerant and competent word processor who valiantly struggled with our numerous drafts that were sent to her in various stages of disarray, and invariably emerged victorious. Finally, we would like to express our gratitude to our editor at Prentice-Hall, Linda Frascino, and for our production editor, Janis Oppelt, for their helpful combination of enthusiastic encouragement and level-headed advice.

F. D. B.
M. A. F.

THE ECONOMICS
OF WOMEN, MEN,
AND WORK

Chapter 1

INTRODUCTION

Courses in economics abound at universities and colleges, and there is an ample supply of texts focusing on the many facets of this discipline. Both these courses and these books increasingly recognize that women play an important role in the economy as workers and consumers and that in many ways their behavior and their problems differ from those of men. However, male patterns often receive the major emphasis and sex differences are, at best, one of the many topics covered. For example, workers are often assumed to enter the labor market after completing their education and to remain until their retirement. Similarly, institutions studied are mainly those involved in traditional labor markets, from businesses to labor unions and relevant government agencies. While women in growing numbers are spending an increasing proportion of their time working for pay, their lives and their world continue to be significantly different from those of men, and much of their time continues to be spent in the nonmarket sector.

In recent years, much attention has been focused on the fact that more than half of all women of working age, and more than half of all married women living with their husbands, are now in the labor market. Much has been made, especially in the popular media, of the often large percentage increases in the number of women in nontraditional occupations, not to mention the publicity received by "the first woman," whether it be stockbroker, jockey, or prime minister. All this tends to obscure the continued importance of traditional nonmarket work for the vast majority of all women, the persistent domination of traditional women's occupations for those in the labor market, the inevitable relationship between these two, and their impact on the status of women. As long as this situation persists, there is a need to address these issues in depth, as is done in this book.

While economic behavior is clearly not isolated from the remainder of human existence, the primary focus of this book is on the economic behavior of women and men, on economic institutions, and on economic outcomes. To refresh the memory of students who have some acquaintance with economics, and to provide a minimal background for those who do not, we begin with a brief introduction to the tools of this discipline. Neoclassical or mainstream economic theory provides the major emphasis of this book. But students should be aware that other schools of thought, such as Marxist and institutional economic theories, also provide valuable insights which we have incorporated to some extent. Students who would like further readings on these alternative approaches will find a useful starting point in some of our references.

WHAT ECONOMICS IS ABOUT

Neoclassical economics is concerned with decision making under conditions of **scarcity**. This means that there are not enough resources to satisfy everyone's wants, and choices have to be made about their use. Given this constraint, it is crucial to recognize that using land, labor, and capital to produce one good results in fewer of these inputs being available for producing other goods. Hence, the real cost of having more of one good is foregoing the opportunity of having more of another.

This concept of **opportunity cost** is fundamental to an understanding of the central **economic problem—how to allocate scarce resources so as to maximize well-being**. In order to make a rational decision whether to spend money to buy a new suit, or whether to spend time going for a hike, it is not sufficient to know how much utility or satisfaction will be derived from each. As long as the amount of money and time is limited, and we cannot buy and do everything, it is crucial also to be aware of how much satisfaction is lost by giving up desirable alternatives. **Rationality**, as economists use the term, involves some knowledge of available opportunities and the terms on which they are available. Only on the basis of such information is it possible to weigh the alternatives and choose those that provide more utility than any others.

It is one of the most fundamental assumptions in traditional economics that people may be expected to behave rationally in this sense. This does not mean, as critics have occasionally suggested, that only monetary costs and benefits are considered. It is entirely rational to take into account nonpecuniary factors since it is *satisfaction,* not, say, money income, that is to be maximized. This definition is so broad that almost everyone might be expected to behave this way. Nonetheless, this cannot be taken for granted. It is not satisfactory simply to argue that whatever a person does must provide more satisfaction than any other alternative course of action would have, because otherwise he or she would have made a different choice. Such an argument amounts to a mere tautology. An individual who does not have the prerequisite knowledge, who blindly follows the traditional course of action without considering costs and benefits, who fails to consider long-run implications or indirect effects, is not necessarily rational. Nor is it uncommon to find persons who, with surprising regularity, make choices which they presently appear to regret. Most of us have probably known someone whose behavior fits one or more of these patterns.

These facts should be kept in mind, lest we accept too readily that whatever people do must be for the best. On the other hand, as a first approximation it is probably more realistic to assume that people tend to try to maximize their well-being, rather than that they are indifferent to it. We shall, for the most part, accept this as a reasonable generalization, while recognizing that it is not necessarily appropriate in every instance. Specifically, it must be kept in mind that the knowledge needed to make optimal decisions is often difficult and costly to obtain. When this cost is likely to exceed the gain derived, it is rational to "satisfice"[1] rather than to insist on maximization. By the same token, however, when additional information can be provided relatively cheaply and easily, it is likely to be useful in improving decision making.

USES OF ECONOMIC THEORY

Assuming that individuals are rational is only one of the many simplifying assumptions economists tend to make in formulating **theories** and building **models**. The justification for this is that much like laboratory experiments in the biological and physical sciences, these abstractions help to focus attention on the particular issue we are attempting to clarify and on the main relationships we want to understand.

---

[1]This concept was first proposed by Herbert Simon, *Models of Man* (New York: Wiley, 1957). He argued that when the knowledge needed to make optimal decisions is difficult and costly to obtain, an individual may be content with selecting a "satisfactory" alternative—one that meets a minimum standard of acceptability.

In many instances, the approach is explicitly to examine the effects of changes in a single variable, say, price or income, while assuming that all else remains the same. This is not to suggest that economists believe that is the case in the real world. An aerospace engineer finds it useful to test a plane in a tunnel where everything except wind speed is artificially stabilized, even though the vehicle will later have to fly in an environment where temperature, atmospheric pressure and humidity will change. Similarly, the social scientist finds it helpful to begin by abstracting from numerous complications.

A theory is not intended to be a full description of the underlying reality. A description is like a photograph which shows reality in all its details. A theory may be likened to a modern painting which, at most, shows the broad outlines of its subject but may provide deeper insight than a more realistic picture would. Hence, a theory or model should not be judged primarily on its detailed resemblance to reality, but rather in terms of the extent to which it enables us to grasp the salient features of that reality. Thus, economic theory, at its best, can help us to understand the present and to correctly predict the future.

Economists should not, therefore, be faulted for making simplifying assumptions or using abstractions, as long as they are aware of what they are doing and test their conclusions against empirical evidence, which is drawn from the real world with all its complexities. Unfortunately, this is not always easy to do. Computers now enable us to process vast amounts of information, and econometricians have made substantial progress in developing better methods for doing so. The availability, timeliness, and quality of the data, however, still leaves much to be desired.

Collecting data is a slow, expensive, and generally unglamorous undertaking. The U.S. government does more and better work in this respect than those of many other countries. Even so, by the time information is collected, compiled, or published, it is not uncommon for it to be as much as two years later. Some data are, in any case, only collected intermittently, others not at all. For a variety of reasons, including the government's appropriate reluctance to invade certain areas, as well as lack of interest in pursuing topics with no strong political constituency, there are some substantial gaps in official data collection. Private research organizations have endeavored to fill these to a degree, but they are even more likely to be constrained by lack of necessary funds. The data from such special surveys are particularly likely to be collected sporadically or at lengthy intervals. In spite of these difficulties, the possibilities for empirical work have improved beyond the wildest dreams of economists of even one or two generations ago.

When suitable data are available, evidence for some relationships can be obtained using such simple devices as averages and cross-tabulations. In other instances, however, very sophisticated statistical methods are required to analyze the data. Such studies are time consuming and rarely are conclusions from any one such study regarded as final. At times there are ambiguities, when different sets of data or various approaches produce inconsistent results. But these too enhance the progress of science, for they help us to identify important areas for future research.

Because of these difficulties of data collection and analysis, timely and definitive answers are simply not available for every question. We have, however, done our best to summarize existing knowledge on each topic considered in this book.

THE SCOPE OF ECONOMICS

Traditionally, and for the most part even today, economics has focused on the market and on the government. In the market, goods and services are sold. Government is itself a major buyer and seller of goods and services and also an agent that regulates and otherwise influences the economy. Only in recent decades have mainstream economists devoted any significant attention to the allocation of time within the household itself, and even now such material is not always included in general economics courses. Also, the value of nonmarket household production is ignored when aggregate indicators of economic welfare, like Gross National Product (GNP), are computed. This is a matter for concern because women play the dominant role in the nonmarket sector.

The typical introductory economics course in its microeconomics section puts primary emphasis on the analysis of product market transactions with the firm as seller, concerned with maximizing profits, and the household as buyer, concerned with maximizing satisfaction or utility. Markets for factors of production, and specifically labor, where it is generally the household that is the supplier and the firm that is the purchaser, are introduced later. As a rule, however, this discussion is a brief portion in the section on factors of production, and most students may well come away with a view of the market as chiefly an institution where goods and services are supplied by businesses, and the demand for them comes from the household.

In this book, our interest is specifically in women and men, their work in the labor market and in the household, the interdependence between individuals within the household, and between the household and the market. Therefore, we briefly review supply and demand in this context.[2]

In a market economy, the forces of supply and demand for labor determine both the jobs that will be available and how much workers will be paid for doing them. Much of our analysis throughout this book will be concerned with the determinants of the supply of labor. We shall examine how in-

---

[2]A more detailed review is provided in the Appendix to this chapter.

dividuals and their families decide to allocate their time between housework and market work and how women's changing roles in this regard are affecting their own well-being and that of their families.

Demand is essentially determined by the behavior of employers, who are in turn influenced by the business climate in which they operate. In the simplest case, their goal is to maximize profits and their demand for labor is related to its productivity in making the goods or producing the services sold by the firm. Thus, the firm's demand for labor is **derived** from the demand of consumers for its final product. It is, however, possible that employers depart from the dictates of profit maximization and consider aspects of workers that are not directly related to their productivity. Discrimination against women in the labor market and its role in producing economic inequality between women and men is another topic that we shall explore in some depth.

On the supply side, workers may influence their productivity by attending school or getting training on the job. We shall also consider the determinants of such human capital investment decisions and their role in producing pay differences between female and male workers.

INDIVIDUALS, FAMILIES, AND HOUSEHOLDS

Throughout this book, we shall at times focus on the behavior of families and at other times on that of individuals. A **family** is defined as consisting of two or more persons, related by blood or marriage, living in the same household.[3] It is, of course, the individual that in the last analysis consumes commodities and supplies labor. Nonetheless, it is often appropriate to treat the family as the relevant economic unit. This is because decisions of various members within a family are interdependent, much of their consumption is joint, and it is common for them to pool income. At the same time, it is important not to lose sight of the fact that the composition of families changes as individuals move in and out and that the interests of members of families may diverge to a greater or lesser extent. We shall return to these issues throughout this book as we discuss the status of women and men within the family and in the labor market.

The broader concept of the **household** is also relevant to economic decision-making and is becoming increasingly more so. A household consists of one or more persons living in one dwelling unit and sharing living expenses. Thus, all families are households, but one person households, or those composed of unrelated individuals, are not families. The use of the term household

---

[3]This is the official definition used in government statistics. The typical **nuclear family** is composed of parents and children, but single-parent families are becoming increasingly common. An **extended family**, a type of unit more common in some other societies, may include grandparents, uncles, aunts, and other relatives.

in this book would have been more general and done greater justice to the increasing prevalence of alternative living arrangements. However, since families still comprise a substantial majority of households that include more than one person, and since the term family is both more familiar and connotes a more uniform set of relationships, we have chosen to use it primarily in this book.

OUTLINE OF THE BOOK

As suggested above, the primary focus of this book is on "economic woman," as she interacts and competes with "economic man." Economic behavior is not, however, treated in isolation from the remainder of human existence. To provide a more comprehensive picture, subsequent chapters will reflect insights from other social sciences, which enhance our understanding of a variety of factors. Such noneconomic factors help to determine economic behavior and how that behavior, in turn, helps to shape other aspects of life.

Chapter 2 deals with the development of the roles of women and men from the earliest days to the present and draws particularly upon the work of anthropologists for the prehistoric period. The contributions of sociologists are especially relevant to the discussion of the family, allocation of responsibilities within it, and allocation of time between the household and the labor market discussed in the following two chapters. Research done by sociologists and psychologists is crucial to the analysis of the impact of women's employment on the family provided in Chapter 5.

The next four chapters deal specifically with women's positions in the labor market as compared to that of men, beginning with an overview of occupations and earnings and going on to an in-depth examination of the various explanations of the existing situation. Chapter 7 reviews the human capital approach, while Chapter 8 concentrates on discrimination as a cause of women's lower economic status. Chapter 9 rounds out the picture by providing information on individuals in the labor market who are unable to find jobs and exploring the reasons for differentials in the unemployment rates of women and men.

In Chapter 10, we compare the economic status of women relative to men in other countries, with special emphasis on similarities and differences between them and the United States. Substantial differences in behaviors suggest that particular outcomes are not inevitable but rather subject to choice by each society. In those instances where a country appears to have impressive achievements to its credit, we may be able to learn from the experiences there.

Throughout this book, but especially in those segments where we deal with policy, as we do in portions of several chapters, we are confronted by a dilemma common to the social sciences. On the one hand, much of what we present is positive, rather than normative, in the sense that we present facts and research results as we find them. Further, we try to avoid normative or prescriptive attitudes, for personal values should not be permitted to intrude upon objective analysis. On the other hand, it is unrealistic to claim that the choice of topics, the emphasis in discussions, and the references provided are, or even can be, entirely value-free. A reasonable solution is to try to present various sides of controversial questions, to make clear that different premises will lead to different conclusions, and that the policies one should adopt depend on the goals one wants to reach. This is the approach we attempt to follow.

Nonetheless, the tenor of this book is undoubtedly colored by our predilection for neoclassical economics and by our feminist perspective. Because of the former, we rely heavily on an analytical framework shaped by mainstream economics. We do, however, take account of institutional factors more than many of our colleagues might and, occasionally, refer to radical and Marxist interpretations. The latter means we recognize the extent to which persons of the same sex may differ, and persons of the opposite sex may be similar. It means we believe that, as much as possible, individuals should have the opportunity to live up to their particular potential, rather than to be forced to conform to stereotypically male or female roles. Most of all, it means that while recognizing differences between women and men, some possibly caused by biological factors and others by the way girls and boys are reared in our society, we are less inclined to emphasize the barriers that divide them than the common humanity that joins them.

A REVIEW OF SUPPLY AND DEMAND IN THE LABOR MARKET

As explained in Chapter 1, supply and demand provide economists with a framework for analyzing labor markets. We briefly review these concepts here in the context of a particular type of labor, clerical workers.

Curve *DD* in Figure 1.1 shows the typical downward sloping **demand curve**. Wage rate (price) is on the vertical axis and quantity is on the horizontal axis. The demand curve represents the various amounts of labor that would be hired at various prices by firms in this labor market over a given period of time. Everything else remaining the same, including methods of production and prices of other inputs, changes in the wage rate cause movements along this curve. There is a change in the *quantity demanded* but demand (that is, the demand curve) remains the same. If, on the other hand, everything else does not remain the same, the entire demand curve may be shifted.

Demand curves normally slope downward to the right, which means that the firm will hire more workers at a lower wage rate and fewer at a higher wage rate. There are several reasons for this. The first is that in the short run there is **diminishing marginal productivity** of labor, meaning that additional units of labor provide progressively less additional output when combined with given

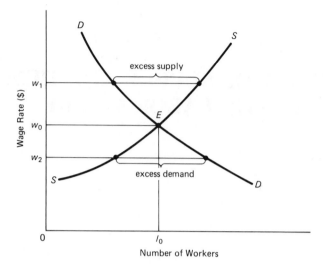

FIGURE 1.1 The Market for Clerical Workers

amounts of capital (plant and equipment). The second is the **substitution effect**. When the price of a particular input changes, while that of a potential substitute remains the same, there will be a tendency for profit-maximizing employers to use more of the one that is now relatively cheaper and less of the one that is now relatively more expensive. In the short run, for example, less-skilled labor may be substituted for skilled workers. In the long run, it may be possible to substitute capital for labor. Last, there is the **scale effect** which may also operate in both the short- and long-run. As wages increase, the price of the product will go up, less of it will be purchased, and fewer workers will be employed. The scale effect is likely to be especially large when wages constitute a substantial part of the costs of production. These are the factors that cause the quantity of labor hired to decrease as the wage rate increases, but the movements are along the given demand curve and do not involve a shift in demand.

The **supply curve** shown by SS in Figure 1.1 slopes upward and to the right. It shows the number of workers who would be willing to do clerical work at all possible prices. The supply is upward sloping because if rewards for one skill increase, while all others remain the same, additional workers will be attracted from other related occupations. So, for example, an increase in the wages of clerical workers may induce individuals who are currently employed in other jobs to improve their clerical skills and compete for clerical positions. Similarly, if pay for clerical work declines relative to others, the quantity of labor supplied to clerical jobs is expected to decline as workers move to other sectors.

It is important to emphasize that the supply curve depicted in Figure 1.1 represents the number of individuals available for a particular line of work. As we shall see in greater detail in Chapter 4, the number of hours supplied to the market by any particular individual may not increase when wages rise. This is because, at a higher wage rate, an individual who participates in the labor market may choose to allocate more of his or her time to nonmarket activities and the satisfactions they bring.

The intersection of the supply and demand curves shown in Figure 1.1 represents a **stable equilibrium**. An equilibrium is a situation where all persons willing to work at the going rate are able to find employment, and all employers willing to hire someone at the going rate are able to find workers. In other words, the quantity demanded and supplied are equal at E so that there are no forces causing the wage to move from its present level, as long as there are no external shocks. In this case, the equilibrium wage is w_0, and the equilibrium quantity of labor employed is l_0.

As noted above, Figure 1.1 shows not only an equilibrium, but a stable equilibrium. Let us assume that, for whatever reason, the wage rate is initially set higher than w_0, say at w_1. At this point, the quantity of labor supplied would exceed the quantity of labor demanded and push wages down toward E. Conversely, if wages were initially set at w_2, the opposite would be true. In short, we have a stable equilibrium where there is no tendency to move away from E. If an external shock did cause a deviation, there would be a tendency to return toward that point.

External shocks may, of course, also cause shifts in either demand, supply, or both, leading to a new equilibrium. Such shocks may come from changes in markets for goods, for nonlabor inputs, or for other types of labor, and are extremely common. Therefore, a stable equilibrium is not necessarily one that remains fixed for any length of time. It merely means that at any given time there is a tendency toward convergence at the point where the quantity of labor supplied equals the quantity of labor demanded, until conditions cause this point to shift.

It may be instructive to consider a couple of examples where there are shifts in the supply or demand curves. These sample situations can help to clarify the difference between factors that cause a movement along an existing supply or demand curve and those that cause a shift in the entire curve. We shall also be able to see how the new equilibrium position is established.

Suppose that the government issues a report on the dangers of credit spending and that it is effective enough to cause a reduction in the demand for such services provided by the banking industry. That is, at any given price of these services, consumers demand less of them. Since this industry employs a substantial number of clerical workers, this would cause a marked inward shift

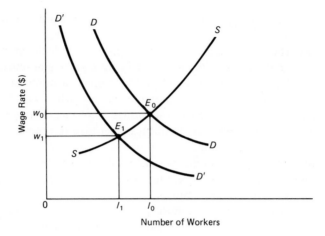

FIGURE 1.2a   A Shift in Demand

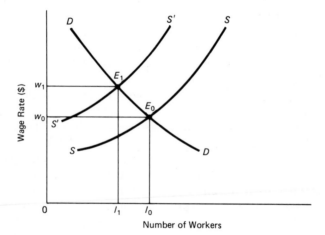

FIGURE 1.2b   A Shift in Supply

in the market-wide demand curve for clerical workers, from *DD* to *D'D'* in Figure 1.2a. That is, at any given wage rate, firms are willing to hire fewer clerical workers. This illustrates that the demand for labor is a *derived* demand: it is derived from the consumer demand for the goods and services that the workers produce. A new equilibrium will occur at E_1, where the quantity of labor supplied again equals the (new) quantity of labor demanded. At E_1, fewer individuals are employed as clerical workers and a lower wage rate is determined for that occupation.

Shifts in supply curves can also alter the market equilibrium as shown in Figure 1.2b. For instance, suppose that the government's antidiscrimination policies increase opportunities for women in managerial jobs, raising their wages, and making it easier for them to obtain such employment. This will result in a reduction in the supply (inward shift in the supply curve) of clerical workers, an occupation primarily staffed by women. At any given wage, fewer women would be willing to work in clerical jobs than previously. At the new equilibrium (E_1), the wages are higher, and the number of workers employed is lower than in the initial situation (E_0). This illustrates that improved opportunities for women in traditionally male jobs can potentially improve the economic welfare even of those women who remain in traditionally female pursuits.

Chapter 2

WOMEN AND MEN: CHANGING ROLES IN A CHANGING ECONOMY

It seems to me that an economic interpretation of history is an indispensable element in the study of society, but it is only one element. In layers below it lie geography, biology and psychology, and in layers above it the investigation of social and political relationships and the history of culture, law and religion.

Joan Robinson, *Freedom and Necessity**

We are constantly told today that we live in an era of rapid change— change in economic conditions, in economic and social institutions, in mores and beliefs. And so we do. Changes in the roles of women and men, their relations to each other, and the nature of the families in which most of them continue to live have been taking place at a speed that, quite possibly, is unprecedented. This situation has inevitably created stresses and strains. Not surprisingly, people who feel insecure in a world of shifting boundaries and values are prone to look back with a great deal of nostalgia to the "good old

---

*Joan Robinson, *Freedom and Necessity: An Introduction to the Study of Society* (London: George Allen and Unwin, Ltd., 1970), p. 5. Reprinted by permission.

days" when women were women, and men were men, and both knew their proper place.

How realistic is this picture some hold of traditional gender roles, unchanging for all time, and pervasive for all places, which is supposed to have existed before the recent era of turmoil and upheaval? The answer to this question has substantial practical implications. If the same roles of women and men have existed always and everywhere, some may conclude that these roles are biologically determined and that they probably cannot, and perhaps should not, be changed. If, on the other hand, there has been a good deal of variation in the roles of men and women over time, it is likely that there is also room for flexibility now and in the future.

For this reason, it is particularly important to gain some insight into the nature of gender roles through the course of human development. There are, of course, other reasons as well. Some awareness of the complexities of history is indispensable for an understanding of the present. It is also crucial if we are to make any progress towards correctly anticipating the future. In our brief historical review, we shall find, while the pace may have been a great deal slower in the past, there has always been change. Societies, throughout time, have been characterized by an astonishing diversity of economic and social institutions.

We begin by considering the biological and anthropological evidence about the nature of males and females. This takes us somewhat far afield from traditional economics but provides valuable background for the historical analysis that follows. Here we consider the changing roles of men and women in the household and in the economy, and the evolution of the family in the course of economic development, into the period of industrialization in the nineteenth and twentieth centuries. While other factors are not ignored, economic causation is assigned the predominant role in the shaping of these changes. The focus during the most recent periods is on the United States.

THE NATURE OF MALES AND FEMALES

As recently as the 1970s, a common interpretation of the behavior of, and relation between, men and women emphasized the importance of the biological maternal function of the female in determining the nature and content of her being.[1] In this view, a woman's early life is a preparation for becoming, and her later life is devoted to being, a successful wife and mother. Accordingly, her nature is compliant, not competitive, nurturant, not instrumental. Her activities, while not necessarily confined to the home at least center around it, for

[1] See, for example, Lionel Tiger, *Men in Groups* (N.Y.: Random House, 1969).

her primary mission is to be a helpmate to her husband and to provide a warm and safe haven for her family. If she does work for pay, she will do best in jobs compatible with her household responsibilities and her "feminine" personality. Men, on the other hand, are not constrained by their paternal function from fully entering the world outside the home. On the contrary, their natural role as provider and protector spurs them on to greater efforts.

The popular perception based, to an extent, on the work of earlier researchers[2] has often been that investigations of male and female roles among nonhuman species provided support for the view that biology is destiny. Therefore, we too begin with a brief look at animals and their behavior. More recent research suggests that no generalization holds for all species and, thus, that extrapolation from animal studies does not support the traditional view. Before summarizing this evidence, we consider the question of why researchers' perceptions of animal behavior have changed over time.

In this area, as in others, scientists confront the problem that their subjective expectations tend to influence how they interpret particular situations and what they notice about them.[3] For example, one male with a group of females is traditionally viewed as the ruler of a dependent harem. Alternatively, it may be a group of dominant females who have no use for more than one male for breeding purposes. Similarly, while attention is frequently focused on individual males who play a dominant role, it goes unnoticed that even the highest ranking ones may be routed by a group of females who gang up to chase them if they, for instance, disturb the young.

When most researchers were male and, whether male or female, held traditional views of appropriate sex roles among humans, they tended to see confirmation of these views in their observations of animal behavior. As more women have joined the ranks of researchers, and as both men and women have been influenced by changing sex roles in human society, perceptions of animal behavior have accordingly been revised. The new view that has emerged, reflecting as it does a process of reexamination and more careful scrutiny of the evidence, probably can be given more credence than earlier ones. The process of re-evaluation and revision is illustrated in more detail in a summary of current developments in the study of primates in the Inset to this chapter beginning on page 18.

Among lower animals, as opposed to mammals, even the minimal distinction that individuals are either male or female does not always hold.[4]

---

[2]Foremost among these have been Robert Ardrey, *The Territorial Imperative* (N.Y.: Athenum Press, 1966); Desmond Morris, *The Human Zoo* (N.Y.: McGraw-Hill, 1969); Lionel Tiger and Robin Fox, *The Imperial Animal* (N.Y.: Holt, Rinehart and Winston, 1971).

[3]This problem is noted in Gordon H. Orians, "On the Evolution of Mating Systems in Birds and Mammals," eds. William van der Kloot, Charles Wolcott, and Benjamin Dane, *Readings in Behavior* (N.Y.: Holt, Rinehart and Winston, Inc., 1974), pp. 232–47; and Jane B. Lancaster, "In Praise of the Achieving Female Monkey," *Psychology Today* 7, no. 4 (Sept. 1973): 3236–99.

[4]Some information on various animal species is provided, for instance, in Janet S. Chafetz,

Hermaphrodites, where each partner in copulation acts as male and female simultaneously, prevail among snails. Some worms are male, until they reach a particular length, then become female.

The extent to which the sexes differ in appearance also varies greatly. Among insects and birds, the female is often much larger. Among birds, the male is often more colorful. Charles Darwin believed, as do many modern sociobiologists, that this developed because of the preferences of females who choose the most decorative species for mating, thus perpetuating the trait.[5] At times, characteristics confined to males among prehistoric species, such as antlers, later appear among females as well. Among many animals, males and females are so much alike in physical characteristics that even experts have difficulty telling them apart.[6]

Similarly, there are extreme variations in male and female behavior by species and often within species depending on their environment. Some are highly male-dominant, some female-dominant, others rather egalitarian. Furthermore, how groups are characterized depends on the type of dominance being measured. In general, males tend to be aggressive about acquiring and defending territory, but females are often extremely ferocious about protecting the young.

Even when it comes to care of their offspring, behavior is far from uniform. In lower animal forms, such as fish, it is common for the young not to receive any care from either parent, while both father and mother birds generally participate in caring for their infants. Female mammals, of course, nurse the new born, but there are species where the mothers hardly bother beyond that. Among many primates, on the other hand, there is at least some "fathering" and the marmoset father carries the infant at all times except when it is feeding.

Much of the research on sex roles among animals has, in fact, concentrated on primates because they are closer to humans than the others. Even there, however, sweeping generalizations are rarely justified. The behavior of these animals is typically dimorphic (that is, certain types of behavior are more typical of one sex than the other). But these differences are generally a matter of degree, not of kind, and there is much overlap. Only among some species, such as rhesus monkeys, are males far more aggressive and belligerent than females. Nor do differences in behavior necessarily mean that females are

Masculine, Feminine, or Human? (Itasca, Ill.: Peacock Publishers, 1978); Lancaster, "In Praise of the Achieving Female Monkey;" and Clarice S. Stoll, *Female and Male Socialization, Social Roles and Social Structure* (Dubuque, Iowa: Wm. Brown Co., 1974).

[5]R. C. Lewontin, Steven Rose, and Leon J. Kamin, *Not in Our Genes* (N.Y.: Pantheon Books, 1984), p. 158. These authors also scathingly attack the whole view that male dominance is the inevitable product of our biology and dispute various types of evidence used—from brain size and structure to hormones.

[6]This is not usually a problem among humans, but for the International Olympic Games chromosomal identification is required to determine the sex of contestants (John Money, *International Encyclopedia of Social Sciences*, 1969, Vol. 14, pp. 209–15).

socially inferior. Only among some species, especially baboons and rhesus monkeys, is there a rigidly hierarchical social structure dominated by highly aggressive males. It is particularly interesting that among chimpanzees, the most socially advanced nonhuman primates, females do not appear to occupy a subordinate position. Harem-like groups with dominant males are entirely unknown.[7]

These examples should suffice to make anyone cautious about the argument that any attribute or behavior is always male or female, even if generalizing from animals to humans were otherwise acceptable. But this is, itself, a debatable point. An alternative approach suggests that what distinguishes "homo sapiens" from other species is that, for humans, it is primarily the norms and expectations of their societies, not blind animal instincts, that are important in shaping their actions and their relations. In this view, biology constrains, but does not determine, human behavior. Human gender roles are no more limited to those of animals than is human behavior otherwise limited to that of animals.[8]

There are, to be sure, physiological and psychological differences between men and women, but, it is argued, they do not adequately explain all existing variations in behavior or why female traits are so often viewed as socially inferior to male traits. Biological nature, which determines the difference between the sexes, is seen as a broad base upon which a variety of structures, with respect to socially determined gender differences, can be built. This hypothesis is consistent with the diverse male and female roles that sprang up under varying conditions in early societies, in spite of the fact that some differentiation of the work and roles of men and women seem to have been present in all known instances. Recently, anthropologists of this school have pointed out that women vary in their social roles and powers, their public status, and their cultural definitions and that the nature, quality, and social significance of women's activities are far more varied and interesting than has often been assumed.

SEX ROLES AMONG PRIMATES: CHANGING VIEWS

As interest in sex roles among humans has been growing, a large number of scholars, many of them women, have also been studying male and female behavior

[7]Edward O. Wilson, *Sociobiology: The New Synthesis* (Cambridge, MA: The Belhuan Press of Harvard University Press, 1975).

[8]See anthropologists such as Ernestine Friedl, *Women and Men. An Anthropologists' View* (N.Y.: Holt, Rinehart and Winston, Inc., 1975), and Michelle Z. Rosaldo and Louise Lamphere, eds., *Women, Culture and Society* (Stanford: Stanford University Press, 1974).

among animals, particularly primates. Excerpts from an interesting report on recent developments in this field* are presented below.

> An explosion of knowledge about monkeys and apes is overturning long-held stereotypes about sex roles and social patterns among the closest kin to humans in the animal world . . . The new body of research has shown that, although male dominance of groups is common, females of many species are fiercely competitive, resourceful and independent, sexually assertive and promiscuous and, in some cases, more prone than males to wanderlust at puberty.
>
> Soon after the advent of modern primate studies in the early 1960's, many scientists believed they had discovered the key to primate social systems when they described hierarchies of aggressive males competing for the right to mate with seemingly passive females, whose roles appeared limited to the bearing of the young . . .
>
> "It was as if scientists had projected onto primates a mirror image of the social structure of an American corporation or university," said Sarah Blaffer Hrdy of the University of California at Davis, a leader in the reappraisal of primate behavior . . .
>
> A common thread through the new findings is that the fundamental evolutionary demand—that parents successfully pass on their genes—imposes different reproductive strategies and behaviors on males and females. But beyond this, Dr. [Jane B.] Lancaster [of the University of Oklahoma] concludes, "It is virtually impossible to generalize about what male primates do or how female primates act." For each species, sex roles have been shaped differently according to its evolutionary history and ecological setting . . .
>
> Efforts to draw lessons about humans from other primates go to the heart of the age-old debate about nature versus nurture—the respective influences of inborn traits and environment on human behavior. This controversy has heated up over the last 15 years with the advent of sociobiology, which studies how evolutionary pressures cause behavior patterns as well as physical traits to become encoded genetically in animals. Though they deny the charge, some sociobiologists, because of their willingness to speculate about innate human behavioral tendencies on the basis of animal studies, have been accused of promoting a new form of biological determinism.
>
> Most scientists, including many who regard themselves as sociobiologists, reject the notion that the genetic component of human behavior can be isolated. They say human genes determine a biological range of capacity, the expression of which is realized only through environmental influences. In the words of Stephen Jay Gould, a professor at Harvard University, "Biology and culture are inextricable and co-determinant."
>
> The recent field studies have raised questions about the extent to which social behavior is genetically fixed even in wild primates. "We used to talk about 'the monkey' or 'the baboon,'" Dr. Lancaster noted, "but now we've seen that all baboons don't act the same."
>
> A group's ecological setting, its demographic makeup and even its history and traditions—transmitted from one generation to the next by learning rather than genetics—have all been found to influence primate behavior . . .
>
> Dr. Hrdy holds the view . . . that evolution has predisposed human

*Erik Eckholm, "New View of Female Primates Assails Stereotypes," *The New York Times,* September 18, 1984, pp. 17-18. Copyright © 1984 by The New York Times Company. Reprinted by permission.

females, like males, not only to intelligence and assertiveness but also to competitiveness. Thus, while attacking old stereotypes that devalue the capacities of women, she also disputes . . . "countermyths that emphasize woman's natural innocence from lust for power, her cooperativeness and solidarity with other women."

. . . The change in perceptions about primates has coincided with ferment in thinking about sex roles in human society and with the entry of women into primate studies in numbers unusually high for the sciences. In addition to the famous field studies of chimpanzees by Jane Goodall and gorillas by Dian Fossey, many women have made important theoretical contributions to primatology. Intriguing questions have been raised about whether social trends and the sex of scientists have affected the course of "objective" science.

Leading primatologists of both sexes agree that men have played key roles in the recent redefining of primate behavior. And the advances in understanding can be explained innocently enough.

Dr. Sherwood L. Washburn of the University of California at Berkeley, who is regarded as the father of modern primate studies, noted that serious field work began only in the early 1960's. "When you get in the field, the obvious creature is the big, dominant male," he said. "The behaviors that were easiest to see were exaggerated in the initial studies. But I don't think this was the result of any bias."

Still, questions about the possible effects on science of a changing social milieu persist. Dr. Hrdy believes that improved methodology, the broad questioning of sexual stereotypes by the women's liberation movement (influencing scientists of both sexes), and the infusion of female scientists have all contributed to the new understanding of primate societies.

FACTORS INFLUENCING WOMEN'S RELATIVE STATUS

In their studies of human societies, anthropologists, particularly the female anthropologists who have given more of their attention to this issue, agree that the relative status of women has varied over time and across societies. There is less consensus on the factors determining their relative position. It is our view that while it may not be possible to definitively answer this question at present, some important insights can be gained by considering existing theories.

One anthropologist, Ernestine Friedl,[9] has emphasized the importance of environmental constraints in shaping human organization. She argues that the technology employed by a society to produce the necessities of life has tended, in the past, to determine the division of labor on the basis of sex. In turn, she

---

[9]Friedl, *Women and Men*. See also Joan Huber and Glenna Spitze, *Sex Stratification: Children, Housework, and Jobs* (N.Y.: Academic Press, 1983).

believes that the more important women's role in production and in controlling distribution outside the family, the higher their status compared to men. Friedl, and others espousing this view, point to the relatively egalitarian situation in primitive societies where men and women shared in providing food, clothing, and shelter for their families, or, in modern days, when both earn an income. In contrast, the status of men and women was very unequal in societies where men provided all the needed resources, and women devoted themselves to transforming these resources into usable form and creating a pleasant atmosphere in which they could be used.

Others tend to disagree, at least with the emphasis on the importance of production roles in determining status. In past epochs, slaves did a great deal of productive work without achieving correspondingly high status, and members of the upper class derived their power and prestige from ownership of wealth rather than any work they did. There is little dispute about the fact that property gives owners power over distribution and that this helps to determine status.

We are inclined toward the view that the structure of social relationships and participation in productive work both play a role. Specifically, in the case of women, it appears that sharing in the provision for the family's needs is a necessary, though not a sufficient, ingredient in achieving a greater degree of equality.[10] Clearly, as Michelle Rosaldo[11] points out, the extent to which women's activities are confined to the home, while men monopolize the public sphere, also plays an important role.

In the remainder of this chapter, we explore different human societies and the effect that changing technology and changing property relations have had on the nature and perception of gender roles.

WOMEN'S ROLES AND ECONOMIC DEVELOPMENT

Hunting and Gathering Societies[12]

In the most primitive economies, food was obtained entirely from what nature provided in the form of plants and animals. In general, women tended to gather berries, seeds, and other vegetable foods, perhaps hunted some small

[10]Joyce M. Nielson, *Sex in Society: Perspectives on Stratification* (Belmont, CA: Wadsworth, 1978).

[11]Michelle Z. Rosaldo, "Women, Culture, and Society: A Theoretical Overview," eds. Rosaldo and Lamphere, *Women, Culture, and Society.* See also, Julie A. Matthaei, *An Economic History of Women in America* (N.Y.: Schocken Books, 1982).

[12]Among the anthropological texts that discuss early societies and emphasize the development of male and female roles are Friedl, *Women and Men,* and Charlotte G. O'Kelly, *Women and Men in Society* (N.Y.: D. Van Nostrand Co., 1980).

animals and did occasional fishing. They also prepared all food and had full responsibility for the care of small children.

Men specialized in hunting large animals and in warfare—activities that required not only physical strength but long absences from home. Most likely, each group produced the relatively primitive tools needed for their pursuits—vessels for gathering and cooking on the one hand, weapons that could be used to slay animals or people on the other. At a time when the birth rate had to be high to maintain a population with a very high death rate, and life expectancy was correspondingly short, women's participation in enterprises taking them far from home may have been incompatible with their reproductive function. Thus, such a division of labor was no doubt expedient when women were pregnant or nursing most of their adult lives, and the greater strength of men gave them a considerable advantage for such activities as hunting large animals and fighting.

The extent to which men and women contributed to the necessities of life differed depending on the availability of various resources. In extreme cases, such as the areas in the Arctic where animals were virtually the only source of food, women's contributions were minimal. In areas where game was scarce, they provided almost all of the provisions that constituted the regular diet.

Two striking facts emerge when these widely varying societies are examined. The greater the share of the necessities of life provided by women, the more modest the difference in the status of the sexes. This was true with respect to the disparity in the right to initiate or to terminate marriage and in the extent of personal autonomy. The larger the contribution of women, the more they were perceived as productive and capable of independent action and independent existence. The common payment of a bride price by men who wanted to acquire a wife is one illustration of the recognition of their economic value. On the other hand, even this transaction took place between men—the father and the groom—with the woman only the object. Nowhere was there complete equality between men and women. Everywhere women were excluded from certain crucial economic and political activities.

It has been suggested that one reason for this disparity was that meat, largely provided by men, was everywhere regarded as the prestige food, possibly because of its high nutritive value. It was generally distributed and exchanged by men both in *and outside* the household, while women only provided for the daily needs of their own families. The opportunity to bestow and barter valuable goods helped men to create larger networks for themselves, and conferred prestige and power upon them. It may also be that the excitement and heroics of big game hunting and fighting promoted an aura and ethic of male dominance over women, whose work must have seemed dull and routine by comparison. Thus, even where women furnished most of the basics, men's contributions were more glamorous, more highly valued, and, perhaps most importantly, more visible outside the family.

Horticultural and Pastoral Societies

As economic development proceeded, plants were cultivated. At first the tool employed was a hoe, which was gradually replaced by a stick plow. A plow, as we think of it today, had not yet been introduced. The plots were relatively small, more like gardens, and were generally located near the home, making it possible for mothers of young children to tend them. Animals began to be domesticated.

In horticultural societies, warfare and slashing and burning to prepare the ground for planting were exclusively male tasks. Women tended to participate in all other kinds of productive activities, including production for market. They also took part in, and not infrequently dominated, trading. Women usually enjoyed relatively high status not only within the family but, to an extent, even in the public sphere.[13]

Full equality, let alone superiority, of women was, however, not achieved. While the hunter was no longer objectively very important, and provided an increasingly smaller share of the food supply, his image continued to cast its shadow over male and female roles and relationships. Further, this lingering male superiority was to receive considerable reinforcement with the development of agricultural societies.

In pastoral societies, on the other hand, men tended to monopolize the herding of large animals, which generally took them far from home and provided the bulk of what was needed for subsistence. Women had no produce of their own to barter or sell, and were beholden to males for the animal products, which not only were the basis of the daily diet but also were the materials from which clothing and shelter were fashioned. Their contributions were largely confined to tending the primitive equivalent of hearth and home, and females never reached more than a subservient status.

Agricultural Societies

With the adoption of the plow, private landholdings came to be the rule. In most societies, ownership was largely, or even exclusively, vested in men. This, together with the fact that men generally did much of the physically exacting work associated with the use of the plow tended to cause the situation of women to deteriorate. Even though women in agricultural societies often "helped" with tasks in the fields,[14] looked after small animals and gardens,

---

[13]This stage perhaps best illustrates the view that while there was always a division of labor by sex, it was not always hierarchical. See Heidi I. Hartmann, ("Capitalism, Patriarchy, and Job Segregation by Sex," *Signs: Journal of Women in Culture and Society* 1, no. 3, Pt. 2 (Spring 1976): 137–69.

[14]Very poor women also hired themselves out as day laborers, and slave women often did hard field work.

and worked long hours in the home taking care of the needs of large families, disparity in power and influence between the sexes reached a very high degree.[15] The dowry, a price paid by the father of the bride to the groom who undertakes to support her henceforth, and purdah, the practice of hiding women from the sight of men, became common in some of these societies. Both may be viewed as ways of subordinating women as well as manifestations of their subordination, for they ensure women's dependence upon the financial largesse of fathers and husbands.

There was one factor that helped to offset the lowly position for at least a small minority of women. As ownership of land, and to a degree of other assets, created an upper class of landed gentry, membership in that class entailed great wealth and power. Under these conditions birth in the right family conferred status even on women. Property was generally owned and inherited by men, but in the absence of a male heir in a ruling family, a woman might even become head of state.[16] Hence, there were ruling queens, Elizabeth I of England being the best known. In general, however, while upper class females enjoyed a rather luxurious lifestyle, they were mainly seen as producers of children, rarely had influence except as behind-the-scenes manipulators, and were typically used as pawns in political and economic alliances. Only in exceptional cases did women achieve important roles in the economy and in the development of culture, aided by achieving high rank in religious orders in some instances, or by the extended absence of fighting men in others.

Women were also more likely to be partners, albeit unequal ones, among the growing class of merchants and artisans in the urban centers that began to grow along with developing agriculture. They participated in what was, in those early days, truly a family enterprise, generally took charge when the men traveled on business, and often continued to do so after their husband died. Household and work places were not rigidly separated, nor were consumption and production. Father, mother, children, perhaps other relatives, and often apprentices, lived and worked together. Yet, their tasks and responsibilities were determined by their age and by their sex. Whenever the father was present, he was the head of the family enterprise.

---

[15]Women continue to have particularly low status in that part of the world where agriculture probably originated, and has since been dominant, namely the Middle East. Their subordinate status was duly incorporated there as long ago as the Code of Hamurabi in the seventeenth century B.C. See Ilse Siebert, *Women in the Ancient Near East* (N.Y.: Abner Schram, 1974).

[16]Only recently have any women become heads of state who were not born into the position, and even today they tend to come from the upper classes. The proposition that women were always relegated to a more or less inferior status in all primitive societies, and that at least a few attained power and prestige when class structure developed is in sharp contrast to the views propounded by Friedrich Engels in *The Origin of Family, Private Property, and the State* (N.Y.: International Publishers, 1884, reprinted 1972, copyright 1942). His contention was that women were powerful matriarchs during the earlier stages of development (primitive communism) and that it was the development of private property that was the root of the subjugation of women. It should be noted, on the other hand, that Engels' emphasis on the mode of production as basic in shaping the roles of women and men underlies our analysis as well.

Industrialization

As we have seen, women tended to have higher status in horticultural societies than in pastoral and agricultural ones where women's activities came to be increasingly centered within the home. Even so, since much production was concentrated in the household, and women were active participants, they were perceived as productive members of the family. With industrialization, much productive activity was shifted from the home to the factory and to the office. Since women, particularly married women, continued to center their activities around the home for the most part, the perceived importance of their productive role tended to decline, as did their relative status.

However, continued industrialization has incorporated ever-increasing numbers of women into paid employment outside the home, paving the way for what one observer has termed a "subtle revolution"[17] in gender roles. In the following sections, we review this process in greater detail, focusing upon the situation in the United States.

The case of the United States is in some respects unique, even in comparison to other advanced industrialized countries. In particular the frontier experience was shared by only a few of these countries, such as Canada and Australia. Nonetheless, the broad contours of the shifts outlined here are to some extent applicable to many of them. Indeed, the alteration in men's and women's work roles occurring in the United States today may be seen as part of a transformation taking place in much of the industrialized world. (Recent developments in other countries are discussed in greater detail in Chapter 10.)

THE U.S. EXPERIENCE

The Preindustrial Period

In Colonial America, as in other pre-industrial economies, the family enterprise was the dominant economic unit, and production was the major function of the family. Most of the necessities for survival were produced in the household, though some goods were generally produced for sale, in order to be able to purchase some market goods and to accumulate wealth. Cooking, cleaning, care of the young, the old, and the infirm, spinning, weaving, sewing, knitting, soap and candle making, and even simple carpentry were carried on in the home. Much of the food and other raw materials were grown on the farm. All members of the family capable of making any contribution participated in production, but there was always some specialization and division of labor.

Among the nonslave population, men were primarily responsible for

---

[17]Ralph E. Smith, "The Movement of Women into the Labor Force," ed. Ralph E. Smith, *The Subtle Revolution: Women at Work* (Washington, D.C.: The Urban Institute, 1979).

agriculture and occasionally trade, while women did much of the rest of the work including what would today be characterized as "light manufacturing" activity. But this sex-role specialization was by no means complete. Slave women were used to work in the fields. Widows tended to take over the enterprise when the need arose, and in very early days, single women were on occasion given "maidplots." Even though men and women often had different tasks, and the former were more often involved in production for the market and generally owned all property, everyone participated in productive activity. Even aged grandparents would help with tasks that required responsibility and judgement, perhaps also supervise children in carrying out small chores they could adequately perform from a very early age.

All family members, except for infants, had the same economic role. They either contributed goods and services directly or earned money by selling some of these in the market. The important economic role of children, as well as the plentiful availability of land, encouraged large families. High infant mortality rates provided a further incentive to bear many children. In the eighteenth century, completed fertility may have averaged as many as eight to ten births per woman.[18]

Wealthy women were primarily managers, not just workers, within the household. This was, no doubt, a less arduous and possibly a more rewarding task but one no less absorbing. For these women, as for the more numerous less affluent ones, there was little role conflict. The ideal of the frugal, industrious housewife, working alongside all her family, corresponded closely to reality. The only women for whom this was not true were very poor women, who often become indentured servants and, of course, black women, who were generally slaves. The former were, as a rule, not permitted to marry during their years of servitude, the latter might potentially have their family entirely disrupted by their owners' choice. Both had to work very hard, and slaves did not even have the modest legal protection of rights that indentured servants enjoyed.

The one thing all these diverse groups had in common was that they were productive members of nearly self-sufficient households. While there was some exchange of goods and services, chiefly barter, it was only well into the nineteenth century that production outside the home, for sale rather than for direct use, came to dominate the economy.

Industrialization

During the early period of industrialization in the late eighteenth and early nineteenth centuries, women in the United States, like elsewhere, worked

---

[18]For a description of demographic trends, see Karl E. Taeuber and James A. Sweet, "Family and Work: The Social Life Cycle of Women," ed. Juanita M. Kreps, *Women and the American Economy: A look to the 1980's* (Englewood Cliffs, N.J.: Prentice-Hall, 1976), pp. 31–60.

in the textile mills and other industries that sprang up in the East. Initially, primarily young farm girls worked in the factories, often contributing part of their pay to supplement family income and using some to accumulate a "dowry" that would make them more desirable marriage partners. The employment of these young women in factories may have appeared quite natural to observers at the time—the same people (women) doing much the same type of work they had done in the home, only in a new location and under the supervision of a foreman rather than the head of the household.[19] Once married, women would generally leave their jobs to look after their own households, which would soon include children.

The earliest available data show that at the end of the nineteenth century, when the labor force participation rate for men was 84 percent, only 18 percent of women were in the paid labor force, and the percentage of married women was 5 percent.[20] The situation was different for black women. Around 25 percent of black wives were employed. Most of these worked either as domestics or in agriculture in the rural South. While such early industries as textiles, millinery, and cigars did employ women, mainly young single ones, the new, rapidly growing sophisticated industries relied from the beginning almost entirely on male workers.

Among some immigrant groups,[21] however, who in the course of the nineteenth century increasingly replaced American-born workers in factories, it was not uncommon even for married women to be employed. Most of these people came to the "New World" determined to improve their economic condition and particularly to make sure that their children would get a better start than they did. At times, the whole family worked. Often if a choice could be made between the children leaving school to supplement family income, or the mother seeking employment, even among groups traditionally reluctant to have women work outside the home, the latter choice was made. By the same token, maternal employment was associated with dire need and was viewed as a temporary expedient to give the family a better start. Few wives remained in the labor force once the husband earned enough for an adequate living. The immigrants' goal of achieving the desired standard of living included what by then was widely considered the American ideal of the family—the male breadwinner who supported his family and the female homemaker who cared for his domestic needs.

[19]This was pointed out by Edith Abbott, *Women in Industry* (N.Y.: Appleton and Company, 1910).

[20]As discussed below, such official figures undoubtedly underestimate the proportion of women who worked for pay. Not only was seasonal work frequently ignored, but work done in the home, such as taking in boarders, bringing home piecework, etc., was often overlooked as well.

[21]Milton Cantor and Bruce Laurie, eds., *Class, Sex and the Women Worker* (Westport, CN: Greenwood Press, 1977) contains a great deal of interesting information on immigrant women.

Industrialization and The Evolution
of the Family

As an ever larger segment of the population began living in urban centers rather than on farms, and family shops were replaced by factories, women found that their household work increasingly came to be confined to the care of children, the nurturing of the husband, and the maintenance of the home. There were no longer a garden or farm animals to take care of, no need for seasonal help with the crops, and no opportunity to participate in a family business. As husbands left the home to earn the income needed to support their families, there came to be a new division into a female domestic sphere and a male public sphere.

Thus, along with industrialization arose the concept of the **traditional family**, which lingered to a greater or lesser degree well into the twentieth century.[22] The family shifted from a production unit to a consumption unit, and the responsibility for earning a living came to rest squarely on the shoulders of the husband. Wives (and children) grew to be dependent on his income. Thus, redistribution of income became a more important function of the family, as it provided a mechanism for the transfer of income from the market-productive husband to his market-dependent wife and children. Not only did specific *tasks* differ between men and women, as was always the case, but men and women now had different *economic roles* as well.

If the wife also entered the labor market, it was assumed that she was compensating for her husband's inadequacy as a breadwinner. It was sometimes viewed as necessary for the wives of poor people, immigrants, or blacks to work. But for the middle-class, white wife, and even for the working class wife whose husband had a steady income, holding a job was frowned upon as inconsistent with her social status, or, in some instances, as selfishly pursuing a career at the expense of her household reponsibilities.

The status of children also changed. Only the children of the very poor would be expected to help to raise the family's standard of living, though others might work in order to be able to spend on extras for themselves or because their parents thought it would be good for their moral fiber. Futhermore, the age when children came to be considered young adults and were expected to become productive members of the household also increased considerably, and, at the end of the nineteenth century, child labor laws were passed that prohibited the employment of "minors."

As a result of industrialization and urbanization, more and more goods and services used by households came to be produced outside the home. Yet much time and effort was still needed to purchase and maintain these goods

[22]Historian Carl N. Degler has termed this the "first transformation." In his view, the second transformation came in the 1940s when married women began to enter the labor market in large numbers. See his *At Odds: Women and the Family in America from the Revolution to the Present* (New York: Oxford University Press, 1980).

and services and to use them to produce the standard of living to which American families aspired. It was the wife's responsibility to do all this and to provide other services needed to maintain the family. Though the husband might "help" with the wife's household responsibilities, this was never to interfere with his "work." The children, too, particularly the girls, might be expected to help but, again, the responsibility for housework rested with the wife.

The net result of these developments was that the number of hours full-time homemakers devoted to housework did not change very much. Data show that no decline occurred at least from the beginning to the latter part of the twentieth century.[23] There were two additional trends which contributed to the continued long hours (over 50 per week) spent by full-time homemakers on housework. One was the decline in the number of household servants, whose presence was not uncommon in middle-class households in the nineteenth and early twentieth centuries. Probably more important was the tendency to use time, which was no longer needed to produce essentials, not to increase leisure but rather to raise the standard of cleanliness, the quality of meals, and, in general, the level of comfort their family could enjoy.

Fertility declined with industrialization, in part due to the diminished economic value of children.[24] As children in urban areas no longer helped on the farm and the number of years of schooling grew in both rural and urban areas, it took increasingly longer before they ceased to be dependents. Also, with growing immigration, hired workers were more readily available as a source of farm labor. Women born in the early nineteenth century still averaged nearly five births—though this was considerably below their eighteenth century predecessors—while those born towards the end of the century averaged about three births. However, as the number of children declined, the years of childhood were substantially prolonged, and the amount of maternal care per child greatly increased.

With soap and bleach purchased at the store and the washing machine doing the scrubbing, laundry became far less of a chore, but it was done far more frequently, and housewives came to take pride in making it "whiter than white." Groceries bought at the supermarket and a gas or electric range made cooking much easier, but homemakers would now serve more elaborate meals rather than a pot of stew. To do otherwise would not have been consistent with

[23]Joann Vanek, "Time Spent in Housework," *Scientific American* 231, no. 5 (Nov. 1974): 116–20, found that even as late as 1966 full-time homemakers were devoting as much time to their work as their grandmothers had in the 1920s. It was not until the late seventies that this situation changed; see Joseph H. Pleck, "Husband's Paid Work and Family Roles: Current Research Issues," eds. Helena Lopota and Joseph H. Pleck, *Research in the Interweave of Social Roles: Families and Jobs* (Greenwich, Conn.: JAI Press, 1983).

[24]Improved methods of birth control are often credited for the declining birthrate. But significant decreases occurred in much of the industrialized world before any important breakthroughs in contraceptive techniques. (Joan Huber, "Toward a Sociotechnological Theory of the Women's Movement," *Social Problems* 23, no. 4 [April 1976] : 371–88).

the role of the dedicated mother and wife, whose every thought was for the well-being of her family, and would have made her unworthy of being supported by her husband.[25]

The responsibility for spending the family's money, and for determining and distributing its savings, was not as clear, but there were accepted norms here as well. The wife usually made most of the everyday purchases but not major ones such as the house and some of the other durables. A husband's authority was supposed to be absolute in all important family decisions.[26] Thus, to some extent, the wife might be viewed as the purchasing agent rather than the decision-maker when she did the shopping.

Unlike the responsibilities that were quite different for every member, the benefits the family could provide were presumably conferred on everyone equally, or according to need, as deemed appropriate. It was, however, the "head of the household" who basically determined the family's lifestyle, both by providing the money income on which it so crucially depended and by making many of the most important decisions. Thus, the husband decided upon the parameters within which the other family members had to operate and was dominant in crucial ways within the household, as well as in the outside world.

As the economic role of women changed within the family, so too did the image of the ideal wife. While the colonial wife was valued for her industriousness, the growing **cult of true womanhood**[27] that developed with industrialization in the nineteenth century equated piety, purity, domesticity, and submissiveness with the femininity to which all women were expected to aspire. Their role was in the now consumption-oriented home—as daughter, sister, but most of all as wife and mother. This ideal particularly extolled the lifestyle of affluent middle- and upper-class women who were to a great extent freed even from their domestic chores by the servants their husbands' ample incomes could provide. Understandably, over-burdened, working class women might come to look longingly at such a more leisurely existence as something to hope for and strive toward. For men of all social classes, it came to be a mark of success to be the sole wage earner in the family.

[25]For instance, William H. Chafe, "Looking Backward in Order to Look Forward: Women, Work, and Social Values in America," ed. Kreps, *Women and the American Economy,* pp. 6–30, suggests that since "woman's divinely ordained task was to support their husbands, care for their children, and provide a haven from the worries of the outside world, the idea that they might wish a career seemed a violation of nature" (pp. 7–8).

[26]Arlene S. Skolnick and Jerome H. Skolnick, *Family in Transition,* 2nd ed. (Boston: Little Brown and Company, 1977), p. 68.

[27]This subject is explored in depth by Barbara Easton, "Industrialization and Femininity: A Case Study of Nineteenth Century New England," *Social Problems* 23, no. 4 (April 1976): 389–401; and Barbara Welter, "The Cult of True Womanhood, 1820–1860," ed. Michael Gordon, *The American Family in Social-Historical Perspective* (N.Y.: St. Martins Press, 1978), pp. 313–33. This attitude was by no means confined to the United States. The German equivalent was "Kuche, Kirche und Kinder," kitchen, church, and children.

This image of the family was fostered not only by the example of the middle and upper middle classes, the envy of the poor woman bearing the double burden of paid and unpaid work[28] or toiling at home to make ends meet on a limited budget, but also by male workers and their trade unions. Initially, the availability of women and children for work in industry was welcomed by national leaders, because they provided cheap, competitive labor, while agricultural production could be maintained by men.[29] However, attitudes changed as workers became more plentiful with the growing influx of immigrants. Male workers and their unions were particularly eager to get wives out of the labor force and women out of all but the lowest paid jobs. Their goals were to reserve the better positions for themselves, make sure they would not be underbid, and give greater force to the argument that a "living wage" for a man had to be sufficient to support a dependent wife and children. Thus, women received little, if any, support from organized labor in trying to improve their own working conditions and rewards.[30]

This was the genesis of the traditional family, once accepted as the backbone of American society. As we have seen, it is in fact comparatively recent in origin, dating back only to the mid-nineteenth and early twentieth centuries. Even in its heyday, it was never entirely universal. Many poor, black, and immigrant married women worked outside their homes and others earned income at home, taking in boarders or doing piece work. Throughout this period, market work was quite common among single women, and a relatively small number of women chose careers over marriage as a lifelong vocation. Nonetheless, exclusive dedication to the role of mother and wife was widely accepted as the only proper and fulfilling life for a women. It was not long, however, before this orthodoxy was challenged for increased modernization brought about dramatic changes in conditions of production and in the economic roles of men and women. Soon there were also changes in ideas and aspirations that made rigid differentiation, let alone ranking of the roles of the sexes, increasingly less appropriate under prevailing conditions.

As family size continued to shrink, the amount of time and energy women needed to spend on childbearing and childrearing declined. At the same time, women lived increasingly longer, giving them a larger number of years after their children grew up to devote to other activities. More and more

[28]As Louise Tilly and Joan Scott, *Women, Work and Families* (N.Y.: Holt, Rinehart and Winston, 1978) forcefully point out, mothers found it very difficult to combine employment outside the home with housework and child care.

[29]George Washington is quoted as writing to Lafayette, "I conceive much might be done in the way of women, children and others [producing yarn and cloth] without taking one really necessary hand from tilling the earth." Cited in Alice Kessler-Harris, *Women Have Always Worked* (N.Y.: McGraw-Hill Book Co., 1981), p. 8.

[30]Alice Kessler-Harris, "Organizing the Unorganizable: Three Jewish Women and their Unions," ed. Cantor and Laurie, *Class, Sex and the Woman Worker* is very eloquent on this point.

of the goods and services that were previously provided within the household for its own use were now mass-produced and available for purchase. New appliances facilitated faster and/or easier production of many of the others. Increasingly, the market also provided many new goods and services desired by consumers that could not readily be produced in the home. Under these conditions, it was only a matter of time before large numbers of women and men would recognize that a second paycheck would make a greater contribution to the family's standard of living than additional time devoted to upgrading the quality of homemaking. Other factors, to be discussed in a later chapter, such as changes in demand for labor and in tastes, were important in facilitating the influx of women into the labor market. However, the shrinking of the household and the household sphere described above were among the basic changes that made it possible.

Women in the Labor Market

As suggested previously, there were always women who were economically active beyond taking care of family and home. Among married women, such activities, however, frequently took place within the confines of the home and, hence, were not counted as labor force participation. It is, for instance, estimated that during the nineteenth century almost one-third of all immigrant families received payments from boarders and lodgers, as did 12 percent of the native born.[31] Piecework brought home and seasonal work done outside the household also went frequently unreported. There is general agreement today that official estimates of women in the labor market were too low.

Nonetheless, the proportion of women who worked for pay outside the home was undoubtedly small. According to census reports, it increased only at a very modest rate between 1890 and 1940 from 18 percent (only one-fourth of them married) to 28 percent (less than one-third of them married). As these data suggest, a considerably larger proportion of single than of married women were employed. In 1890, 41 percent of single women worked outside the home, in comparison to 5 percent of married women. In 1940, this was true of 46 percent of single women and 16 percent of married women.

Not only were relatively few women, particularly married women, employed, but they were also largely concentrated in a very few occupations. According to census data at the turn of the century, 42 percent of men were in agriculture, but the remainder were widely distributed across many occupations—38 percent in blue collar jobs, fairly evenly distributed among skilled, semi-skilled, and unskilled; 18 percent were in white collar jobs, with the largest share in the category of managers and proprietors, followed by sales

---

[31]These data, as well as much other useful information on the economic status of women in the United States prior to World War II, are found in Matthaei, *An Economic History of Women in America.*

occupations, professionals, and clerical occupations. On the other hand, 39 percent of all employed women were in domestic service, about one-third of them black, one-third foreign-born white, and one-sixth Asian. This occupation may plausibly be seen as an extension of what women do at home. Another 25 percent were in manufacturing, virtually all in textiles, clothing, and tobacco. As many as 18 percent were in agriculture, by far most of these black. Lastly, 8 percent were in the professions, almost entirely comprised of school teachers and nurses. The female professions, again, may be regarded as extensions of women's roles within the home, although, interestingly enough, teaching was intially a male occupation. Ninety percent of all women in the labor force were in these occupational categories.

It was not until after 1900, when clerical work was becoming less of an apprenticeship for managerial positions, that women began to enter clerical fields to any significant extent. Like teaching, this was originally a primarily male occupation, and as late as the turn of the century, 76 percent of clerical workers were men. In time, however, as more women sought employment, this sector became predominantly female and as it expanded absorbed a very substantial proportion of employed women.

A variety of factors, no doubt, contributed to this development. The growth of large corporations increased the volume of paperwork and, thus, the demand for clerical workers. It is also thought to have helped to separate purely clerical from apprentice-training functions. Employers did not have to provide much on-the-job training for clerical workers and would, therefore, be more willing to hire women, even though they were not expected to stay for a long time. A high proportion of young women were high school graduates with the general skills necessary to perform this work. Women were likely to find these jobs attractive because relevant skills did not depreciate much during periods out of the labor force, and re-entry was relatively easy. In addition, they might prefer such white collar positions to the often dirtier, noisier, and physically more demanding blue collar jobs and, in fact, had few other white collar opportunities at that time.[32] The growth in the demand for labor in clerical occupations undoubtedly facilitated the rapid influx of women into the labor force that began in the 1940s and has continued ever since.[33] The causes of this increase in female labor force participation are considered in greater detail in Chapter 4.

[32]For analyses of women's occupational choices and of their entry into clerical work see, Claudia Goldin, "The Historical Evolution of Female Earnings Functions and Occupations," *Explorations in Economic History* 21, no. 1 (Jan. 1984): 1–27; and Margery Davies, "Woman's Place is at the Typewriter: The Feminization of the Clerical Labor Force," eds. Richard C. Edwards, Michael Reich, and David M. Gordon, *Labor Market Segmentation* (Lexington, MA: D.C. Heath and Co., 1975), pp. 279–96.

[33]Valerie Oppenheimer, *The Female Labor Force in the United States: Demographic and Economic Factors Governing its Growth and Changing Composition,* Population Monograph Ser. 5, Berkeley, CA: 1970.

CONCLUSIONS

The overview provided here has been very general. The importance of the technology employed to produce the basic necessities of life was emphasized as a determinant of the roles of men and women and the nature of the family. This does not mean, however, that other factors—social, political, religious, etc.—are not relevant as well. Various combinations of these make each situation unique, to a greater or lesser extent. In Chapter 10, we will examine the contemporary situations in a variety of countries throughout the world. The lessons we have learned so far are summarized below.

The roles of men and women and the social rules that prescribe appropriate behavior for each are not shaped by biology itself. Rather they are determined by the interaction of biology with the technology of production—the way goods and services are produced under given circumstances. When men are the providers while women specialize in childbearing and homemaking, the latter tend to be viewed as dependents, to some extent even as possessions. They may be put on a pedestal, protected, and sheltered, and the affluent may be permitted to enjoy luxuries and leisure. But they tend not to achieve any significant degree of independence or status apart from their family.

When, on the other hand, "productive" work is shared by women, they are less likely to be primarily defined in terms of their maternal and family role. They are not excluded to the same extent from the public sphere and lead far more autonomous and less subordinate lives. Participating in productive activities beyond housekeeping has tended to bring women a greater measure of equality, but they have also generally worked very hard under these conditions, since they have always been responsible for household and children, no matter what else they did.

While the roles of men and women are influenced by the technology of production, it is entirely likely that gender roles that develop as a rational response to conditions at one time in the course of economic development continue their hold long after they have ceased to be functional.[34] Among tribes where men did the hunting while women looked after planting and harvesting, women continued to do most of the horticultural work long after hunting ceased to be a major economic activity. The view that women should devote themselves entirely to homemaking, once a full-time occupation when life was short, families large, and housekeeping laborious, lingered long after these conditions changed substantially.[35] Jobs originally allocated to men, because they required great physical strength, often continued as male preserves when

---

[34]"Although stereotypes are often based on fact, they are seldom revised as quickly as the facts change." Ralph Smith, "The Movement of Women into the Labor Force," p. 3.

[35]Even in the 1980s these ideas are not yet dead. In 1984, Judge Melvin Duran of New Orleans awarded custody of a four-year-old girl to her father. For three years prior to that—since her parents had separated—she had been living with her mother. The reason was that her mother

mechanization did away with the need for musclepower. The possibility that such lags in adjustment are not uncommon should be kept in mind when we come to analyze the current situation.

Our review also suggests that neither the role of "housewife," nor that of "working woman" is without significant problems for women. Men's work in the public sphere, (that is, outside the family), has usually enjoyed higher status than women's domestic work within the family circle. But even when women have succeeded in entering the world beyond the household to a greater or lesser extent, men have not shown much inclination to share in household work.[36] This, in turn, has made it difficult for women to achieve substantial equality in the public sphere. It has also caused many of those who *have* tried to be confronted by the problem of "the double burden" of responsibility for home and market work, or to make a choice between a career and marriage.[37] In modern times, machines have largely done away with the need for muscle, and physical strength is no longer required for the most highly valued work. At the same time, childbearing absorbs an increasingly smaller proportion of a woman's adult life and can, for the most part, be timed at will. It is entirely possible that, under these conditions, it is the unequal distribution of labor in the home, rather than women's lesser ability to perform other types of work, that is the main obstacle to equality.

SUGGESTED READINGS

ARDREY, ROBERT. *The Territorial Imperative.* N.Y.: Atheneum Press, 1966.
CHAFETZ, JANET S. *Masculine, Feminine or Human?* Itasca, IL.: F. E. Peacock Publishers, 1978.

---

had accepted a position with the National Labor Relations Board in Washington. The judge described her as a selfish, ambitious woman, "who wants to be a lawyer more than she wants to be a mother." The father of the child was a urologist (*American Bar Association Journal* 69, (December 1983), p. 1808).

[36]It is interesting to note that even Marx, who extolled the beauty of not just specializing in one type of work but rather of participating in a variety of different activities, never included "woman's work" among them. Thus, he suggests that under the ideal conditions of full communism, man will be able to hunt in the morning, fish in the afternoon, rear cattle in the evening, and criticize after dinner. (Karl Marx and Friedrich Engels, *The German Ideology.* Translation by W. Loach and C. P. Magill, London: Lawrence and Wishart, 1938.) Nowhere does he suggest that man might also share in house cleaning, preparing dinner, or putting the children to bed.

[37]Not only does the woman who is employed and retains the primary responsibility as homemaker work long hours, but she is also confronted by a substantially different set of values in the two spheres. In the home, there is emphasis on nurturing, mutual aid and service to others. In the marketplace competitive, individualistic behavior is rewarded. Thus, the person whose identity is grounded in the family, who tends to give priority to cooperation and seek approval rather than gain, may well be at a disadvantage. See Clair (Vickery) Brown, "Home Production for Use in a Market Economy," *Rethinking the Family: Some Feminist Questions,* ed. Barrie Thorne (New York: Langman, Inc., 1981), pp. 151-67.

FRIEDL, ERNESTINE. *Women and Men. An Anthropological View.* N.Y.: Holt, Rinehart and Winston, 1975.

MATTHAEI, JULIE A. *An Economic History of Women in America.* N.Y.: Schochen Books, 1982.

MORRIS, DESMOND. *The Human Zoo.* N.Y.: McGraw-Hill, 1969.

O'KELLY, CHARLOTTE G. *Women and Men in Society.* N.Y.: D. Van Nostrand Co., 1980.

ROSALDO, MICHELLE Z. and LOUISE LAMPHERE (eds.). *Women, Culture and Society.* Stanford: Stanford University Press, 1974.

STOLL, CLARICE S. *Female and Male. Socialization, Social Roles and Social Structure.* Dubuque, Iowa: Wm. Brown Co. Publishers, 1974.

TIGER, LIONEL and ROBIN FOX. *The Imperial Animal.* N.Y.: Holt, Rinehart and Winston, 1971.

TILLY, LOUISE and JOAN SCOTT. *Women, Work and Family.* N.Y.: Holt, Rinehart and Winston, 1978.

WELTER, BARBARA. "The Cult of True Womanhood, 1820-1860. In *The American Family in Social-Historical Perspective,* edited by Michael Gordon. NY: St. Martins Press, 1978, pp. 313–33.

Chapter 3

THE FAMILY AS AN ECONOMIC UNIT: THE DIVISION OF LABOR BETWEEN HUSBAND AND WIFE

For a long time neoclassical economics largely concerned itself with the behavior of "economic man." It was, of course, acknowledged that this man interacted with others, in competition or in cooperation, but it was his individual well-being that he would attempt to maximize. Consumer economics had recognized the existence of the family and its importance as a unit of consumption. However, not until the 1960s, with the path-breaking work of Gary Becker and Jacob Mincer did mainstream economists begin to concern themselves with the issues confronted by men and women in allocating their time and wealth so as to maximize family well-being.[1] Since then, using

---

[1]See Gary S. Becker, "A Theory of the Allocation of Time," *Economic Journal* 75, no. 299 (Sept. 1965): 493-517; and Jacob Mincer, "Labor Force Participation of Married Women," ed. H. Greg Lewis, *Aspects of Labor Economics,* Universities National Bureau of Economic Research Conference Series, no. 14 (Princeton, N.J.: Princeton Univ. Press, 1962), pp. 63-97. An early pioneer was Margaret G. Reid, *Economics of Household Production* (N.Y.: Wiley, 1934) but her interesting ideas had little impact on economists before they were revived in the 1960s, a time when large numbers of women were entering the labor market. Home economists were influenced to a greater extent. A large number of authors have contributed to the growing literature of the "New Home Economics," but much of this work has been conveniently summarized by Gary S. Becker in *A Treatise on the Family* (Cambridge, Mass.: Harvard University Press, 1981).

sophisticated theory and advanced econometric methods, models have been developed and tested that have produced important insights in this area. Yet, these models are not altogether satisfactory for there is a tendency to treat even this multiperson family as a single-minded, indivisible, utility-maximizing unit.

In this chapter, we draw heavily upon neoclassical economic analysis, with appropriate simplifying assumptions, to better understand the determinants of the division of labor in the family.[2] At the same time, we also present an evaluation and critique of that approach and introduce a more complex reality. In particular, the simple neoclassical model suggests that there are considerable efficiency gains to the traditional division of labor in which the husband specializes in market work and the wife specializes in home work. While this may be true, it is also the case that this arrangement is becoming less and less prevalent. We shed light on the reasons for this change by extending the simple model in two ways.[3]

1. We point out that there are other types of economic benefits to forming families besides specialization. Thus, couples may discard specialization and still reap economic gains from living in families.
2. We examine the *disadvantages* of the traditional division of labor, particularly for women, which are not considered in the simple neoclassical model.

Throughout, however, we operate within the framework of neoclassical economic analysis. There are alternative approaches, including that of radical feminists and Marxists. One example is offered on page 52 in this chapter based on the work of Heidi Hartmann.[4]

Our emphasis upon economic analysis does not mean that we believe families are established or dissolved entirely, or even primarily, for economic reasons. Human need for companionship, sexual attraction, affection, the urge to perpetuate one's life through children all play a part in family forma-

---

[2] We discuss the division of labor between husbands and wives because a substantial majority of people continue to live in families. Much of the analysis is, however, also applicable to unmarried individuals living together in a household. At one time, it would have been suggested that such arrangements tend to be less permanent because they do not involve marriage. But marriages are no longer as enduring as they used to be, so the distinction is not as important as it once was.

[3] Much of this material was first developed in Marianne A. Ferber and Bonnie G. Birnbaum, "The New Home Economics: Retrospect and Prospects," *Journal of Consumer Research* 4, no. 4 (June 1977): 19-28.

[4] See Heidi I. Hartmann, "Capitalism, Patriarchy, and Job Segregation by Sex," *Signs: Journal of Women in Culture and Society* 1, no. 3 (Spring 1076, pt. 2): 137-70, and Heidi I. Hartmann, "The Family as the Locus of Gender, Class and Political Struggle: The Example of Housework," *Signs: Journal of Women in Culture and Society* 6, no. 3 (Spring 1981): 366-94. For another analysis in the Marxist tradition, see Julie A. Matthaei, *An Economic History of Women in America: Women's Work, the Sexual Division of Labor and the Development of Capitalism* (New York: Schocken, 1982). For an institutional approach to the family, see Clair Brown, "Consumption Norms. Work Roles, and Economic Growth," paper presented at the Conference on "Gender in the Workplace," Brookings Institution, November 1984.

tion. Human need for independence and privacy, preference for a variety of partners, disappointment when children do not live up to expectations all play a part in family breakups. Nonetheless, it is our belief that economic factors also play an important part and that focusing upon them considerably enhances our understanding of the determinants of the division of labor in the family.

As we saw in Chapter 2, with industrialization in the nineteenth century, men and women adopted distinct economic roles within the family. Married men, by and large, were viewed as the breadwinners, that is, as having primary responsibility for earning an adequate market income to support the family. Married women, for the most part, were expected to be homemakers, that is, to be responsible for nonmarket work performed in the home. Yet, throughout this century and particularly in recent decades, married women have been entering the labor market and increasingly sharing responsibility for producing an adequate income for the family. In Chapter 4, we examine the trends in female labor force participation in greater detail. Here we need only note that the traditional division of labor, which developed with industrialization, appears to be in the process of dramatically changing as married women assume greater responsibility for work outside the home.

So far, however, considerably less change has occurred in the division of household responsibilities. It was not until the late 1970s that the average amount of housework done by husbands started to increase and, for the most part, husbands continue to do little housework. Married women, including those who are employed outside the home, continue to retain primary responsibilities for housework. The way in which the amount of housework done by men and women has been affected by the increased employment of wives outside the home is explored in greater depth in Chapter 5. At this point, we simply emphasize that responsibility for housework remains fairly unequally divided between men and women within the family.

We may be moving, albeit very slowly, toward a greater acceptance of the egalitarian marriage, where both spouses share the duty for earning a living and for being homemakers. Such families are most likely to have few, but highly educated, children, who are increasingly less likely to ever make an economic contribution to their family of origin.[5] This family will not, in the main, be a unit of production or of redistribution of income (except from parents to children) but rather a unit for pooling income and facilitating consumption. As we shall see, much progress has been made in explaining the operation of the family as it has been, somewhat less in enhancing our understanding of the new type of family which may be emerging.

---

[5]Today's children will be tomorrow's adults, who will then support the older generation through their contributions to the social security system. But for any family, the contribution of their own children is only a tiny and entirely insignificant portion of the whole. Hence, people cannot be expected to have children merely in order to provide their fair share, any more than most of them would voluntarily pay for any public good.

THE SIMPLE NEOCLASSICAL MODEL: SPECIALIZATION AND EXCHANGE

The basic underlying assumptions of the neoclassical analysis of the family are that it is a unit whose adult members make informed and rational decisions that result in maximizing the utility or well-being of the family. Beginning with these premises, economists have applied the tools of their discipline to the analysis of the division of labor within the family. Models employing these basic economic concepts have also been used to explain women's increasing labor force participation rates, their growing divorce rates and declining fertility, the family's greater emphasis on education of children, and a good many other aspects of human behavior. In this chapter, we single out the division of labor within the family to illustrate both the strengths and weaknesses of such models. In later chapters, we utilize the insights of economic analysis to explain recent trends in female labor force participation, marriage, divorce, and birth rates.

As noted above, in the simplest model of the family, it is assumed that the goal is to maximize its utility or satisfaction. This is accomplished by selecting the combination of **commodities** from which the family derives the greatest possible amount of utility. Commodities are produced by combining the home time of family members with goods and services purchased in the market, using labor market earnings.

Virtually all market-purchased goods and services require an infusion of home time to transform them into the commodities from which we may derive utility—from food that needs to be bought and prepared and furniture that needs to be purchased, arranged in the home, and maintained, to day-care centers where children must be dropped off and picked up. Similarly, even time spent in leisure generally requires the input of market goods and services to be enjoyable—from television sets and stereos to concerts and baseball games. Thus, time spent on paid work produces the income necessary to purchase market goods, which in turn are needed together with home time to produce commodities. A crucial question for the family is how time should be allocated between home and market most efficiently in order to maximize satisfaction.

Comparative Advantage

Under certain conditions, commodity production is carried out most efficiently if one member of the family specializes, to some extent, in market production while the other specializes, to some extent, in home production. They may then exchange their output or pool the fruits of their labor to achieve their utility-maximizing combination of market-purchased goods and home-produced goods. In order for this to be true, it is only necessary for the two individuals to have differing **comparative advantages** for home and market production. That is to say, one must have a higher value of time spent at home *relative to* market earning power as compared to the other person.

Is it generally the case that women are relatively more productive in the home and men are relatively more productive in the market? Whether or not one assumes that women are biologically better suited for housework because they are the ones who bear children,[6] it will frequently be the case that women have a comparative advantage in household production and that men have a comparative advantage in market work. This can be true because men and women are traditionally raised with different expectations and receive different education and training. Or it may be the case that women have been discriminated against in the labor market, lowering their market earnings. Or, even if women and men have identical skills initially, the traditional division of labor itself is likely to generate differences in skills, because both homemaking and market skills tend to increase with experience "on the job."

While each of the above factors tends to produce sex differences in the comparative advantage for homemaking, it is not necessarily the case that the traditional division of labor is the optimal outcome. Treating children according to sex rather than individual talents and discriminating against women workers in the labor market clearly introduce distortions. Even more obvious is the fact that circular reasoning is involved when women supposedly specialize in housework because they do it better, but, in fact, they do it better because they specialize in it. To the extent that women's relative advantage for homemaking is socially determined and reflects unequal access to market opportunities, the traditional division of labor is not always efficient, let alone desirable, particularly when, as we shall see, it entails many disadvantages for women.

In the following discussion, we assume that women have a comparative advantage in housework relative to men because the reality that we seek to explain is one in which women generally have primary responsibility for housework. We do not mean to imply, however, that the traditional division of labor is inevitable or that it will persist indefinitely into the future. Indeed, we are also concerned with better understanding the reasons why traditional patterns are changing.

Specialization and Exchange:
Numerical Examples

Two examples will help to clarify the notion of comparative advantage and to illustrate the efficiency of specialization and exchange. The analysis is

---

[6]Some sociobiologists suggest not only that women's childbearing function is crucial but, also, that women are better suited than men to the far more time-consuming task of childrearing. Their views were discussed in Chapter 2.

TABLE 3.1a   An Illustration of the Gains From Specialization and Exchange

Case 1: Absolute Advantage

SEPARATE PRODUCTION

	Value of Market Goods		*Value of Home Cooking*		*Total Income*
John	(6 hrs. × $10) $ 60	+	(2 hrs. × $5) $10	=	$ 70
Jane	(7 hrs. × $5) $ 35	+	(1 hr. × $10) $10	=	$ 45
Total (John & Jane)	$ 95		$20		$115

SPECIALIZATION AND EXCHANGE

	Value of Market Goods		*Value of Home Cooking*		*Total Income*
John	(8 hrs. × $10) $ 80	+	(0 hrs. × $5) $ 0	=	$ 80
Jane	(5 hrs. × $5) $ 25	+	(3 hrs. × $10) $30	=	$ 55
Total (John & Jane)	$105		$30		$135

analogous to the standard proof of gains from international trade and is illustrated in Tables 3.1a and b.

Absolute advantage. The simplest case is when one individual has an absolute advantage in market work and the other individual has an absolute advantage in household production. Suppose John could earn $10 for working one hour in the labor market or could produce a mediocre dinner worth about $5 at home during the same period of time. A second individual, Jane, would earn only $5 an hour in the labor market but is able to prepare an excellent dinner at home worth about $10 in one hour. In this case, it is clear that John and Jane's combined level of economic well-being can be increased if they each specialize. John, who has an *absolute advantage* in market work, can spend all his time in the labor market earning money while Jane, who has an *absolute advantage* in cooking, prepares the dinners.

This is illustrated in the top section of Table 3.1a. Initially, John and Jane are each self-sufficient and both allocate some time to market work and the preparation of home-cooked meals. John devotes six hours to earning income and two hours to cooking. His total income (including the value of home-cooked meals) is $70. Jane spends seven hours in the market and one hour on cooking. Her total income is $45. The sum of their two incomes (although they are not necessarily sharing at this point) is $115. If they collaborate, they have the option of each specializing to some extent in one or the other activity and exchanging (or pooling) their output.

The bottom section of Table 3.1a shows that they can produce a higher value of both market goods and home-cooked meals through specialization and exchange and, thus, increase their total income. The concept of *opportunity cost* is useful in understanding this. It may be recalled from Chapter 1 that opportunity cost is the benefit foregone in the next best alternative. John's opportunity cost of obtaining $10 worth of market goods in terms of the value of meals foregone ($5) is lower than Jane's ($20). On the other hand, a home-cooked meal valued at $10 is cheaper for Jane to produce in terms of the value of market goods foregone ($5) than it is for John ($20). Suppose John decides to devote all his time to the market, and Jane transfers two additional hours from market work to cooking. By reallocating their time, the couple is able to raise their total income from $115 to $135.

Comparative advantage. Less obvious is the case where one individual not only earns more in the labor market but is also a better cook. In other

TABLE 3.1b   An Illustration of the Gains From Specialization and Exchange

Case 2: Comparative Advantage

SEPARATE PRODUCTION

	Value of Market Goods		Value of Home Cooking		Total Income
Dave	(6 hrs. × $10) $ 60	+	(2 hrs. × $5) $10	=	$ 70
Diane	(7 hrs. × $15) $105	+	(1 hr. × $15) $15	=	$120
Total (Dave & Diane)	$165		$25		$190

SPECIALIZATION AND EXCHANGE

	Value of Market Goods		Value of Home Cooking		Total Income
Dave	(8 hrs. × $10) $ 80	+	(0 hrs. × $5) $ 0	=	$ 80
Diane	(6 hrs. × $15) $ 90	+	(2 hrs. × $15) $30	=	$120
Total (Dave & Diane)	$170		$30		$200

words, one individual has an absolute advantage in both types of work. In this situation, the crucial question is for which type of work each has a *comparative advantage.*

This is illustrated in Table 3.1b. Dave earns $10 per hour for time spent in the labor market or can produce a meal worth, say, $5 for an hour spent cooking. Diane is more efficient than Dave in both activities. Her market wage is $15, while she can produce a meal worth $15 in an hour's time. The important point here is that while Diane is a bit more efficient than Dave in the labor market, she is a far better cook than he is. The opportunity cost (in terms of market goods foregone) of a home-cooked meal worth $10 is lower when Diane produces it than when Dave does. It takes Dave two hours (valued at $20) to produce such a meal while Diane can do so in 40 minutes (valued at $10). Table 3.1b shows that through specialization and exchange, the couple can increase their total output of both market goods and home-cooked meals and raise their total income from $190 to $200.

Gains to Specialization and Exchange

These examples serve to illustrate the potential gain in output of specialization and exchange. However, the goal of the family is to maximize utility or satisfaction. Thus, the value attached to various commodities, and the time allocation actually chosen by each couple, will depend on their preferences for market- versus home-produced goods. Many outcomes are possible. For example, it might be that Jane and John would have such a strong preference for market goods that their well-being would be maximized by both of them working for pay and eating all their meals out. Or Diane and Dave might have such a strong preference for home production that she would entirely specialize in housework, and he would divide his time between market and home. In the Appendix to this chapter, we present a fuller treatment of the decision-making process that explicitly takes into account both the production possibilities available to the couple and their preferences for each type of good.

In any case, however, each couple will seek to produce their desired combination of market and home goods in the most efficient way. Thus, as long as they produce some of each type of good, if the wife has a *comparative* advantage in housework (relative to the husband) and the husband has a *comparative* advantage in market work (relative to the wife), the analysis suggests that they will choose to specialize to some extent.

It would appear then that this analysis provides a perfect explanation for the traditional family with a male breadwinner and a female homemaker. One may help the other if the demand for the production he or she is not particularly qualified for is very high, but each has a clearly defined sphere of primary responsibility. For whenever such specialization does not take place, the couple will not succeed in maximizing their output and potentially their well-being. Of course, if the husband and wife do not have different comparative advantages, this conclusion no longer follows. It is then not clear, within the framework of this simple analysis, what the couple gains from collaborating. For their pooled income will presumably be no greater than the sum of their separate incomes. However, specialization and exchange is not the only economic rationale for joint production and consumption. Further, the traditional division of labor results in a number of disadvantages, particularly for women, that are not considered in this simple model. We now consider each of these points in turn.

OTHER ADVANTAGES OF JOINT PRODUCTION AND CONSUMPTION

In this section, we review a number of other reasons why individuals may increase their economic well-being by forming families. Where husband and wife do not differ in relative abilities, or do not differ significantly, these provide alternative reasons why they may still find it in their economic self-interest to form families.

Economies of scale. Economies of scale exist when an increase in the scale of operation of a productive unit can result in increased output at decreasing incremental cost. To the extent that a couple is able to benefit from economies of scale in the production of some market and/or home goods, there are economic gains to their living together. For example, ample housing for two may cost less than the combined amount each was paying for their housing separately. Meals for two may take less than twice as much time to prepare as meals for one and so forth.[7]

Public goods. A public good has the unique characteristic that the consumption or enjoyment of the item by one of the partners does not diminish the consumption or enjoyment of it by the other partner. Within the family, this is likely to be the case with many goods. For example, one partner's enjoyment of a television program is unlikely to be reduced at all by the fact that the other partner is also watching. Similarly, the delight of a parent in his or her child's adorable antics is not apt to be diminished by the other parent's enjoyment. Many aspects of housing—the views from the windows, the decoration of the rooms—also have public goods aspects. In fact, the enjoyment of these goods by one partner may even enhance that of the other. To the extent that public goods are important, the gains to joint consumption are increased. This is because two individuals may derive more total satisfaction from sharing a

[7]Economies of scale also explain the advantages of larger groups living together. The fact that such arrangements are not common in affluent societies suggests that most people value additional privacy highly once they can afford it.

given stock of public goods and services by living together than by living separately.

Externalities. Externalities occur when the consumption of a good or service by one of the partners has an impact on the well-being of the other. For example, a husband's purchase of a new suit may increase his wife's utility as well as his own. Both members of a couple may enjoy their summer vacation more because they are traveling together than they would if each were traveling alone. To the extent that these externalities are positive—one person derives enjoyment from the other's consumption—gains will be greater than indicated by the simple model. When two people care for one another, one partner may derive satisfaction simply from the enjoyment and happiness of the other. This also greatly enhances the gains from joint consumption.

The economic benefits of families. This discussion suggests that the economic gains to individuals joining together to form couples may derive from other factors than simply specialization and exchange. This further implies that, from the perspective of economic considerations, even as men and women are becoming less differentially specialized in market and home production, marriage may continue to be an important economic institution. However, the decline of specialization does remove one of the economic benefits of marriage. From this perspective, it is not surprising that the increased employment of married women has been accompanied by a rising divorce rate.

THE DISADVANTAGES
OF SPECIALIZATION

We have just pointed out a variety of sources of economic benefits from family formation. We now return, however, to the issue of specialization and exchange, which the simple model suggests is the economic foundation of marriage. Here we consider the possibility, frequently ignored in the standard models, that such specialization and a gender-based division of labor may not always be desirable, particularly for women.[8]

Sharing of Housework

One correct prediction of the simple model is that, given sex differences in comparative advantage, women's employment outside the home is not necessarily accompanied by an increase in the amount of housework done by

---

[8]These points are stressed in Ferber and Birnbaum, "The New Home Economics." It is also suggested there that more sophisticated models could incorporate many of these complexities.

her husband. Nonetheless, the simple assumption that women have a comparative advantage in all household tasks seems unrealistic.

The problem here may be that the simple model assumes there is only one type of home good. In our numerical example, it was home-cooked meals; more generally it is simply an aggregate category "home goods." In fact, tasks typically performed within the household vary from child care, house cleaning, cooking, and shopping to gardening, washing the car, and taking care of the family finances. It is not particularly likely that the wife will be better at all of these things than the husband. It is entirely possible that the husband has a comparative advantage in at least some of them, even taking his larger market earnings into account. Of course, once the wife is at home because she is better at some, or many, of the household tasks, it may be more efficient for her to undertake other related work as well. But the husband also spends a good bit of time in the home, and not all household tasks are performed in or around the house (for example, shopping, going to the bank). Thus, it seems likely that even a fairly traditional family will find it efficient for the husband to do a bit more housework than suggested by the simple model.

So far we have only been concerned with maximizing utility derived from the consumption of market-produced or home-produced goods. Yet, most people spend much of their time working, and their well-being is very much influenced by the satisfaction or dissatisfaction associated directly with their work. If people always enjoyed more (or disliked less) the kind of work they do more efficiently, the gains from specialization would be even greater than indicated by the simple model; and this may to a degree be the case. But this line of reasoning ignores the possibility that how we feel about doing particular tasks depends on how much time we have to spend on them. Persons who dislike market or home work to begin with are likely to hate additional time spent on it more as they do increasingly more of it. And even those who like what they are doing are, nonetheless, likely to become less enthusiastic. The stronger this effect, the less likely there are to be the gains in utility from specialization suggested by the simple model.

A similar issue arises with respect to the utility each individual derives from leisure. The model fails to consider adequately that leisure is likely to be more highly valued by the partner who has less of it and that the one who has a great deal of leisure may become bored and also come to feel useless. Thus, the situation in which the wife works in the market and retains full responsibility for housework is not likely to be optimal if, as is often the case, it results in considerably less leisure for her than for her husband; this is especially true during the childrearing years. Alternatively, the diminished responsibilities the full-time homemaker experiences as her children grow up (discussed below) may create more leisure for her than she finds desirable.

Another consideration is that some tasks are more efficiently performed by two people together and that many people may enjoy housework more when they do not have to do it alone. Frequently, homemakers spend much of their time isolated, with little possibility for interaction with other adults. For all these reasons, complete specialization by the husband in market work, whether or not the wife specializes completely in housework, may not maximize utility for the family. Nonetheless, the simple model does seem to square with reality to the extent that, on average, husbands devote relatively little time to housework.

Tastes and Bargaining Power

In our development of the simple model, we did not consider how the couple determines how much of various goods to produce. This decision will be relatively easy to make if they both have the same tastes or preferences. Then they will each opt for the same combination of goods to be shared. However, if their tastes differ significantly (and this is more likely to be the case as the spouses are more specialized), the question arises as to how they will decide on the combination of commodities to be produced and consumed. Putting the matter somewhat differently, whose preferences (husband's or wife's) will receive greater weight?

Considerable flexibility exists in the case where the couple may pool production but then choose different bundles of commodities for individual consumption, although even here the share of the total going to each partner could be a matter of dispute. But more difficult problems arise in the case of public goods or where commodities have significant externalities. We saw earlier that for people with similar tastes, public goods and positive externalities increase the gains from joint consumption and collaboration. However, where one person's public good is another's public "bad" or where negative externalities exist, consumption of the commodity by one individual may reduce the well-being of the other. For example, one partner may derive enormous satisfaction from the presence of children, while the other dislikes having them around. Or, the consumption of onions at dinner by one individual may have a negative effect on the enjoyment of the evening for the other.

These difficulties are relevant to the conclusions we derived from the simple model regarding the benefits of specialization. They suggest that conflicts of interest may arise between husband and wife and that relative bargaining power could play a role in resolving these conflicts. In this case, specialization in home work on the part of the wife could have negative consequences for her.

Since the husband earns the money, he may be viewed as having the "power of the purse." He may, thus, be accorded a greater say in spending decisions. A number of sociologists suggest that decision-making and task responsibility are built into the traditional husband-wife roles based on cultural norms and unrelated to individual skills and interests. Power resides in the position rather than the person. Accordingly, the husband determines what car they will buy, and the wife decides what to serve guests for dinner.[9]

Further, in a money economy, adherence to the traditional division of labor results in the wife being financially dependent on the husband. Since she has more to lose if the marriage breaks up, she may be under greater pressure to subordinate her wishes to her husband's. Indeed, it has been found that the more successful the husband in fulfilling his economic role, the more the wife tends to give him power to define the norms for decision-making.[10] This may reflect not only the greater financial costs to the wife of marital breakup in this case but also that the husband's market success, in a sense, validates his claim to greater competence in familial decision-making.

Finally, the lesser outside contacts of the full-time homemaker in comparison to her working husband may make her more dependent on his counsel and judgment than he is on hers. For these and other reasons, a number of studies tend to confirm the dominance of the husband in decision-making, given the traditional division of labor.[11]

Life Cycle Changes

A very serious shortcoming of the simple model is that it ignores the fact that the comparative advantage of an individual does not necessarily remain the same over the life cycle. As will be explained in greater detail in Chapter 4, the value of home production for women peaks during the childrearing years and then declines as children grow up and become more self-sufficient. At the same time, labor market earnings tend to increase with experience and decline while a person is not employed. If a woman withdraws from the labor force for a considerable period of time for childrearing, she is likely to pay a high price in terms of career advancement and potential earnings. Hence, specializing in home work may not be advantageous to the wife or even to her family in the long run, even if it maximizes family well-being in the short run. Unfortunately, many couples may not be aware of this. Hence, they would fail to realize that it might be worthwhile for the family to make some sacrifices of utility during the early years to keep the wife in the labor market, in order to

[9]Harry L. Davis, "Decision Making Within the Household," ed. Robert Ferber, *Selected Aspects of Consumer Behavior. A Summary from the Perspective of Different Disciplines.* Prepared for National Science Foundation, Directorate for Research Applications, RANN-Research Applied to National Needs (Washington, D.C.: U.S. Government Printing Office, 1976), pp. 73-97.

[10]John H. Scanzoni, *Opportunity and the Family* (New York: Free Press, 1970).

[11]For instance, Marianne A. Ferber, "Labor Market Participation of Young Married Women: Causes and Effects," *Journal of Marriage and Family* 44, no. 2 (May 1982): 457-68; Dair L. Gillespie, "Who has the Power? The Marital Struggle," *Journal of Marriage and the Family* 33, no. 3 (August 1971): 445-58; and Hartmann, "The Family as the Locus of Gender, Class, and Political Struggle".

maximize her long-run career prospects and lifetime earnings. The negative effects of women's shorter, and more discontinuous, labor force participation on their earnings and occupational attainment are considered in greater detail in Chapter 7.

It might be argued that offsetting these disadvantages for the wife's career and the lifetime income of the family is the higher quality of children produced when there is a full-time mother at home. However, recent research concerning the effects that alternative ways of caring for children have on their well-being and achievement levels shows that much depends on the quality as well as the quantity of time mothers spend with children, on the quality of the substitutes provided, on social attitudes toward the family's lifestyle, and on the age and sex of the children.[12] An exhaustive review of this work concluded that "taken by itself, the fact that a mother works outside the home has no universally predictable effects on the child."[13] This issue is considered in greater detail in Chapter 5.

Costs of Interdependence

Whatever the probability that the well-being of husband and wife will be maximized by specialization as long as the ongoing arrangement continues, it is not likely to be true in case one or both are faced with the need to fend for themselves. This may happen because of divorce, separation, or the disability or death of one partner. The difficulties encountered are closely related to the points made above regarding the financial dependency of the wife and the negative effect on her potential earnings of time spent out of the labor force. As long as the relationship lasts, both husband and wife may gain from the greater proficiency each acquires in the area in which he or she specializes. However, their skills in the other area are likely to deteriorate, or, at any rate, fail to increase.

This problem will be especially serious for the homemaker. The husband who has concentrated on market work may be seriously inconvenienced because of a lack of household skills. But he has market earnings that may be used to purchase household services. The woman who has specialized in household production, on the other hand, is left with no earnings and market skills that may be obsolete. In view of the high divorce rate and the substantially higher life expectancy of women than men, the risk of becoming a "displaced homemaker" is serious.[14] The special problems of female-headed families are discussed more fully in Chapter 5.

---

[12]Alison Clarke-Stewart, *Child Care in the Family: A Review of Research and Some Propositions for Policy* (N.Y.: Academic Press, 1977).

[13]Urie Bronfenbrenner and Ann. C. Crouter, "Work and Family Through Time and Space," eds. Sheila B. Kamerman and Cheryl D. Hayes, *Families That Work: Children in a Changing World* (Washington, D.C.: National Academy Press, 1982), p. 51.

[14]For example, 7 out of 10 women 55 years old and over live alone, and more than one-third

There are also potential difficulties for a full-time homemaker even if the partnership lasts until her death or until a time when she is adequately taken care of by a pension or inheritance. As pointed out earlier, the value of the homemaker's contribution to the family is greatest while the children are young. Now that the average number of children is about 2 and female life expectancy is 78, this period is relatively early in a woman's life. After that the value of her contribution at home declines. Since during the time she was out of the labor market her earnings ability (generally lower than her husband's to begin with) also declined, her contribution during the latter part of her life is likely to be considerably smaller than her mate's.

One way of looking at this is that the husband's increasing earnings in the market compensate for her declining productivity, and she can now enjoy her share of the family's total income and a good deal of leisure. Yet, even if her partner is very fond of her, is happy to share his largesse, and/or is grateful to her for the considerable contributions she made earlier, she may come to wonder about her present worth to the family. (Who has not heard of the empty nest syndrome?) But she may not be so lucky. Her spouse may ask what she has done for him lately, and take advantage of his increasingly greater bargaining power. This may take the form of his appropriating a larger share of family income for commodities only he uses or only he wants and, in general, adopting a lifestyle that conforms to his, but not necessarily her, preferences.

Disadvantages of Specialization: A Summary

Thus, we find that the traditional family where husband and wife each specialize in a separate sphere is not as advantageous as the simple economic model presented at the beginning of this chapter suggests. Specializing in homemaking is a particularly high-risk undertaking for the value of home production peaks early in the life cycle. Market skills tend to decline when a person is out of the labor market, and a woman is often socially isolated in the home. Therefore, the homemaker's bargaining power within the family is likely to decline over time, and she will find it difficult to manage on her own if the need arises. But there are risks for the wage earner as well. If the marriage breaks up, he will be confronted with the need to pay alimony or face the problem of avoiding it. Also, he may lack even the minimal skills to keep house for himself. Last, but not least, children of divorced parents may have to live in poverty with a mother unable to earn a decent living or, in rare cases, with a father quite inexperienced in child care.

One may speculate why so many couples continue to opt for a lifestyle that raises so many potential problems. A number of obvious answers come to

of them have incomes that fall below the poverty line ("Old at 40: Women in the Workplace," A report from the Institute of Gerontology, University of Michigan, April 1984, p. 2).

mind. First, there can be little doubt that most young people in full awareness of the high divorce rate nonetheless expect their own marriage to succeed. This is not so different from the person who starts a small business, fully expecting to make a go of it in spite of the formidable bankruptcy rate. Second, important initial decisions are made at a relatively young age when concerns for well-being in middle and old age may not loom very large. Third, pressures from relatives and peers toward adoption of traditional family arrangements cannot be entirely discounted. Among some groups it may still take a strong-willed, confident, young person to withstand these pressures. There is, however, no doubt that all this is changing and that surely helps to account for the rising proportion of couples who are rejecting the old breadwinner-homemaker dichotomy.

A MARXIST-FEMINIST VIEW OF THE FAMILY

Substantially different interpretations of the existing division of labor within the family, and its relation to the position of women and men in the labor market, are offered by a variety of radical economists, Marxists, and Marxist-feminists. While there are many disagreements among the proponents of these alternative views, there tends to be considerable emphasis on the role of either capitalism, patriarchy, or both.

Capitalism describes an economy where the preponderance of capital is privately owned and controlled, even though government may also play a large part, as is the case in the United States. Marxists see such an economy as one in which capitalists wield power over workers who do not own the means of production and are, thus, forced to sell their labor. Patriarchy is the name given to a system in which men are dominant over women.

What follows is a synopsis of the analysis of one prominent exponent of Marxist-Feminist theory, Heidi Hartmann.* It differs from this text's neoclassical approach in its emphasis on power relationships both between men and women in the family and between capitalists and workers in the labor market. market.

In this model, the family is seen as a primary source of women's oppression and as a locus of struggle. Even though there are often strong emotional ties within the family, it is not primarily shaped by such kinship relations. Rather, it is a unit where production and redistribution of income take place, with emphasis on material aspects of gender relations. The organization of this production within the family, as well as that outside it, has been shaped by

*Adapted from Heidi I. Hartmann, "Capitalism, Patriarchy, and Job Segregation by Sex," *Signs: Journal of Women in Culture and Society* 1, no. 3, Pt. 2 (Spring 1976): 137–70; and Heidi I. Hartmann, "The Family as the Locus of Gender, Class and Political Struggle: The Example of Housework," *Signs: Journal of Women in Culture and Society* 6, no. 3 (Spring 1981): 366–94. Adapted by permission.

both patriarchy and capitalism. Hence, according to this model, production in the family is based on unequal division of labor by class and gender, inevitably bringing about conflict and change.

Individuals within the family are mutually dependent and to a degree their interests are unified. However, they also act as members of gender categories so that there is room for conflict about many issues. Who does the housework, and how much of it is to be done? Should the woman work outside the home? How should the money be spent? Data that indicate that women do the vast majority of the housework, even when they are employed outside the home, and that men are dominant in decision-making power are offered as evidence of patriarchy in the family.

Marxist-feminists argue that capitalism was preceded by a patriarchal system that, in turn, shaped the form modern capitalism took. The primary mechanism for maintaining male superiority in the capitalistic economy is occupational segregation, the restriction of women in the labor market to a small number of predominantly female jobs. Job segregation reinforces the traditional division of domestic labor because it results in lower wages for women and, thus, makes them economically dependent on men. At the same time, the traditional division of labor in the home reinforces occupational segregation by weakening women's position in the labor market.

The present status of women in the labor market and the current arrangement of sex-segregated jobs are seen as the results of a long process of interaction between patriarchy and capitalism. The actions of male workers and their unions have been an important factor in bringing this about. If women's subordination is to end and if men are to begin to escape their own class oppression and exploitation, men will have to be forced to give up their favored positions in the division of labor—in the labor market and at home. Capitalism grew on top of patriarchy; patriarchal capitalism is stratified society par excellence. If non-ruling-class men are to be free, they will have to relinquish their patriarchal benefits as well as struggle against capitalism. If women are to be free, they must fight against both patriarchal power and the capitalist organization of society.

POLICY ISSUE: SPECIALIZATION AND TAXES

Up to this point, we have been comparing home production and market earnings as though families received the full benefit of each. In fact, the benefits that families actually receive and retain depend upon government transfer and tax policies. Two of the federal government's major programs in this area, income taxes and the social security system, have been particularly criticized as being biased in favor of the traditional, one-earner family. The argument is made that these programs, which evolved when the one-earner family was the norm, need to be modified in the face of the changing structure of American families.

One of the primary rules economists have proposed for fair taxation is

horizontal equity which means simply that *equals should be treated equally.*[15] That is, those in similar circumstances should be treated the same. Do current government policies offend against this rule in their treatment of one-earner and-two-earner families? We consider this question below for income tax and social security policies.[16]

Income Taxation Policy

It is claimed that government policy in this area is inequitable because the value of goods and services produced in the home is not taxed, while money income is subject to taxation. As a result, two families with the same level of economic well-being are not treated the same way. Suppose one couple, Ellen and Ed, who are both employed, together earn $40,000 and produce $10,000 worth of goods and services for the family during time spent at home. In the case of a second couple, Jim earns $30,000 in the market and Jane, a full-time homemaker, produces $20,000 worth of goods and services at home. While both couples enjoy the same total income (including the value of home-produced goods and services) of $50,000, Ellen and Ed will be taxed on a money income of $40,000, while Jane and Jim will be taxed on a money income of $30,000. Assuming that each couple has two children, Ellen and Ed would have paid $2,263 more in taxes in 1984.[17]

One of the concerns with such a policy is that it creates a disincentive for married women to participate in the labor force. Hence, it provides incentives for families to adopt the traditional division of labor. This is the case, not only because market earnings are taxed, while home production is not. The disincentive to market work is further increased by the **progressivity** of the tax system, meaning that higher levels of family income are taxed at a higher rate than lower levels. In general, progressivity is believed to be a good idea because it is supposed to result in wealthier families bearing a higher share of the tax burden. However, it also means that a married woman can face a relatively high marginal tax rate on her potential income when deciding whether or not to work outside the home.

To see this, consider the case of Bob and Sue. Suppose that Bob earns

---

[15] "There is a generally accepted standard of equity or fairness with respect to public finance measures: equal treatment of those equally circumstanced." Carl S. Shoup, *Public Finance* (Chicago: Aldine Publishing Company, 1969), p. 23.

[16] These topics are discussed in Nancy R. Gordon, "Institutional Responses: The Federal Income Tax System" and "Institutional Responses: The Social Security System," ed. Ralph E. Smith, *The Subtle Revolution,* (Washington, D.C.: The Urban Institute, 1979), pp. 201-21, 223-55; and Richard V. Burkhauser and Karen C. Holden, eds., *A Challenge to Social Security: The Changing Roles of Women and Men in American Society* (New York: Academic Press, 1982).

[17] In all the examples provided in the text, it is assumed that married couples file a joint tax return and take the standard deduction. In this particular example, it is further assumed that Ellen earns $15,000, and Ed earns $25,000. It is necessary to know how much each earns in order to compute the deduction available to a married couple in which both spouses work. This deduction is discussed below.

$25,000 in the market and that Sue is considering taking a market job for $15,000. Sue's earnings will push the family into a higher tax bracket and reduce her potential benefits of market work. Assuming the couple has no children, taxes on their $25,000 income would be $3,113 (12.5 percent of their gross income) in 1984. Sue's entry into the labor force would *increase* their tax liability by $3,590. Putting this differently, Sue would owe 23.9 percent of her $15,000 earnings in federal taxes. Taking into account social security taxes, work-related expenses, and the reduction in the value of her home production, she may conclude that labor force participation is not worthwhile.

The unfavorable tax treatment of the two-earner family vs. the one-earner family is also illustrated by the fact that, under existing tax laws, a two-earner couple may pay a tax penalty for being married, while a one-earner family generally receives a tax advantage. This is because a married couple pays a lower tax rate than a single individual with the same income. So, if a man marries and his wife does not work, his tax liability is reduced. On the other hand, when two individuals marry and both continue to work, their combined income will place them in a higher tax bracket than each would have been in individually, and their (combined) tax liability will be increased. This is the so-called "marriage penalty" that affects working couples.

In the case of Bob and Sue, for example, their tax liability would be $637 higher as a married couple with a family income of $40,000 than it would have been if they filed separately as two unmarried individuals—with Bob earning $25,000 and Sue earning $15,000.[18]

As another example, if Steve and Pat (who each earn $35,000) had married, they would have owed an additional $2,322 in taxes in 1984 than if they had remained single. In general, the higher and the more equal the earnings of the married people, the higher the marriage penalty they would pay. Such policies could deter career-oriented couples from marrying.

In terms of potential solutions to these perceived inequities, the possibility of taxing household production has received almost no attention. It is doubtful such a proposal would command much popular support. Moreover, it would be extremely difficult to implement since it would be almost impossible to obtain reliable estimates of the value of household production.

An alternative proposal, which would eliminate both the work disincentive and the marriage penalty, would be to tax each person as an individual. This would equalize tax rates for individuals with equal income, regardless of their marital status. Individual taxation has been adopted in Sweden but has not received much support in this country. Whether it is viewed as more equitable in its treatment of *money* income than the current arrangement (in terms of our definition of horizontal equity) depends on whether the individual or the family is viewed as the appropriate tax unit. Such a change

---

[18]Bob and Sue cannot get around this problem by filing separate tax returns. The tax rates for "married individuals filing separately" are higher than the tax rates levied on "single individuals."

would benefit two-earner couples but would increase tha tax liability of one-earner families, even though these families still benefit because in-kind income is not taxed.

The adoption of a so-called "flat tax," which taxes all income at the same rate, would be another possible way of eliminating the work disincentive. The marriage penalty would also be eliminated if married couples and single individuals paid the same tax rate.

A law introduced in 1981 took a step in the direction of reducing the tax advantages of one- versus two-earner families. This legislation provided that, by 1983, 10 percent of the income of the lower earning partner (up to $30,000) was to be tax exempt. Even with this law in effect, however, the examples provided above show that the work disincentive and marriage penalty problems remained substantial.[19] The continued growth of the two-earner family may generate support for further measures, possibly including individual taxation, to reduce the relatively unfavorable tax treatment of this group.

Social Security System

The social security system, which covers 9 out of 10 American wage earners, also poses problems of equity between one- and two-earner families. As presently constituted, proportional taxes to a specified maximum of earnings are levied, half to be paid by the employer, half by the worker. One controversial aspect of the system centers on the provision of spouse and survivor benefits.

The spouse benefit is equal to 50 percent of the covered worker's benefit, and the survivor benefit is equal to 100 percent. The spouse of a covered worker is entitled to receive a spouse or survivor benefit *or* a benefit based on his or her own earnings record, whichever amount is greater. Since many married women have substantially lower wages and shorter work lives than their husbands, they are often better off collecting spouse or survivor benefits than benefits based on their own earnings. The additional taxes, which they have paid into the system as workers, have yielded them no increase in benefits. Even those wives who get somewhat higher benefits because of their own participation in the system get a relatively low return on their tax payments. One-earner families get the highest returns on their payments into the system—only the husband pays social security taxes and the wife receives a spouse or survivor benefit.

This situation may be considered to violate one rule of horizontal equity—equal contributions into the system do not secure the same return for all individuals (or both types of families). Further, under such circumstances, social security taxes are likely to be a deterrent to labor force participation among wives. For, again, while they are required to pay social security taxes

---

[19]The deduction available for working couples was included in our calculations of married couple's tax liability. The 1981 law also expanded the child care credit to 20 percent of the first $2400 spent, thus affording some additional tax relief to working couples with small children.

on their market earnings, they get little or no return on their payments.

One proposed solution to these problems is "earnings sharing" in which an equal share of total household earnings is assigned to each spouse. This proposal recognizes that the division of labor in the home represents a familial decision and that both spouses contribute to family welfare through their market and/or nonmarket work. Earnings sharing is neutral with respect to the work roles of the husband and wife and would, thus, be more encouraging of labor force participation than the current system. The social security system would move in the direction of greater horizontal equity in that equal contributions yield equal benefits. At the same time, two-earner families would gain at the expense of one-earner families because spouse benefits would be eliminated. As in the case of individual taxation, support for such a policy is likely to increase with the continued growth of the two-earner family.

CONCLUSION

We have seen in Chapter 2 that the "traditional family" evolved with the man as the breadwinner and the woman as the homemaker, combining her time with the goods and services purchased with the husband's earnings to satisfy the family's needs and wants. The simple neoclassical model explains how such a division of labor may be advantageous under appropriate conditions. But as we have also seen, it cannot be taken for granted that these conditions are satisifed at any given point in time, let alone that they will be for the rest of each person's life.

The traditional specialization may have come about because conditions that existed at that time made such an arrangement more nearly optimal than it is today. There are several obvious reasons for this. When cloth was spun, bread was baked, and soap was produced at home, the family was large, and there were few opportunities for women to earn a decent market wage, her relative advantage for home work was great. With many children, and a shorter life expectancy, the problem of the decline in the value of housework after the children grew up was far less serious. With severe social and religious sanctions against divorce, women were less likely to find themselves, and their children, dependent on a recalcitrant ex-husband for a living.

However, as these factors have changed, the advantages of the traditional division of labor have decreased while the costs associated with it, particularly for women, have increased. Growing recognition of the drawbacks of the traditional division of responsibilities between husband and wife may be one of the factors that has contributed to the decline in the proportion of families following this pattern. These developments will be analyzed further in the next chapter. Increasing awareness of the potentially high costs of specialization should enable young people to make better informed decisions and should cause policymakers to reconsider social policies that favor one-earner families and, thus, inhibit more rapid change.

Appendix

SPECIALIZATION AND EXCHANGE: A GRAPHICAL ANALYSIS

As discussed in Chapter 3, a complete analysis of the division of labor between the individuals who make up a couple takes into account both their production possibilities and their preferences. In this appendix, we do this by providing a fuller examination of the simple neoclassical model in the context of a graphical analysis. The same conclusions are reached as to the value of specialization and exchange.

For simplicity, we assume that individuals derive utility from only two types of goods—home goods, produced with inputs of home time, and market goods, purchased with market income. In Figure 3.1, H and M measure the dollar value of household output and market goods, respectively. Two persons, Kathy and Jim, each allocate their time between market work (M production) and housework (H production).[20]

If Kathy and Jim are each dependent on their own output, their consumption opportunities are limited to their individual *production possibility*

---

[20]We also assume fixed proportions production functions for H and M for each individual. This means, for example, that an additional hour spent on the production of H by Kathy increases output by the same amount, regardless of how much H she has already produced. This simplifying assumption results in the straight line production possibility frontiers shown in Figure 3.1.

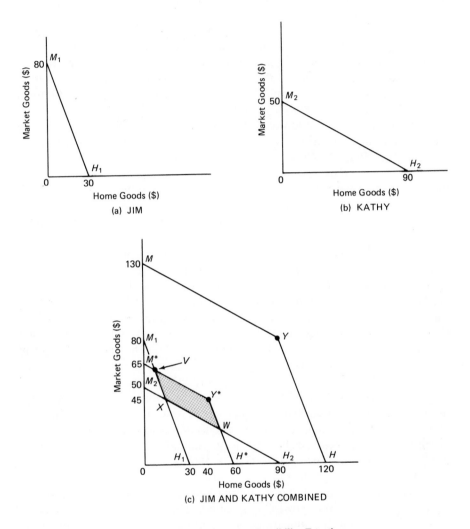

FIGURE 3.1   Separate and Combined Production Possibility Frontiers

frontiers. The production possibility frontier shows the largest feasible combinations of the two outputs that can be produced with given resources (e.g., in this case, time inputs) and know how. M_1H_1 indicates the combinations of household and market outputs available to Jim, while M_2H_2 shows the best options from which Kathy can choose. For example, if Jim devotes full time to market work (*M* production), he can produce a maximum of $80 worth of market goods. If he spends all his time on household activities, he can produce $30 worth of home goods.

The slope of the line, M_1H_1, tells us the money value of the market goods Jim must give up to get an additional dollar of home goods. The fact that M_1H_1 is more steeply sloped than M_2H_2 means that Jim must give up more market goods to get an additional dollar of home goods than Kathy. Specifically, Jim must give up $2.67 of market goods to get an additional dollar of home goods ($80/$30), while Kathy needs to give up only $.56 of market goods to get an additional dollar of home goods ($50/$90). Viewing the matter somewhat differently, Kathy must forego more home goods to get an additional dollar of market goods than Jim. Kathy would have to give up $1.80 worth of home goods to get an additional dollar of market goods ($90/$50), while Jim needs to give up only $.38 worth of home goods to get an additional dollar of market goods ($30/$80). Thus, Jim has a comparative advantage in market work, while Kathy has a comparative advantage in home production.

If Jim and Kathy decide to collaborate, their combined production possibility curve will be MYH as shown in panel c. At point M both Jim and Kathy specialize entirely in market work, producing $130 ($80 + $50) of market goods. If they prefer to have some home goods, it will pay for only Kathy to do housework, up to the point where she does no market work at all (point Y), because she adds more to home production ($1.80) for every dollar of market goods given up than Jim would add ($.38). Therefore, the segment MY has the same slope as M_2H_2, showing that as long as only Kathy is dividing her time between market and home, it is Kathy's slope that is relevant. Jim will do some housework only if a mix of more household production and fewer market goods are desired than it represents. Beyond that point, it is the slope of M_1H_1 that becomes relevant, since it is only Jim who is dividing his time between home and market. At the extreme, at point H, both Jim and Kathy work only in the home, producing $120 ($30 + $90) of home goods.

The combined production possibility frontier (MYH) makes feasible combinations of M and H that would not be attainable by Kathy and Jim on their separate production possibility frontiers. These gains from specialization and exchange may be illustrated by putting the output combinations represented by production possibility frontier MYH on a per capita or per person basis. Dividing MYH by two we obtain $M^*Y^*H^*$, which may be compared to the options represented by Jim and Kathy's individual production possibility frontiers, M_1H_1 and M_2H_2 (panel c). The shaded area $WXVY^*$ represents the increased per capita output that is now available. This gain in output may potentially be distributed between Jim and Kathy so as to make them both better off than they would have been separately. To obtain the gains represented by $WXVY^*$, the couple must produce a nontrivial amount of both market- and home-produced goods, for it is the production of both commodities that gives each of them the opportunity to specialize in the area of their comparative advantage.

This analysis also illustrates that the gains to specialization will be larger, the more the individuals that make up the couple differ in their comparative advantages. To see this, imagine the extreme case in which Kathy and Jim both have the same production possibility frontier, say M_1H_1. The combined production possibility frontier would then be $2 \times M_1H_1$. On a per capita basis (dividing the combined production possibility frontier in half), we would simply be left with M_1H_1. Kathy and Jim would do no better combining forces than they would each do separately. Based on this simple analysis alone, it is not clear what the economic gains to collaborating are. However, as we saw in Chapter 3, there are likely to be economic gains even in this case, mainly because two people can use many goods and services more efficiently than a single person can. Here, we focus on the couple that can potentially increase its income through joint production.

To provide a link between the potential increase in output due to collaboration and the goal of maximizing satisfaction, we need to introduce an additional tool of economic analysis and pursue our inquiry one step further. So far we have only established the various combinations of the two types of outputs that Kathy and Jim could produce. Which of these they would choose depends on their tastes, that is to say, on their preferences for market goods compared to home goods. To considerably simplify the analysis, we will

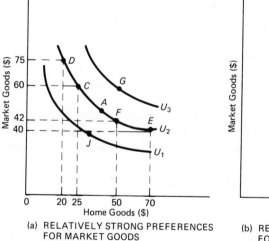
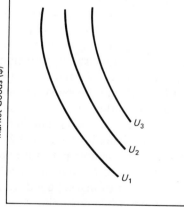

(a) RELATIVELY STRONG PREFERENCES FOR MARKET GOODS

(b) RELATIVELY STRONG PREFERENCES FOR HOME GOODS

FIGURE 3.2 Indifference Curves

assume that they both have identical tastes. If home goods are valued more highly than market goods, the couple will be willing to give up a considerable amount of market goods in order to get an additional dollar of home goods, and vice versa if market goods are valued more highly. This relationship can be illustrated using **indifference curves,** as seen in Figure 3.2.

Let us assume that Kathy and Jim have been told that they could have the combination of market and home goods represented by point A in panel (a). They are then asked to find various other combinations of H and M from which they would derive exactly the same amount of satisfaction or utility. These other points can all be connected into one indifference curve, U_2, called that because the couple is indifferent about being at various points on the curve. The U_2 curve is *negatively sloped.* This means that if the amount of market or home goods is decreased, the amount of the other good must be increased for the couple to remain equally well-off.

Notice too that indifference curve U_2 is convex to the origin. That is, it gets steeper as we move to the left and flatter as we move to the right. What this means is that at a point like C where M goods are relatively plentiful and H goods are relatively scarce, it takes a fairly large amount of M ($15 worth) to induce the couple to give up a fairly small amount of H ($5 worth) and still remain equally well-off. On the other hand, at a point like E where M goods are relatively scarce and H goods are relatively plentiful, the couple is willing to give up a fairly large amount of H ($20 worth) to get even a small additional amount of scarce M ($2 worth). This is generally realistic to the extent that relatively scarce goods are valued more highly.

However, Kathy and Jim do not have just one indifference curve but rather a whole family of higher or lower indifference curves. For it is possible to choose a point like G on curve U_3 that offers more of both M and H and, hence, is clearly preferable to point A on curve U_2. Hence, all points on curve U_3 will, by extension, be preferable to (give more satisfaction than) all points on curve U_2. Similarly, it is possible to choose a point like J on curve U_1 that offers less of both M and H than at point A. Point J is clearly less desirable than Point A and, by extension, all points on curve U_1 are less desirable (give less satisfaction) than all points on curve U_2.[21]

On the other hand, another couple's preferences might look like those depicted in panel b of Figure 3.2. These indifference curves are steeper and show that this couple places a relatively higher value on home goods, compared with market goods than Kathy and Jim do. In general, it would take a larger amount of market goods to induce them to give up a dollar's worth of home goods while remaining equally well-off.

[21]It should be clear that indifference curves can never intersect. All points on any one curve represent an equal amount of utility, while any point above (below) represents a larger (smaller) amount of utility. At the point where two curves intersect, they clearly represent the same amount of utility, yet at all other points they do not. This is a logical impossibility.

To determine the division of labor (or time allocation) a couple will actually choose, we must consider both their production possibilities and their tastes or preferences. In Figure 3.3, we superimpose the couple's hypothetical indifference map on the production possibility frontier shown in Figure 3.1, panel (c). It is then readily possible to determine the combination of home-produced and market-produced goods that a rational couple with those tastes (indifference curves) will choose. It will always be the point where the produc-

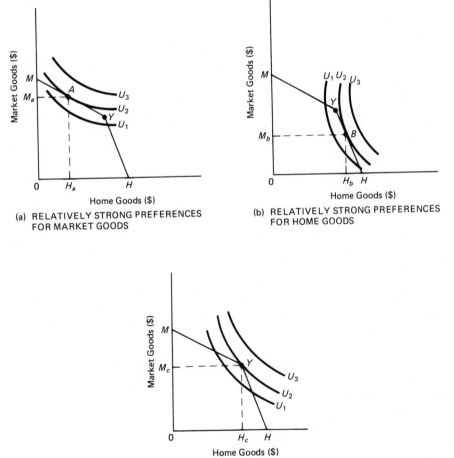

(a) RELATIVELY STRONG PREFERENCES FOR MARKET GOODS

(b) RELATIVELY STRONG PREFERENCES FOR HOME GOODS

(c) INTERMEDIATE PREFERENCES

FIGURE 3.3   **The Role of Tastes in Determining the Household Division of Labor**

tion possibility curve just touches the highest indifference curve it reaches. The reason is simple—the couple always prefers to be on a higher indifference curve (by definition, as we have seen), but since they are constrained to the possible combinations of output represented by the production possibility frontier, there is no realistic way they can reach an indifference curve that at all points lies above the frontier.

In Figure 3.3, we illustrate the impact of the couple's preferences on their time allocation. The combined production possibility curve for the couple, MYH, shows the various combinations of H and M the couple can produce while taking full advantage of their combined resources and the comparative advantage each has in producing one of the goods. Let us continue to assume that the wife has a comparative advantage in home production and that the husband has a comparative advantage in market work.

As may be seen in panel (a), a couple with relatively strong preferences for market goods will maximize satisfaction at point A along segment MY. The husband will specialize entirely in market production and the wife will do all the housework and also supply some time to the market. They will consume M_a dollars of market goods and H_a dollars of home goods.

Panel (b) shows a couple with stronger preferences for home-produced goods. They will maximize utility at point B. The wife will devote herself entirely to household production, while the husband will do some housework as well as supplying time to the market. Such a couple will consume fewer market goods (M_b) and more home goods (H_b) than a couple with stronger preferences for market goods.

Finally, panel c shows a couple with intermediate tastes. They will maximize utility at point Y. Both wife and husband will each fully specialize in home and market production, respectively, and will consume M_c dollars of market goods and H_c dollars of home goods.

Couples may differ in their allocation of tasks within the family, not solely due to differences in tastes. The relative productivity of each member of the family in the production of market and home goods will also be an important factor. We have already noted that if both husband and wife are equally productive in each endeavor, there will be no gains to specialization or division of labor within the family. However, even if we assume that the wife has a comparative advantage in household production and that the husband has a comparative advantage in market work, the relative productivities of each individual in home and market production are still relevant. This is illustrated in Figure 3.4.

Panel (a) shows two hypothetical production possibility functions. In MYH, the segment corresponding to the wife's frontier (MY) is relatively flat indicating that she is considerably more productive in the home than in the market. For given tastes (represented by indifference curve U), the couple maximizes utility at point Y, where the wife specializes entirely in home production and the husband specializes completely in market work. However, if the couple's production possibility frontier were $M'Y'H'$, even with the same tastes (indifference curve), they would choose point A along segment $M'Y'$. Here the wife will continue to do all the housework but will do some market work as well. This is because $M'Y'$ is steeper than MY, indicating a higher ratio of the wife's market productivity relative to her home productivity. The opportunity cost of home goods in terms of market goods foregone has increased and as a result the family consumes less of them.

Similarly, as shown in panel b, the couple's time allocation may also depend on the husband's relative productivity in the home and the market. For given tastes (represented by indifference curve U), the couple will choose point Y when the husband's productivity in the home is extremely low relative to his market productivity. (This is indicated by the relatively steep slope of segment YH on frontier MYH.) They are more likely to choose a point like B along the flatter segment $Y'H'$ on frontier $M'Y'H'$, where he does some housework as well as market work, when his market productivity is lower relative to his home productivity. At B, the couple consumes more of the now relatively cheaper home-produced goods than at Y.

Figure 3.4 shows how the relative productivity of the husband and the wife in the home and the market influence the division of labor in the family and the combination of home- and market-produced goods that they choose to

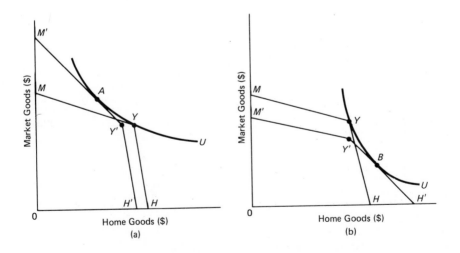

FIGURE 3.4   The Role of the Production Possibility Frontier in Determining the Household Division of Labor

consume. Nonetheless, as long as the comparative advantages of husband and wife differ in this simple model, specialization will be efficient. As we have seen, the greater the difference between the two in their comparative advantage, the greater the gains to specialization and exchange.

Thus, the fuller analysis presented here supports the conclusions reached on the basis of the numerical example provided in Chapter 3. In this case too, however, the same qualifications hold. First, there are other potential economic benefits to marriage besides specialization and exchange, and, second, there are disadvantages, particularly for women, to the traditional division of labor.

SUGGESTED READINGS

BECKER, GARY S., *A Treatise on the Family.* Harvard University Press, 1981.
FERBER, MARIANNE A. and BONNIE G. BIRNBAUM, "The 'New Home Economics: Retrospects and Prospects," *Journal of Consumer Research* 4, no. 1 (June 1977): 19-28.
GILLESPIE, DAIR L., "Who Has the Power? The Marital Struggle," *Journal of Marriage and the Family* 33, no. 3 (August 1971): 445-58.
HARTMANN, HEIDI I., "The Family as the Locus of Gender, Class and Political Struggle: The Example of Housework," *Signs: Journal of Women in Culture and Society* 6, no. 3 (Spring 1981): 366-94.

THE ALLOCATION OF TIME BETWEEN THE HOUSEHOLD AND THE LABOR MARKET

The continued and increasingly rapid growth in women's labor force participation has been one of the most significant economic and social developments in this country and elsewhere. It is, therefore, important to understand the meaning and nature of this phenomenon before going on to examine its causes and to discuss some of its effects. In this chapter, we first review the definition of the labor force and summarize female and male trends over time in labor force participation. We shall see that while female participation rates have been increasing, particularly in the post-1940 period, male rates have been declining, albeit not as dramatically. As a consequence of both types of changes, men's and women's labor force participation rates and their patterns of involvement in market work over the life cycle have been becoming increasingly similar. We then turn to the development of some economic concepts for analyzing these trends, and use them to provide a better understanding of the reasons for the remarkable influx of women into the labor market. Essentially, the dramatic rise in women's labor force participation is attributed to an increase in the value of their time in the market relative to the value of time spent in the home. In Chapter 5, we examine the consequences for the family of women's increasing employment outside the home.

THE LABOR FORCE: SOME DEFINITIONS

Each month, the U.S. Bureau of the Census conducts a survey to gather statistics on the labor force. According to the official definition, the **labor force** includes all those individuals 16 years of age and over who worked for pay or profit during the reference week or actively sought paid employment during the four weeks prior to the reference week. That is, the labor force is comprised of both the employed and the unemployed.

The **employed** group includes all those who worked one hour per week or more as paid employees or were self-employed in their own business or profession or on their own farm. This includes part-time workers who worked less than 35 hours per week, as well as those who worked full-time, 35 hours or more. It also includes all those temporarily absent from paid employment because of bad weather, vacation, labor-management disputes, or personal reasons, whether or not they were paid. An exception to the emphasis on paid employment is that those who worked at least 15 hours as unpaid workers in an enterprise operated by a family member are also included.[1] The **unemployed** include those who do not have a job but who have made specific efforts to find a job within the past four weeks, as well as those not working but waiting to be called back to work or to report for a new job within 30 days.

The **labor force participation rate** of a particular group is equal to the number of its members who are in the labor force divided by the total number in the group who are of working age. Thus, for example, a labor force participation rate of .53 for women means that 53 percent of women 16 years of age and over are labor force participants.

A careful reading of the definition of the labor force makes it clear that being in the labor force is not synonymous with working. Persons who work less than 15 hours a week as unpaid family workers, and those who work only in the household or as volunteer workers, no matter how many hours, are excluded. On the other hand, persons temporarily not working, or unemployed, are included. In large part, this results from the emphasis (in the official definition of the labor force) on being employed in or seeking *market* work. Since women have tended to have primary responsibility for nonmarket work, they constitute a high proportion in the categories that are left out. Thus, their share of the labor force considerably understates their share of work. This was particularly true in earlier days when family enterprises were more common

---

[1]The labor force excludes illegal activities such as prostitution and drug trafficking. In the nature of the case, no data are available that would enable us to obtain reliable estimates on the extent of these activities. Further, employment ranging from baby sitting to yard work, which is paid for in cash and not reported for tax purposes (the so-called "underground economy"), is likely to be under-reported in labor force statistics.

and when most married women were homemakers.[2] In spite of these reservations, women's labor force participation rate is probably an important indicator of their status in a market economy, for work done outside the labor market seldom offers as much prestige, let alone money income, and is sometimes not even viewed as real "work."[3]

TRENDS IN LABOR FORCE PARTICIPATION

The purpose of this section is to briefly review the trends in female and male labor force participation. The reasons for the observed changes are considered later. But here we may obtain an overview of how dramatic these changes have been. Labor force participation rates for selected years since 1890 are shown in Table 4.1. The figures indicate a relatively slow rate of increase in the labor force participation rates of women in the pre-1940 period. In the years since 1940, however, more dramatic changes in women's labor force status have occurred. In 1940, 27.9 percent of women were in the labor force; by 1984, the figure had risen to 53.7 percent. During this time, women workers increased from one quarter to over two-fifths of the total labor force.

This rapid influx of women into the work force is by no means unique to the United States. On the contrary, as we shall see in Chapter 10, it is typical for most industrialized countries and for many developing countries as well. Further the labor force participation rate of women is considerably higher than in the United States not only in Eastern Europe and some developing countries, but also among some nations in Western Europe.

[2] It has been suggested that such activities as taking in boarders, piecework done at home, and even seasonal work done in factories frequently went unreported, especially when it was the husband who was interviewed. (See, for instance, Milton Cantor and Bruce Laurie, eds., *Class, Sex, and the Woman Worker* (Westport, Conn: Greenwood Press, 1977.) How important this undercount may have been is suggested by the fact that when the Census enumerators in 1910 were given instructions to take special care not to overlook women workers, especially unpaid family workers, the participation rate was found to be about 4 percentage points higher than would be expected based on earlier and immediately subsequent decades. It is for this reason that the year 1910 is normally omitted from historical series on women's labor force participation. We follow this practice in Table 4.1.

[3] Most of us have heard a woman say in response to the question whether she works, "No, I am a housewife." Other aspects of the official definition of the labor force have also been the object of criticism at various times. For example, the definition of the unemployed excludes those who would like a job but who have given up searching because they believe no work is available, so-called discouraged workers. While no definition is likely to be equally satisfactory to all, adherence to a reasonably consistent definition over a long period of time provides useful data for analyzing trends. In some cases, criticism has been accommodated by providing additional data that may be used to construct labor force measures based on different definitions. We take advantage of such data on discouraged workers in our discussion of unemployment in Chapter 9.

TABLE 4.1   Labor Force Participation Rates of Men and Women, 1890-1984[a]
(Total Labor Force)

	PERCENT OF MEN IN THE LABOR FORCE	PERCENT OF WOMEN IN THE LABOR FORCE
1890	84.3	18.2
1900	85.7	20.0
1920	84.6	22.7
1930	82.1	23.6
1940	82.5	27.9
1945	87.6	35.8
1947	86.8	31.5
1950	86.8	33.9
1960	84.0	37.8
1970	80.6	43.4
1980	77.9	51.6
1984	76.8	53.7

[a]Prior to 1947 based on population 14 years of age and over; thereafter 16 years and over.

Sources: U.S. Department of Commerce, Bureau of the Census, *Historical Statistics of the United States, Colonial Times to 1970,* Bicentennial Edition, Part 1, 1975, pp. 131–32; U.S. Department of Labor, *Employment and Training Report of the President,* 1982, Table A-1, pp. 147–48; U.S. Department of Labor, Bureau of Labor Statistics, *Employment and Earnings* 32, no. 1 (January 1985), p. 16.

Table 4.1 also indicates the dramatic effect that the mobilization for World War II had on female labor force participation. As males left their civilian jobs to join the armed forces, women entered the labor force in unprecedented numbers. Between 1940 and 1945, the female labor force participation rate increased from 27.9 to 35.8 percent. As suggested by the 1947 figures, some decline occurred in the immediate post-World War II period. However, since that time, the female participation rate has continued to increase and at a pace considerably in excess of the pre-1940 period.

In contrast to the situation for women, male labor force participation rates began to decline in the 1950s, from 86.8 percent in 1950 to 76.8 percent in 1984. As a consequence of these opposing trends, the *difference* between the male and female participation rates has declined sharply from 54.6 percentage points in 1940 to 23.1 percentage points in 1984.

We gain a fuller picture of the trends in labor force participation by examining them separately for different subgroups. Table 4.2 shows trends in labor force participation since 1955 by race and Hispanic origin. The participation rate has declined for all groups of men but considerably more so for nonwhites (mostly blacks), who have now fallen considerably behind. Hispanic men, however, are more likely to be in the labor force than other white or nonwhite males. The rate has risen for all groups of women but substantially more so for whites and Hispanics. Nonwhite women have tradi-

TABLE 4.2   Labor Force Participation Rates of Men and Women by Race and Hispanic Origin, 1955-1984[a]

(percent)

	MALES			FEMALES		
	White	*Nonwhite*	*Hispanic[b]*	*White*	*Nonwhite*	*Hispanic[b]*
1955	85.4	85.0	n.a.	34.5	46.1	n.a.
1965	80.8	79.6	n.a.	38.1	48.6	n.a.
1973	79.5	73.8	81.5	44.1	49.1	40.9
1981	77.9	70.6	80.6	51.9	53.6	47.5
1984	77.1	71.4	80.5	53.3	55.3	49.9

[a]Civilian labor force, includes population aged 16 and over.
[b]Hispanics are also included under the relevant racial category.
n.a. Not available.

Source: 1955-73 U.S. Department of Labor, Bureau of Labor Statistics; 1977, *U.S. Working Women: A Databook,* pp. 44-5; 1981, U.S. Department of Commerce, Bureau of the Census, *Labor Force Statistics Derived from the Current Population Survey: A Databook;* and 1984, U.S. Department of Labor Statistics, *Employment Earnings* 32, no. 1 (January 1985), pp. 157, 159.

tionally had considerably higher labor force participation rates than white women. The gap has now almost closed, but it should be noted that nonwhite women still tend to work longer hours. Hispanic women continue to have a lower labor force participation rate than other white or nonwhite women.

The influx of women into the labor market that has occurred since 1940 has been accompanied by pronounced changes in the patterns of female labor force participation over the life cycle. Before 1940, the typical female worker was young and single, since women tended to leave the labor force permanently upon marriage and childbearing. As Figure 4.1 shows, at that time, the peak age-specific participation rate occurred among women 20 to 24 years of age and declined for each successive age group after that. Over the next 20 years, older married women entered or re-entered the labor force in increasing numbers, while the labor force participation rates of women between 20 and 34 years of age remained relatively constant. Married women comprised 30 percent of women workers in 1940 and 54 percent in 1960. The World War II experience may have played some part in encouraging this shift in the behavior of married women, since it was during the war that for the first time large numbers of older married women worked outside the home.[4]

---

[4]William H. Chafe (*The American Woman: Her Changing Social, Economic, and Political Role, 1920-1970,* Oxford: Oxford University Press, 1972), argues that the notion that woman's appropriate sphere was in the home was so deeply embedded that it took a cataclysmic event like World War II to break down this normative barrier. This is an instance where a significant change in tastes is likely to have come about as a result of women's experience during World War II. Such shifts are generally ignored in economic models that tend to simply take tastes as given.

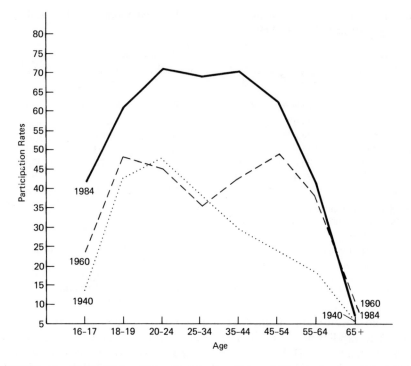

FIGURE 4.1   Civilian Labor Force Participation Rates of Women by Age, Selected Years, 1940-1984.

    Since 1960 there has been a sizable increase in the participation rates of all women under 65, particularly among women aged 20 to 44. This increase in part reflects declines in the birth rate and increases in the divorce rate over this period. Most notable, however, has been the large increase—from 18.6 percent in 1960 to 51.8 percent in 1984—in the labor force participation rate of married women, spouse present, with children under 6 years of age.

    As a result of these changes, the pattern of labor force participation by age among women has come to more closely resemble the male pattern shown in Figure 4.2. Figure 4.2 also shows that the decline in male labor force participation rates that occurred during the post-World War II period was concentrated among younger men under 24 (particularly those under 19) and among older men, aged 55 and over. Since the 1960s, there has also been a small decrease in the participation rates of men in the so-called prime working ages, not only those 45 to 54 but even those 25 to 44. Participation rates for these age groups remain extremely high, however, with over 90 percent of men in the 25 to 54 age group in the labor force.

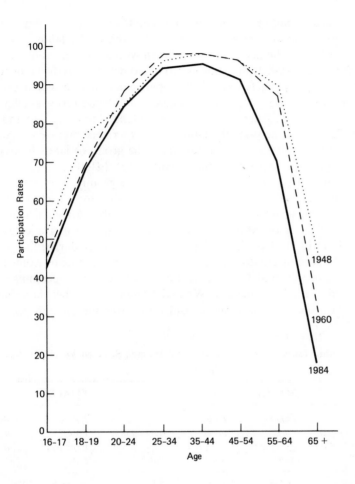

FIGURE 4.2   Civilian Labor Force Participation Rates of Men by Age, Selected Years, 1948-1984

TRENDS IN LABOR FORCE ATTACHMENT

The changes in the pattern of women's labor force participation (by age) that have occurred since 1940 suggest that rising female participation rates have been associated with an increase in the labor force attachment of women over the life cycle. That is, women are tending to remain in the labor force more consistently over a period of time.

Some indication of women's increasing labor force attachment is provided in Table 4.3. This table shows the **labor force participation rate**, which, it may be recalled, is the percentage of a particular group (say, women) who are in the labor force *at a point in time.* It also shows the **labor force experience rate,** which is the percentage of women who are in the labor force *at some time during the year.* If the same group of women were in the labor force consistently over the year, the labor force participation rate would exactly equal the labor force experience rate, and there would be no *turnover* (change) of the labor force group. Alternatively, if women tended to move into and out of the labor force over the year, the labor force experience rate would exceed the labor force participation rate. In this case, the group of labor force participants would include some different individuals at different points in time (that is, there would be *turnover* in the labor force group). The **labor force turnover rate** is equal to the difference between the labor force experience rate and the labor force participation rate divided by the labor force participation rate. It is an indicator of labor force attachment and tells us the extent to which the composition of the labor force group *turns over* during the year.

As may be seen in Table 4.3, the labor force turnover rate of women has been declining since the mid-1960s, indicating that women are becoming more firmly attached to the labor market. While the rate is still higher than that of men, the sex differential has fallen considerably over the past 30 years. A

TABLE 4.3   Labor Force Turnover of Men and Women Selected Years, 1957-81[a]
(percent)

	MALES			FEMALES		
Year	*Labor Force Participation Rate[b]*	*Labor Force Experience Rate[c]*	*Labor Force Turnover Rate[d]*	*Labor Force Participation Rate[b]*	*Labor Force Experience Rate[c]*	*Labor Force Turnover Rate[d]*
1957	81.9	88.2	7.8	35.8	47.3	32.1
1962	78.4	85.1	8.5	36.6	48.7	32.9
1967	80.4	86.7	7.8	41.1	53.1	29.2
1972	79.0	86.7	8.5	43.9	54.3	23.9
1977	77.7	83.4	7.4	48.4	58.2	20.1
1981	77.0	81.2	5.5	52.1	59.4	14.0
1983	76.4	79.8	4.5	52.9	59.6	12.7

[a]Civilian labor force
[b]The proportion of individuals in the labor force during the reference week (annual averages)
[c]The proportion of individuals in the labor force at some time during the year
[d]The difference between the labor force experience rate and the labor force participation rate divided by the labor force participation rate

Source: 1957-1977 data are from Cynthia B. Lloyd and Beth T. Niemi, *The Economics of Sex Differentials* (N.Y.: Columbia University Press, © 1979), Table 2.6, p. 71, reprinted by permission of the publisher; 1981 data are from U.S. Department of Labor, *Employment and Training Report of the President* (1982), Table A-5, p. 155 and Sylvia L. Terry, "Work Experience, Earnings and Family Income in 1981," *Monthly Labor Review* 106, 4 (April 1983), Table 4, p. 17 and p. 19; and 1983 data are from Ellen Sehgal, "Work Experience in 1983 Reflects the Effects of the Recovery," *Monthly Labor Review* 107, no. 12 (December 1984), Table 1, p. 19.

further indication of women's increasing labor force attachment is that the percentage of women who were full-time, year-round workers has been increasing steadily over the past 20 years. In 1983, 48 percent of women held such jobs in comparison to 64 percent of men.

This growing labor force attachment of women has contributed to the increase in their labor force participation rate. The labor force group is increased by entries into the labor force and decreased by exits from the labor force; therefore, when the number of entrants exceeds the number of those who leave the labor force, the size of the labor force is increased. Thus, *both increases* in flows of *entrants* and *decreases* in flows of *exits* may contribute to the growth of the female labor force. And, indeed, the data in Table 4.3 suggest that both these factors have played a role in increasing the female participation rate. That is, labor force experience rates have risen showing that entries have increased. However, experience rates have declined *relative to* participation rates indicating that women are remaining in the labor force more continuously (that is, exits have decreased).

As we shall see in greater detail in Chapter 7, work experience is an important determinant of labor market earnings. This is true for women as well as men, though their rewards have not been as great. The lesser amount of work experience of women relative to men has traditionally been cited as an important reason for their lower earnings. It is not clear whether recent increases in women's labor force participation have been associated with increases or decreases in their *average* amount of work experience. This is because two changes, which would tend to have opposite effects, are going on here. On the one hand, the growing number of new entrants, who have worked only a short time, has a negative effect on the average labor market experience of women workers. On the other hand, the growing tendency for women to remain in the labor force for longer periods of time has a positive effect.

Unfortunately, the usual published statistics on labor force participation do not help to answer the question of what the net effect of the increased labor force participation on experience has been. From time to time, estimates have, however, been made using longitudinal data that provide information for the same individuals over a period of time, as well as various other types of information. The evidence suggests that before the late 1960s, rising female labor force participation rates were associated with constant or slowly increasing average levels of work experience among women workers. In recent years, notable gains in experience have occurred, particularly among younger women.[5]

[5]See for example, Francine D. Blau, "Longitudinal Patterns of Female Labor Force Participation," eds. Herbert S. Parnes, *et. al., Dual Careers: A Longitudinal Analysis of the Labor Market Experience of Women,* Vol. 4 (Columbus, Ohio: Center for Human Resource Research, Ohio State University, December 1978), pp. 27-55; Claudia Goldin, "Life-Cycle Labor Force Participation of Married Women: Historical Evidence and Implications," NBER Working Paper, no. 1251 (December 1983); June O'Neill, "The Trend in the Male-Female Wage Gap in the United States," *Journal of Labor Economics* (January 1985, Supp.); and James P. Smith and Michael P. Ward, "Times Series Changes in the Female Labor Force," *Journal of Labor Economics* (January 1985, Supp.).

For the female population as a whole, rising labor force participation rates have unambiguously worked to increase the average number of years women tend to spend in the labor force over their lifetime.[6] In 1940, a 20-year-old woman had an estimated work life expectancy of about 12 years. This was 30 percent of the male expected work life of about 40 years. In 1980, the most recent year for which this information is available, the work life expectancy of a 20-year-old woman had risen to 27 years or 74 percent of the male figure of 37 years.

THE LABOR FORCE
PARTICIPATION DECISION

In Chapter 3, we examined the division of household and market work between husband and wife. Here we focus upon the closely related question of how an individual decides on the allocation of his or her time between the home and the labor market. We again use a neoclassical model and assume that the goal is to maximize utility or satisfaction.[7] Individuals decide whether or not to participate in the labor force by comparing the value of their time in the market (w) to the value they place on their time spent at home (w^*). If w is greater than w^*, they participate in the labor force; if w is less than w^*, they remain out of the labor force. In the next section, the long-run increase in women's labor force participation is analyzed in terms of factors that have increased their value of market time and lowered their value of home time.

Now let us examine this model in greater detail. Individuals are viewed as deriving utility from the consumption of *commodities* (goods and services) that are produced using inputs of market goods and nonmarket time.[8] For example, the commodity, a gourmet meal, may be produced using inputs of

---

[6]U.S. Department of Labor, Bureau of Labor Statistics, "New Worklife Estimates," Special Labor Force Report, no. 2157 (November 1982); and Shirley J. Smith, "Revised Worklife Tables Reflect 1979–80 Experience," *Monthly Labor Review* 108, no. 8 (August 1985): 23–31.

[7]Again, the underpinnings of the analysis are derived from the work of Gary S. Becker ("A Theory of the Allocation of Time," *The Economic Journal* 75, no. 299 (Sept. 1965): 493–517) and Jacob Mincer ("Labor Force Participation of Married Women," ed. H. Gregg Lewis, *Aspects of Labor Economics,* Universities National Bureau of Economic Research Conference Studies, no. 14 (Princeton, N.J.: Princeton University Press, 1962), pp. 63–97). Major early empirical work on this topic includes Glen G. Cain, *Married Women in the Labor Force* (Chicago: University of Chicago Press, 1966) and William Bowen and T. Aldrich Finegan, *The Economics of Labor Force Participation* (Princeton, N.J.: Princeton University Press, 1969). Both Reuben Gronau and James Heckman have contributed greatly to the development of statistical techniques for estimating the theoretical relationships; see, for example, the collection of papers in James P. Smith, ed., *Female Labor Supply: Theory and Estimation* (Princeton, N.J.: Princeton University Press, 1980).

[8]Students who have read the Appendix to Chapter 3 where a graphical analysis of specialization and exchange was presented will recognize that the basic approach employed here is quite similar. However, in this analysis, we do not need to make the rigid distinction between home goods (produced exclusively with inputs of home time) and market goods (produced entirely with market purchased goods) that was used to simplify the analysis in the Appendix to Chapter 3. In-

market goods (like groceries, cooking equipment, etc.) and the individual's own time in preparing the meal. In order to keep this model reasonably simple, we make the following three additional assumptions.

First, we assume that all income earned in the labor market is spent on market goods. This avoids the need to consider the determinants of savings and also means that we may use the terms market income and (the money value of) market goods interchangeably.

Second, we assume that all nonmarket time is spent in the production of commodities, whether the output is a loaf of bread, a clean house, a healthy child, or a game of golf. This approach not only avoids the need for analyzing a three-way choice among market work, housework, and leisure but also makes the often difficult distinction between nonmarket work (including volunteer work) and leisure unnecessary.[9] We do not wish to suggest, however, that in reality there is no difference between the two. Indeed, one of the concerns about the impact of married women's increased labor force participation on their welfare is that it has not been accompanied by a comparable reallocation of household chores. As a result, women are often saddled with the "double burden" of home and market work. This may reduce the leisure time available to them, impede their ability to compete with men in the labor market, or both. These issues are examined more closely in Chapter 5.

Third, and perhaps even more crucially, we focus here on the individual rather than on the family as a whole. This is quite realistic when the individual is the only adult in the family. However, as we saw in Chapter 3, where more than one adult is present, the division of labor among them and, thus, the labor supply decision of each is reasonably expected to be a family decision. However, we cannot introduce all the complexities of family decision-making without causing the exposition to become unduly complex and unwieldy. We do continue to view the individual in a family context by taking into account the impact of the earnings of other family members on each person's labor supply decision, but the labor supply of other members of the household is taken as given and is assumed not to be influenced by the individual's own choice. This assumption is probably not too unreasonable when we consider women's labor supply decisions since, in most American families, husbands are likely to remain in the labor market full-time in any case.[10]

deed, not only can we recognize that market goods and nonmarket time are both inputs into the production of commodities but also that there may in many, though not in all instances, be more than one way to produce the same commodity.

[9] Market work is relatively easy to distinguish as any activity for which there is material, usually monetary, reward. But it is quite problematic to determine whether preparation of a gourmet meal, going to a League of Women Voters meeting, growing flowers, or taking a child for a walk is work or leisure.

[10] However, the willingness of husbands to do overtime work and their selection of a job with longer (e.g., 40) vs. shorter (e.g., 37.5) full-time hours are more likely to be affected by their wife's labor force participation and earnings. Further, the labor supply decisions of other family members, such as older children or grandparents, are likely to be more sensitive to the wife's labor supply decision.

Since both market goods and nonmarket time are used in the production of the commodities from which the individual derives satisfaction, his or her task is to select the utility-maximizing combination of market goods and non-market time. Since market goods are purchased with income earned by market work, and all time available is spent either on market work or nonmarket activities, this is the basis of the labor supply decision. In making this choice, the individual must take into account both options that are open to him or her, given by the *budget constraint* shown in panel (a) of Figure 4.3, and his or her

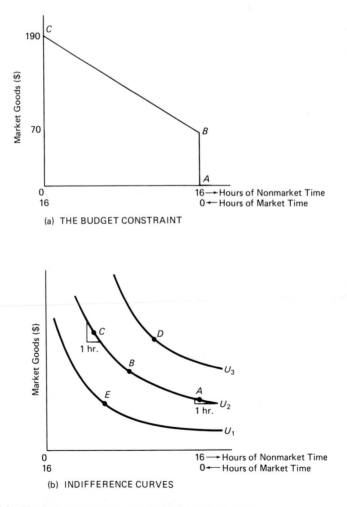

FIGURE 4.3   The Budget Constraint and the Indifference Curves

tastes or preferences expressed in the family of *indifference curves* shown in panel (b) of Figure 4.3. Let us trace out this decision for the hypothetical case of a married woman named Mary.

The Budget Constraint

The budget constraint shown in panel (a) gives the various combinations of nonmarket time and market goods Mary has at her disposal, given her potential market wage rate and the nonlabor income available to her. By nonlabor income we mean income other than her own earnings and, hence, unrelated to the amount of time she devotes to the labor market. This may include her husband's earnings, as well as income from interest, dividends, or rental property. Government transfer payments, such as welfare or unemployment insurance, for example, may also be considered nonlabor income, although the amount of income received from such sources is influenced by the amount of time a person supplies to the labor market. Hours of *nonmarket time* are measured from left to right along the horizontal axis. We assume that Mary has a total of 16 hours available to her in a day to allocate between market and nonmarket activities (allowing 8 hours for nondiscretionary activities like sleeping). Since any of this time that Mary does not spend in nonmarket activities is spent in the market, hours of *market time* are measured from right to left along the horizontal axis.

Mary's nonlabor income is $70 a day. The vertical segment *BA* of the budget constraint shows that Mary has this income available to her even if she supplies no time to the labor market. She may further increase her money income by participating in the labor force. For each additional hour she supplies to the market, she must give up an hour of nonmarket time. In return she receives $7.50, her hourly market wage (w). Thus, segment *CB* is negatively sloped. Its slope is equal to -7.5 or $-w$. If Mary devotes all her time to the market, her total earnings will be $120 ($7.5 $\times$ 16). Her total income, including her nonlabor income, will be $190 ($120 + $70).

Indifference Curves

Mary's preferences for market goods and nonmarket time are represented by her indifference map shown in panel (b). As discussed above, we can incorporate the family context of decision-making into the budget constraint by including the income of other family members as part of the individual's nonlabor income. The matter is thornier when we consider the indifference curves. One possibility would be to view the indifference curves in Figure 4.3 as representing the family's preferences for various combinations of market goods and Mary's nonmarket time. We do not adopt this approach because, as we saw in Chapter 3, preferences among family members may differ, and the process of arriving at family decisions is complex. However, it is important to recognize that our discussion of indifference curves as representing the individual's preferences is only an approximation. In fact, we expect the individual's decisions are made in the context of the family and that the preferences of other family members have been taken into account in the decision-making process. Bearing this in mind, we now take a closer look at the indifference curves.

Suppose Mary is told that she could have the combination of market goods and nonmarket time represented by point *B*. She is then asked to find various other combinations of market goods and nonmarket time from which she would get exactly the same amount of satisfaction or utility. She then identifies the combinations represented by points *A* and *C*. These and other points, which represent equal satisfaction, can all be connected into one indifference curve, called that because she is indifferent about being at various points on the curve. Thus, each indifference curve indicates the various combinations of market goods and nonmarket time that provide Mary with the same amount of utility or satisfaction.

Mary, however, has not just one indifference curve, but a whole family of higher or lower curves. A point like *D* on indifference curve U_3 is clearly preferable to *B* since it offers more of both market goods and nonmarket time. Thus, by extension, all points on U_3 are preferred to all points on U_2. Similarly, *B* is preferred to *E* and, thus, all the points on U_2 are preferred to all the points on U_1.[11] As we move out from the origin in a northeasterly direction, consumption possibilities and, thus, potential satisfaction increase.

Indifference curves are generally assumed to be convex to the origin. That is, they become flatter as we move from left to right and steeper as we move from right to left. This is the case because it is believed that individuals generally value relatively scarcer commodities more highly than relatively more plentiful ones. At point *A*, where nonmarket time is relatively plentiful and market goods are relatively scarce, Mary would be be willing to exchange an hour of nonmarket time for a relatively small amount of income (market goods) and still feel equally well-off. However, at a point like *C* where market goods are relatively plentiful, it would take a lot of income (market goods) to induce her to give up an additional hour of scarce nonmarket time.

It is interesting to consider more closely the way in which an individual like Mary may substitute market goods for nonmarket time (or vice versa) along an indifference curve while still remaining equally well-off. It is important to recognize that we assume she does not derive satisfaction directly from market goods and nonmarket time. Rather, she values them only insofar as

[11]It should be clear that indifference curves can never intersect. All points on any one curve represent an equal amount of utility while any point above (below) represents a larger (smaller) amount of utility. At the point where two curves intersect, they clearly represent the same utility. Yet at all other points they do not. This is a logical impossibility.

they can be used to produce commodities.[12] Thus, broadly speaking, two types of substitution are involved.

Substitution in consumption. Some commodities are relatively *goods intensive* to produce. That is, they are produced using relatively large amounts of market goods and relatively little nonmarket time. Examples of these include buying expensive antiques, furniture, and clothing or recreational activities such as dining out at an elegant restaurant or flying to the Riviera for a short vacation.

Other commodities are relatively *time intensive.* That is, they are produced using relatively large inputs of nonmarket time and relatively fewer inputs of market goods. Examples of these include recreational activities like hiking, bird watching, going to a baseball game, or taking a cycling trip across the country. Also, as anyone who has spent time caring for youngsters can attest, small children are a relatively time-intensive "commodity."

Substitution in production. In many instances, the same commodity can be produced using a relatively time-intensive technique or a relatively goods-intensive technique. For example, a meal may be prepared from scratch at home, made with the use of convenience foods, or purchased at a restaurant. A clean house may be produced by an individual doing the work himself or herself or by hiring cleaning help. A small child may be cared for entirely by a parent, have a babysitter for a few hours a day, or spend all day at a child care center.

As an individual like Mary moves from point *A* to point *B* to point *C* along indifference curve U_2 in Figure 4.3, she will exploit opportunities for substitution in consumption and production. That is, she will substitute goods-intensive commodities for time-intensive commodities, and/or goods-intensive for time-intensive production techniques. As she continues to do so, she will exhaust many of the obvious possibilities. It will take larger increments of market goods to induce her to part with her scarcer nonmarket time. This is why the indifference curves are believed to get steeper as we move from right to left.

Substitution between market goods and nonmarket time. Comparing across individuals, the steepness of the indifference curve is influenced by how difficult or easy it is for them to substitute market goods for nonmarket time,

---

[12]Students who read the Appendix to Chapter 3 will recognize that this was not the case in the analysis presented there. In that case, families derived utility directly from market and home goods. The indifference curves used in this chapter are a graphical representation of what has been termed the individual's "indirect utility function," see Becker, "A Theory of the Allocation of Time."

while remaining equally well-off. This, in turn, will depend on their opportunities for substituting one for the other in production or consumption, or both. For example, those who enjoy hiking very much will not easily be induced to decrease the time they spend on it. They will have steeper indifference curves, reflecting that they have greater difficulty in substituting market goods for nonmarket time in consumption than those who care less for such time-intensive activities.

Similarly, we would expect those whose services are in greater demand in the home (say because small children are present) to have steeper indifference curves, reflecting their greater difficulty in substituting market goods for nonmarket time in production. Tastes and preferences will be a factor here, too. People who feel very strongly that children should be cared for full-time by their own parent and that alternative care is an extremely poor substitute will have steeper indifference curves than those who believe that adequate alternative care can be provided.

This analysis assumes that there is some degree of substitutability between market goods and nonmarket time. However, it has been pointed out, quite correctly, that there are some commodities that cannot be purchased in the market. Various personal services and management tasks provided in the home may be of this nature. Similarly, there are some commodities available in the market that cannot be produced at home. Examples of this range from sophisticated medical care and advanced education to means of transportation and communication, insurance, and many consumer durables.[13] Nonetheless, it is highly likely that when all commodities are aggregated together (as in the indifference curves shown in Figure 4.3) some substitution possibilities between market goods and nonmarket time exist. Given that, the ease or difficulty of substitution is represented by the steepness of the indifference curves.

Tastes. Beyond considerations of this kind, economists generally do not analyze the determinants of individuals' preferences for income (market goods) versus nonmarket time. However, it is important to point out that individuals do not operate in a social vacuum. Their tastes and behavior are undoubtedly influenced by social attitudes and norms.[14] For example, the willingness of a woman to substitute purchased services for her own time in child care is undoubtedly influenced by the social acceptability of doing so. Yet, it is probably true that attitudes follow behavior to some extent, as well. Thus, it is likely, for example, that it has become more acceptable for mothers of small children to work outside the home in part because it has become more common for them to do so, as well as *vice versa*.

[13]Clair (Vickery) Brown, "Home Production for Use in a Market Economy," ed. Barrie Thorne, *Rethinking the Family: Some Feminist Questions* (New York: Longman, Inc., 1981).

[14]The importance of social norms is particularly emphasized by Clair Brown, "Consumption Norms, Work Roles, and Economic Growth," paper presented at the Conference on "Gender in the Workplace," Brookings Institution, November 1984.

A woman's relative preference for income (market goods) versus non-market time reflects a variety of other factors not generally emphasized by economists. As we saw in Chapter 3, women may value earning their own income for the economic independence it brings and to enhance their relative power position in the family. Increasingly more women value career success in much the same way their male counterparts do, which also affects the shape of their indifference curves.

While such considerations do not invalidate the use of this model in analyzing women's labor supply decisions, they do serve to make us aware that the term "tastes" (or preferences), as economists use it, covers a lot of ground. This is particularly important as we attempt to explain women's rising labor force participation over time.

The Participation Decision

Let's suppose that Mary's indifference curves and her budget constraint are shown in panel (a) of Figure 4.4. Mary will maximize utility or satisfaction at point Y where the budget constraint just touches the highest possible indifference curve, U_2. At Y, the amount of income she is willing to accept to give up an additional hour of nonmarket time, given by the slope of the indifference curve at Y, exactly equals the market wage she is offered for that hour, given by the slope of the budget constraint. Mary, therefore, supplies 8 hours per day to the market and spends 8 hours on nonmarket activities. Her daily earnings of $60 ($7.50 x 8) plus her daily nonlabor income of $70 give her (and her family) a total income of $130 per day.

It is interesting to compare the situation at point Y to that at point A, where Mary would supply no time to the labor market. At A, indifference curve U_1 is *flatter* than the budget constraint. This means that Mary values her nonmarket time *less* than the wage the market is willing to pay her for it. Thus, she will certainly choose to supply some time to the market.

Another woman, Joyce, faces the same budget constraint as Mary but has steeper indifference curves (shown in panel (b) of Figure 4.4). This may be because, for example, she has more young children to care for than Mary does. In Joyce's case, the budget constraint touches the highest possible indifference curve at point A, where the indifference curve is steeper than the budget constraint. This means that Joyce sets a *higher* value on her nonmarket time than does the market. She will maximize her utility by remaining out of the labor force, spending all 16 hours available to her on nonmarket activities. Her consumption of market goods will be limited to her nonlabor income of $70 per day.

The slope of the indifference curve at zero hours of market work (point A in panels (a) and (b) of Figure 4.4) is termed the **reservation wage** (w^*). It is equal to the value the woman places on her time at home. If the market wage (w) is greater than the reservation wage (w^*), as in panel (a), the individual will choose to participate in the labor market. If the market wage (w) is less than

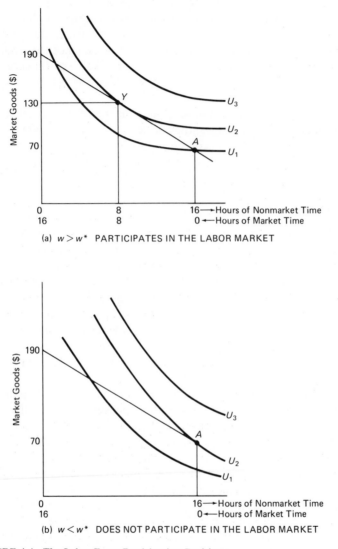

(a) $w > w^*$ PARTICIPATES IN THE LABOR MARKET

(b) $w < w^*$ DOES NOT PARTICIPATE IN THE LABOR MARKET

FIGURE 4.4   The Labor Force Participation Decision

the reservation wage (w^*), as in panel (b), the individual will choose not to participate in the labor market. Factors that increase w, or the value of market time, while all else remains equal, tend to increase the probability that the individual will choose to participate in the labor force. That is, labor force participation is *positively related* to the wage or the value of market time. On the other hand, factors that increase the value of nonmarket time (w^*), tend to lower the probability of labor force participation, other things equal. That is, labor force participation is *negatively related* to w^* or the value of nonmarket time.

The Value of Nonmarket Time (w^*)

As our previous discussion suggests, the value of nonmarket time is influenced by tastes and preferences and also by the demands placed on an individual's nonmarket time. Given the traditional division of labor in most families, the presence of small children, and other circumstances which increase the need for housework, particularly influence women's participation decisions. Over time, the availability of good market substitutes for home time would be a potential factor increasing women's labor force participation.

Another factor that influences the value placed on nonmarket time is the availability of income from sources other than the individual's own work efforts. Figure 4.5 shows the impact of changes in nonlabor income on the labor force participation decision. Let's suppose that the figure represents the budget constraint and indifference curves for Susan, a married woman with two small children. Suppose that her husband is unemployed and that initially her budget constraint is *ABC*. This represents $30 of nonlabor income (from

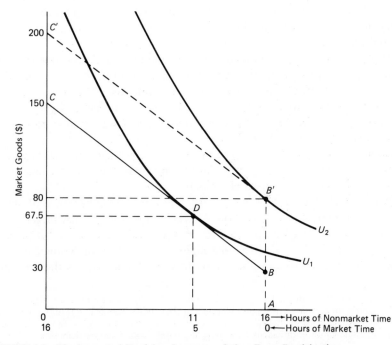

FIGURE 4.5   The Impact of Nonlabor Income on Labor Force Participation

interest on some bonds the family owns) and her market wage of $7.50. She maximizes utility at point D, where she supplies five hours a day to the market and earns $37.50. This brings the family's total daily income to $67.50. Now suppose Susan's husband finds a job. When his earnings ($50) are added to the interest received from the bonds ($30), her nonlabor income becomes $80. Her new budget constraint is $AB'C'$. Note that segment $B'C'$ is parallel to (has the same slope as) segment BC. This is because Susan's (potential) market wage rate remains unchanged at $7.50.

At the higher income level, Susan's consumption possibilities have increased, and she is able to reach a higher indifference curve. She maximizes utility at B' where she consumes more of both market goods and nonmarket time, and supplies less time to the market; in fact, she withdraws from the labor force entirely. This represents the impact of the **income effect**. The reason is that ordinarily as a person has more income he or she will be able to afford more of a variety of good things. To the extent that nonmarket time is used to produce them, higher income will increase the demand for nonmarket time and result in the person choosing to spend less time in the labor market. The income effect will be relatively large when the demand for time-intensive commodities increases sharply with income. The individual then needs to transfer more time from market to nonmarket activities in order to produce them. This is likely to occur when market goods are not considered to be very good substitutes for home-produced items. So Susan, whose wage rate has not changed while her income increased, may choose to consume more recreation, to spend more time caring for her children, and possibly even baking more cakes and pies, etc.

Table 4.4 illustrates the impact of the value of nonmarket time (w^*) on women's labor force participation decisions. Marital status reflects in part the availability and level of alternative sources of income. Thus, we see that women who are married and whose spouse is present, are generally less likely to work outside the home than those in other marital status categories. (The low participation rate of widowed women is largely due to their being an older population, many of retirement age.) Further, studies have found that within the married, spouse present group, labor force participation is negatively related to husband's income, all else equal.[15]

Within each marital status category, we see that the presence of small children deters women's participation. This is because they greatly increase the value of time spent at home. (The lower participation rates for most groups with no children under 18 reflect the higher average age of women in that category.) Of course, the causation may, to some extent, run in the opposite

---

[15]See, for example, the studies reported in James P. Smith, ed., *Female Labor Supply*. The negative relationship between wife's participation and husbands's income is not fully revealed in simple tabulations, because of the impact of other variables. In particular, wife's education is positively associated with both husband's income and wife's labor force participation.

TABLE 4.4 Labor Force Participation Rates of Women by Marital Status, and Presence and Age of Youngest Child, 1966 and 1984[a]

MARITAL STATUS	TOTAL	NO CHILDREN UNDER 18	CHILDREN 6-17, NONE YOUNGER	CHILDREN 3-5, NONE UNDER 3	CHILDREN UNDER 3
1966					
Never married	40.8	n.a.	n.a.	n.a.	n.a.
Married, husband present	35.4	38.4	43.7	29.1	21.2
Other ever married	39.5	34.7	65.9	57.5	38.6
1984					
Never married	63.3	64.8	70.2	51.0	40.1
Married, husband present	52.8	47.1	65.4	57.6	48.3
Other ever married	44.9	35.8	77.5	68.4	51.1
Married, husband absent	61.1	59.3	70.2	60.3	48.5
Widowed	20.4	18.3	60.4	n.a.	n.a.
Divorced	74.3	70.6	84.1	74.8	55.5

[a]Data are for March of each year and include women 16 years of age and over in 1981 and 14 years of age and over in 1966. n.a. = Not available.

Source: U.S. Department of Labor, Bureau of Labor Statistics, *Special Labor Force Report, no. 2163*, Table B-5, p. 16 and Bureau of Labor Statistics data reported in Bureau of National Affairs, *Daily Labor Report*, no. 145 (July 27, 1984), p. B-3.

direction. That is, women who are more committed to the labor market and/or face more attractive labor market opportunities may choose to have fewer children. Evidence suggests both that such reverse causation does exist and that the presence of children also has a negative effect on women's labor force participation.[16]

Table 4.4 also shows that while marital status and presence of children continued to be important determinants of women's labor force participation, married women (husband present) and those with small children were considerably more likely to work outside the home in 1984 than in 1960s. For example, in 1984, 48.3 percent of married women with children under three years old were in the labor market, compared to only 21.2 percent in 1966. Similarly, 57.6 percent of married women with children between the ages of three and five were labor force participants in 1984 compared to 29.1 percent in 1966.

Policy Issue: Government Subsidy of Child Care[17]

As we have seen, young children are still a significant deterrent to the entry of their mothers into the labor market. At the same time, the labor force participation rate among these women has been increasing more rapidly than for any other group. Hence, availability of suitable and affordable child care is an important issue because it would encourage more young women to enter and stay in the labor market and because the children of mothers who are employed in any case will be better cared for.

Public policy encouraging and subsidizing purchased child care could increase its supply and reduce its cost. Official approval might also increase its social acceptability. The crucial questions are whether and how this should be done. The outlays involved are potentially very large, and there is little agreement about who should bear them. The effects on fertility and child quality need also to be considered. These issues will be discussed in Chapter 5. It may be noted that available evidence, with respect to the effect of various types of care on children's development, provides little reason for concern about unfavorable effects of high quality substitutes for family care. Unfortunately, not all child care is of high quality.

[16]For efforts to disentangle this complex causation, see Glen Cain and Martin Dooley, "Estimation of a Model of Labor Supply, Fertility and Wages of Married Women," *Journal of Political Economy* 84, no. 4, pt. 2 (August 1976): S179-S200; Belton M. Fleisher and George F. Rhodes, Jr., "Fertility, Woman's Wage Rates and Labor Supply," *American Economic Review* 69, no. 1 (March 1979): 14-24; and Linda J. Waite and Rafe M. Stolzenberg, "Intended Childbearing and Labor Force Participation of Young Women: Insights from Nonrecursive Models," *American Sociological Review* 41, no. 2 (April 1976): 232-52.

[17]For further consideration of these issues, see James J. Heckman, "Effects of Child Care Programs on Women's Work Effort," *Journal of Political Economy* 82, no. 2 (March/April 1974, supp.): S136-S163; and Myra H. Strober, "Formal Extra Family Child Care—Some Economic Observations," ed. Cynthia B. Lloyd, *Sex, Discrimination, and the Division of Labor* (New York: Columbia University Press, 1975).

In the meantime, the short-run effect of subsidizing child care on labor force participation is quite clear. Suppose panel (b) of Figure 4.4 represents the situation of Nancy, a woman with small children, before the government subsidy. As we can see, she chooses not to participate in the labor force. When suitable child care becomes available at a lower cost, Nancy's home time becomes relatively less valuable. This is shown by the flatter indifference curves in panel (a). In this particular example, the government subsidy results in Nancy deciding to enter the labor force. And, in general, we would expect the availability of child care at a lower price to increase the labor force participation rate of women with small children.

The policy is also likely to have long-run effects on the women who are influenced by it. Since they would experience fewer (and/or shorter) work force interruptions, they would accumulate longer and more continuous labor market experience. This is expected to have a favorable effect on the quality of jobs they are able to obtain, and on their earnings, and would in turn further reinforce the tendency toward spending more time in the labor market. Therefore, in the long run, child care subsidies are likely not only to raise women's labor force participation, but also to enhance their occupational attainment and earnings. Thus, child care subsidies could contribute to a reduction in labor market inequality between men and women. Whether or not they are desirable on other grounds is considered in Chapter 5.

The Value of Market Time (w)

As discussed above, in addition to the impact of the value of nonmarket time, the labor force paricipation decision is influenced by the labor market opportunities an individual faces, particularly the wage rate available in the labor market. To see this in greater detail, let us consider the case of Ellen who initially faces the budget constraint, ABC, shown in Figure 4.6. Her potential market wage is $4.50 per hour while her nonlabor income (say, equal to her husband's earnings) is $40 per day. Given her tastes (indifference map), she maximizes utility at point B where she devotes all her time to nonmarket activities. Note that at point B the indifference curve is steeper than the budget line (BC)—Ellen's reservation wage (w^*) is higher than the wage rate offered to her by the market (w).

Now suppose that Ellen's market opportunities improve and her potential market wage increases to $8.00. Her new budget constraint is ABC'. Segment BA of her budget constraint remains unchanged, because it is still the case that if she remains out of the labor market entirely she (and her family) will receive $40 a day of nonlabor income. However, BC' is steeper than BC because now she will receive $8.00 for each hour she supplies to the market rather than $4.50. Another way to see this is to realize that C' must lie above C because if Ellen devotes all her time to market work her total income will be

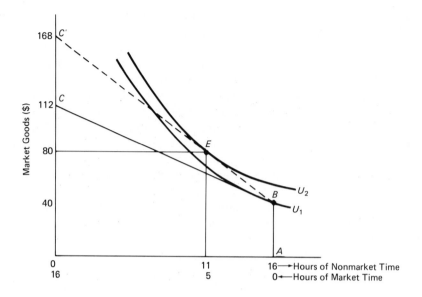

FIGURE 4.6 **The Impact of the (Potential) Market Wage on Labor Force Participation**

higher at a wage of $8.00 per hour than it would have been at a wage of $4.50 per hour.

At the higher wage, the budget constraint (*BC'*) is now steeper than the indifference curve at point *B*—the market wage (*w*) is greater than the reservation wage (*w**), and Ellen maximizes her utility at point *E* on indifference curve U_2 where she supplies five hours to the market. Thus, Ellen chooses to participate in the labor force.

This illustrates the *substitution effect*. An increase in the wage rate, all else equal, raises the opportunity cost of time spent in nonmarket activities and, hence, the "price" of nonmarket time. Individuals are expected to respond by supplying more time to the market and substituting market goods for nonmarket time in consumption and/or in production. Since the wage increase has clearly enabled Ellen to reach a higher indifference curve, we may conclude that she feels better off with the combination of commodities represented by point *E*, even though she has less nonmarket time available at *E* than at *B*.

Some indication of the impact of the potential market wage on labor force participation may be gained by examining the association between educational attainment and labor force participation (Table 4.5). As we shall see in greater detail in Chapter 7, education appears to increase market productivity and, hence, earnings. This would lead us to expect that education would be positively associated with labor force participation.

For women, in particular, the positive effect of education on labor force participation may be reduced to the extent that additional education also raises the productivity of their nonmarket time. This would be the case if, for example, the time that more-educated women spend with their children contributed more to their children's achievement levels than time spent by less-educated women.

The figures in Table 4.5 suggest, however, that the impact of education on market earnings is greater than on the value of home time. Women with higher levels of education are more likely to be in the labor force. The positive relationship between education and labor force participation may also reflect the fact that younger women who initially plan to spend a relatively high proportion of their mature years in the labor force are more likely to invest in education. Further, given a trend toward rising educational attainment, the fact that women at the lowest levels of education have such very low participation rates is in part attributable to the high representation of older individuals among them. Finally, we may note that the jobs held by more educated individuals may have greater nonpecuniary (or nonmonetary) attractions—such as a more pleasant environment, more challenging work, etc.—as well as offering higher wages. This serves to call attention to the fact that the "value of

TABLE 4.5 Labor Force Participation Rates of Women by Years of Schooling Completed, 1964 and 1983[a]

YEARS OF SCHOOLING COMPLETED	LABOR FORCE PARTICIPATION RATES	
	1964	*1983*
Elementary School		
8 years or less	28.0	20.9
High school		
1-3 years	38.3	39.2
4 years	44.6	57.5
College		
1-3 years	42.2	62.8
4 years	53.0	67.8
5 years or more	72.1	75.8

[a]Data are for March of each year and include women 18 years of age and over in 1964 and 16 years of age and over in 1983.

Source: U.S. Department of Labor, Bureau of Labor Statistics, *Special Labor Force Report,* no. 2191, Table B-2, p. 11, and *Special Labor Force Report,* no. 53, Table B, p. A-7.

market work'' should ideally take into account not only pecuniary benefits but also other aspects of the job. Table 4.5 also shows that while education was an important determinant of labor force participation in both 1964 and 1983, participation rates of high school educated and college educated women increased over the period.

Policy Issue: Taxes and the Decision to Work

As previously discussed in Chapter 3, not all money earned is actually at the disposal of the worker. Some of it has to be paid out in taxes. Since earnings are taxed but the value of home production is not, labor force participation among married women is discouraged. This effect is increased by the progressive nature of the tax system. Since the family (rather than the individual) is the tax unit, married women, generally regarded as second earners, face relatively high tax rates on their labor market earnings.

These points may be illustrated in Figure 4.6. Suppose Joan earns $8.00 and faces budget constraint ABC'. If she has to pay out 44 percent of her income in taxes, her after-tax wage (or hourly take home pay) will be $4.50. This situation is represented by budget constraint ABC. At this lower wage Joan chooses to stay out of the labor market. In general, the higher the tax rate, the lower the after-tax wage and the more likely a woman is to decide not to participate in the labor force.[18]

Economic Conditions

Fluctuations in economic conditions also affect labor force participation. These effects are likely to be largest among demographic groups that contain a relatively high proportion of individuals who are loosely attached to the labor force. This would include teenagers of both sexes, older men, and women. Economists view the response of labor force participation to the changing level of economic activity as being the net result of two opposing effects.

The **added worker effect** predicts that during economic downturns, if the primary earner becomes unemployed, other family members may enter (or postpone their exit from) the labor force in order to maintain family income. Essentially, the decline in their nonlabor income due to the unemployment of the primary earner lowers the value of other family members' nonmarket time (w^*). Such individuals may leave the labor force when economic conditions improve and the primary earner is again employed on a regular basis.

---

[18]A more detailed discussion of the tax issue is presented in Chapter 3, p. 53. Note that we have simplified the representation of the tax in Figure 4.6 in that we only consider one tax rate. In fact, since the tax system is progressive, as Joan works more hours her higher total income would most likely push her into a higher tax bracket. Thus, the after tax budget constraint would be "kinked," its slope becoming flatter each time she entered a higher tax bracket.

Alternatively, the **discouraged worker effect** holds that during times of high unemployment, when individuals become unemployed, they may become discouraged and drop out of the labor force after a fruitless period of job search. Others who are outside the labor market may postpone labor force entry until economic conditions improve. Discouragement is due to the decline in the perceived reward to market work (*w*) because of the difficulty of locating an acceptable job. As economic conditions improve, previously discouraged workers may become encouraged and enter the labor force.

Both these effects can operate at the same time for different households. The *net* effect of economic conditions on labor force participation depends on whether the discouraged or added worker effect predominates in the aggregate. This is an empirical question. The data suggest that for the labor force as a whole the discouraged worker effect is probably dominant. One study finds that cyclical sensitivity is particularly pronounced for teenagers, older men, and women under 35. The evidence for older women is less strong. Other researchers report that the cyclical sensitivity of female labor force participation seems to have declined in the 1970s.[19] This finding is consistent with the observation that women appear to be getting more firmly attached to the labor force. This means they are less likely to move in and out of the labor force with the ups and downs of the business cycle.

THE HOURS DECISION

The impact of a change in the wage rate on the number of hours supplied to the market by those who are already labor force participants is a bit more complex than the impact of a wage change on labor force participation. As may be seen in Figure 4.7, an increase in the wage rate corresponds to a rotation of the budget constraint from *CD* to *CD'*, since more market goods can now be purchased for every hour worked. In both panels a and b, the individual initially maximizes utility at point *A* on indifference curve U_1. At a higher wage, he or she is able to reach a higher indifference curve and selects point *B* on indifference curve U_2. This may result in either an increase (panel a) or a decrease (panel b) in hours supplied to the market[20] because, for those who are labor force participants, an increase in the wage rate has two distinct effects.

On the one hand, the increase in the wage is in one respect like an increase in their income. For any given amount of time supplied to the market

[19]See Kim B. Clark and Lawrence H. Summers, "Demographic Differences in Cyclical Employment Variation," *Journal of Human Resources* 16, no. 1 (Winter 1981): 61-79; and Cynthia B. Lloyd and Beth Niemi, "Sex Differences in Labor Supply Elasticity: The Implications of Sectoral Shifts in Demand," *American Economic Review* 68, no. 2 (May 1978): 78-83.

[20]The diagrammatic representation of the effect of a wage change on work hours is shown in greater detail in the Appendix to this chapter.

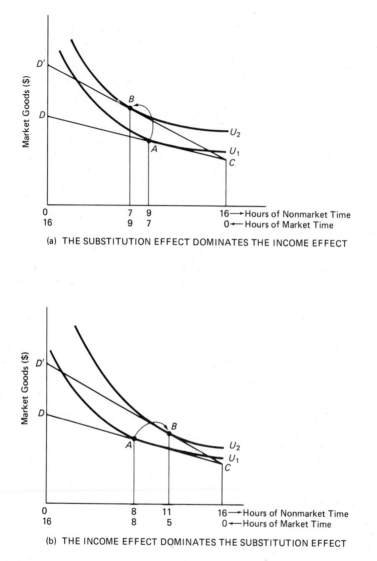

(a) THE SUBSTITUTION EFFECT DOMINATES THE INCOME EFFECT

(b) THE INCOME EFFECT DOMINATES THE SUBSTITUTION EFFECT

FIGURE 4.7   The Impact of the Market Wage on Labor Hours

greater than 0 hours, income is higher along *CD'* than along *CD*, as shown by the fact that higher indifference curves can be reached. This gives rise to an **income effect** that, other things being the same, increases the demand not only for most market goods, but also for nonmarket time, and tends to lower the hours supplied to the market. The increase in the wage, however, also raises the opportunity cost of nonmarket time in terms of market goods that could be purchased. This results in a **substitution effect** that, other things being the same, would cause a reduction in nonmarket time and an increase in the supply of hours to the market.

Thus, when the wage rate rises, the substitution effect will work to increase labor hours supplied, but the income effect will work to reduce labor hours supplied. The net effect is indeterminate. If the substitution effect dominates the income effect, work hours are increased (panel a). If the income effect dominates the substitution effect, work hours are reduced (panel b). Again, it may be recalled that a wage increase unambiguously raises the probability of labor force participation because, in this case, there is no offsetting income effect, but only a positive substitution effect.

With respect to the hours decision, empirical evidence indicates that for men the income effect generally tends to offset or even dominate the substitution effect and that they do not decrease, or may even increase, the amount of nonmarket time as their wage rate goes up. This may be the case because as a group, men generally have worked full-time in the market and have traditionally devoted most of their nonmarket time to recreation rather than other types of household production. While it is possible to substitute market goods for nonmarket time in recreational activities, these possibilities are necessarily limited. Thus for men, the substitution effect is likely to be no greater than the income effect.

The situation is quite different for women. For the most part, they spend a great deal of nonmarket time doing housework. This means that they may substitute market work for housework, rather than for recreational activities. To the extent that purchased goods and services are useful substitutes for nonmarket time in producing the commodities the family wants, an increase in the wage rate is very likely to have that result. Hence, the substitution effect is more likely to dominate for women than men. Even so, the situation is complex and empirical findings differ depending on the group studied.[21] Findings also differ depending on whether the concern is with labor force participation or number of hours worked[22] and whether the focus is on labor supply at a point in time or over the whole life cycle.[23] Nonetheless, empirical studies for

---

[21]Black and white wives were found to respond differently to changes in take-home pay (Jane H. Leuthold, "The Effect of Taxation on the Probability of Labor Force Participation by Married Women," *Public Finance* 33, no. 3 [August 1978]: 280-94) and to varying work incentives provided by AFDC (Frank Levy, "The Labor Supply of Female Household Heads, or AFDC Incentives Don't Work Too Well," *Journal of Human Resources* 14, no. 1 [Winter 1979]: 76-97).

[22]As we have seen, an increase in wages always increases the probability that an individual will be in the labor market but, because of the income effect working in the opposite direction, will not necessarily have a positive effect on the number of hours worked.

[23]A thorough discussion of why the two are not the same is found in James J. Heckman, "A Partial Survey of Recent Research on the Labor Supply of Women," *American Economic Review* 68, no. 2 (May 1978): 200-207.

the most part find that women's labor supply is strongly positively related to the wage rate,[24] confirming the dominance of the substitution effect.

‸
•

THE CONTRIBUTION OF NONMARKET PRODUCTION
TO GROSS NATIONAL PRODUCT

Gross National Product (GNP) is the total money value of all the goods and services produced in the economy over a one-year period. No one doubts that unpaid activities like housework and volunteer work are valuable to households, and to the community, but at the present time these contributions are not included in GNP. The results of this omission are potentially serious. GNP is considerably underestimated. Comparisons of GNP between countries are distorted to the extent that the relative size of household and market sectors differ. Finally, within a country, the growth in GNP is overstated if women reduce home production as they work more in the labor market.

A major obstacle to including these contributions in GNP is lack of agreement on an acceptable way to estimate the value of time spent in nonmarket production.* There are two fundamentally different methods, each with its own strengths and drawbacks. One is the **opportunity cost approach,** which sets the value of unpaid work equal to the income the person could earn in the labor market. It meshes well with the theory of labor supply in which individuals who participate in the labor force equate the value of nonmarket time to the market wage rate. For individuals who do not participate in the labor market, the value of nonmarket time must be at least as great as the potential market wage.

However, despite its theoretical appeal, there are a number of difficulties with this approach. First, for those who are out of the labor force, we have the nontrivial problem of estimating their potential market earnings. Second, while the market wage is known for those who are employed, the presumption that it accurately represents the value of nonmarket time may not be correct. Few workers have the option to work precisely as long as they wish but often must work a specified number of hours or

---

[24]This is the case both for studies that investigate the gross effect of wage changes and even more so for those that estimate the net effect when the change in income is compensated for. Among the former are Orley Ashenfelter and James J. Heckmann, "The Estimation of Income and Substitution Effects in a Model of Family Labor Supply," *Econometrica* 42, no. 1 (January 1974): 73-85; Michael J. Boskin, "The Economics of Labor Supply," eds. G. G. Cain and H. W. Watts, *Income Maintenance and Labor Supply* (Chicago: Markham, 1973), pp. 163-81; Robert E. Hall, "Wages, Income and Hours of Work in the U.S. Labor Force" eds. Cain and Watts, *Income Maintenance,* pp. 102-62. Among the latter are Ashenfelter and Heckman, "The Estimation of Income and Substitution Effects;" Boskin, "The Economics of Labor Supply;" Jane H. Leuthold, "An Empirical Study of Formula Income Transfers and the Work Decision of the Poor," *Journal of Human Resources* 3, no. 3 (Fall 1968): 312-23. For a helpful review of the empirical findings, see Mark R. Killingsworth, *Labor Supply* (Cambridge: Cambridge University Press, 1983).

*For a thorough review of the literature on this subject, see Luisella Goldschmidt-Clermont, *Unpaid Work in the Household: A Review of Economic Evaluation Methods* (Geneva: International Labor Office, 1982). For a fuller consideration of some of the theoretical issues, see Carmel U. Chiswick, "The Value of a Housewife's Time," *Journal of Human Resources* 17, no. 3 (Summer 1982): 413-25.

forego an otherwise desirable job. Hence, they may not be able to divide their time so that the value of the last hour spent at home is exactly equal to their wage rate.

In addition to these problems, while correct application of the opportunity cost approach may identify the value of the nonmarket production to individuals and their families, it results in a higher value being placed on the nonmarket production of those whose (potential) *market* productivity is higher. So, for example, an hour spent scrubbing floors by a college graduate is valued more highly than an hour spent by a high school gratuate in the same activity. This is the case even if the quantity and quality of their *nonmarket* production is identical. Such estimates are, therefore, not entirely acceptable.

The main alternative to the opportunity cost approach is the so-called **market cost approach,** which sets the value of nonmarket production equal to the cost of hiring someone to do it. This method is not free of difficulties either. The main one is the need to make sure that the purchased item is of equal quality and, for that matter, that it is possible to purchase it. What qualifications must a housecleaner, a cook, a gardener, and a baby sitter have to adequately replace the services of a homemaker and parent? Is it possible to delegate such tasks as directing children's upbringing and planning and budgeting for the household?

One approach to estimating market value is to first determine how much time is spent on each individual activity, itself a very difficult task, and then to use the wages of such specialists as cooks, home decorators, chauffeurs, and even child psychologists to estimate the value of nonmarket time. However, this is unrealistic in that it is unlikely that the typical homemaker has all these skills to the same extent that such specialists do. Another alternative is to value unpaid home work at the wage of a domestic worker. But this is not likely to satisfy everyone, especially traditionalists who believe that "a loving wife and mother" will do the job better than any hired help.

Despite these difficulties, both the opportunity cost and the market cost approach have yielded useful estimates of the value of nonmarket production. These estimates suggest that the extent to which we understate GNP by ignoring nonmarket output is 25 percent or more. This also gives some idea of the extent to which real incomes of families are underestimated and their relative size distorted when, as under our current federal income tax laws, the value of non-market production (particularly of full-time homemakers) is not included.

ANALYZING TRENDS IN WOMEN'S PARTICIPATION: AN OVERVIEW

Having examined how the labor supply decision is made will help us to better understand why women's labor force participation has developed as it has over time. In this section, we give an overview of the factors responsible for the long-term increase in women's labor force participation with industrialization. In the following sections, we take a closer look at a number of subperiods of particular interest.

Why has female labor force participation been rising over the course of the present century? Drawing upon the analysis presented earlier in this chapter, the obvious answer to this question is that a shift toward more market work by women can be explained by a rise in the wage rate (w) and/or a decrease in the value of time spent in the home (w^*). There is considerable evidence of developments that would be expected to have these effects and also of complex interactions, reinforcing the original results.

Factors Influencing the Value of Market Time (w)

A variety of factors caused the real (inflation adjusted) wages of women to increase over time. The result was a rotation of the budget constraint as shown in Figure 4.6. Under these circumstances, more women would be expected to find that the wage offered them by the market exceeded their reservation wage and to choose to enter the labor force.

Education. As young women received more education, the wage rate they were able to earn by working in the market also went up and they were more likely to work outside the home. At the same time, once women were more inclined to work for pay, they were likely to want to obtain more market-oriented schooling, in order to be able to obtain better-paying jobs.

The magnitude of this phenomenon can be gauged by the enormous changes in the proportion of the population that graduated from high school or obtained college degrees. Between 1900 and 1980, the female population more than tripled, but the number of high school graduates per year went up 27 fold. The rate of increase for men was even greater, since in the early period only two-thirds as many boys graduated from high school as girls, while by 1980 their numbers were almost equal. During this same period, the number of female college graduates went up 66 times. For men, the increase was 22 times. This reflects the fact that traditionally, more young men than young women completed college and pursued graduate study. However, this differential declined, particularly during the late 1960s and the 1970s. During this period, women substantially increased their share of college, graduate and professional degrees awarded, as well as their representation in traditionally male fields of study. (Data on this are presented in Chapter 7.) Hence, although men's educational attainment has also increased over time, sex differences in patterns of educational attainment have been narrowing dramatically, especially in recent years.

A second development that increased the returns to education was the growing number of years women could expect to live. Life expectancy at birth for women went up from 48 years at the turn of the century to over 78 years in 1983. By that time, a woman aged 20 could expect to live 59 more years. Though most individuals retire by age 65, this increase in life expectancy meant that women were able to reap considerably higher rewards for education and on-the-job training over their lifetime, even if they took some time out for homemaking. As women responded to this increased incentive to invest in education and on-the-job training, their potential lifetime market earnings were increased. The effect was much the same as that of an increase in the wage rate, raising the opportunity cost of nonmarket activities and, thus, increasing labor force participation.

The demand for female labor. It is also frequently suggested that, first with industrialization and then with the movement to the post-industrial economy, the demand for workers in traditionally female clerical and service jobs increased and caused their wages to be higher than they otherwise would have been. The fact that women's occupations, and more recently sex-integrated occupations, have increased more rapidly than male occupations tends to support this view.[25] More recently, anti-discrimination legislation has quite likely increased the demand for women in traditionally male jobs as well.

Overall productivity increases. Women, like male workers, have benefited from increases in labor productivity due to growth over time in the capital stock and technological change. This also exerted upward pressure on women's wages, all else equal.

Factors Influencing the Value of Nonmarket Time (w^*)

It would be a mistake, however, to ascribe the impetus for the persistent influx of women into the labor market entirely to higher wage rates and to overlook those changes which influenced the relative value of nonmarket time. The net result of these factors was to lower the value of nonmarket time relative to market time and, thus, to raise the proportion of women working for pay.

Availability of market substitutes. Among the most obvious of these was the increase in the availability of goods and services that had previously been produced in the home but that more and more came to be available for purchase in the market. Not only did fruits and vegetables, in earlier days grown in the family garden, come to be available at the grocery, but in time they were cleaned, canned, frozen, and eventually often included in prepared dishes or even meals. First yarn, earlier spun at home, became commonly available, next it was cloth, and then ready-made clothing, now most often of the easy-care variety. Schools extended the hours and years of care provided.

---

[25]Valerie Oppenheimer, *The Female Labor Force in the United States: Demographic and Economic Factors Governing its Growth and Changing Composition,* Population Monograph Ser. 5, (Berkeley, CA, 1970) was the first to emphasize the expansion of female occupations. June O'Neill, ''The Trend in the Sex Differential in Wages,'' was among those to point to the increase in mixed occupations.

For young children, nursery schools and recently day-care centers became more prevalent, while hospitals increasingly care for the sick, and various types of care for the infirm and aged are becoming more common.

These are only a few examples of commodities that in earlier days were produced with large inputs of home time but that today require mainly expenditure of money. Some changes did have the opposite effect, such as the considerably higher cost and greater difficulty of finding domestic help. But by and large, market goods have become more substitutable for nonmarket time. As a result, women would be expected to be more willing to give up time at home in order to be able to do more market work, a change illustrated in Figure 4.4 by the flatter indifference curves shown in panel (a) as compared to the steeper indifference curves shown in panel (b). Thus, we see that the greater availablility of goods and services for purchase has resulted in a decrease in the value of women's nonmarket time (w^*) and caused their labor force participation to increase. At the same time, women's rising labor force participation tends to increase the demand for market goods and services which substitute for their time in the home, further encouraging development and production of such products.

Urbanization. Closely related to these changes in households and lifestyles was the growing urbanization of the population. The movement from country to city reduced the opportunity for household production (say, growing and processing vegetables) and increased the convenience of market purchases as well as access to market work. Even leisure activities changed from those that mainly required time—hiking, swimming in the waterhole, and chatting on the front porch—to others that required substantial expenditures—going to the theater, pedalling an exercycle, and watching television.

Demographic trends. Another important change that influenced relative preferences for home vs. market time was the long-run decline in the birth rate alluded to earlier, from 30.1 per 1000 population in 1910 to 15.5 per 1000 by 1983. Since the rearing of young children, generally considered to be women's responsibility, is very time-intensive, especially in the absence of adequate provision for their care outside the home, their presence used to be one of the strongest barriers to women's entry into the labor market. As we have seen, it is only since the 1960s that mothers of preschoolers are working outside the home to any significant extent, and even now their representation is low relative to that of other groups.

Not only is the period during which there are young children in the home more protracted as their number goes up, but the longer the woman is at home the less favorable the terms she is likely to encounter in the labor market upon her return and the more likely she is to remain out permanently. As we have noted, women are, of course, aware of this and to some extent adjust family size to their work plans, as well as vice versa.

Just as women's labor force participation is influenced by, and in turn influences, their fertility, the same is true of marital stability. The divorce rate per 1000 population per year went from .9 in 1910 to 5.0 in 1983. At the same time, women's labor force participation rates have been increasing. This is, in part, because divorced women have considerably less nonlabor income and are thus more likely to participate in the labor force. Married women's behavior is affected by rising divorce rates as well. As they have increasingly become aware of the extent to which full-time homemakers are dependent on their spouses for financial support, their preference quite likely has shifted toward market time as a means of safeguarding their standard of living in case of a marital breakup. The other side of the coin is that a two-earner couple can more readily afford to get divorced. The woman can count on her own income, rather than being completely dependent on the often grudging and uncertain support of an ex-husband. The man need not spend resources to fully support, or to avoid support of, an ex-wife.

Rising husband's income. Not all changes have operated in the direction of lowering the value of nonmarket time. In particular, earnings of men have increased more rapidly than the cost of living with very brief interruptions throughout the period we are concerned with. As the husband's real income goes up, all else equal, married women's labor force participation is reduced due to the income effect (Figure 4.5). Our previous discussion suggests, however, that, for women, the positive substitution effect of their own rising real wages is likely to offset the negative income effect due to the increasing real incomes of their husbands.[26]

Tastes. Over time, the development of many desirable market products that could not be produced efficiently in the home, like automobiles, air conditioning, television and stereos, and most recently personal computers, increased people's preferences for market-produced goods and reduced the relative value placed on nonmarket time.[27]

Last, it is also entirely possible that the trend towards rising female participation rates itself was also responsible for further changes in tastes. To the extent that people tend to be conformist, it was far more difficult for women to enter the labor force when this was the exception than today when it has almost become the rule. Shifting cultural norms, encouraged in part by the ex-

[26]This was first pointed out by Jacob Mincer in "Labor Force Participation of Married Women."

[27]This factor is particularly emphasized by Clair Brown, "Consumption Norms, Work Roles, and Economic Growth."

ample of more women working in the market, have led women to place a higher value on the independence and autonomy that their own earnings bring. Finally, to the extent that people want to keep up with the Joneses in their consumption standards, it takes two paychecks to keep up with the two-earner families of today.

THE WORLD WAR II EXPERIENCE

As noted earlier, during World War II, there was a sharp rise in the female labor force participation rate, particularly among married women. In the immediate post-World War II period, the female participation rate declined sharply, although it remained above pre-War levels (Table 4.1) and began a long-term increase shortly after that. This experience illustrates the importance of economic and social factors in causing changes in female labor force participation.

As men were mobilized for the armed forces and the need for workers rose at the same time, there was a large increase in demand for women to fill the available positions. This increase in labor market opportunities, which included relatively high-paying, traditionally male jobs, increased the potential market wages of women. At the same time, married women were urged to work outside the home to contribute to the war effort. This raised the nonpecuniary benefits of market work for women and lowered their subjective assessment of the value of nonmarket time. In addition, the birth rate, which was already relatively low in the Depression years of the 1930s, remained low during the war because many young men were away in the armed forces.

A further factor that worked to lower the value of home time for married women was that the government and some employers opened day-care centers for children of working mothers.[28] Even though there were not sufficient places for all such youngsters, this action increased both the supply, and the acceptability, of alternative care of children, at least for the duration of hostilities. Thus, the combination of an increase in the value of market time and a reduction in the value of nonmarket time induced a large increase in the proportion of women working outside the home.

In the immediate post-War period, each of these factors was reversed, helping to bring about the observed decline in participation rates. As men returned to the civilian labor force, many were able to reclaim their former

---

[28]Given the public conern, both about stimulating maternal employment in war industries and about possible neglect of children, the federal government provided $52,000,000 during 1941–1943 in matching funds to induce states to provide day-care centers. It has been estimated that 1,600,000 children attended these programs. The best known centers established by large private employers were those by Curtiss-Wright in Buffalo and by Kaiser in Portland. See Bernard Greenblatt, *The Changing Role of Family and State in Child Development.* (San Francisco: Jossey Bass, Inc., Publishers, 1977), pp. 58–60.

jobs from the women who had held them during the war. This was the case because many union contracts reserved their former jobs for men who had left them for military service. Even in the absence of union agreements, some employers may have voluntarily done this because they felt it was the appropriate recompense for the veteran's wartime contribution. Moreover, whether or not a returning veteran claimed a specific job that had been held by a woman, the influx of returning males into the labor market certainly lowered the demand for women workers.

In addition, social values changed and the employment of married women outside the home was once again frowned upon, now that the wartime emergency was over. Indeed, after enduring the major dislocations of the Great Depression of the 1930s followed by a World War of unprecedented dimensions, there may understandably have been a desire to return to "normalcy," including traditional roles. This swing in attitudes may have also played a role in producing the upsurge in birth rates during the post-War period, discussed in the next section. Finally, the wartime labor shortage over, day-care centers were perceived to be no longer needed and were closed. These changes combined to lower the benefits of market work relative to the value of home time and to reduce women's labor force participation rate in the immediate post-World War II period.

The long-term operation of the factors discussed in the preceding section meant that the post-War participation rate, while lower than the wartime peak, exceeded prewar levels. We see the long-term rise in participation rates which followed the war as being primarily due to the fundamental economic and social factors identified above. Yet the wartime experience may well have hastened this process by helping to break down the attitudinal barriers to married women's employment outside the home[29] and giving many women a taste of getting their own income.

THE POST-WORLD WAR II
BABY BOOM

As noted above, the long-run, downward trend in birth rates was interrupted by the post-World War II baby boom. From 1946 to the mid-1950s, birth rates rose steadily, and they remained at relatively high levels until the early 1960s. While some of this rise in birth rates was simply a response to the postponement of childbearing that had occurred during the Depression and the war years, much of it did indeed reflect an increase in family size in comparison to earlier periods. At the height of the baby boom, women averaged three births, considerably more than the replacement-level fertility rates of their Depression-era mothers. This means that the decline in the birth rate, which

[29]This argument is made by William H. Chafe, in *The American Woman*.

contributed to the rise in female labor force participation over the long-run, does not help to explain it during the Baby Boom era.

Why did participation rates increase despite the negative effect of the high birth rate? The first point to be made is that the increase in birth rates would principally affect younger women (under age 35) in the prime childbearing ages, who would be most likely to have small children present. It may be recalled that this was precisely the group for whom labor force participation rates did *not* increase over the 1940 to 1960 period (Figure 4.1). The rising participation rates were primarily due to the entry of older women (over age 35) with school-age or grown children. Many of these women had acquired experience in and, quite possibly a taste for, paid work during the war. They were also from a generation that benefitted from considerably more education than their elders had received. The rate of high school completion jumped from 29 percent in 1930 to 49 percent in 1940. While the baby boom meant that young children would cause mothers to stay home, this was not so as the children grew older and more self-sufficient. Indeed, it might be argued that teenagers, and especially college students, need more money, rather than time.

Second, during this period, economic factors were particularly favorable for rising female participation rates. Real wages were steadily increasing and economic conditions, particularly by current standards, were relatively good. Thus, both the continued rise in participation rates and the pattern of the increase appear explainable in terms of economic and demographic factors.

THE 1960s TO THE 1980s:
A PERIOD OF CHANGE

The post-World War II Baby Boom was followed by the Baby Bust during which birth rates fell. By the late 1970s, total fertility rates had fallen below the replacement level. In addition, increasing numbers of women began to postpone the birth of their first child into their late 20s or even 30s. This pattern of childbearing appears to be associated with a stronger attachment to the labor market and a reduction in time spent out of the labor force for childrearing. A further demographic trend, which encouraged rising participation rates, was the sharp increase in the divorce rate. Currently, it appears to be leveling off but at a very high level. On the basis of past trends, demographers predict that one-third to one-half of new marriages will end in divorce. It may be recalled that the younger women (under age 44), who would be most affected by these demographic factors, have posted the largest gains in participation rates since 1960.

During much of the 1960s, rising real wages and relatively low unemployment rates also contributed to the increases in female labor force participation rates. However, since that time, the persistent problem of stagflation has resulted in frequent periods of high unemployment rates and relatively constant real wages. This raises the question of why female participation rates have continued to rise despite these unfavorable economic conditions.

One obvious explanation is that favorable demographic factors, as well as the continued impact of the other long-run forces we have discussed, outweighed the negative effect of economic conditions. In view of the importance of level of education and presence of young children for women's labor force participation, both the continued increase in years of schooling and the decline in the family size would be expected to have made important contributions. However, one study found that such factors, even together with the effect of the woman's own wage rate, accounted for only about half of the increase in young women's participation rates during the 1970s.[30]

One may speculate that changes in the work expectations of younger women help to explain the portion of their participation increase that was not caused by the above-mentioned factors. It may be recalled that in the pre-World War II period, most women left the labor force permanently upon marriage and childbearing. It is quite likely that the older married women who entered or re-entered the labor force during World War II and the early post-War period had not anticipated working during this stage of the life cycle but were drawn into the labor market by prevailing economic and social forces.

As the re-entry pattern of labor force participation became firmly established, most younger women could anticipate spending a substantial portion of their mature years in the labor force. They must also have learned, by observing the experiences of older women, that time spent out of the labor force was costly in terms of career advancement and earnings. To maximize their labor market earnings and to secure intrinsically more interesting and attractive jobs, which were becoming somewhat more accessible for women, they would have to keep work force interruptions to a minimum. Thus, the increases in younger women's labor force participation rates, including those of mothers with small children, probably were in part a response to their growing expectation of working for a substantial period of time at a later stage in the life cycle. Further, once it had become socially acceptable for mothers of older children to work outside the home, it was not long before it was socially permissible for women with small children to do so as well.[31]

[30]See David Shapiro and Lois Shaw, "Growth in the Labor Force Attachment of Married Women: Accounting for Changes in the 1970's," *Southern Economic Journal* 50, no. 2 (October 1983): 461–73.

[31]One more factor thought to have played a part in explaining younger women's rising participation rates is that the entry of the large baby boom cohort into the labor market depressed the wages of younger men. It has been argued that, in order to attain the consumption standards they aspired to, younger couples needed to be two-wage earners. See, Valerie Kincade Oppenheimer, "The Easterlin Hypothesis: Another Aspect of the Echo to Consider," *Population and Development Review* 2, nos. 3 and 4 (September/December 1976): 433–57.

ANALYZING TRENDS IN MEN'S PARTICIPATION

The changes in male labor force participation patterns, while less dramatic, are also of interest. The decline in the participation rates of younger men (Figure 4.2) reflects their tendency to remain in school longer. This in turn reflects the ever-increasing skills demanded by our advanced economy. Expenditures on education are more profitable to the individual when they are made relatively early in the life cycle, since this results in a longer period over which to reap the returns to this investment in the form of higher earnings. Finally, with rising real incomes, families no doubt demanded more education for their children. They were better able to afford to pay the bills and also to forego the contribution their children might otherwise have made to family income.

The declining participation rates of older males are often viewed as evidence of the dominance of the income effect over the substitution effect. As real wages have risen over time, men's demand for nonmarket time appears to have increased. One indicator of this is that the full-time work week declined from 60 hours at the turn of the century to about 40 hours in the 1940s and remains at about that level today. Further, *annual hours* of full-time workers have declined as paid vacations, holidays, and sick leave have become more prevalent.[32] The increased propensity of men to retire, and to retire at earlier ages, is seen as part of this pattern. In addition, the provision of social security and the growing coverage of private pension schemes, while in part a transfer of income from earlier to later years, also created an income effect that encouraged older males to retire.

The small decline in the participation rate of prime-age males is less well understood. To some extent, it may reflect the greater provision in recent decades of disability income under government programs to older men below conventional retirement age.[33] In the absence of such programs, more disabled men would probably have sought work. It has been argued that black males were particularly affected by programs that provide help for those in need, because they tend to be concentrated at the lower end of the wage distribution, where the opportunity cost to leaving the labor force is relatively low. This, in addition to their high unemployment rates, may help to explain why the participation rates of black males have been declining at a faster pace than those of white males.

The decline in male labor force participation in the prime working years may also, to some extent, reflect the impact of the increased employment of

---

[32]For an analysis of these trends, see Thomas J. Kniesner, "The Full-Time Work Week in the U.S.: 1900–1970," *Industrial and Labor Relations Review* 30, no. 1 (October 1976): 3–15.

[33]Donald Parsons, "The Decline in Male Labor Force Participation," *Journal of Political Economy* 88, no. 1 (February 1980): 117–34.

women outside the home. As the two-earner family has become the norm, the additional income may induce some (still relatively few) males to leave the labor force for periods of time, say to retool for a mid-life career change.

BLACK AND WHITE PARTICIPATION DIFFERENTIALS: AN ANALYSIS

In our earlier discussion of labor force participation trends, we noted that black male participation rates have been declining faster than those of white males, while black female participation rates have been increasing at a slower pace than those of white females. As a result, black male participation rates have fallen considerably below those of white males, while black female participation rates are now only slightly higher than those of white females.

Table 4.6 compares the participation rates of blacks and whites by marital status in 1966 and 1983. Males who are married, with their spouse present, are more likely to be in the labor force than those in other marital status categories. Given traditional sex roles in the family, married men living with their wives tend to assume greater financial responsibilities than either never married or other ever married men who have been separated, divorced, or widowed. They are also more likely to be in the prime working ages than never married men who are considerably younger on average. In both years, participation rates of black and white males are quite similar within the married, spouse present, category. The decrease in the black male participation rate relative to that of white males is associated with the relative decline in the proportion of black men who are married, spouse present. In 1966, 51.9 percent of black men were married and living with their wives in comparison to 66.7 percent of white men. In 1983, this was true of 42.0 percent and 63.2 percent respectively.

Marital status also is associated with the declining racial differential in participation rates among women. It has traditionally been the participation rate of married women, spouse present, that has been particularly high among black as compared to white women, in part because of the substantially lower average income of black males, especially during an earlier period.[34]

[34]Labor force participation of married black women has, however, been found to be higher than that of white women even when husband's income is held constant. For analyses of racial differences in women's participation see Duran Bell, "Why Participation Rates of Black and White Wives Differ," *Journal of Human Resources* 9, no. 4 (Fall 1974): 465–79; Claudia Goldin, "Female Labor Force Participation: The Origin of Black and White Differences, 1870 and 1880," *Journal of Economic History* 37, no. 1 (March 1977): 87–108; and Cain, *Married Women in the Labor Force.*

As in the case of males, there has been a considerable decrease in the proportion of black women relative to white women who are married, spouse present. In 1966, 46.1 percent of blacks and 61.3 percent of whites were in this marital status category, in comparison to 33.5 percent and 58.3 percent in 1983. (These proportions are lower for women than for men, because there are more women than men in the population, particularly among blacks.) In addition, the gap in the participation rates of black and white married women narrowed over the period. This may in part be due to the increase that occurred in the earnings of black men relative to white men during this time. On the other hand, the earnings of black women also increased relative to those of white women. Such a change would be expected to increase their relative participation, all else equal, but appears to have been outweighed by other factors, including the relative increase in husband's income.

The reasons for these shifts in racial patterns of labor force participation and marital status in recent years have not been fully identified.[35] However, the disadvantaged economic status of blacks undoubtedly plays a role. In 1983, the unemployment rates among whites were 8.8 percent for males and 7.9 percent for females, but among blacks they were 20.3 percent and 18.6 percent, respectively. The rates for teenagers were considerably higher, and the differential between the races even greater. This dismal situation may well impede family formation among young blacks.

Higher unemployment rates among black youths may also account for the considerably lower labor force participation rates of black than white never-married individuals—a gap that increased substantially between 1966 and 1983. As we saw earlier, the net effect of high unemployment rates, particularly for young people, is likely to prove very discouraging for them and must be expected to inhibit their labor force participation. The higher unemployment rates of blacks, relative to whites in all age groups, may also contribute to marital breakup as well as to labor force withdrawals associated with the increased provision of disability benefits.

Finally, the provision of welfare to female-headed families by the Aid to Families with Dependent Children (AFDC) program may reduce the incentive of lower income women to marry or remarry, especially to the extent that husband-wife families are less likely to receive such aid, and may discourage labor force participation among recipients. This program expanded greatly in the 1960s and the early 1970s and the concentration of blacks at the lower end of the wage distribution would make them particularly susceptible to its effects.

[35]The controversial *Moynihan Report* (Daniel P. Moynihan, "The Negro Family: The Case for National Action," Washington, D.C.: Office of Policy Planning and Research, U.S. Department of Labor, 1965) initially focused public attention on the causes and consequences of the higher incidence of female headship among blacks. See also Heather Ross and Isabel Sawhill, *Time of Transition: The Growth of Families Headed by Women* (Washington, D.C.: The Urban Institute, 1975), pp. 67–92.

TABLE 4.6   Labor Force Status by Marital Status, Sex, and Race, 1966 and 1983[a]

MARITAL STATUS	1966		1983	
	BLACKS[b]	WHITES	BLACKS	WHITES
Males				
Total	70.2	75.1	68.1	76.3
Never married	48.0	49.9	61.8	71.7
Married, spouse present	86.6	87.3	76.3	79.4
Other ever married[c]	62.7	54.5	63.5	69.6
Females				
Total	44.1	36.5	54.0	52.0
Never married	32.7	41.9	52.0	65.3
Married, spouse present	47.6	34.3	60.8	51.0
Other ever married[c]	48.1	37.8	49.2	42.7

[a]Data are for March of each year. The 1966 data are for individuals 14 years of age and over; the 1983 data refer to individuals 16 years of age and over.
[b]Data are for nonwhites, the great majority of whom are black.
[c]Includes individuals who are separated, divorced or widowed.

Sources: U.S. Department of Labor, Bureau of Labor Statistics, *Special Labor Force Report,* no. 80, Table B-1, p. A-7, and *Families at Work: The Jobs and the Pay,* Bulletin 2209, Table B-1, p. 35.

CONCLUSION

We began by reviewing the trends in male and female participation rates. We found that while female labor force participation rates have been increasing over the course of the present century—20 percent in 1900; 28 percent in 1940; 54 percent in 1984—male participation rates have been declining from 87 percent in 1950 to 77 percent in 1984. We then turned to the economic theory of labor supply to gain insight into the determinants of labor force participation in order to better understand these trends, as well as differences in participation across various groups. Last, we applied this theory to an analysis of recent trends.

We conclude this chapter with a fuller consideration of the outlook for the future. Predicting the trend of things to come is always hazardous, and the past record of economists and demographers in this respect is not particularly encouraging. Nonetheless, we shall venture some predictions about changes in labor force participation over the next few decades. In order to do that, however, we must first forecast the variables that are particularly important in influencing labor force participation.

Among the factors particularly relevant to women's entry into the labor market are the rates of marriage, fertility, and divorce. We do not expect any of these to change radically in the foreseeable future. While there has been a trend toward later marriages, we see no convincing evidence that significantly more people will remain single throughout their lifetime. Though the birthrate has been declining, relatively few couples appear to be choosing to remain childless. Here, too, the evidence is far stronger that the choice is to postpone having children, though they may end up having a smaller number as well. On the other hand, we believe that the recent "baby boomlet," interpreted by some as portending further increases to come, is merely a result of these couples having the babies they chose not to have earlier.[36] Although the divorce rate had been rising sharply, this increase appeared to level off in the early 1980s. A continued constancy of the divorce rate, possibly even a small decline, might be expected in the future as the expectations of men and women come more into line with their new, less traditional work roles. The tendency toward later marriages, entered into less because of social pressures and more deliberately than before, should have a similar effect.[37]

Increasing education contributed to the impetus toward greater labor force participation in the past, but there is not much room for further increases in the extremely high proportion of young women who finish high school. Recent trends in enrollments suggest that the number of college graduates is not likely to go up much further either, at least for the near future and the rise in the percentage of students who are women must also be expected to level off now that they make up about half of the undergraduates. On the other hand, there is the possibility for further entry of women into nontraditional fields and for further increases in their participation in professional and advanced degree programs.

One factor that may be expected to continue to encourage more women to enter employment is the growing acceptance of career aspirations of women and the declining pressure on them to become full-time homemakers. The concomitant tendency for young women to prepare themselves for more rewarding jobs will in turn result in greater labor force attachment, which will further increase their (potential) market earnings.

Other variables that have been important in the past may continue to exert some influence. New and better household appliances and more goods

[36]The total fertility rate per 1,000 women (the number of births that a cohort of 1,000 women would have if they experienced the age-specific birth rates occurring in the current year, throughout their childbearing career) was 1,760 in 1978 but rose to 1,808 in 1979 and to 1,840 in 1980. (However, it declined slightly to 1,829 in 1982.) Even during the period of small increase, the rate remained below the replacement level (estimated under mortality conditions that prevailed in 1980) of 2,100 (Department of Commerce, Bureau of the Census, *Statistical Abstract of the United States, 1984,* Table No. 83, p. 63).

[37]The determinants of demographic factors are discussed in greater detail in Chapter 5.

and services that may be purchased in the market, so that they need not be produced at home, would continue to raise the value of market income compared to home time. Most significant in this category would be greater availability of adequate infant and child care at lower prices, but this may not come about for some time. Nor is there any likelihood that household help will become either more plentiful or less expensive.

Turning from supply-side to demand-side issues, the availability of jobs, and jobs attractive enough to be preferable to full-time homemaking, is of course, crucial. Protracted periods of high unemployment, such as we experienced in the early 1980s, would be expected to slow down the influx of women into the labor market and may even cause some women to leave it. Of all the variables we are concerned with, this is one of the most unpredictable.

It is not, however, only the general level of unemployment that is important in determining the demand for female labor. There are also the questions of the extent to which specifically female occupations are likely to expand or contract and whether women's entry into mixed occupations and male occupations will continue and, perhaps even accelerate. With the possibility that the impending microcomputer revolution will reduce the need for clerical workers, where women have been so heavily concentrated, the outlook in this respect may not appear very rosy. On the other hand, with the continued expansion of traditionally female service jobs, declining competition from a shrinking group of teenagers, and young women increasingly preparing for and entering nontraditional occupations, women are likely to avail themselves of growing opportunities wherever these arise, assuming that their ability to enter continues to be safeguarded by the government.

What does all this add up to? We consider it extremely unlikely that women's participation rate will decline in the foreseeable future. At a minimum, we would expect the proportion of women in the labor force to continue at the present level. Even that seems very unlikely, if only because the young women who have a far higher labor force participation even during their childrearing years are much more likely to remain employed up to retirement age than were the older cohorts. Therefore, we would expect a continued upward trend in women's labor force participation, though perhaps at a somewhat slower rate than during the 1970s. Only a real labor shortage, as in World War II, or a dramatic shift toward policies encouraging women to enter the labor market, for instance, heavy subsidies for infant and child care, would be likely to result in further acceleration of the rate of increase in labor force participation beyond that of the 1970s. Thus, the "middle growth" projection of the Bureau of Labor Statistics (BLS) that 60.3 percent of adult women will be in the labor force by 1995 appears quite reasonable. Even their "high growth" projection of 66.7 percent may not be excessive.[38]

[38]See Howard N. Fullerton and John Tschetter, "The 1995 Labor Force: A Second Look," *Monthly Labor Review* (November 1983).

As for the labor force participation of men, as long as present attitudes do not change dramatically, many of the factors important for women are not especially relevant here. For instance, marital and parental status and level of education are likely to have considerably less influence on men's participation. One factor is even likely to have the opposite effect on men as opposed to women. As noted earlier in this chapter, rising real income appears to have encouraged men to retire earlier and may do so again as real wages begin to rise consistently once more. But the serious fiscal problems of the social security system, which have resulted in legislation to gradually increase the age when full benefits become available, may offset much or all of this impact.

Unemployment is an important unpredictable variable for men as well as women. We have already discussed its impact on black men and young black men in particular. Other groups may react similarly if confronted by long periods of job shortages. Short of a disastrous depression, however, unemployment rates for whites are not likely to rise to the levels presently experienced in the black community.

Weighing these considerations, we would expect men's labor force participation to continue at the present level or possibly to decline somewhat further, but very little. The BLS projects, by 1995, an additional small decrease of less than one percentage point in the male participation rate under its "middle growth" scenario. Should there be a dramatic shift toward acceptance of men and women as being equally responsible for earning income and homemaking, there could be a larger decline, but we do not anticipate such a change.

Combining the two projections, we fully expect a further reduction in the differential in labor force participation between men and women, though we do not expect it to disappear entirely for a long time to come. Under the BLS's "middle growth" projections, the gap between the male and female participation rates would decline from 23.8 percentage points in 1983 to 15.8 percentage points in 1995. The full impact of this change becomes clear when we remember that this differential was 65.7 percentage points at the turn of the century.

THE INCOME AND SUBSTITUTION EFFECTS: A CLOSER LOOK

As discussed in Chapter 4, for labor force participants, an increase in the wage rate has an uncertain effect on hours supplied, all else equal. This is illustrated in greater detail in Figure 4.8. The *overall* effect of the wage change is shown (in panels a and b) by the move from point A to point C. It may be broken down into distinct components, attributable to the income and substitution effects.

The income effect is represented by a hypothetical increase in income just large enough to get the individual to the higher indifference curve, U_2, leaving the wage rate unchanged. This would result in a move from point A to point B. For the reasons discussed earlier, the impact of the increase in income, all else equal, is unambiguously to reduce labor hours supplied to the market. The substitution effect is given by the impact of a hypothetical change in the wage (the slope of the budget constraint) *along a given indifference curve, U_2.* This results in a move from B to C. The effect of an increase in the opportunity cost (or price) of nonmarket time, all else equal, is unambiguously to increase labor hours supplied.

The overall effect of the wage change may be either positive or negative depending on whether the substitution effect dominates the income effect

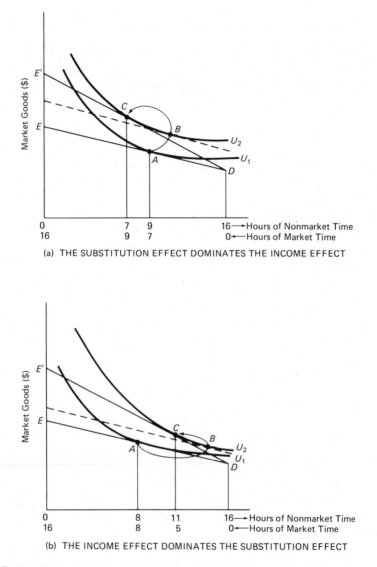

(a) THE SUBSTITUTION EFFECT DOMINATES THE INCOME EFFECT

(b) THE INCOME EFFECT DOMINATES THE SUBSTITUTION EFFECT

FIGURE 4.8   The Impact of the Market Wage on Labor Hours: A Closer Look

(panel a) or the income effect dominates the substitution effect (panel b). Since the prediction of economic theory is ambiguous in this case, empirical evidence is required to resolve this issue in any given case. Such evidence was discussed in Chapter 4.

SUGGESTED READINGS

BECKER, GARY S., "A Theory of the Allocation of Time." *The Economic Journal* 75, no. 299 (September 1965): 493–517.

BOWEN, WILLIAM and T. ALDRICH FINEGAN, *The Economics of Labor Force Participation,* Princeton, N.J.: Princeton University Press, 1969.

BROWN, CLAIR, "Consumption Norms, Work Roles, and Economic Growth," paper presented at the conference on "Gender in the Workplace," Brookings Instituion, November 1984.

CAIN, GLEN G., *Married Women in the Labor Force,* Chicago: University of Chicago Press, 1966.

KILLINGSWORTH, MARK R., *Labor Supply,* Cambridge: Cambridge University Press, 1983.

MINCER, JACOB, "Labor Force Participation of Married Women," ed. H. Greg Lewis, *Aspects of Labor Economics,* Universities National Bureau of Economic Research Conference Studies, no. 14, Princeton, N.J.: Princeton University Press, 1962, pp. 63–97.

OPPENHEIMER, VALERIE, *The Female Labor Force in the United States: Demographic and Economic Factors Governing its Growth and Changing Composition,* Population Monograph Ser. 5, Berkeley, CA, 1970.

SMITH, JAMES P., ed., *Female Labor Supply: Theory and Estimation,* Princeton, N.J.: University Press, 1980.

Chapter 5

THE CONSEQUENCES OF WOMEN'S EMPLOYMENT FOR THE FAMILY

In earlier chapters, we discussed the family as an economic institution and the allocation of time of husband and wife between the household and the labor market. We now turn our attention to the impact a woman's employment has on her family. Since the typical family today is one where both spouses participate in the labor force, at least for part of their married life, this topic is of considerable importance. There is also a growing proportion of families where the woman is the head of the household and the sole wage-earner. Such units have particular problems because there is generally only one adult in the family and because that adult is a woman. Therefore, we devote special attention to them.

There is one basic difference between our approach here and in Chapter 4. There we accepted marital status and fertility as given, exogenous to our models, and focused on the effects of these factors on women's labor force participation. In this chapter, we turn the tables and examine the impact that women's labor force participation has on marriage, number of children, and the well-being of family members.

The first sections of this chapter deal with family formation, childbearing, divorce, and the relationship of these to women's labor force participa-

116

tion.[1] After that, we look first at how much time wives and husbands spend on nonmarket work, particularly housework, whether or not both are in the labor market. Secondly, we examine how much the wife contributes to family earnings. We go on to examine the impact of women's work on satisfaction within the family and conclude with a consideration of the problems of female-headed families.

MARRIAGE

What would be the expected effect of women's increased labor force participation on family formation? From the viewpoint of neoclassical economics, the determining factor in the marriage decision would be whether the benefits exceed the costs. Thus, the question is what effect rising female labor force participation has had on this cost/benefit calculus—do more or fewer couples find it in their economic self-interest to marry?

The answer to this question is not obvious from a theoretical point of view. That is, there are forces operating both to reduce and to increase the benefits of marriage, and their net effect is uncertain. The issue of costs is a bit more difficult to speculate intelligently about, but there may have been changes here as well. We first consider these theoretical issues and then review the empirical evidence.

On the one hand, women's increased opportunities for earning their own livelihood may have a negative effect on their incentives to marry. For market work presents a woman with a viable alternative to marriage, making it economically feasible to postpone or altogether forego such a commitment. One may speculate that it has become more socially acceptable to do so as well.

Women's increased tendency to work outside the home may have reduced some of the economic benefits to marriage accruing to the couple as well. It may be recalled from Chapter 3 that one of the gains to marriage is that it makes possible the specialization and exchange that may potentially increase the couple's productivity and economic well-being. In general, the more the comparative advantage in producing home and market goods *differs* between the two partners, the larger the potential gain. For each may then specialize in his or her area of higher relative productivity. As women have been acquiring more market-oriented education and training, their market productivity has been rising relative to their home productivity. The traditional specialization of the husband in wage-earning and of the wife in homemaking has become in-

[1]Seminal work by neoclassical economists on the economics of the family was first done by Gary S. Becker and has been summarized by him in *A Treastise on the Family,* (Cambridge, MA: Harvard University Press, 1981). A great deal of interesting work by some of the best known researchers in this area is contained in *Economics of the Family,* a conference report of the National Bureau of Economic Research, ed. Theodore W. Schultz (Chicago: University of Chicago Press, 1974).

creasingly less advantageous. And, in general, the gains to marriage from specialization are reduced.[2]

On the other hand, as we also pointed out in Chapter 3, specialization and exchange is not the only economic benefit to marriage. Some of the other benefits need not be affected one way or the other by women's increased labor force participation. Such is the case for economies of scale and the consumption of public goods. Other benefits may be increased. For example, the externalities of joint consumption may be enhanced if an employed wife and her husband have more similar tastes. And, to the extent that the tastes of two-earner couples are more similar than those of traditional couples, potential disagreements over the combination of commodities to consume would be reduced.

Moreover, a working woman's income can have a positive effect on her propensity to marry because she can supplement her husband's earnings. When a traditional marriage is planned, it cannot occur unless or until the potential husband earns enough income to "support" his wife. A working woman's income may potentially make her a more attractive partner, at least to a man who values that income more than the services of a full-time homemaker.

With respect to the costs of marriage, the greater acceptability of market work for married women may have reduced these costs for women. For women today no longer choose between employment on the one hand or marriage on the other. While many women continue to accommodate their paid work to what are still perceived to be their household responsibilities, they are far less likely than in the past to cut short their education or leave the labor market at the time they get married.

Only empirical evidence can show what the balance of these forces appears to be. The large increase in the proportion of single people between 1970 and 1982, from 35.8 percent to 53.4 percent for those between ages 20 and 24 and from 10.5 percent to 23.4 percent for those between ages 25 to 29, suggests that for relatively young people the propensity to marry has declined. At the same time the proportion of those 40 years of age or older who had never married actually declined slightly from 6.2 percent in 1970 to 4.7 percent in 1982.

It appears that young women with increasingly acceptable alternatives are less likely to rush into marriage early on but that most of them do opt for it eventually. Even so, it is projected that the proportion of people who never marry in their lifetime may show a modest increase from the low of 5 percent in the early eighties to about 7 percent by the end of the century as this large proportion of young singles moves through the life cycle.[3]

---

[2]The gains from specialization and exchange are not entirely eliminated unless there is no difference at all in the comparative advantages of the two members of the couple.

[3]Bureau of the Census, *Marital Status and Living Arrangements; March 1982,* Current Population Reports Series P-20, no. 380 (May 1983).

Economic considerations are not the only ones that play a role in these demographic changes. One factor that undoubtedly has contributed to the growing number of young people who are not married is the change in attitude toward sex outside of marriage and the corresponding increase in cohabitation. The really dramatic rise occurred after 1970. At that time, 523,000 unmarried couples were living together. This figure increased to 1,137,000 by 1978 and 1,988,000 in 1984.[4]

By sharing housekeeping, informal living arrangements provide the same possibility for economies of scale as marriage does, though they certainly do not provide the same legal guarantees for a partner who specializes in homemaking and foregoes the opportunity to maintain and increase labor market skills. But this is less important as fewer partnerships are based on the husband's specializing in market work and the wife's specializing completely in housework, and the proportion of two-earner couples continues to grow. Furthermore, the status of a woman no longer seems to be solely determined by her marriage but, rather, is enhanced by her own educational and occupational accomplishments. Even so, cohabitation does not appear to be a substitute for marriage but, rather, a prelude to it.[5]

The high rate of remarriage is another indication that, despite all the changes, marriage is still the cornerstone of American life. About four out of five divorced persons eventually remarry.[6] The proportion is lower among those who are widowed, in part because they are older, but is still substantial. Furthermore, there is a trend toward shorter intervals before remarriage.

CHILDBEARING

We have seen that neoclassical economic theory contributes to our understanding of marriage. Similarly, it helps to shed light on the decision of whether to have children, how many to have, and to what extent scarce resources should be allocated to them. To make such decisions rationally, costs must be weighed against benefits.

The costs of raising children include not only the expenses incurred in feeding, clothing, housing, and educating them, substantial though these have

---

[4]Data for the earlier years are from Paul C. Glick and Graham B. Spanier, "Married and Unmarried Cohabitation in the United States," *Journal of Marriage and Family* 4, no. 1 (February 1980): 19–30; the figure for 1984 is from the *New York Times,* September 16, 1985, p. 11.

[5]In some instances, cohabitation also follows the termination of marriage among the elderly. Most likely this is spurred on by social security rules that would often severely reduce the incomes of such couples if they married.

[6]The proportion is somewhat higher for men because, among the elderly, they are considerably outnumbered by women. Paul C. Glick and Arthur J. Norton, "Marrying, Divorcing and Living Together in the U.S. Today," *Population Bulletin* 32, no. 5 (October 7, 1979): 3–39.

become. A very large part of total costs consists of the time parents devote to childrearing, for children require a great deal of personal attention. Even when some child care is delegated to paid help, the final responsibility for finding suitable caretakers, taking care of emergencies, and providing affection and stability rests with the parents, most often particularly the mother. The time and energy she devotes to these purposes could otherwise be used to get more education or training for herself, to earn money, or to enjoy leisure. Giving up some or all of these constitutes the opportunity cost of rearing children.

In view of these considerations, women's growing potential for market earnings increases the opportunity cost of children and would, accordingly, be expected to have a negative substitution effect. This may well be one of the main determinants of fertility. At the same time, however, greater earnings would also be expected to have a positive income effect, since the family can now afford more children in terms of the money-costs associated with them. So long as fathers are not expected to give us much of their time for child care, their higher earnings would be expected to have predominantly such a positive effect.[7] For women, on the other hand, the either/or choice between labor force participation and children is still common enough that the substitution effect is likely to predominate.

As we have seen in Chapter 4, far more mothers of young children are employed now, but the proportion of full-time homemakers is nonetheless higher among them than for other women. This has been found to be especially true for the first two years. Also, mothers of preschoolers who are in the labor force are more likely to work part-time. Further, those who work full-time nonetheless spend less time on the job and tend to make less progress on the job.[8] This is as would be expected in terms of the economic theory of the family, for the value of the woman's contribution in the home is high relative to her (potential) market earnings during this period. Thus, young children continue to be an impediment to a woman working outside the home.

At the same time, there is also reason to believe that women's work plans influence their intended childbearing.[9] Women in the labor force, and particularly those who are highly educated and tend to have a stronger career

---

[7]The importance of both the substitution and income effect has been confirmed by research, such as William P. Butz and Michael P. Ward, "The Emergence of Countercyclical U.S. Fertility," *American Economic Review* 69, no. 3 (June 1979): 318–28. Another study, Michael Hout, "The Determinants of Marital Fertility in the United States, 1968–70, Inferences from a Dynamic Model," *Demography* 15, no. 2 (May 1978): 139–60, suggests that women's employment responds to the presence of children in the short run but that the total number of children a family has is determined by the women's employment status.

[8]Gus W. Haggstrom, Linda J. Waite, David E. Kanouse, and Thomas J. Blaschke, *Changes in the Lifestyles of New Parents* (Santa Monica, CA: Rand, 1984).

[9]Two studies that establish this relationship are Linda J. Waite and Ross M. Stolzenberg, "Intended Childbearing and Labor Force Participation of Young Women: Insights from Nonrecursive Models," *American Sociological Review* 41, no. 2 (April 1976): 235–52; and Michael Hout, "The Determinants of Marital Fertility in the United States, 1968–70."

orientation, have fewer children.[10] Accordingly, families have become smaller as women's education and labor force participation has been increasing. The growing demand for higher quality children, with better health and more education, that is related to rising incomes would reinforce this effect.[11]

Table 5.1 shows the fertility rate since the 1940s. It has been declining since the baby boom years. As may be recalled from our discussion in Chapter 4, there was little change in the labor force participation rates of younger women until the early 1960s. The sharp drop in the number of children and the large increase in employment of young women have both occurred since then. In 1982, the fertility rate of 1829 per 1000 women was below the replacement level of 2100.

As mentioned earlier, these trends can be explained in part by the higher cost of reduced time in the labor market among women with a strong labor force attachment. One may also speculate that such women are inclined to hold less traditional values and are most likely to find their work absorbing and fulfilling. It should be noted, however, that the decline in the birth rate appears to have leveled off,[12] and that as of the early 1980s, there was only scant evidence of a trend toward more childlessness. The percent of married women who do not intend to have any children continues to be quite modest, not exceeding 10 percent, except among the highly educated.

Nonetheless, since it is highly educated and career-oriented women who tend to have the fewest children, or even none, and both level of education and career orientation are continuing to increase, it may be that the long downward trend in family size will once again resume. There are those who predict that as young women continue to find the costs of childbearing increasingly unattractive, and alternative uses of their time and energy increasingly inviting, there will be a further decline in birthrates.[13] Such a trend would also be

[10]Kristin A. Moore and Sandra L. Hofferth, "Women and Their Children," ed. Ralph Smith, *The Subtle Revolution,* (Washington, D.C.: The Urban Institute, 1979), pp. 128–32. Evidence on very highly educated women is found in Marianne A. Ferber and Betty Kordick, *Industrial and Labor Relations Review* 31, no. 2 (January 1978): 227–38. Evangelos M. Falaris, "An Empirical Study of the Timing and Spacing of Childbearing" (unpublished paper, Ohio State University, August 1984) also found that higher potential earnings cause women to have their first child later but then space additional children closer together.

[11]Becker, *A Treastise on the Family.*

[12]There was even conjecture about a reversal. In fact, the increase in the birthrate—births per 1000 population—in the late seventies was very largely caused by the rise in the proportion of the population of women in childbearing years and, as mentioned in Chapter 4, some women having babies they chose not to have earlier, rather than a rise in the total number of children during a woman's lifetime. (*Estimates of the Population of the United States by Age, Sex, and Race, 1980 and 1983,* Current Population Reports. Population Estimates and Projections, Series P-25, no. 949, May 1984). The proportion of women between the ages of 20 to 24 who were married, or had been married, and did not have any children rose from 24 percent in 1960 to 43 percent in 1982. Also, by that time, 14 percent of women between the ages of 35 and 39 were childless. (Trish Hall, "Many Women Decide They Want Their Careers Rather Than Children," *The Wall Street Journal* (Oct. 10, 1984): 35).

[13]See, for instance, Joan A. Huber and Glenna Spitze, *Sex Stratification, Children, Housework and Jobs* (NY: Academic Press, 1983).

TABLE 5.1   Total Fertility Rates

YEAR	TOTAL FERTILITY RATE[a]
1940-44	2523
1945-49	2985
1950-54	3337
1955-59	3690
1960-64	3449
1965	2913
1975	2480
1980	1840
1982	1829

[a]The number of births that a cohort of 1,000 women would have if they experienced the age-specific birth rates occurring in the current year, throughout their childbearing career.

Sources: Department of Commerce, Bureau of the Census, *Statistical Abstract,* 1984; National Center for Health Statistics, *Monthly Vital Statistics Report* 33, no. 6, (September 28, 1984).

reinforced by increasing recognition that children cannot be viewed as investment goods in modern societies. Not only are the costs of raising and educating them very high, but they are increasingly being replaced by such institutional arrangements as insurance, pensions, and social security as caretakers of the aged. On the other hand, the attraction of children as consumer goods may surely be expected to continue, possibly even to increase as fathers become better acquainted with them. Further, to the extent that fathers undertake a larger share of child care and organized child care becomes more readily available, such developments would tend to reduce the burden on young women. In this case, fertility may continue to remain at around the replacement level, or only slightly below it, in the future.

DIVORCE

Two people who marry in anticipation of improving their well-being may nonetheless find that one or both of them later feel they would be better off if they terminated their relationship. This can occur because everything does not always work out as anticipated at the time the initial decision is made. This is all the more likely to happen during a period when long-accepted standards and norms are rapidly changing. If, however, only one partner wants a divorce, it may be necessary to find a way to get the other partner to agree.

When considering the effect of women's labor force participation on marital dissolution, we are, therefore, confronted, once again, by a complex situation. On the one hand, the great interdependence of the breadwinner husband and the homemaker wife clearly deters divorce. The wife earns no money and needs her husband's income to buy whatever she requires of market goods and services. The husband has little time and no training for household tasks and needs the wife to look after home and children. As this traditional division of labor breaks down, the economic incentives for remaining married are reduced. Also, the stress of overcommitment and possible role conflict in the two-earner family may cause additional strains on a marriage.

On the other hand, couples in which the wife works enjoy to an equal, or even to a greater extent, the other benefits of marriage that we have discussed—economies of scale, public goods, joint consumption, etc. Moreover, while such couples have less time, they have more money than those with only one paycheck. Not only does their higher income permit them to consume more of the market goods and services that they desire, it also presumably reduces at least one area of potential stress and disagreement—conflicts over allocating scarce dollars. Their higher income also gives them the opportunity to accumulate more assets. This tends to inhibit marital dissolution because of the problems that are often encountered in dividing illiquid assets. Furthermore, sharing both market work and housework might be expected to create greater understanding and empathy between husband and wife.

In fact, the divorce rate in the United States has sharply increased as can be seen in Table 5.2, from .9 per 1000 population in 1910 to 2.0 in 1940 to 5.2 in 1980. The increase was particularly marked between 1960 and 1980. Although the data suggest a leveling off of the increase in the early 1980s, it is estimated that about 40 percent of new marriages may end in divorce.[14] Accordingly, the chances of a child living in the same family until he or she

TABLE 5.2   Divorce Rate per 1000 Population, 1910-1982

YEAR	DIVORCE RATE
1910	0.9
1920	1.6
1930	1.6
1940	2.0
1950	2.6
1960	2.2
1970	3.5
1980	5.2
1982	5.1

Source: U.S. Department of Commerce, Bureau of the Census, *Statistical Abstract,* 1984.

[14]Such projections are necessarily hazardous because they are based on assumptions about future rather than merely past and present behavior. For each cohort, we only know their actual divorce rate up to their present age. Quite different conclusions may be reached about the proportion of their marriages that will eventually break up depending on projections for the future. Among four cohorts of women born between 1890 and 1920 for whom data were available up to age 55, the ratio of divorces by age 55 as compared to divorces by age 30 ranged from 1.9 to 2.5. Among the cohorts born in 1950, 27 percent were divorced by the age of 30. Using the lower figure would result in an eventual divorce rate of 51 percent; using the higher one it would be 67 percent. (Robert Schoen, William L. Urton, Karen Woodrow, and John Bay, "Marriage and Divorce in 20th Century American Cohorts," *Demography* (forthcoming).

establishes an independent household and of marrying only once in a lifetime have been rapidly decreasing.[15]

Because of the conflicting considerations discussed above, it is not clear how the existing evidence of a rising divorce rate should be interpreted or what future developments are likely to be. While, as was pointed out earlier, most people continue to live in families most of the time, there has been a radical change in family stability. This growing trend is usually regarded both as a symptom and a cause of society's malaise, for it is widely believed that two people who live together "forever after" are most likely to be happy and that children raised by such a couple are most likely to grow up well-adjusted and successful.[16] There can, indeed, be no doubt that the breakup of a marriage, which generally begins with high hopes and excellent intentions, is at best sad and regrettable and often entails recrimination and bitterness. To the extent that women's work outside the home is associated with the high divorce rate, it may, therefore, have some undesirable effects.

This is, however, only one side of the story. First, empirical evidence on whether wives' employment tends to raise the divorce rate is rather mixed.[17] Thus, although rising labor force participation rates of married women over time have been associated with rising divorce rates, it has not been conclusively established that the former has caused the latter. However, even if this is to some extent the case, one might argue that similar lifestyles of husbands and wives enhance the quality of some marriages, even if by reducing interdependence, they facilitate the breakup of unsatisfactory ones. In such instances, divorce may be preferable to an unhappy marriage.

In terms of the future, it seems probable that any positive impact of married women's labor force participation on the divorce rate should diminish. First, strains are likely to be greatest when tradition still has a strong grip and is in conflict with existing reality. Once women and men have had the opportunity to adjust to new standards and norms, there should be fewer surprises and thus fewer problems. Second, the decreasing economic and social pressures to marry associated with women's rising labor force participation

[15]U.S. Department of Commerce, Bureau of the Census, *Current Population Reports,* "Divorce, Child Custody, and Child Support," Series P-23, no. 84, p. 2. On this subject, see also Saul Hoffman and John Holmes, "Husbands, Wives, and Divorce," eds. G. J. Duncan and J. N. Morgan, *Five Thousand Families* 4, (Ann Arbor, MI: Institute for Social Research, 1976), pp. 23–76.

[16]Interestingly, the increase in the proportion of children living in one-parent homes because of the rapid rise in the divorce rate has been at least partially offset by the decline in early deaths. The extent to which this is true can be gauged from the fact that among ever-married women less than 45 years old, the group most likely to have children still at home, 6.1 percent were widowed and 0.8 percent divorced in 1890, while in 1983 only 1.2 percent were widowed, but 12.1 percent were divorced.

[17]A good summary of studies on both sides of this issue can be found in Sandra L. Hofferth and Kristin A. Moore, "Women's Employment and Marriage," ed. Ralph E. Smith, *The Subtle Revolution,* pp. 108–10.

have lead young people to postpone marriage. This should promote marital stability in that couples who get married at older ages are less likely to break up.[18] The evidence that the divorce rate began to level off in the early 1980s would tend to support such speculations. It may even decline somewhat in the future, although it is not likely to fall to the levels that prevailed when husbands and wives were highly economically dependent on each other and when social attitudes towards divorce were extremely negative.

Whatever the pros and cons of divorce, it is clear that when it does occur it is the full-time homemaker, along with her children, who is particularly vulnerable. She has been dependent on her husband not only for money income but also for her social status and even, at times, for much of her circle of friends. She continues to be most likely to obtain custody of the children, and while she may be awarded alimony[19] and/or child support by the courts, the amounts involved are often inadequate and are frequently not paid. In 1981, only 15 percent of the 17 million ever-divorced or separated women received alimony, and of the 4 million women due child support, only 47 percent received the full amount.

As would be expected in the light of these facts, many women, especially those who have not previously been working outside the home, find themselves in poverty after a divorce. The ones who were employed while they were married are also at a disadvantage because even women with labor force experience earn less than men and because they generally continue to be responsible for child care. We shall discuss the problems of female-headed families at greater length in the last section of this chapter. In the meantime, we will consider various other issues related to the employment status of the wife.

NONMARKET WORK

As we have seen in Chapter 4, economists have traditionally focused their analyses and interest upon market work. Yet, much work is peformed outside the market that substantially contributes to the well-being of the individual, his or her family, and the society at large. In this section, we consider the two most important categories of nonmarket work—housework and volunteer work—and how women's and men's involvement with them has changed with women's rising labor force participation.

[18]Alan Booth and Lynn White, "Thinking About Divorce," *Journal of Marriage and Family* 42, no. 3 (August 1980): 605–16.

[19]Alimony mainly represents continued support for a dependent spouse and compensation for the reasonably expected economic benefits of marriage but may also be a means of punishing particularly reprehensible behavior on the part of the other spouse. Data from U.S. Bureau of the Census, Current Population Reports, Series P-23 (May 1983).

Work at Home

A number of surveys have provided information on the extent to which husbands and wives share in paid and unpaid work. Their estimates of hours worked, however, show a considerable range. An examination of the individual studies shows why this might be expected. They are based on different samples, some are drawn from different populations. Methods of collecting data and samples vary, as does the definition of what is considered work. Nonetheless, the data presented in Table 5.3, based on four of the most widely cited studies, reveal some interesting patterns, and the fact that they cover years between 1965/66 and 1975/76 enables us to discern some changes over time.

The evidence indicates that nonemployed wives worked the fewest total hours. This was true during both periods but more so during the latter. While they still did far more housework than their husbands, and more than employed wives, they devoted considerably less time to this activity in the

TABLE 5.3 Range Estimates of Time-Use Data on Housework and Market Work (Hours per Day)

| | WIVES | | | |
| | Nonemployed | | Employed | |
	1960s	1970s	1960s	1970s
Housework	7.6-8.6	4.6-6.8	4.0- 5.3	2.3-4.0
Market work	0.0-0.6	0.1-1.9	4.8- 5.3	5.0-6.5
Total work	7.6-8.6	6.5-6.8	9.3-10.1	7.9-9.3

| | HUSBANDS | | | |
| | Nonemployed wives | | Employed wives | |
	1960s	1970s	1960s	1970s
Housework	1.0-1.6	0.6-1.8	1.1- 1.6	0.6-1.9
Market work	7.5-7.8	7.0-7.7	6.3- 6.9	6.9-7.1
Total work	8.4-8.5	8.3-8.9	7.9- 8.0	7.7-8.8

Sources:
Martin Meissner, Elizabeth W. Humphreys, Scott W. Meis, and William J. Scheu, "No Exit for Wives: Sexual Division of Labour and the Cumulation of Household Demands," *Canadian Review of Sociology and Anthropology* 12, no.4 (November 1975): 424–39.

Joseph H. Pleck, "Husband's Paid Work and Family Roles: Current Research Issues," *Research in the Interweave of Social Roles: Jobs and Families* 3, (1983): 251–333.

John P. Robinson, *Changes in America's Use of Time* (Cleveland: Communications Research Center, Cleveland State University, 1977).

Kathryn E. Walker and Margaret E. Woods, *Time Use: A Measure of Household Production of Family Goods and Services* (Washington, D.C.: American Home Economics Association, 1976).

1970s, while still spending (by definition) very little time in the labor market.[20] In the 1960s, the total work time of employed wives was considerably higher than that of any of the other groups, including their husbands. But they also reduced time spent on housework considerably over the decade so that they too worked fewer total hours during the latter period, only very slightly more than their husbands. At the same time, the number of hours employed women spent on market work increased somewhat. Husbands of women in the labor market spent somewhat less time on paid work than other husbands but, nonetheless, considerably more than their employed wives. The number of hours spent on housework was small and about the same for husbands of employed and nonemployed wives during both decades.

While these data suggest that the total workload of husbands and wives in two-earner families became more equal between the 1960s and the 1970s, they also suggest that the division of labor remained quite traditional, with women doing considerably more housework and less market work than men. There is, however, more recent evidence that the differences in allocation of time between married men and married women are beginning to narrow significantly. A study that compared data from 1975/76 and 1981/82 surveys found that men's market work declined by one hour per week, from 36.3 to 35.3, and their work in the home increased by about the same amount, from 13.4 to 14.7. During the same period, women's work in the market rose by one and a half hours per week, from 16.9 to 18.4, and time spent on housework went down by about the same amount, from 30.8 to 29.3. (It should be noted, however, that these data are for all women, not only those in the labor force. Hence the changes in average hours of market work in part reflect increased labor force participation.) Further, the changes were considerably larger for the younger group, 25 to 44 years of age. These men worked one hour less in the market and three hours more at home; women worked three and one half hours more in the market and one hour less at home.[21]

Unfortunately, this study did not report data separately for families with employed and nonemployed wives. However, it seems reasonable to infer that the trend towards more housework for husbands held for both groups or, if anything, was stronger for working couples where there is a greater rationale for husbands taking on more household tasks. This speculation is supported by the fact that a recent study found that husbands of employed women were likely to spend more time on child care.[22] As heartening as these trends are for

---

[20]The reason they do report some time in this category is that someone who is employed, but working less than one hour per week, is not included in the labor force, nor are unpaid family workers who put in less than 15 hours.

[21]F. Thomas Juster, "A Note on Recent Changes in Time Use," eds. F. Thomas Juster and Frank P. Stafford, *Time, Goods, and Well-Being,* (Ann Arbor: Institute for Social Research, The University of Michigan, 1985).

[22]The survey was carried out by Joseph Pleck and James Levine. The results were reported in the Wellesley College Center for Research on Women, *Research Report* 4, no. 1 (Fall 1984): 1, 4.

proponents of an egalitarian division of labor, it is important to bear in mind that such data, as well as those shown in Table 5.3, tend to underestimate the problems of employed wives.

First, in 1984, 29 percent of employed married women worked part-time, the other 71 percent full-time. The former are likely to face a smaller and less attractive choice of jobs, lower earnings, less fringe benefits, and fewer opportunities for promotion. The latter face a considerably higher work overload.[23] Second, the sample includes women with and without young children. The former, who are also likely to be at the age when workers need to prove themselves on the job and to begin to show that they are upwardly mobile if they are to make much progress, face a far heavier burden. Moreover, these extra responsibilities are apt to make it more difficult for them to compete with their male counterparts, at least to some extent. Thus, whichever route employed wives choose, be it part-time or full-time work, the unequal division of labor in the home is likely to adversely affect their success in the labor market.

On the other hand, it has been argued that the unequal division of labor is in some ways less of a problem than it superficially seems to be. First, many tasks women perform are no longer as physically exacting as those their grandmothers did. Second, such activities as shopping and, to a considerable extent, child care, may be enjoyable enough to be regarded as quasi-leisure.[24] But much of paid work has also become less onerous, and such time on the job as chatting with fellow workers and entertaining clients is as much quasi-leisure as any family work. In fact, a recent study indicates that, on the whole, people enjoy child care more than any other activities included in a comprehensive list, but enjoy their jobs far more than any other types of housework and considerably more than many leisure activities.[25]

While the unequal division of tasks between men and women in the home remains a problem, the evidence suggests that as women are spending increasing amounts of time on paid work, men are finally increasing their participation in housework. The proportion of time spent on the two different types of work moved more rapidly toward equality for the sexes during the 1975/76 to 1981/82 period than during the preceding decades. It is likely that the utimate locus of responsibility for household work continues to rest with women and that they are accordingly the ones who are expected to give family needs priority over market work when unexpected problems and small emergencies come

[23]Joann Vanek, "Household Work, Wage Work, and Sexual Equality," ed. S. F. Berg *Women and Household Labor,* Beverly Hills, CA: (Sage, 1980): pp. 75–89.

[24]These points are discussed by Glen G. Cain, "Women and Work: Trends in Time Spent in Housework," Institute for Reseach on Poverty, University of Wisconsin, Discussion Paper 747–84 (April 1984).

[25]F. Thomas Juster, "Preferences for Work and Leisure," eds. Juster and Stafford, *Time, Goods and Well-Being.*

up.[26] Nonetheless, the more egalitarian distribution of unpaid work would be expected to have a positive impact on women's occupational attainment and earnings. These topics are discussed further in Chapters 7 and 8.

Whatever the precise amount of time employed wives and their husbands spend on housework, there is no doubt that it is considerably less than that devoted to work at home by families with nonemployed wives. It is less clear exactly how this reduction is accomplished.

It has often been assumed that families with wives who work outside the home compensate for less household time by purchasing more labor-saving devices and more services available in the market. Research does not fully support this view, however. While child care expenditures are higher for working wife families, a number of recent studies have failed to find any other marked differences in expenditures between employed and nonemployed-wife families at the same income level, except for outlays on directly work-related items such as transportation.[27]

Part of the story is that employed women have, on the average, fewer and older children. It is, therefore, plausible to assume that, even though there is little evidence that children of employed mothers do more housework, they at least take care of their own needs to a greater extent. This tends to be substantiated by detailed time diaries that show that when the wife enters the labor market, she reduces time spent in the care of other family members more than on other types of housework.

It has also been suggested that homemakers' behavior illustrates Parkinson's law—they tend to stretch out their work to fill the available time.[28] This would make it easier to get more work done in a shorter time when the need arises. Or women may reduce the amount or quality of services they offer their family. No evidence is available to date that would enable us to determine to what extent each of these possible solutions is used.

Two other interesting developments with respect to the allocation of time in the family are that, since 1965, men have reduced the number of hours spent on the job, and full-time homemakers have reduced the amount of time spent on housework. The former is readily explained. Both rising real-wage rates of

[26]"A Recent Wellesley College study of 160 middle-class families in the Boston suburb of Dedham, Massachusetts, found that fathers with working wives spent more time alone with their children than other fathers, but that nearly all of the women were in charge of remembering, planning and scheduling children's activities." ("Working Fathers Feel Pressure Deriving from Child-Rearing Duties," *Wall Street Journal,* [Sept. 7, 1984].) It also is still the case that men who feel role strain because of their participation tend to blame it on their wives' employment, while women tend to blame such strain on their own labor force participation.

[27]See particularly Myra H. Strober and Charles B. Weinberg, "Strategies Used by Working and Nonworking Wives to Reduce Time Pressures," *Journal of Consumer Research* 6, no. 4 (Mar. 1980): 338–48; Myra H. Strober, "Wives' Labor Force Behavior and Family Consumption Patterns," *American Economic Review* 67, no. 1 (Feb. 1977): 410–17.

[28]Joann Vanek, "Time Spent in Housework," *Scientific American* 231, no. 5 (Nov. 1974): 116–20.

men and the earnings of the growing proportion of women who are in the labor market reduce, at least to some extent, the incentive for the husbands to work long hours for pay. The latter might be considered more surprising in view of the failure of hours worked in the household of nonemployed women to decrease over about 50 years prior to the 1960s.[29] It might be conjectured that women who choose or agree to be full-time homemakers will increasingly do so only on favorable terms, i.e., that they too are "liberated" from some of the household chores that were formerly expected. This would help to explain why their families spend as much on many purchased services and on labor-saving durables as do two-earner units at the same income level. In any case, while evidence of a major shift in the allocation of household work among the general population is at best scanty to date, the conclusion that a gradual move toward a more egalitarian division of labor may at least have begun is not without foundation.

Volunteer Work

In addition to market work and housework, many people also spend an appreciable amount of time on volunteer work. To qualify for this category, the chief beneficiaries must not be members of the immediate family, there must be no direct material reward, and the work must be part of an organized program. This definition is intended to make a clear distinction between volunteer activities as opposed to such tasks as performing services for children and spouse, doing an assigned job for wages, commission, or payment in kind, and spending time with a sick friend.

It is clear from this description that such voluntary activities are not an integral part of homemaking.[30] Nonetheless, anything that enhances life in the community influences the family at least indirectly and often the connection is a fairly close one. In fact, the precise line between volunteer work on the one hand and activities intended to benefit an individual's family or career is often difficult to draw. A person is most likely to participate in the PTA or scouting when he or she has children who are involved. People participate in unions at least in part to improve their own working conditions and in the symphony guild so that they will be able to hear concerts. Attending a garden club is at least to some extent a leisure activity. Much business is transacted, and many profitable contacts are made at the meetings of the Rotarians. In principle, the distinction is made in terms of which is the dominant purpose, but it is obvious that any data on the amount and value of volunteer time must be accepted with

---

[29]Vanek, "Time Spent in Housework."

[30]For women, this may be thought of as "social homemaking" or women extending the services they generally perform for their own families to the community. See, for instance, Julie A. Matthai, "Capitalism and Sexual Division of Labor: An Essay in U.S. Economic History," *Social Concepts* 1, no. 2 (Sept. 1983): 13–35.

some caution. There is, however, no doubt that much valuable work is performed on a volunteer basis.

It is estimated that in 1973 one quarter or more of all women, and approximately the same proportion of men, participated in volunteer activities for a total of nearly 6 billion hours. Women constituted a substantial majority in recreational, charitable, and religious organizations. Men involved in volunteer organizations were more highly represented in civic and political groups and dominated among volunteer workers in professional organizations and labor unions.[31]

Many reasons have been given for doing work that, by definition, brings little or no direct material rewards. True altruism, contact with congenial people, dedication to a particular cause, desire for recognition, and furthering business and career interests of oneself or a spouse all play a part to a greater or lesser extent. Research also suggests that women who are out of the labor force may believe that volunteer activities will help them to get better jobs when they re-enter. While experience gained in volunteer work is probably not as valuable, in general, as that acquired on the job, a woman with young children particularly will often value the more flexible schedule, and others may enjoy the greater choice of the type of work they prefer to do.[32] Experience in volunteer work is also particularly useful for persons interested in running for political office, both because of the skills acquired and the valuable contacts often made. In spite of all these possible advantages, it has been found that most people only join voluntary organizations upon being invited, and even urged, to do so.[33]

From the point of view of society, voluntary organizations also serve a number of useful functions. They offer the opportunity for mediation, integration of subgroups, affirmation of values, and distribution of power. All of these are important, especially in a democratic society. Beyond this, it appears that volunteers provide free services. It is frequently argued that as more and more women enter the labor market and have less time to spend on unpaid

[31]ACTION American Volunteer 1974 (ACTION Pamphlet 4000-17), (Washington, D.C.: U.S. Government Printing Office, 1975). Other estimates would suggest a higher figure. Helen Z. Lopata, *Occupation Housewife* (London: Oxford University Press, 1971) found 64 percent of her sample of married women belonged to at least one organization. No comparable data are available for more recent years than 1973, but Jessica Reynolds Jenner, 'Participation, Leadership, and the Role of Volunteerism Among Selected Women Volunteers," *Journal of Voluntary Action Research* 11, no. 4 (Oct.–Dec. 1982): 27–38 concludes, on the basis of scattered information, that participation has not changed substantially.

[32]For a discussion of this subject see Marnie W. Mueller, "Economic Determinants of Volunteer Work by Women," *Signs: Journal of Women in Culture and Society* 1, no. 2 (Winter 1975): 325–38 and Francine D. Blau, "How Voluntary is Volunteer Work? Comment on 'Economic Determinants of Volunteer Work by Women,'" *Signs: Journal of Women in Culture and Society* 21, no. 1 (Autumn 1976): 251–54.

[33]David L. Sills, "Voluntary Associations: Sociological Aspects," *International Encyclopedia of Social Sciences* (NY: The Macmillan Company and the Free Press, 1968): 362–76.

work, their contributions to worthy causes will be greatly missed. While there is a grain of truth in this, it must not be overlooked that these women now earn an income. They will, therefore, be able to contribute more money to worthwhile causes, which incidentally might be considerably more efficient than baking and selling cookies or collecting money door-to-door. Employed women also pay taxes, which make additional expenditures for public services possible. Thus, workers could be hired to do much of what is now done by volunteers.

WIFE'S CONTRIBUTIONS TO EARNINGS

As we have seen in Chapter 4, by the early 1980s more than half of all married women with husbands present were working for pay. The labor force participation rate for comparable blacks was as high as 61 percent, while it was somewhat less than half for Hispanics.

The earnings of these married women make a substantial contribution to the money income of their families. In 1981, wives who worked part-time contributed on the average 25 percent and those who worked year-round, full-time, contributed 38 percent. For low-income families, the proportion was as high as 50 percent for those with an income between $10,000 and $15,000 and 64 percent for those with an income less than $10,000. The contribution was substantially greater among blacks than among whites.[34]

These data make it abundantly clear that the earnings of married women serve to bring a considerable number of families out of poverty status. In many other instances, they make the difference between a barely adequate and comfortable living. Even if we take into account the increased expenses of two-earner households, the loss of the services of the full-time homemaker, and the fact that such families may well be "time-poor,"[35] the standard of living of these families is likely to be much improved.

As discussed earlier, a woman is expected to enter the labor market when the value of her earnings exceeds the value of her time at home. Therefore, it would appear that the well-being of her family must be increased when she decides to work for pay, presumably in response either to increased wages or to a decline in her usefulness at home. This approach, however, ignores the possibility that any change may improve the situation for some members of the family but cause others to be worse off. We, therefore, turn to a more detailed examination of the impact of women's growing labor force participation on various family members.

[34]Bureau of the Census, Current Population Reports, Consumer Income Series P-60, no. 142, Money Income of Households, Families and Persons in the U.S., 1982.

[35]This term was first introduced into the literature by Clair (Vickery) Brown, "The Time-Poor: A New Look at Poverty," *Journal of Human Resources* 12, no. 1 (Winter 1977): 27–48. The issue is also discussed in Clair (Vickery) Brown, "Women's Economic Contribution to the Family," ed. Smith, *The Subtle Revolution*, pp. 159–200.

SATISFACTION WITHIN THE FAMILY

Considerable work has been done to learn about the impact of women's labor force participation on their own and their husband's satisfaction with various aspects of life and on the development of their children. It is not easy to summarize the results of these studies concisely, for the issues involved are very complex and findings are not always consistent.[36] One of the unresolved questions is the extent to which reporting on this sensitive subject is reliable.[37]

How the woman herself feels about taking a job outside the home depends on such considerations as the nature of the work; her health and energy level; supportiveness of her co-workers, friends and family; the number and ages of her children; and the availability of services to replace those of the homemaker. The husband's attitude is likely to be influenced by many of the same factors but will be particularly affected by the extent to which his job requires his wife's involvement, his own taste for housework and leisure, and perhaps most of all whether he wants a partner whose independence and accomplishments he can respect or a helpmate who devotes herself to creating a warm and relaxed home for him. The children's well-being is likely to depend on the extent to which the mother's work interferes with their demands on her time and energy, whether their friend's mothers are also employed, and, last but by no means least, the quality of the alternative arrangements that are made for their care.

Given the involvement of a number of individuals and a multitude of variables, it would be expected that the impact of the woman's labor force participation on the family will be quite different, depending on the context of various personalities, family situations and social environments. There are also such methodological problems as possible selection bias. For instance, women who are particularly family-centered are probably more inclined to become full-time homemakers, while those who have less patience with

[36]Most of the research on this subject has been done by psychologists and sociologists. Some of the best-known among these studies are Ronald J. Burke and Tamara Weir, "Relationship of Wives' Employment Status to Husband, Wife and Pair Satisfaction and Performance," *Journal of Marriage and Family* 38, no. 2 (May 1976): 278–87; Myra M. Ferree, "Working Class Jobs: Housework and Paid Work as Sources of Satisfaction," *Social Problems* 23, no. 4 (Spring 1976): 431–41; Francis I. Nye and Lois W. Hoffman, *The Employed Mother in America* (Chicago: Rand McNally, 1963); James D. Wright, "Are Working Women Really More Satisfied? Evidence From Several National Surveys," *Journal of Marriage and Family* 40, no. 2 (May 1978): 301–13; and Ronald C. Kessler and James A. McRae, Jr., "The Effect of Wives' Employment on the Mental Health of Married Men and Women," *American Sociological Review* 47, no. 2 (April 1982): 216–26.

[37]Frank M. Andrews and Stephen B. Withey, *Social Indicators of Well-Being. Americans' Perceptions of Life Quality* (New York: Plenum Press, 1976) report that fully 60 percent of respondents in their survey claimed they were "delighted" with their children, 58 percent with their spouse, and 50 percent with their marriage, but only 22 percent were equally positive to all three combined. The authors suggest as one possible explanation that people are likely to be reluctant to express reservations about any individuals in their family but more willing to do so in response to more general questions.

children and less tolerance for housework and are more interested in a career are likely to enter the labor market. Given all these complications, the results of different studies can be inconclusive and even contradictory. Hence there is good reason to avoid hasty conclusions.

Wife

It has generally been found that employed women enjoy better physical and mental health, have higher self-esteem, and on the average live longer than those who do not work for pay. This may show that the additional stimulation and rewards associated with market work have a positive effect but could in part also be the result of stronger, more confident women entering the labor force to begin with.

The findings on the relationship between women's employment and marital satisfaction have been mixed, some indicating it is positive, others suggesting it is negative, but most conclude that it is neutral.[38] In part, the problem here is that such important factors as whether the woman works by choice or necessity, full-time or part-time, how much education and what type of job she has, etc. are often not taken into account. Part of the difficulty, no doubt, also is that the issue of bias arises once again. In this instance, the sample selection bias may be negative because those who have higher ambitions and more demanding standards and those who are specifically dissatisfied with their marriage are, everything else being the same, the ones most likely to work for pay.

To the extent that any conclusion can be drawn, it appears that mothers, especially those working full-time, frequently complain of being overcommitted and experience more anxiety and guilt. Regrettably, we have no evidence how much of this is caused by societal pressures. At the same time, employed women also have a better self-concept and enjoy their children more. It is not far-fetched to ascribe the latter to diminishing utility of additional time spent with children. As was suggested in Chapter 3, even the most pleasurable activity palls when a great deal of time is devoted to it and what may at first be a minor nuisance is likely to become a major annoyance over a long period. Hence, the quality of time may well be quite different for a parent who looks forward to spending time with his or her children on evenings and weekends than one who spends more or less seven days a week with them. Last, it is also interesting to note that education is positively related to satisfaction with paid work but negatively to satisfaction with homemaking. Thus, the picture for working women is not all rosy, but the pluses appear to outweigh the minuses for most of them.

---

[38]Sociologists, rather than economists, have done research on these questions. Much of the best known work is summarized in Hofferth and Moore, "Women's Employment and Marriage."

COPING WITH HOME AND JOB RESPONSIBILITIES:
A MANAGERIAL APPROACH

Though combining career and family is not easy, growing numbers of women are finding that the benefits outweigh the costs. In this column from the *Wall Street Journal,** a "managerial approach" to coping with family responsibilities is advocated—and one need not be a professional manager to benefit from the advice offered. While it is assumed in this piece that the working mother will be hiring a nanny, other arrangements, like organized day-care centers, can provide the quality and reliability advocated.

A September article in this paper described a working mother—a major account executive for an advertising firm—who almost missed an important meeting because she had to dash out into the snow to buy diapers for her child. Her housekeeper called and said they had run out. The mother left the office, spent $20 on cab fare for a $10 box of diapers and arrived back at the office feeling as if she'd "been to California and back."

The tone of the article was summed up by an "expert" who was quoted as saying that most women find combining career and family an impossible situation. "I'm not sure," said the expert, "how any woman can avoid being overwhelmed. Simply dropping out may be the only alternative."

Maybe. But there are many women with children doing very well out there in law firms, accounting offices, government and other professional capacities. Of course it is difficult for a professional woman to manage a successful career and be a mother. But women in management have an edge they might not be using to the full advantage: They can put their management skills to use in managing their lives as working mothers.

Taking a managerial approach to home life doesn't mean you have to haul in McKinsey & Co. to do a work-flow study on your kids. And it certainly isn't recommending a tough-cookie approach to home and hearth. Far from being callous, an effective management approach to childrearing is the most loving, caring and respectful course a professional woman can take. When arrangements are slapdash, when no one knows what to do next, when Mommy is too torn and crazed to be effective either as an investment banker or as a mother, then everyone suffers.

If the woman who almost missed her meeting had paid more attention to managing her inventory (diapers) and to hiring an employee who could take expected initiative (going out and buying the diapers), she probably would not have ended up in such a frazzled state.

A three-step management approach is required for the effective manager-mother:

1. *A feasibility study.* Some jobs in some companies may not be compatible with family life. Sixty-hour weeks, a two-hour commute and a heavy

---

*Claudia P. Feurey, "Manager's Journal: Kids Plus Careers Needn't Keep Mom in Arrears," *Wall Street Journal,* June 4, 1984, p. 20. Reprinted by permission of the *Wall Street Journal,* ©Dow Jones & Company, Inc. (1984). All rights reserved.

travel schedule don't leave much time for kids. (Of course, this is true for men as well as women.)

Does the culture of your organization support families? Management attitudes can make or break a company as a place where women can have both families and careers. While management should not be expected to go out of its way to accommodate unreasonable demands, it is generally in a company's interest to ease the transition when its employees become parents.

2. *Making your decision and setting your priorities.* If you decide you can work, do you still want to? They may not get into this at Wharton, but if you have other sources of income, you do not have to work at a particular job. There is no disgrace in not working or in working part time and devoting the rest of your time to family and home.

If you decide to go to work, however, get your priorities straight. As a managerial mother, you may not be able to keep up your previous social life, be den mother to the Cub Scouts or see every play that comes to town. If family and career come first, carefully evaluate the costs and benefits of other claims on your time.

3. *Implementation.* The next step is organizing your life so that you can combine home, children and career with the minimum strain.

• Decide what your child-care needs are. If your job involves late nights, early meetings or extensive travel, then be sure your husband or your help can cover for you during these times. Or make standing arrangements with reliable sources.

• Bite the bullet and pay for the best child care you can afford. It is astonishing how many high-income families try to make do with ad hoc arrangements or bottom-of-the barrel help. Would you trust the person you hire to deal with an emergency or get a sick child to the doctor? If not, you have made a mistake. Hire the best person you can afford, treat her well and let her do the job.

• Have a reliable temporary agency or nurses' registry on call for those days the nanny is ill. These agencies exist in virtually every community and may be a lot less hassle than getting your mother to come over on a snowy Tuesday.

• Ferret out every neighborhood store that delivers and set up local charge accounts at these stores.

• Learn to appreciate the virtures of take out food.

Even with the most sophisticated management approach, there will be times when your husband is out of town, when your three-year-old has thrown up on your best suit and you are late for work. It is easy to succumb to playing the part of the working heroine, a martyr for the movement. When this happens, it is wise to think of the many, many women who are working—and often raising their kids alone—without the privileges and the psychic and financial rewards of management positions. At these times, look at your family, look at your accomplishments and count your blessings . . .

Husband

The consequences of the wife's employment on the husband have been found to be, overall, less favorable.[39] A number of studies report less marital

[39]Again summarized in Hofferth and Moore, "Women's Employment and Marriage."

satisfaction, less physical and mental well-being, and even greater job pressures. These negative effects are especially strong for men in the lower class, though less so when the wife works by choice or works less than full-time. Such results seem rather puzzling since we know the husband shares in the benefits of the additional income, and the wife normally carries the main burden of the additional work. But there are a number of reasonable explanations.

Once again, the likelihood of a negative bias exists, because wives may be especially likely to enter the labor market when the marriage is not satisfactory. Furthermore, wives of unsuccessful husbands are more likely to seek to supplement family income. Beyond that, it is widely accepted that many husbands perceive the shift to the two-earner family as a loss of status and power for themselves. Any increase in household responsibilities is viewed as demeaning and as interfering with their work. They see recent changes as eroding their secure position and even as threatening their masculinity. The wife, on the other hand, believes she is expanding her sphere, as well as increasing her influence and her security.

Several studies confirm that the status and power of the wife within the family increases vis-a-vis that of the husband when she too is a wage earner.[40] Men have a more dominant role in important family decisions when their wives do not work for pay. The fact that women who do work are more likely to have their own credit cards and bank accounts points in the same direction. One may also conjecture that the sole breadwinner has more bargaining power because an angry, "if I do not like it, I do not have to put up with this" or an impatient, "if you do not like it, you can go" has far more credibility coming from him than from his "dependent" wife.

Past research necessarily included many men who would not have anticipated at the time they married that their wife would be in the labor market. There is much evidence that unanticipated changes tend to cause problems, and these results are likely to be more negative than will be the case for younger cohorts.[41] It is entirely possible that, in time, men may come to enjoy a partnership marriage more than they ever did the traditional one. They will no longer need to shoulder the total responsibility of financial support of the family. Many surely will enjoy getting to know their children better. They will

---

[40]See Marianne A. Ferber, "Labor Market Participation of Young Married Women: Causes and Effects," *Journal of Marriage and Family* 44, no. 2 (May 1982): 457–68. Dair L. Gillespie, "Who Has the Power? The Marital Struggle," *Journal of Marriage and Family* 33, no. 3 (Aug. 1971): 445–58.

[41]Alan Booth, "Wife's Employment and Husband's Stress: A Replication and Refutation," *Journal of Marriage and Family* 39, no. 4 (Nov. 1977): 645–50, reports that stress is caused by a change in the wife's labor force status in either direction, not by the wife being in or out of the labor force. Further evidence on this point is provided by Catherine E. Ross, John Mirowsky and Joan Huber, "Dividing Work, Sharing Work, and In-Between: Marriage Patterns and Depression" *American Sociological Review* 48, no. 6 (December 1983): 809–23. They found that those husbands of employed wives who preferred her to be a full-time homemaker tended to be depressed but that this was definitely not the case for those husbands who preferred that their wife work for pay. They conclude that it is the transition, when the wife's employment status has changed but the husband's traditional attitudes have not, that causes the problem.

be better prepared to fend for themselves in emergencies. Last, but not least, they will often have a happier wife.

CHANGING SEX ROLES: A MALE PERSPECTIVE

A small but increasing number of men are actively sharing responsibility for home as well as market work. This excerpt from an article in the *New York Times** summarizes some of the costs and benefits of these changes from a male perspective.

Change is not easy, and many men have come to feel a good deal of anger and resentment in their lives. There is a sense that somehow we have been deprived of the chance to become the sort of men we expected to be as we grew up—men who, like those of earlier generations, possess a sure-footed sense of what is expected and of how to meet those expectations.

Contradictions increasingly rule our lives. On the one hand, a majority of people now believe that both sexes should enjoy equal employment opportunities. On the other, most believe that children may be harmed psychologically if their mothers work outside the home. Says Dr. Joseph Pleck, a prominent researcher in this field: "One fundamental American value is that family and parenthood are important, and this belief is now being extended to include men to a much greater degree. This contradicts the traditional belief, however, that a man should be mainly the breadwinner."

The result can be considerable strain and tension . . . I, too, am often beset by such anxieties. My wife now works more than 40 hours a week, mostly in the afternoon and evening. As a result, I frequently must cut short my own workday in order to pick up our 18-month-old son from day care or to spend time with my older child. Often, I am also the one who is on call in case of illness, who prepares many of the meals and who keeps the house clean.

I have many fewer hours available for work than I wish, and sometimes I am too exhausted at the end of a day to resume my work when the children have gone to bed. I cannot pretend to feel comfortable about this, and at times I explode with rage or I withdraw into sarcasm and moodiness. There is no question that the rewards of sharing career achievement and child rearing with one's spouse are great, but the price paid can be high. It is a price, finally, that many of us never imagined we would have to pay, and therein lies much of the trouble.

Maybe some of us might be able to do this. Maybe we might learn—in the words of my departmental colleague—to give up the amenities of life in order to concentrate on the essentials, adhering not only to precise daily schedules but working late into the night (a major ingredient in the success of

*Donald H. Bell, "About Men: Conflicting Interests," *New York Times Magazine* (July 31, 1983), p. 32. Copyright ©1983 by The New York Times Company. Reprinted by permission. For further discussion of the strains, pulls, penalities, and rewards of two-career lives, see Donald H. Bell, *Being a Man: The Paradox of Masculinity* (Lexington, MA.: Stephen Greene/Lewis Publishing Co., 1982).

many men who seem to be able to combine the demands of work and family). We might, in addition, learn to exult in the career attainment of our wives, even if we must sacrifice some of our own professional ambitions. We might find the time, as well, to be with our children and to be involved as a matter of course in the necessary household chores. We might even learn to give up the anger and resentment that is often engendered by the need to do all of these things, and to do them well.

We might. But most of us, as yet, cannot hope to follow such a program, nor should we berate ourselves if we do not live up to the "superman" image. Despite the things we did learn from our own fathers, we usually did not find out how to balance full participation in work and in family. Now we are exploring uncharted territory, with all of the missteps and false starts that such exploration requires.

Still, if we think about it, we might ultimately come to gain from the new requirements in our lives. On the morning I was to begin writing this column, my 18-month-old son woke up with a low-grade fever. My wife had a full schedule at the office, and this sick child clearly could not go to his baby sitter. The only solution was for me to alter my plans and to stay home, where I diapered, played with, worried over and comforted a still-energetic but cranky baby. I could feel my bitterness and resentment boiling—for lost hours at work, for missed deadlines, for unprepared classes. "Men today," I found myself thinking, "really have a raw deal."

Then I discovered that my son had learned something new. For the first time, he was able to give a proper kiss, puckering up his lips and enfolding my face in his arms. "Kees Dada," he said as he bussed me on the nose and cheeks. No amount of gratification at work could have compensated for that moment. I found out another thing that morning, a discovery that came as a bit of poetic justice. I suddenly realized that in sacrificing my workday, I had learned a lot about how fathers might care for their sons. And I found that I had learned something further about what it means to be a man, something that goes beyond simply bringing home the paycheck.

Children

The most emotionally charged issue is the question of the effect of maternal employment on children. While in principle the question should be asked about parental employment in general, it is still commonly accepted that the father will be working in any case and, as of now, that is a realistic assumption. It is more difficult to understand why most research on this subject goes so far as to ignore the role of the father entirely, since he can do much to compensate for the reduced home-time of the mother.

This is only one of the many variables that needs to be taken into account when the effect of the mother's labor force participation on her children is to be investigated. Some of the others are the age, sex, number of children, the affection they receive from relatives and other friends, the quality of care they receive from hired sitters and teachers, and the quality of time the family spends together. As noted in previous chapters, it is not obvious that the mere fact a mother works has any clearly predictable effects on her children.[42]

Some more specific conclusions are also instructive. No evidence has been found of any adverse effects of quality day care (with an adequate number of qualified personnel), even for infants and preschoolers, and a number of studies discovered favorable results, especially with respect to social adjustment. The impact on school-aged and older children when mothers are successful in their paid work appears to be overwhelmingly favorable, perhaps because she herself is more satisfied, is likely to have more structured and consistent rules in her relationship with her children, is less passive and fosters greater independence in her family. Daughters, particularly, hold their mothers in higher esteem and adopt them as role models, but their sons also are more likely to favor equality for women. There are some indications of negative influence on the academic achievement of sons[43] but not on daughters, where some evidence of a favorable effect has been found.

These findings should prove useful in helping individuals make better-informed decisions about childrearing. They should also reduce controversy about the usefulness of quality day-care centers. They cannot, however, be regarded as definitive. For one, little research has been done so far on the long-term consequences of maternal employment apart from educational attainment. Such questions as the impact on career, marital problems, and success in raising their own children remain to be fully investigated.

Policy Issue: Child Care Subsidies

Public subsidies for child care, common in many other countries, have received consideration in the United States as well. As discussed in Chapter 4, such subsidies are likely to raise women's labor force participation, all else equal. There is also great interest in the impact of such policies on the welfare of children.

Those who believe parental care is better for children often oppose day-care subsidies because they tend to encourage maternal employment. The

[42]See Urie Bronfenbrenner and Ann. C. Crouter, in one of the most thorough reviews in recent years, "Work and Family Through Time and Space," eds. S. B. Kamerman and C. D. Hayes, *Families That Work: Children in a Changing World.*(Washington, DC: National Academy Press, 1982.)

[43]See, for instance, O. D. Duncan, D. L. Featherman, and B. Duncan, *Socioeconomic Background and Achievement* (New York: Seminar Press, 1972); Lois W. Hoffman, "Effects of Maternal Employment on the Child," eds. Lois W. Hoffman and Francis I. Nye, *Working Mothers* (San Francisco: Jossey-Bass Publishers, 1974); Belton M. Fleisher, "Mothers' Home Time and the Production of Child Quality," *Demography* 14, no. 2 (May 1977): 197–212; and Sheila F. Krein and Andrea H. Beller, "Family Structure and Educational Attainment of Children: Difference by Duration, Age and Gender," unpublished paper, University of Illinois (Jan. 1985).

evidence we have reviewed, however, suggests that adequate substitute care need not be harmful to children. Further, a substantial proportion of mothers already work outside the home, and their numbers are likely to increase to some extent, regardless of government policy. Those concerned with child welfare might thus more fruitfully focus their attention on how best to provide good alternative child care, rather than on whether or not it should be provided.[44] However, given strongly held and often emotional beliefs, negative attitudes on this subject are likely to remain a factor. In spite of the sharp decline in birth rates, opposition to subsidies also continues because it is commonly believed that reducing the costs of raising children will encourage people to have more of them and that, in any case, parents should be responsible for all of the expenses. Both these points deserve careful examination.[45]

Economic analysis tells us that reducing the price of any good will generally result in an increase in the quantity demanded, and there is no reason to assume this effect would not exist in the case of children. Thus, from this perspective, subsidized child care could increase the number of children women have. But this is not likely to be the only effect. As we have seen, providing subsidized care will also encourage mothers to enter the labor market. To the extent that women acquire more, and more market-oriented education in anticipation of this, and accumulate more work experience, they will have higher earnings. Hence, the opportunity cost of additional children will also increase. Further, it may be that women, after working, become addicted to market goods, or perhaps to having their own income, and a greater feeling of independence.[46]

It is not possible to determine, a priori, which set of forces is likely to be stronger. However, in the various advanced industrialized countries that have introduced child care subsidies, none have experienced a large increase in the birthrate. In particular, Sweden, which among Western countries provides the most financial support, has a significantly lower birthrate and a substantially

---

[44]How good some of this care can be is obvious when one reads about schools for "nannies" where the students, many of them college graduates, are trained in nutrition, child development, cardiopulmonary resuscitation, and even party planning. Trainees from such schools, however, are reported to receive about $600–$800 a month, which puts them out of reach of most parents (*Newsweek,* May 21, 1984, pp. 63–64). At the other extreme there are families, mostly those in dire poverty, who permit even quite young children to be home alone for extended periods of time. Estimates of the numbers of such "latchkey" children range from 4 to 10 million, although not all of that group should necessarily be considered too young to care for themselves (*The New York Times,* March 19, 1984, p. C-10). A course for parents and children on coping strategies for self-care is described in the Inset on p. 144.

[45]A thorough discussion of these issues is found in Myra H. Strober, "Formal Extrafamily Child Care—Some Economic Observations," ed. Cynthia B. Lloyd, *Sex, Discrimination, and the Division of Labor,* (N.Y.: Columbia University Press, 1975).

[46]Glen G. Cain, "The Effect of Income Maintenance Laws on Fertility in the United States," Discussion Paper #117, (Madison, WI: Institute for Research on Poverty, University of Wisconsin, 1972).

higher labor force participation rate of women than the United States. On the other hand, it is widely believed in Sweden that these arrangements, together with generous provisions for parental leave, have helped to arrest the decline in fertility that might otherwise have occurred.

The question of how the costs of raising children should be divided is also quite complex. Children's parents, undoubtedly, do have a special responsibility for their care. It is generally recognized, however, that the nation benefits from a healthier, better educated, and better trained population. This is true even in narrowly economic terms. These people will be more productive, will contribute more both as workers and as taxpayers, and are less likely to be a burden on the public. In other words, there are significant positive externalities when children are better cared for that benefit both their parents, and the whole community.

Another long-run economic advantage resulting from subsidized child care is that more mothers will be able to take jobs that offer valuable experience and on-the-job training opportunities, even if the initial wages paid are low. Thus, instead of permitting their human capital to deteriorate, they would be adding to it, enabling them to become taxpayers rather than, in some cases, welfare dependents. Such women will also provide better role models for their children. Greatly expanded day-care facilities would even help to provide jobs for many women, especially for trained teachers, and also for relatively unskilled women, who would often make excellent teacher's aids.

Those who believe that all individuals deserve as nearly an equal chance in life as can be provided would find this another argument for public subsidies for child care. Nor is such a view unprecedented, even in the United States, which lags considerably behind other advanced industrialized countries in this respect. For this country does have a long, and apparently well-nigh universally accepted, policy of paying out public funds for primary and secondary education.[47] In recent years, the government has also contributed substantially to public institutions of higher education. One might argue that it makes little sense to do all that for youngsters from age five or six on, but to permit many younger children to live under conditions that do not enable them to benefit equally from these advantages when they reach school age.

In addition to parents and the public, employers have a potential interest in child care. In the long run, they also benefit from any arrangements that help today's children become more productive workers. But more immediately subsidized child care helps to make more workers available to the firm, to increase women's labor force attachment (making them more stable workers),

---

[47]Vocal opponents of public schools, among whom Milton Friedman is perhaps one of the best known, do not advocate that the government should stop paying for education but rather that it should do so by giving parents vouchers. They could then send their children to any school of their choice. See Milton Friedman, *Capitalism and Freedom* (Chicago: University of Chicago Press, 1962), pp. 85–107.

and to reduce absenteeism brought about by undependable arrangements for children. Also, to the extent that other employers do not provide similar services, job changing is reduced. This is why, in 1985, about 2000 corporations—triple the number of just three years previously—provided some form of child care assistance. While this represented only a tiny fraction of the nation's 6 million employers, it did include such trend-setting firms as I.B.M., A.T.&T., and Polaroid.[48]

Some firms directly provide child care services, while others give employees payments which help defray the costs of such care. Among the advantages to workers of direct employer provision of child care, apart from the free or subsidized price of the service, are that parents do not have to make a separate trip to take the children elsewhere and that they are nearby. Thus, they can see the children during breaks or in case of emergencies.

Since, as we have seen, parents, employers, and the public all potentially stand to gain from good child care, a reasonable solution to the dilemma of who should bear the burden of providing it would be to find an equitable way of sharing the costs. Parents might be asked to pay tuition on a sliding scale, depending on their income. Large employers might provide facilities but receive reimbursements for a portion of the costs; smaller ones could subsidize employee use of centers located elsewhere. The government could make up the remainder of the expenses. There would, no doubt, be a good deal of disagreement about any precise formula, but if arrangements could be worked out where each of the three parties received benefits that exceeded their contributions, it should be possible to reach a consensus. One of the effects of making progress in this direction would be to enable more mothers of young children to remain in, or to enter, the labor market.

Given the extremely low levels of support for child care from either government or employers, parents have resorted to whatever means of providing for their children they have been able to afford. Table 5.4 displays data on the various kinds of child care in the United States in recent decades. They show a very substantial decline in the proportion of young children of employed mothers who were cared for in their own home between 1965 and 1982. In the latter year, a substantial proportion, 43.8 percent, were cared for in the homes of others. The share in group centers was still less than one in five but had increased considerably since 1965. In contrast, two-fifths of children of working guardians in Sweden were being cared for in their own homes and slightly over half were in public day-care centers.

[48]The *New York Times* (August 4, 1985): p. F 1. A Study of employer-sponsored child care conducted by Renne Y. Magid for the American Management Association found that employers who did provide such facilities claimed that benefits far outweighed costs. The gains reported included less employee absenteeism, improved morale, and greater ability to attract and keep superior employees. Reported in Bureau of National Affairs, *Daily Labor Report,* no. 39., February 28, 1984, pp. A-5, A-6.

TABLE 5.4   **Child Care Arrangements of Working Mothers in the United States and Sweden for Children under Age 7**[a]

	UNITED STATES		SWEDEN
	1965	1982	1980
Care in child's home	47.2	25.7	40.8
By father	10.3	10.3	13.4
By others	36.9	15.4	27.4
Care in another home	37.3	43.8	n.a.
Group care center	8.2	18.8	50.8
All other arrangements	7.3	11.7	8.4

Swedish data are for "guardians."
n.a. not separately available.

Source: U.S. Department of Commerce, Bureau of the Census, Current Population Reports, Special Studies P-23, no. 117.

Some individuals who take youngsters into their homes do, of course, provide excellent care. But there is much evidence that parents who can afford it prefer to have small children cared for in their own home. Further, the quality of day-care centers is at least somewhat better regulated than individual arrangements in private homes.

AN INNOVATIVE EMPLOYER PROGRAM: SELF-CARE INSTRUCTION FOR CHILDREN

No one advocates that young children should be left without an adult to take care of them, but all children need to learn to take care of themselves sooner or later, whether or not both parents are employed. Employer programs that are supportive of families make it easier for workers, particularly women, to combine job and household responsibilities. This, in turn, is likely to make them more productive employees. One such program is described below.*

The question is every parent's nightmare, but it was raised matter-of-factly enough in the room full of children:

"Problem: You are walking home alone from school and you think that a man in a car is following you," Evie Herrmann-Keeling read from her work sheet, as 11 children followed the question on their own printed sheets. "What would you do? (A) Stand still and see what he does. (B) Walk quickly home and lock yourself in the house. (C) Walk to a neighbor's home and stay there.

*Glen Collins, "Course for 'Latchkey' Children and Parents, *New York Times,* March 19, 1984, p. C-10. Copyright ©1984 by The New York Times Company. Reprinted by permission.

(D) Stop and ask the person what he wants. (E) Other."

"Well," Mrs. Herrman-Keeling asked, "what do you think?"

A hand shot up, and Mrs. Herrmann-Keeling called on Kristin, an 11-year-old. "I think that if you go to a neighbor's house, well, an adult you know will be there—and they can help if you need it." She paused for a moment "But if you go home and lock yourself in the house, you could be followed, and there might not be anyone there to help you."

A murmur of voices signaled agreement from the children, all of whom were between 9 and 13 years old. They began talking animatedly, and soon agreed that to "Stop and ask the person what he or she wants" was a very, very bad idea indeed.

It was a typical exchange in the weekly courses for "latchkey" children run by Mrs. Herrmann-Keeling, executive director of Parents Anonymous of Connecticut. What made the session unusual was that it took place in the offices of a large corporation—the Phoenix Mutual Life Insurance Company—and was offered free to the company's 1,900 employees in the Hartford area. . . . The course of five 90-minute sessions at Phoenix Mutual is intended to make both children and parents aware of the problems—and the opportunities for growth—that confront millions of American families who have "latchkey" children, those who spend time not directly supervised by a parent or adult.

Studies have estimated that there are between 4 and 10 million such children, but there are no reliable statistics on the phenomenon. Since the term "latchkey child" has become something of a pejorative, Parents Anonymous and other groups prefer the term "self-care" to describe children who are on their own, usually after school.

These children are the shock troops of a family revolution that has seen a dramatic increase in two-career marriages and single-parent families. Although only 19 percent of mothers were working in 1947, 58 percent of all mothers with children under 18 were in the work force by 1980.

"It's very logical to approach the problem of latchkey children through the work place," said Mrs. Herrmann-Keeling. "Corporations are the very places where parents most need this service. It's very important for companies to be supportive of families."

A small but rapidly increasing number of corporations accept that premise, including companies as varied as Bankers Trust, Exxon, Philip Morris and Phoenix Mutual. They have been hosts to a variety of parent-education programs, have offered referrals to local social-service agencies and have established child-care networks among employees.

"At most companies, from 3 P.M. on," said Mrs. Herrmann-Keeling, "there is much covert telephoning going on. Parents feel they have to call to see if their children are safe. Yet it's so silly for this kind of thing to have to be underground. The more supportive the company can be of family life, the more productive workers will be." . . .

The positive aspects of "self-care," she said, can make it a growth experience for families that develops children's sense of responsibility and involves parents in monitoring the progress of their independence. "We want parents and children to understand that they are working together to achieve a common goal," said Mrs. Herrmann-Keeling.

FEMALE-HEADED FAMILIES[49]

While there has been considerable interest in families with working mothers, special concern has focused on those where the mother is the main breadwinner and often the only adult. Such attention is appropriate in part because the proportion of families in this category has been rising rapidly and because they experience a disproportionate share of economic problems.

There has been a substantial increase in female-headed households, composed of:

1. Individuals living alone or with nonrelatives
2. Families of persons related by birth or by marriage.

Between 1950 and 1983, female-headed households of unrelated individuals increased from 10.7 to 16.0 percent of households, while female-headed families rose from 7.7 to 11.6 pecent of households. The unrelated individuals are often older women, widowed or divorced. Their numbers have been growing with their longer life expectancy and as they are increasingly less likely to live with their adult children. More than half of women over 65 now live in such households. There are also childless younger women, divorced or never married, who are now also more likely to live in their own household.

Female-headed families are generally comprised of women and dependent children. Historically, there were always children without a father in some homes, but the main cause used to be death. It is primarily divorce and separation today with the greater number of births to unmarried women also a contributing factor. Mothers and their young children also are more likely to form separate families today, rather than to live with other relatives. Table 5.5 shows the relatively high incidence of poverty among female-headed families, providing some evidence why there is much discussion about the "feminization" of poverty. These data also show that the poverty problem is particularly serious in the black community.

Among blacks fully two-thirds of those in poverty live in households headed by women. In addition, the incidence of poverty among blacks is disproportionately high and increasingly more so. While blacks constituted about one-fourth of the poor in 1959, this figure had increased to one-third in 1982. Another indication of the seriousness of this situation is that more black children under 18 are living with their mothers only than with both parents, and three-fourths of black children born in the early 1970s are now expected to spend at least some time in a female-headed household. The comparable figure

[49]Much of the information in this section comes from Suzanne M. Bianchi and Daphne Spain, "American Women: Three Decades of Change," (U.S. Department of Commerce, Bureau of the Census, Special Demographic Analysis, Aug. 1983). We use the term "female-headed" because it represents general usage. Technically it should be "single-parent family headed by a woman."

TABLE 5.5   Incidence of Poverty by Type of Household, 1983

	NUMBER (THOUSANDS)	MEDIAN INCOME	PERCENT IN POVERTY
All households	85,407	$20,885	14.6
White	74,376	21,902	12.1
Black	9,236	12,429	34.0
Spanish origin[a]	4,326	15,906	26.8
Family households	61,997	24,783	12.3
Married couple families	50,090	27,329	7.6
Male householder, no wife present	2,030	22,882	13.0
Female householder, no husband present	9,878	12,239	36.0
White	6,784	14,353	28.3
Black	2,874	8,190	53.8
Spanish origin[a]	810	8,005	53.5
Nonfamily households	23,410	12,010	20.7
Male householder	9,752	16,107	16.6
Female householder	13,658	9,842	23.6

[a]May be of any race.

Source: U.S. Department of Commerce, Bureau of the Census, Current Population Reports, Consumer Income Series P-60, no. 148, *Characteristics of Households and Persons Receiving Selected Noncash Benefits: 1983.* Table 1.

for white children is one-third, not a negligible fraction either, and white female-headed families, too, are far more heavily represented in the poverty group than in the population.

It has been noted that the income figures used to determine poverty status do not include such items as food stamps, Medicaid, housing subsidies, and other in-kind transfers so that they understate real income. Less attention has been drawn to the fact that families with a single adult are at a great disadvantage compared to mother-father families because all household responsibilities fall upon that person, in addition to whatever work she does for pay. This double burden can be a serious constraint on the woman's labor force participation, not to mention reducing her leisure time.

It is not surprising that female-headed households, and particularly families, generally have economic problems. As we shall see, women in general earn considerably less than men with comparable qualifications and often have been confronted by a relatively higher unemployment rate. Married women also tend to accumulate less labor market experience than their husbands, and this is especially so for those with children. Hence, such women are ill-equipped to cope with the double role of single parent and breadwinner.

In recognition of these difficulties, women may receive alimony to compensate for their reduced earning power and child support as payment of the father's share of the expense of childrearing. Everyone has at one time or another heard of very large divorce settlements. These tend to convey the erroneous impression that generous payments are common. In fact, as we have seen, a very small proportion of separated and divorced women are awarded any alimony, only about half of those with children are awarded child support, and enforcement is notoriously inadequate. Little wonder that one out of four female-headed families is on welfare.

Many factors no doubt contribute to this dismal situation. In some instances, the father has died; more frequently, he is himself poor and genuinely unable to pay more. There is little that can be done in such cases, except to offer public assistance. But there are other causes for inadequate support by the father that might be amenable to appropriate changes in legal arrangements and, particularly, to more conscientious enforcement of existing laws. This issue is an important one because it is generally the women who are least able to stand on their own, with little education, little or no labor market experience, and few other resources, that are also least likely to receive any support from their ex-husbands.

A recent study found that during the first year after the marriage was terminated, the income of the female-headed family was only 66 percent of that of the family before the divorce, leaving the woman and her children substantially worse off financially even when the smaller number of individuals left in the family is taken into account. On average, three-fifths of the income of those families consisted of the earnings of the mothers whose labor force participation rose substantially from the previous year, only one-tenth was contributed by the fathers, and one-twentieth came from welfare.[50] This reality differs substantially from the popular image of the lady of leisure supported generously by her ex-husband or the lazy welfare mother taking advantage of the taxpayer.

Policy Issue: Raising the Incomes of Female-Headed Families

The preceding discussion suggests a variety of measures that would improve the economic status of female-headed families. Their primary sources of income are threefold:

1. Private transfers
2. Public transfers
3. Their own labor market earnings.[51]

[50]Greg J. Duncan and Saul D. Hoffman, "Economic Consequences of Marital Instability," ed. Martin David, *Horizontal Equity, Uncertainty and Well-being,* (NBER Conference Volume, Chicago: University of Chicago Press, forthcoming).

[51]Evidence of the potential effectiveness of these various approaches is reported and discussed in Barbara R. Bergmann and Mark D. Roberts, "Work and the Single Parent: Work, Child Support and Welfare," paper presented at the Conference on "Gender in the Work Place," Brookings Institution, November 15–16, 1984.

TABLE 5.6   An Illustration of Alternative Welfare Programs

PROGRAM A (100% tax rate)

Labor Market Earnings	*Government Welfare Payment*	*Total Family Income*
(1)	(2)	(1 + 2)
$ 0	$3,500	$3,500
2,000	1,500	3,500
3,500	0	3,500

PROGRAM B (50% tax rate)

Labor Market Earnings	*Government Welfare Payment*	*Total Family Income*
(1)	(2)	(1 + 2)
$ 0	$3,500	$3,500
2,000	2,500	4,500
3,500	1,750	5,250
7,000	0	7,000

Private transfers are comprised of court-awarded alimony and child support payments. Federal legislation to enforce child support obligations more stringently was passed in 1984. State enforcement services are now available to mothers, regardless of whether or not they are on welfare. In cases of overdue child care payments, withholding of wages, as well as of state and federal income tax refunds may be obtained. However, improved collection of currently owed child support by itself would bring about only very modest improvements in the economic status of female-headed families. Nor is there likely to be much public support for a policy to substantially raise the level of such awards, since this would likely be considered too great a burden on the fathers.

Public transfers stem from a variety of sources, particularly the federal welfare program, Aid to Families with Dependent Children (AFDC). While such programs do provide a minimum level of support, they generally leave the family with an income below the poverty level. Given the attitudes of taxpayers towards such arrangements, more generous welfare provisions are unlikely. Further, in contrast to private transfers, there are work disincentives associated with these public payments. This is because payments are reduced as labor market earnings increase.

Assume that a female-headed family receives $3,500 when the mother is not employed, and these payments are reduced by an amount equal to what she is paid when she takes a job. This amounts to a 100 percent implicit tax rate on her wages up to $3,500. Such an arrangement ensures saving a full dollar of public funds for every dollar a welfare recipient earns but, as illustrated by Program A in Table 5.6, will also greatly reduce the incentive to work for pay, especially for women who can earn little more than $3,500. This is all the more so because working outside the home generally involves job-related expenses such as commuting, better or special clothing, and child care.

The disincentives will be smaller if the reduction in payments is only a fraction of earnings, particularly if such provisions for retaining a share of earnings are generous. This is illustrated by Program B in the table. In this case, a woman's welfare payment is reduced by only one-half the amount of labor market earnings (an implicit tax rate of 50 percent). Such an arrangement substantially increases the incentive to work, as indicated by the increases in the total income of the family that occur in this case. The government's outlay to the welfare family is also reduced as market earnings increase. While this reduction is not as rapid as under Program A, as noted earlier, an individual receiving welfare is unlikely to work in that case. On the other hand, under Program B, families with considerably higher incomes, up to $7,000, are eligible for welfare. This would be expected to reduce their incentives to work to some extent.

Thus, a reduction of the implicit tax rate potentially reduces program costs by encouraging welfare recipients to supplement their transfer payments with market earnings and, perhaps, shorten the period of time until they can find jobs that pay enough to enable them to leave the welfare roles entirely. But, a reduction of the implicit tax rate potentially increases program costs by making a larger number of families (at higher income levels) eligible for some welfare payment.

It has been difficult to get agreement on the proper balance between these conflicting considerations. It was no doubt concern over the disincentives for employment of welfare recipients that led to a change in 1967 from reducing welfare payments dollar-for-dollar with market earnings to allowing them to retain $30 per month, plus one-third of their earnings. In 1981, however, there was a policy change in the opposite direction. The more liberal provisions were restricted to the first four months of employment, after which the dollar-for-dollar deduction once again applied.[52] Thus welfare outlays may have declined in the short run, but the cost of any savings achieved was the loss of incentives to welfare recipients to enter the labor market and to gain useful skills that would eventually enable them to rise above the poverty level.

The preceding discussion suggests that though private and public transfers undoubtedly have a role to play, they neither have been, nor are likely to be, sufficient to substantially improve the economic status of female-headed families. Thus, other measures, which would raise the market earnings power

---

[52]Ronald G. Ehrenberg and Robert S. Smith, *Modern Labor Economics: Theory and Public Policy,* 2nd ed. (Glenview, Ill.: Scott Foresman, 1985), pp. 181–190.

of these women, are most likely necessary. At present, their potential market earnings are too low to enable many of these families to achieve a decent standard of living.

Since all women (and their children) are at risk of living in a female-headed household, policies to benefit female heads are, in the last analysis, the same as those needed to raise the earnings of women in general. Such measures, discussed at various points in this book, range from ending preferential tax and social security treatment of one-earner families (to encourage women to acquire more labor market experience), to encouraging women to invest in market-oriented education and training and to combatting labor market discrimination.

CONCLUSION

This chapter has considered the effect of a woman's labor force participation on the formation, operation, and possible breakup of families, as well as the special problems of households where the woman is a single family head. While this continues to be a highly controversial subject, we interpret the preponderance of the evidence to show that the dominant effects of the wife working outside the home are likely to be benign for the whole family and particularly so for her and the children. Perhaps the chief negative effect of women's employment is its apparent association with the rising divorce rate. Here we would point out that though a divorce inevitably is fraught with disappointment and problems, in some instances ending an unhappy marriage may be the lesser of evils. In any case, it is clear that should a marriage terminate, whether because of death or divorce, it is the woman who has maintained her labor market skills and contacts who will be able to best fend for herself and for her children.

SUGGESTED READINGS

BECKER, GARY S., *A Treastise on the Family.* Cambridge, MA: Harvard University Press, 1981.

HARTMANN, HEIDI I., "The Family as the Locus of Gender, Class and Political Struggle: The Example of Housework," *Signs: Journal of Women in Culture and Society* 6, no. 3 (Spring 1981): 366–94.

HUBER, JOAN A. AND GLENNA SPITZE, *Children, Housework and Jobs.* N.Y.: Academic Press, 1983.

KAMERMAN, SHEILA B. AND CHERYL B. HAYER (eds.), *Families that Work: Children in a Changing World.* Washington, DC: National Academy Press, 1982.

SCHULTZ, THEODORE W. (ed.), *Economics of the Family,* A conference report of the National Bureau of Economic Research. Chicago: University of Chicago Press, 1974.

SMITH, RALPH E. (ed.), *The Subtle Revolution.* Washington, DC: The Urban Institute, 1979.

Chapter 6

DIFFERENCES IN OCCUPATIONS AND EARNINGS: OVERVIEW

While the main focus so far has been on the roles of men and women in the family, Chapter 4 reviewed the dramatic increase in women's labor force participation that has occurred in the post-World War II period. This increase, in conjunction with a decline in male labor force participation rates, has resulted in a steady narrowing of sex differentials in the extent of involvement in market work. Furthermore, the labor force attachment of women has increased as women have become more committed to work outside the home. These substantial increases in women's participation in paid work do not appear, however, to have been accompanied by anything like comparable improvements in their economic status as compared with men.

In Chapters 7 and 8, we consider alternative theoretical explanations for the observed differences in economic outcomes between men and women. In Chapter 7, we focus on supply-side explanations, particularly the human capital model, which emphasize the role of women's preferences and the choices they make to invest less in job-related education and training, as well as to spend a smaller proportion of their adult years in the labor force. These explanations can also encompass premarket, or "societal" discrimination, in which various types of social pressures influence women's choices adversely.

In Chapter 8, we go on to consider demand-side explanations of the present situation of women. Emphasis will be on the possible results of sex discrimination in the labor market which occurs when men and women with equal qualifications find work in different occupations and/or at different wage rates. We also consider that labor market discrimination can indirectly lower women's economic status by reducing their incentives to acquire education and training. Meanwhile, in this chapter, we review the extent of sex differences in the two main indicators of economic status—occupational attainment and earnings.

As we shall see, although some improvement has taken place in recent years, there continue to be substantial differences in the occupational distributions of men and women. In particular, women who have succeeded in reaching the highest levels in business, unions, government, or academia are still extremely rare. But their success is likely to have an impact out of proportion with their small numbers, because they are proving to employers, fellow workers, and clients, as well as to young women who may want to follow in their footsteps, that it can be done. They also continue to face some special problems as women, as well as those successful men have always faced. They have to "fit in," have to work their way up, have to find time for themselves and their families. In the insets to this chapter, we illustrate these difficulties and present profiles of three women who have overcome them and achieved outstanding success.

INVESTMENT BANKER: KAREN VALENSTEIN*

In a manner of speaking Karen Valenstein discovered her passion for business in Filene's Basement . . . Now a 38-year-old first vice president at E. F. Hutton and Company and one of the preeminent women in investment banking, Mrs. Valenstein was then a rebellious college student whose family offered to reimburse her if she shed her jeans for a more ladylike wardrobe. She would shop for Villager or John Meyer outfits at the Boston bargain bazaar, accept repayment at the retail price and then resell most of the clothes to her classmates at a 10 percent discount . . .

"It's the thrill of beating the system," Mrs. Valenstein says . . . It can be said that [she] has similarly beaten the system by rising to her current level at Hutton, where she is the highest-ranking woman in the public-finance department. For, while the number of women on Wall Street has increased dramatically in the last 20 years, few have risen as high as Mrs. Valenstein . . .

---

*Jane Gross, "Against the Odds: A Woman's Ascent on Wall Street," *New York Times Magazine,* January 6, 1985, pp. 16 ff. Copyright ©1985 by The New York Times Company. Reprinted by permission.

"People my age are only now getting to the level where we can dispel the myth that we are not capable of doing business," says Mrs. Valenstein, who began her career as a municipal analyst, first at the Bank of New York and then at Citibank. She moved to the investment-banking firm of Lehman Brothers Kuhn Loeb Inc., where she was the first woman in the company's history to become a vice-president; a year and a half ago, she went to Hutton as a vice-president.

"It's not pleasant, and you're always bucking," says Mrs. Valenstein. "You have to be 30 percent better than a man to be considered equal. But, when you work in a subjective business like this, you just have to display, with competence, patience and professionalism, that you're more than capable of the task."

Women like Mrs. Valenstein confront not only the difficulties of rising in a profession that has traditionally been closed to them, but also the adjustment to a corporate environment that makes few concessions to those with gentle natures. And, for the most part, these women seem to be responding in kind, modeling themselves after the hard-driving men who have preceded them on the fast track. The women who succeed are doing it, in the main, the way it has always been done: with brutally long hours and burdensome amounts of travel, with political savvy that advances their careers and with single-mindedness that can disrupt families and friendships. The women who embrace this model are often scorned for behavior that is applauded in men

In the corridors of Wall Street, a word heard often is "fit." Can you "fit" into the team concept of the firm, where groups of bankers conceive and execute financial transactions? Can you "fit" with the clients who provide the new business that is ultimately the measure of an investment banker's success and compensation?

While some women turn themselves inside out with varying degrees of success in order to co-exist in such a setting, Karen Valenstein is a natural. She has an intuitive understanding of masculine culture, with all its aggressiveness, competition and politics; she also has a genuine enthusiasm for living by its fierce rules. By her own admission she can trade locker room vulgarities, belt back stingers until dawn and recite National Football League scores on Monday morning. She skis fast and plays to win in mixed doubles. She rejected basketball during a tomboy childhood because "girls rules are stupid." . . . "I never go out of my way to screw someone," Mrs. Valenstein says, "but I'm always looking over my shoulder." . . . She thrives on a frenzied schedule that in a recent two-month period included five round trips to the West Coast, 39 office meetings, 26 business-related meals and 21 days that stretched from one sunrise to the next . . .

Mrs. Valenstein recalls her hiring interview with Lew Glucksman, a firebrand in staid Wall Street circles, who prides himself on championing minorities because of what he calls the "sharp sting" he once felt as a Jew in a Gentile world. "I'm not going to pay you like a broad, and I'm not going to treat you like a broad, so don't act like a broad," Mrs. Valenstein reports he said, mimicking his delivery . . . "Glucksman rewarded aggressive behavior that I was penalized for my whole life. I saw I could be myself, make money and be respected." . . . "Clients love me," [she] says, matter-of-factly. "I listen to them and vary my behavior and wardrobe. I make them feel smart without intimidating them. They ask me questions they'd never ask a man because I go out of my way not to be threatening."

The Valensteins have a live-in housekeeper, but it is John [a second vice president and manager of trust and estate real estate at Chase Manhatten

Bank] who takes the children [aged 7 and 11] to school, supervises their activities, cooks their meals on weekends, dispenses tissues for runny noses and builds jungle gyms for his son and doll houses for his daughter. "He's the nicest man I ever met," Mrs. Valenstein says. "He's sensitive, much more sensitive than I am. If I was married to any other kind of man . . ."

"There's something very special about dealing with a child, especially when they're young like this," Mr. Valenstein [says. He adds] that his wife is "usually very good" about her obligations to her children, "but there are times when she just can't do it." . . . [Mrs. Valenstein] boasts that "I'm the disciplinarian, the tough guy who enforces manners . . . These kids are normal, well-adjusted and very secure . . ., and there's none of that hiding behind mommy."

. . . [Her] steely confidence did not protect Mrs. Valenstein from sexism . . . At her first job [she] recalls being told, "This is not a suitable job for a woman of your breeding and background." . . . At Lehman Brothers . . . she was routinely asked "Whose secretary are you?" and battered with "filthy jokes" which she returned in kind. During her pregnancies . . . male colleagues were trotted past her office as if she were a tourist attraction. . . . " They gave me tasks and I completed them," Mrs. Valenstein says, . . . "They found I had half a brain even if I was a woman, but they never asked me to lunch."

Then, there are the overtures from clients and colleagues, which Mrs. Valenstein's boss says she handles with uncommon aplomb . . . In [one] situation, Mrs. Valenstein felt a hand on her knee. "What I wanted to do was punch him in the face." She says, "What I did was say, real quietly, 'I think your hand is lost.'" In the second situation [one of her supervisors invited her to dinner. She declined and] the following day, three months pregnant and wearing a maternity dress for the first time, she paid a visit to the offender's office. She leaned sweetly against the door frame until he said "touche!" in an appreciative salute.

"You have to deal with it with humor," Mrs. Valenstein says. "If I made a scene, I'd probably have been fired. Instead I turned a potentially devastating situation into a bond between us and gained a very powerful ally."

[For young women starting out] veterans offer solace when they can through organizations like the Financial Women's Association. Mrs. Valenstein is a recent—and somewhat reluctant—member of the group, choosing more often to help younger women already at Hutton, like a receptionist she is recommending for a post on the trading floor, or those she is recruiting. "Men don't become door-openers until they're well past 40, so that's just a mirror image of the men," says [the head of the association] . . . "Karen will be a mentor, one of the best mentors, at 50."

OCCUPATIONAL DIFFERENCES

One way of determining the extent to which men and women do different types of work is to compare the percent of male workers and the percent of female workers in various occupational categories. As can be seen by examining the data in Table 6.1, in 1984, women were very heavily concentrated in the ad-

TABLE 6.1 Distribution of Men and Women by Major Occupational Categories, November 1984[a]

OCCUPATIONAL CATEGORY	NUMBER OF MEN	NUMBER OF WOMEN	PERCENT FEMALE WORKERS	PERCENT OF ALL MEN IN THE LABOR FORCE IN EACH OCCUPATION	PERCENT OF ALL WOMEN IN THE LABOR FORCE IN EACH OCCUPATION
	(thousands)	(thousands)			
Executive, administrative, and managerial	7,769	3,951	33.7	13.1	8.5
Professional specialty	6,996	6,548	48.3	11.8	14.0
Technicians and related support	1,616	1,495	48.1	2.7	3.2
Sales occupations	6,543	6,387	49.4	11.0	13.7
Administrative support, including clerical	3,356	13,525	80.1	5.6	28.9
Service occupations	5,543	8,620	60.9	9.3	18.4
Precision production, craft and repair	12,124	1,106	8.4	20.4	2.4
Operators, fabricators and laborers	12,574	4,613	26.8	21.1	9.9
Farming, forestry, and fishing	2,990	492	14.1	5.0	1.1
Total civilian labor force	59,511	46,736	44.0	100.0	100.0

[a]Data refer to workers 16 years of age and over.

Source: Department of Labor, Bureau of Labor Statistics, *Employment and Earnings*, Dec. 1984, Tables A-22, A-23, pp. 27-28.

ministrative support (including clerical) and service occupations. Accordingly, as can be seen in the far right-hand column, 47 percent of all women workers were in these two predominantely female occupations. Women were also more likely than men to be professionals and sales workers. Men were more heavily represented in executive, managerial, and administrative positions, in operator and laborer jobs, and even more so in precision production, craft and repair occupations, which are the strongholds of skilled blue collar workers, as well as agriculture, forestry, and fishing.

While the situation was similar in earlier years, some improvements occurred over the 1970s and early 1980s. Women were less concentrated in administrative support and service occupations in 1984 than they had been in 1972, when 53 pecent held such jobs. Women also made significant inroads into executive and managerial jobs over the period, increasing their share of those positions from 20 percent in 1972 to 34 percent in 1984.[1] Nonetheless, the figures in Table 6.1 amply demonstrate that considerable sex differences in occupational distributions remained.

In order to examine the same relationships by race and ethnicity as well as by sex, Table 6.2 provides data for black, white, and Hispanic workers also. There were substantial differences both by race and ethnicity, as well as by sex.

Black and Hispanic men and women were much less likely than whites of the same sex to be employed in the prestigious, high-income executive, administrative, and managerial category or to work in professional and sales jobs. At the other end of the scale, they were over-represented in service occupations as well as among operators, fabricators, and laborers.

Within each race or ethnic group, however, the patterns of occupational differences by sex showed considerable similarities. Women were heavily over-represented in administrative support and service occupations and, especially among minority workers, were more likely than men to be in professional and sales jobs. At the same time, women were under-represented among managerial and craft workers, operatives and laborers, and those employed in farming, forestry, and fishing. Overall, sex differences in occupational distributions were larger than racial or ethnic differences. Further, since the 1960s, racial differences in occupational attainment have been declining at a faster pace, particularly among females. (Long-term trends for Hispanics are not known, since data for this group have been available for a shorter period of time.)

Occupational Segregation

So far we have discussed sex differences in occupational distributions in a rather general way. Occupational segregation refers to a situation where two

---

[1]It may be that, in the face of government pressure to increase the representation of women in higher-level positions, some women were moved into managerial jobs without being given corresponding responsibility and pay. There can, however, be little doubt that there also has been genuine change.

TABLE 6.2   Distribution of Workers by Occupation, Race, Hispanic Origin, and Sex, 1982[a]

OCCUPATIONAL CATEGORY	WHITE		BLACK		HISPANIC	
	MEN	WOMEN	MEN	WOMEN	MEN	WOMEN
Executive, administrative, and managerial	12.8	8.0	5.8	4.0	6.6	4.8
Professional specialty	11.8	14.1	5.6	10.2	4.2	6.5
Technicians and related support	2.8	3.1	1.9	2.9	1.7	1.9
Sales occupations	10.9	13.5	4.0	7.6	5.9	10.9
Administrative support, including clerical	5.6	29.9	8.5	25.2	6.5	26.4
Service occupations	8.7	18.1	18.2	30.6	14.0	21.8
Precision production, craft and repair	21.2	2.0	15.6	2.0	20.6	3.3
Operators, fabricators, and laborers	20.9	10.1	34.6	16.3	32.4	21.1
Farming, forestry, and fishing	5.3	1.2	5.8	1.2	8.1	3.3
Total civilian labor force	100.0	100.0	100.0	100.0	100.0	100.0

[a]Data refer to workers 18 years and older.

Source: Bureau of the Census, Population Reports, Consumer Income Series P-60, no. 142, *Money Income of Households, Families, and Persons in the United States: 1982.*

groups, in this case men and women, tend to work in a different set of occupations. The **index of segregation** is a widely accepted measure of the degree of segregation.[2] It gives the percentage of female (or male) workers who would have to change jobs in order for the occupational distribution of the two groups to be the same. The index would equal zero if the distribution of men and women across occupational categories were identical; it would equal 100 if all occupations were either completely male or female. In terms of the data in Table 6.1, the index of occupational segregation by sex equals 37.8.

The same approach may be used to calculate an index of segregation by race and ethnicity. Using the figures presented in Table 6.2, the index of segregation is 26.6 between black and white men, and 20.5 between Hispanic and white men; for women it is 18.7 and 18.1, respectively. Comparing these results with the index of sex segregation, which is 38.9 for whites, 38.3 for blacks, and 35.2 for Hispanics, confirms that, as suggested earlier, there are greater differences in the occupational distribution of men and women than between whites, blacks, and Hispanics of the same sex.

However, data on major occupational categories do not reveal the full extent of occupational segregation by sex. For example, among sales workers, women tend to be employed as retail sales clerks while men are more likely to be manufacturing sales representatives. In fact, the Census also provides information on a far larger set of detailed occupations. The precise number has varied over time but is well in excess of 400. The proportion of women in these more narrowly defined occupations within the broader groupings examined above does indeed tend to vary considerably. This is illustrated in more detail in Table 6.3, which shows a selection of professional specialty occupations, chosen because we tend to be familiar with the nature and function of the various professions and because both men and women are substantially represented in the category as a whole.[3]

In 1980, 56 percent of all women professionals were in the five predominantly (75 percent or more) female professions shown in the table—dietician, librarian, nurse, prekindergarten and kindergarten teacher,

---

[2]See Otis Dudley Duncan and Beverly Duncan, "A Methodological Analysis of Segregation Indexes," *American Sociological Review* 20, no. 2 (1955): 210–17. The index of occupational segregation by sex is defined as follows:

$$S = \tfrac{1}{2} \sum_i \left| M_i - F_i \right|$$

where M_i = the percentage of males in the labor force employed in occupation, and F_i = the percentage of females in the labor force employed in occupation i.

[3]We use decennial census data for this purpose because they are based on the largest sample and, hence, are the most accurate, especially for detailed occupations.

TABLE 6.3 Percent Female in Selected Professional Specialty Occupations, 1970, 1980[a]

	1970		1980	
	TOTAL	**PERCENT FEMALE**	**TOTAL**	**PERCENT FEMALE**
Architects	53,670	4.0	107,693	8.3
Biological and life scientists	27,897	33.1	46,079	37.8
Chemists except biochemists	95,386	11.7	102,239	20.1
Computer systems analysts and scientists	107,580	13.6	202,651	22.5
Dentists	95,241	3.5	125,291	6.7
Dieticians	43,275	92.0	67,270	89.9
Economists	63,230	15.9	95,565	29.7
Editors	155,446	41.6	210,831	49.3
Engineers	1,249,255	1.7	1,400,973	4.6
Lawyers	273,083	4.9	501,834	13.8
Librarians	130,389	82.1	187,379	82.5
Operations and systems researchers and analysts	65,008	11.1	80,876	27.7
Pharmacists	115,544	12.1	145,637	24.0
Physicians	296,988	9.7	433,255	13.4
Physicists and astronomers	21,258	4.5	22,473	5.4
Psychologists	29,575	38.8	92,929	47.2
Registered nurses	762,298	97.3	1,285,299	95.9
Social workers	239,357	63.3	459,984	64.9
Statisticians	24,269	41.6	30,200	48.1
Surveyors and mapping scientists	13,213	0.0	31,634	4.2
Teachers, except post-secondary				
Prekindergarten and kindergarten	134,390	97.9	183,338	96.4
Elementary school	1,510,037	83.9	2,319,370	75.4
Secondary school	1,062,742	49.6	860,806	56.5
Special education	1,584	100.0	32,818	69.1
Teachers, postsecondary[b]	510,523	29.1	637,149	36.6
Veterinarians	20,420	5.3	34,355	13.3

[a]Data are for the experienced civilian labor force aged 16 and over.
[b]This category is at a higher level of aggregation.

Source: Bureau of the Census, *Detailed Occupation of the Experienced Civilian Labor Force by Sex for the United States and Regions: 1980 and 1970,* Supplementary Report PC80-S1-15, March 1984.

or elementary school teacher. At the same time, 40 percent of all male professionals were in the nine predominantly (80 percent or more) male occupations
shown—architect, chemist, dentist, engineer, lawyer, physician, physicist,
surveyor, and veterinarian.

A number of studies have calculated the index of occupational segregation for various years using the detailed breakdown of all occupations for
various census years. They have found levels of occupational segregation in excess of 60 percent for all census years since 1900.[4] But even these calculations
underestimate the real extent of segregation. Job categories used by employers
are far more detailed than the census occupations, and researchers have found
that particular firms often employ only men or women, even in occupations
where both sexes are substantially represented.[5] Restaurants, for instance,
commonly employ only waiters, or waitresses, but not both. The impact of
both these factors is revealed in a study of California firms. Using the
employers' own job classifications, it was found that 51 pecent of firms were
completely sex-segregated by job category; no men and women shared the
same job title. An additional 8 percent of the firms were single-sex
establishments. The mean index of segregation in the remaining firms was
84.1.[6]

Hierarchies Within Occupations

In addition to differences in the distribution of men and women among
occupations, they also tend to be employed at different levels within occupations. This is often referred to as vertical segregation. No adequate data are
available that would enable us to construct economy-wide quantitative
measures, but there can be little doubt that such hierarchical differences are
substantial.

A good example of this is the hierarchy on university faculties, because
they generally use a clear and widely understood set of titles. Table 6.4 provides data on the distribution of men and women by rank in academic year

---

[4]See, for instance, Andrea H. Beller, "Trends in Occupational Segregation by Sex and
Race: 1960-1981," ed. Barbara F. Reskin, *Sex Segregation in the Workplace: Trends, Explanations and Remedies,* (Washington, D.C.: National Academy Press, 1984), pp. 11-26; Edward
Gross, "Plus Ca Change . . . ? The Sexual Structure of Occupations Over Time," *Social Problems*
16, no. 1 (Fall 1968): 198-208; Francine D. Blau and Wallace E. Hendricks, "Occupational
Segregation by Sex: Trends and Prospects," *Journal of Human Resources* 14, no. 2 (Spring 1979):
197-210.

[5]See, for example, Francine D. Balu, *Equal Pay in the Office* (Lexington, MA: Lexington
Books, 1977).

[6]James N. Baron and William T. Bielby, "A Woman's Place is With Other Women: Sex
Segregation in the Work Place," ed., Reskin, *Sex Segregation in the Workplace,* pp. 27-55.

TABLE 6.4 Full-Time Instructional Faculty in Institutions of Higher Education by Academic Rank and by Sex, 1981-82

	TOTAL (MEN & WOMEN)	PERCENT FEMALE OF FACULTY MEMBERS IN EACH RANK	PERCENT OF ALL MALE FACULTY IN EACH RANK	PERCENT OF ALL FEMALE FACULTY IN EACH RANK
Professors	108,594	10.4	33.1	10.5
Associate professors	98,189	21.2	26.3	19.4
Assistant professors	95,912	35.5	21.0	31.7
Instructors	30,421	52.2	4.9	14.8
Lecturers	6,436	46.6	1.2	2.8
Undesignated rank	62,024	36.3	13.4	20.9
Total	401,576	26.8	100.0	100.0

Source: *Digest of Education Statistics 1983/84*, National Center for Education Statistics, Washington D.C.: U.S.Government Printing Office.

1981–82 and shows large differences between the two.[7] Women were clustered at the lower end of the occupational hierarchy, as Assistant Professors, Instructors, Lecturers, and those with undesignated rank, while men were more highly represented in the upper ranks, as Professors and Associate Professors—the only ones that tend to have job security in the form of tenure.

This case is not unique. While the number of women managers and administrators more than doubled between 1972 and 1980, a period during which the number of men increased only 22 percent, women's representation in top positions is still extremely sparse. At the end of the 1970s, only one of the 500 largest U.S. industrial corporations on *Fortune's* list, had a woman chief executive.[8] Of the 6,400 officers and directors (those listed in the proxy statements) of the 1300 companies covered by *Fortune,* only 10 were women. No wonder that when Herman Kahn, the futurist, was asked how long it would take before 25 percent of the chief executives of the *Fortune* 500 companies were women, his estimate was about 2000 years. On the other hand, he also suggested they might reach 10 percent in 20 years.[9]

Last, Table 6.5 illustrates the importance of hierarchical segregation in a variety of other occupations. It also shows that women tend to earn less than men in the same occupation more because of their concentration at the lower levels of the hierarchy than because they are paid much less than men who are at the same level. As we have seen, of course, women also tend to be in different occupations. The reasons for the sex difference in earnings will be discussed at much greater length later.

Evaluating the Extent of Occupational Segregation

However segregation is measured, and whatever the numerical value of the index arrived at, how can it be determined whether any figure in excess of zero and short of 100 is modest or excessive? The answer depends in part on one's perception of how great the differences are in men's and women's talents, tastes, and motivation and how relevant these are to their occupational distribution and achievements.

[7]When such data were first published in 1974, the general interpretation was that women were seriously under-represented at the higher ranks because many of them had presumably been hired recently. It was, accordingly, expected that in time the female distribution would become more similar to the male distribution as women advanced in the ranks. In fact, the proportion of full professors who are women has remained at about 10 percent, and the proportion that women comprise of associate professors has risen from 16.9 to 21.2 percent. Their proportion of assistant professors rose from 27.1 to 35.5 percent, and of instructors from 40.7 to 52.2 percent.

[8]Katherine Graham of *The Washington Post.* This was reported by Susan Fraker, "Why Women Aren't Getting to the Top," *Fortune* 109, no. 8 (April 16, 1984): 40–45.

[9]Cited by J. Benjamin Forbes and James E. Piercy, "Rising to the Top: Executive Women in 1983 and Beyond," *Business Horizons* (Sept.–Oct. 1983): 38–47.

TABLE 6.5 Female-Male Earnings and Employment Ratios By Occupational Work Level, 1981

OCCUPATIONAL WORK LEVEL		AVERAGE MONTHLY SALARY[a]	FEMALE-MALE EARNINGS RATIO	PERCENT FEMALE
Accountant	I	1,377	99	46
	II	1,679	98	34
	III	1,962	96	19
	IV	2,402	95	11
	V	2,928	90	5
Auditor	I	1,364	98	36
	II	1,651	97	27
	III	2,033	92	21
	IV	2,456	90	8
Attorney	I	1,873	103	28
	II	2,338	99	24
	III	3,031	95	13
	IV	3,738	94	9
Chemist	I	1,508	96	38
	II	1,757	94	29
	III	2,120	93	15
	IV	2,567	92	10
Buyer	I	1,350	96	52
	II	1,689	95	23
	III	2,100	92	9
Director of personnel	I	2,321	101	21
	II	2,933	94	10
	III	3,574	90	7
Job analyst	I	1,412	87	75
	II	1,525	92	85
	III	1,900	90	66
	IV	2,393	94	29
Engineering technicians	I	1,137	97	24
	II	1,307	98	17
	III	1,527	97	9
Drafter	I	923	103	34
	II	1,075	101	26
	III	1,301	96	18
	IV	1,611	94	8
Computer operator	I	906	99	37
	II	1,049	102	49
	III	1,220	97	35
	IV	1,475	97	24
	V	1,733	92	17

[a]Includes data for workers not identified by sex.

Source: Earl F. Mellor, "Investigating the Differences in Weekly Earnings of Women and Men," *Monthly Labor Review* 107, no. 6 (June 1984): 17–28.

Those who argue that occupational segregation is natural and appropriate are at one extreme. In this view, efforts to change the existing situation will merely lead to economic inefficiency and personal frustration. Its proponents emphasize the similarities among individuals within each sex and the differences between the two groups. Those who emphasize the variations among individuals within each sex and similarities between the two groups are at the other extreme. In this view, if men and women were not constrained by gender stereotyping and various barriers to individual choice but were free to follow their own inclinations, they would be far less concentrated in separate occupations. The fact that there are occupations that are predominantly male in some countries but female in others lends some support to the view that socially imposed restrictions play a role in the sex typing of jobs.[10] In this case, removing existing barriers would presumably increase efficiency and decrease frustration, since individuals could seek work suited to their particular aptitudes.

It should be emphasized that even if present occupational segregation is deemed excessive, it would be unreasonable to conclude that the optimal situation would necessarily be a precisely proportional distribution of men and women. Apart from whatever innate differences there may be, past socialization and the prevalent allocation of household responsibilities would make such an outcome unlikely for some time to come.

In addition, the rate of change is limited by the extent to which new people can be hired. Large numbers of people cannot be expected to change jobs on short notice as the computation of the segregation index perhaps implies. The most that could reasonably be expected is that the under-represented group would be more highly represented among new hires, to the extent that they are qualified for the available positions, than among those presently employed in the occupation. Especially during periods of recession and retrenchment this may be, at best, a very slow process.

TRENDS IN OCCUPATIONAL SEGREGATION

The same issues confronted in measuring current occupational segregation also arise in determining the precise extent to which it has changed over time. However, in addition to the concern over how detailed the categories are, or whether hierarchical segregation is taken into account, there is also the question of whether the same occupational definitions are used for the various periods to be compared. The main difficulty is that the occupational categories used, both their definition and their number, undergo frequent changes. Given

[10]This subject will be discussed at greater length in Chapter 10.

constant flux in the economy, this is inevitable. For example, had the Census Bureau rigidly adhered to the occupational categories of an earlier era, jobs like computer systems analyst and programmer, as well as computer operator and data entry keyer, would not be included. In spite of the best efforts of the people who compile the data and the researchers who use them, data are not entirely comparable over the years and the less so as the years are further apart.

In spite of these limitations, there is no reason to question the unanimous findings of the studies on this subject, all of which point to little change over a number of decades. The index of segregation was actually reported to have increased by 1.1 percentage points between 1950 and 1960, as predominantly female clerical and professional jobs grew in relative size. Between 1960 and 1970, an inflow of men into female professions and of women into male sales and clerical jobs produced a modest drop in the segregation index of 3.1 percentage points.[11]

Between 1972 and 1981, a larger decrease in the segregation index of 6.6 percentage points was found.[12] During this period, women increased their share of traditionally male professional jobs. This is illustrated in Table 6.3. A comparison of the data for 1970 and 1980 shows that women have made notable progress in precisely those professional occupations that were most preponderantly male in 1970. With the exception of physicists and astronomers, their proportion increased rapidly in all fields where it had been less than 15 percent in the earlier year. There were similar large increases in many executive, administrative, and managerial occupations during this period. Extreme examples are a rise in the representation of women from 0.0 percent to 25.6 percent for administrators in public administration, from 0.0 percent to 9.4 percent for administrators in protective services, and from 7.9 percent to 17.6 percent for managers in marketing, advertising, and public relations.

Nonetheless, many highly segregated occupations remain. This can be seen when examining Table 6.6, which shows occupations that are either more than 90 percent or less than 5 percent female. Many of the latter are from the category of precision production, craft and repair occupations. Overall, relatively little change occurred in the sex composition of blue collar jobs during the 1970s.

Thus, the figures indicate that some decline in the amount of segregation occurred since 1960 and that the pace of change accelerated in the 1970s. However, the magnitude of segregation remained substantial. As we have seen, it was still the case that more than 60 percent of women (or men) would

---

[11]Blau and Hendricks, "Occupational Segregation."

[12]Beller, "Trends in Occupational Segregation by Sex."

TABLE 6.6 Selected Occupations Less Than 5 Percent or More Than 90 Percent Female, 1980[a]

OCCUPATIONS	LESS THAN 5 PERCENT FEMALE
Airplane pilots and navigators	1.4
Captains and other officers, fishing vessels	3.6
Construction laborers	3.2
Construction trades	2.1
Engineers	4.6
Extractive occupations	2.3
Firefighting and fire prevention occupations	2.0
Garbage collectors	3.0
Helpers, construction and extractive occupations	4.3
Material moving equipment operations, other than miscellaneous	3.0
Mechanics and repairers	3.4
Plant systems operators	3.8
Rail transport occupations	1.6
Sales engineers	3.2
Stevedors	1.4
Supervisors, forestry and logging workers	3.2
Supervisors, protective service occupations	4.3
Surveyors and mapping scientists	4.2
Timber cutting and logging occupations	2.5
Truck drivers, heavy	2.3

	MORE THAN 90 PERCENT FEMALE
Bank tellers	91.1
Child care workers, except private household	93.2
Data entry keyers	92.4
Dental hygienists	98.5
Health record technologists and technicians	91.3
Licensed practical nurses	96.6
Private household occupations	95.3
Receptionists	95.8
Registered nurses	95.9
Secretaries, stenographers, and typists	98.3
Teachers' aides	92.5
Teachers, prekindergarten and kindergarten	96.4
Telephone operators	91.0

[a]Data are for the experienced and civilian labor force aged 16 and over. Not all occupations are at the same level of aggregation.

Source: Bureau of the Census, *Detailed Occupation of the Experienced Civilian Labor Force by Sex for the United States and Regions: 1980 and 1970,* Supplementary Report PC80-S1-15, March 1984.

have had to change jobs in 1981 in order for the detailed occupational distribution of the two sex groups to be the same. One reason for this is that the relatively rapid changes in managerial and professional jobs have not been matched in most of the other occupations. Continued change, even at the recent higher rate, would require 100 years for the index of occupational segregation to reach zero.

A question that must also be raised is to what extent the observed trends reflect real improvements in opportunities for women.[13] In some cases, firms have responded to government pressures by placing women into nominal management positions that involve little responsibility and little contact with higher levels of management. In other instances, jobs have become increasingly female when skill requirements declined because of technological changes. In such cases, integration may turn out to be a short-run phenomenon as women increasingly come to dominate such occupations. One example of this trend is the case of insurance adjusters and examiners. Women increased their share of this occupation from 29.6 percent in 1970 to 60.2 percent in 1980. Yet, they are employed primarily as "inside adjusters" whose decision-making has, to a considerable extent, been computerized and involves little discretion.[14] "Outside adjusters," a better paid and more prestigious group, remain largely male.

In yet other instances, women may gain access to a sector of an occupation that was always low-paying. For example, the representation of women among bus drivers increased from 28.3 percent in 1970 to 45.8 percent in 1980. But men continue to comprise the majority of full-time workers in metropolitan transportation systems, while women are concentrated among part-time school bus drivers.

Nonetheless, it is likely that much of the observed decline in occupational segregation does represent enhanced labor market opportunities for women and that the decrease will continue in the future. The group that can most readily respond to new opportunities, given the difficulty in changing occupations in mid-career, is younger women. And, indeed, the decrease in occupational segregation has been particularly pronounced among this group. This means that change is necessarily something of a slow process but may be expected to gain momentum as more recent cohorts of women who are less occupationally segregated replace older ones.

---

[13]These examples are from Barbara F. Reskin, "Status Hierarchies and Sex Segregation" (unpublished paper, February 1985).

[14]For a study of the insurance industry, see Barbara Baran and Suzanne Teegarden, "Women's Labor in the Office of the Future. Changes in the Occupational Structure of the Insurance Industry," ed., Lourdes Beneria, *Women and Structural Transformation: The Crisis of Work and Family Life* (New Brunswick, N.J.: Rutgers University Press, forthcoming).

UNION LEADER: KAREN NUSSBAUM*

When Karen Nussbaum met a group of top union men for the first time, she told her fellow labor leaders to think of her organizing efforts "as a cross between George Meany and Dolly Parton."

It is an apt description. Ten years ago, trying to prod clerical workers to fight for better working conditions, Ms. Nussbaum was afraid to use the word "organize." Now she runs 9 to 5, the National Association of Working Women—which inspired the movie "Nine to Five" with Dolly Parton as a harassed secretary—and is the president of a national union affiliated with the Service Employees International union.

In a labor movement dominated by male leadership, 34-year-old Ms. Nussbaum is part of a small but growing nucleus of women wielding real power . . .

These women labor leaders are part of a new generation, younger and more activist than most of the path-cutters who preceded them. They speak the language of the women workers whom unions increasingly are trying to recruit. "Ultimately," Ms. Nussbaum says, "the key to improving the conditions for women lies in organizing the private sector."

In a nation where white males lost their majority in the work force for the first time in 1983—and where more than 1.5 million women are entering the work force each year—many unions must actively seek out women members to survive. The problem is dispelling the notion that unions are ailing institutions run by and for men.

The new female labor leaders, while they also represent male workers, have special appeal to unorganized white-collar women workers in such industries as health care, banking and insurance that traditionally have kept unions at bay . . .

"Karen's the kind of person who builds things," says Robert Welsh, a top operative in the Service Employees Union. "Part of what she's building is a perception, the way people think of women workers, not only in the public at large but in the labor movement itself."

An exterminator's daughter from Chicago, Ms. Nussbaum was a 30-year-old college dropout working as a clerk-typist at Harvard University when, in the early 1970s, she began to sense the powerful force women were becoming in the workplace. She and her fellow clerical workers yearned for better pay, advancement opportunities and respect. (Ms. Nussbaum recalls that a young student once entered her office, looked around and asked, "Isn't anyone here?") They formed a group of office workers, initially 300 strong, that was to become 9 to 5.

"Over a period of 10 years, Karen has painstakingly built an organization that's unique in the labor movement," says Kim Fellner, the communica-

*Cathy Trost, "Dynamic Trio: Three Labor Activists Lead a Growing Drive to Sign Up Women," *The Wall Street Journal* (January 29, 1985), pp. 1, 18. Reprinted by permission of the *Wall Street Journal*. ©Dow Jones & Company, Inc. (1985). All rights reserved.

tions director for the Screen Actors Guild. The national 9 to 5 association has 12,000 members in 25 chapters. In 1981, Ms. Nussbaum aligned the group with District 925 of the Service Employees, which claims about 6,500 members.

Ms. Nussbaum lives in Cleveland with her husband and infant son, but spends half her time traveling: to conferences on automation in the office, to organizing campaigns, and to lobby for health and safety laws for workers who use video display terminals.

In organizing campaigns, "we use videos that show workers talking and Karen talking on different talk shows, and then we bring her into town and it's bigger than life," says Bonnie Ladin, District 925's organizing director. "She has very high recognition among office workers."

In the beginning, though, Ms. Nussbaum was as wary of unions as they were of her. "There was a bias among clericals that said unions were for blue collar workers," she says, "and a bias among unions that said clericals just never organized." But she grew to understand that 9 to 5 could use a union's structure to give it more power, while retaining its own character. District 925 has won 24 of its last 26 certification elections and has several organizing campaigns in progress now.

Her ideas about women workers might have ended in the 1960s junkyard of failed idealism were it not for the surge of women into the work force and her adroit manipulation of the media. One of the first places organized was Educators Publishing Service, a small company outside Boston. Workers picketed with signs that bellowed: "Every Person a Slave." Ms. Nussbaum says the company sued for defamation but the union got a contract. (A spokesman for Educators Publishing Service says officials there don't recall details of the case.)

More recently, hundreds of women marched outside Equitable Life Assurance Society's Manhattan headquarters to protest the company's long battle against unionization of one of its offices. District 925 won an election there in 1982, but contract bargaining had stalled. In November, Equitable signed a contract that Ms. Nussbaum calls a breakthrough, both in gaining a foothold in the insurance industry and in giving the mostly female claims-processors more control over working conditions while using video display terminals. The Equitable contract will make the industry "think twice before investing millions of dollars to defeat us," she says.

Critics say the victories are small—the Equitable contract covers 54 employees—and the battles long. But Ms. Nussbaum thinks one of the union's best assets is its staying power. A slight woman who friends say neither raises her voice nor crows about successes, she sits in her small office over an art-supply store in Cleveland and says: "I am surprised every day by what this has turned into."

EARNINGS

The single best known statistic relevant to the economic status of women in this country probably is that for about 30 years women who worked year-round, full-time earned about 60 cents to every dollar men working year-round, full-time earned.[15] One reason this fact has penetrated people's consciousness to such an extent is that the same gap persisted for so long with modest fluctuations and no significant trend. As the data in Table 6.7 show, womens' median annual earnings fluctuated between 59 and 64 percent of those of men from 1955 to 1982.[16] The ratio was actually highest in 1955. But in 1983, the 1955 figure of 64 percent was again attained. Perhaps more

TABLE 6.7 **Median Annual and Usual Weekly Earnings of Full-Time Women Workers as Percent of Men's Earnings, Selected Years, 1955-1985**

	ANNUAL[a]	WEEKLY[b]
1955	63.9	
1960	60.8	
1965	60.0	
1970	59.4	62.3
1975	58.8	62.0
1976	60.2	62.2
1977	58.9	61.9
1978	59.7	61.3
1979	60.0	62.4
1980	60.2	63.4
1981	59.2	64.6
1982	61.7	65.0
1983	63.6	65.6
1984		64.8[c]
1985 (1st quarter)		66.3[c]

[a]Includes year-round, full-time workers only. Includes income from self-employment.
[b]Includes all full-time workers, regardless of weeks worked. Excludes income from self-employment.
[c]The median earnings figure is calculated using $10 rather than the $50 intervals previously used and, thus, is not completely comparable to prior years.

Source: Bureau of Labor Statistics, Bulletin 1977, *U.S. Working Women: A Databook* (annual earnings 1955-1975); Earl F. Mellor, "Investigating the Differences in Weekly Earnings of Women and Men," *Monthly Labor Review* 107, no. 6 (June 1984): 17–28 (weekly earnings 1970-1983); Bureau of the Census, Population reports, Consumer Income Series P-60, Money Income of Households, Families and Persons in the United States (annual earnings 1976-1983), various issues; U.S. Department of Labor, Bureau of Labor Statistics, *Press Release,* January 30, 1985 (weekly earnings 1984); BNA, *Daily Labor Report* 91, April 10, 1985 (weekly earnings, 1985).

[15]Since considerably more women than men work less than year-round, defined as 50 weeks or more per year, and less than full-time, defined as 35 hours or more per week, the gap would be considerably larger if earnings of all workers were compared.

[16]The median, rather than the mean, income is shown because more government data are presented this way. The definition of the median is that half the cases fall above and half below it. In this case, the implication is that half of the individuals concerned have a higher income, half a lower income. The mean, more properly called the arithmetic mean, is calculated by adding up total income of all individuals concerned and dividing by their number. Since there is a relatively small number of persons who have an extremely high level of income, the mean tends to be higher than the median.

significantly, the ratio had risen for two consecutive years. Was this the beginning of a trend or merely a short-term fluctuation?

Inspection of the data on weekly earnings of full-time workers, available only more recently, suggests it may indeed have been the beginning of a trend. In each year, the earnings ratio computed on the basis of weekly earnings is higher than the annual figure. There are a number of possible reasons for this. First, the weekly data refer to *usual* weekly earnings from primary employment. Thus, they exclude income from overtime work when it is performed on an irregular basis and income from moonlighting for those with more than one job. Since men are more likely than women to work overtime and to moonlight, the ratio of women's to men's earnings is lower for annual than for weekly earnings. Second, although both data sets refer to wage and salary workers, additional income from self-employment is included in the annual, but not in the weekly, data. Men are more likely than women to be in occupations like physician and dentist where such income is more likely to be important. Finally, the weekly data include individuals who worked full-time only part of the year. It is possible that the exclusion of this group in the computation of annual earnings raises the earnings of men more than women.[17]

Whatever the reasons for the differences between the male-female earnings ratios based on the weekly and annual data, of more interest is that the data for weekly earnings show a fairly consistent upward trend since 1978, having risen by 3.5 percentage points between 1978 and 1984. This suggests that the more recent upturn in the ratio of annual earnings may indeed be the beginning of an upward trend as well.[18]

On the other hand, the female-male earnings ratio based on annual earnings data was highest in 1982 and 1983, two years of exceptionally high unemployment. Male earnings may have been more adversely affected by the recessionary conditions, both because men were somewhat more likely to be unemployed than women and because men generally work more overtime hours than women. (Overtime hours are reduced in times of economic downturn.) In the recovery year of 1984, the ratio of women's to men's weekly earnings slipped from 65.6 percent in 1983 to 64.8. However, data from the

[17]The reasons for the differences in the weekly and annual series are discussed in Nancy Rytina, "Comparing Annual and Weekly Earnings from the Current Population Survey," *Monthly Labor Review* 106, no. 4 (April 1983): 32–8. Women's weekly earnings are estimated to be an even higher percentage of men's, even among full-time workers (those working 35 hours or more per week) when an adjustment is made for actual hours worked. June O'Neill reports a figure of 72 percent for 1983 after this adjustment ("The Trend in the Male-Female Wage Gap in the United States," *Journal of Labor Economics* 2, no. 4 [Jan. 1985, pt. 2]). This figure must, however, be viewed with some caution because of the inevitable lack of accuracy of estimates of hours worked; see George J. Borjas, "The Relationship Between Wages and Weekly Hours of Work: The Role of Division Bias," *Journal of Human Resources* 15, no. 3 (Summer 1980): 409–23.

[18]As we shall see in Chapter 10, the earnings gap has been closing in many advanced industrialized nations to a considerably greater extent than has been the case in the United States so far.

first quarter of 1985 suggest that the ratio has once again begun to increase.

Based on this review of the evidence, we tentatively conclude that a trend towards a narrowing of the female-male earnings ratio did begin in the late 1970s or early 1980s. The size of the reduction, however, may be somewhat exaggerated by the data from 1982 and 1983, due to the exceptional economic conditions prevailing during those years.

Given the substantial earnings gap for women and men overall that nonetheless persists, the question arises of how particular groups within the population have been faring. Accordingly, we shall examine the situation for workers with various levels of schooling, in different occupations, and of different race and age. Unfortunately, the relevant data in several instances are only available for income, not earnings. The former includes such items as interest, dividends and transfer payments as well as earnings. But for the great majority of the working population, these items are quite small. In 1982, for instance, when median earnings for men were $21,077 and for women were $13,014, the corresponding figures were $21,655 and $13,663 for income.[19] Accordingly, women's earnings were 62 percent of men's, while women's income was 63 percent of men's. This difference is not large enough to cause serious concern.

As can be seen in Table 6.8, education has a strong positive effect on the income of both groups, but it took considerably more years of schooling for women to achieve the same earnings as men. For instance, in both 1967 and 1983, males with only an elementary school education made more than female high school graduates; male high school graduates had higher incomes than women who had graduated from college. Also, there was no clear tendency for the percent that women earned to increase with years of schooling. Hence, a rising level of education for both men and women cannot be expected of itself to reduce the income gap. Despite the similarities in the patterns of sex differentials in the two years, it is worth noting that the ratio of women's as compared to men's income increased for all levels of schooling between 1967 and 1983.

Table 6.9 presents information on earnings in 1983 for the same nine major occupational categories that were discussed in the previous section. There were, of course, differences in earnings across these groups for both men and women. More surprising, perhaps, were the large differences in earnings between men and women in the same group. Two factors previously discussed help to explain this. First, within the broad categories, women tend to be in different detailed occupations—they are nurses, men are doctors, they are elementary school teachers, men are professors, they are retail sales clerks, men are wholesale representatives. Second, vertical segregation, even within detailed occupations, is important and influences earnings considerably.

We turn next to Table 6.10, which provides information on workers by

---

[19]If mean, rather than median income and earnings were compared, the very large amounts of income received by a relatively few individuals would make for a larger difference.

TABLE 6.8 Median Income of Men and Women Working Year-Round, Full-Time, by Years of Schooling 1967 and 1983[a]

YEARS OF SCHOOLING	1967 INCOME ($) MEN	1967 INCOME ($) WOMEN	1967 WOMEN'S INCOME AS PERCENT OF MEN'S	1983 INCOME ($) MEN	1983 INCOME ($) WOMEN	1983 WOMEN'S INCOME AS PERCENT OF MEN'S
Elementary:						
Less than 8	4,831	2,820	58.4	14,093	9,385	66.6
8	6,133	3,343	54.5	16,438	10,337	62.9
High school:						
1–3	6,891	3,704	53.8	17,685	11,131	62.9
4	7,732	4,499	58.2	21,823	13,787	63.2
College:						
1–3	8,816	5,253	59.6	24,613	16,536	67.2
4	11,571	6,796	58.7	29,892	18,452	61.7
5 or more	12,510	7,823	62.5	34,643	22,877	66.4

[a]Data refer to workers 25 years of age and older.

Source: Bureau of the Census, Current Population Reports, Consumer Income Series P-60, no. 145, Money Income of Households, Families and Persons in the United States: 1983. (Advance data from the March 1984 Current Population Survey.)

race and ethnicity as well as sex. Within each group, women earned less than men in 1982, but the female-male income ratio was higher among blacks (75.2 percent) and Hispanics (72.9 percent) than among whites (62.3 percent). This represented a considerable increase in the earnings of black women relative to black men from 55.1 percent in 1955. The trends in income differences among whites closely mirror the trends we previously discussed for the population as a whole (of which they comprise the majority), showing little tendency towards a narrowing of the income gap until the early 1980s. A moderate decrease in income differences by sex is also discernable among Hispanics since the mid-1970s when data became available for this group.

Minority individuals of both sexes earned less than their white counterparts in 1982, but the differential was considerably smaller among women than among men. In 1982, the median income of black males was 75.2 percent and of Hispanic males 70.1 percent of white males. The income ratios were 90.8 percent for black women and 82.1 percent for Hispanic women, respectively. This reflected a considerable improvement in the incomes of blacks relative to whites, dating from the 1950s for women and from the 1960s for men. The

TABLE 6.9   Median Earnings of Men and Women Working Year-Round, Full Time by Major Occupational Category, 1983[a]

OCCUPATIONS	MEN	WOMEN	EARNINGS OF WOMEN AS PERCENT OF EARNINGS OF MEN
	($)	($)	
Executive, administrative, and managerial	30,476	18,277	60.0
Professional specialty	29,547	19,202	65.0
Technical and related support	24,573	16,555	67.4
Sales occupations	23,128	11,979	51.8
Administrative support, including clerical	20,833	13,473	64.7
Service occupations	14,688	9,228	62.8
Precision production, craft, and repair	21,520	13,245	61.5
Operators, fabricators, and laborers	18,085	11,371	62.9

[a]Data refer to workers 15 years and older.

Source: Bureau of the Census, Current Population Reports, Consumer Income Series P-60, no. 145, Money Income of Households, Families, and Persons in the United States: 1983. (Advance Data from the March 1984 Current Population Survey)

TABLE 6.10   Median Income of Year-Round, Full-Time Workers by Race, Hispanic Origin, and Sex, 1955-82[a]

YEAR	INCOME OF WHITE WOMEN AS A PERCENT OF INCOME OF WHITE MEN	INCOME OF BLACK WOMEN AS A PERCENT OF INCOME OF BLACK MEN	INCOME OF HISPANIC WOMEN AS A PERCENT OF INCOME OF HISPANIC MEN	INCOME OF BLACK MEN AS A PERCENT OF INCOME OF WHITE MEN	INCOME OF BLACK WOMEN AS A PERCENT OF INCOME OF WHITE WOMEN	INCOME OF HISPANIC MEN AS A PERCENT OF INCOME OF WHITE MEN	INCOME OF HISPANIC WOMEN AS A PERCENT OF INCOME OF WHITE WOMEN
1955	65.3	55.1	n.a.	60.9	51.4	n.a.	n.a.
1960	60.6	62.2	n.a.	66.1	62.2	n.a.	n.a.
1965	57.9	62.5	n.a.	62.8	67.9	n.a.	n.a.
1970	58.6	70.3	n.a.	70.3	84.2	n.a.	n.a.
1975	58.5	74.8	68.6	76.7	98.2	72.5	85.0
1980	59.3	74.4	71.7	74.7	93.7	69.9	84.5
1982	62.3	75.2	72.9	75.2	90.8	70.1	82.1

[a]Blacks include blacks and other non-whites. Data refer to workers 15 years of age and older, except for blacks in 1982 it is 14 years and older.

Source: Bureau of the Census, Current Population Reports, Consumer Income Series P-60, Money Income of Households, Families and Persons in the United States, various issues.

TABLE 6.11   **Median Income of Women Working Year-Round, Full-Time as a Percent of Men's Income, by Age, 1983**

AGE	MEN	WOMEN	WOMEN'S EARNINGS AS PERCENT OF MEN'S
	($)	($)	
15–19	8,204	7,857	95.8
20–24	12,822	11,062	86.3
25–29	18,865	14,239	75.5
30–34	22,264	16,056	72.1
35–39	25,328	16,624	65.6
40–44	26,479	14,893	56.2
45–49	26,839	15,088	56.2
50–54	27,046	15,171	56.1
55–59	26,013	14,829	57.0
60–64	24,836	15,606	62.8

Source: Bureau of the Census, Current Population Reports, Consumer Income Series P-60, no. 145. Money Income of Households, Families and Persons in the United States, 1983. (Advance data from the March 1984 Current Population Survey.)

gains were particularly large for black women whose median income was only 51.4 percent of white women's in 1955. However, little narrowing of minority-white income differentials appears to have occurred since the mid-1970s.

The 1983 earnings profiles for men and women over the life cycle are shown in Table 6.11. Women earned less than men in all age groups, but the extent to which this was the case varied considerably. The differential was only 4 percent for the youngest group but increased to 44 percent for those between ages 40 and 54. This clearly indicates that young women do relatively better than older ones.[20]

Does this merely show that men's earnings tend to rise more steeply with age than do women's, or does it show that young women are doing better now than their predecessors did? If the former is true, we would expect the women who were, say, age 25 to 29 in 1983, and earned 76 percent as much as men at that time, to earn only 66 percent as much as their male contemporaries 10 years later in 1992 when they would be 35 to 39 years old. If, however, the latter is the case, these women would be expected to still earn 76 percent as much

[20]The increase in women's earnings relative to men's after age 54 may be explained by the larger proportion of men who partially retire for a time before going into full retirement. This often involves a reduction in earnings, even when they do not reduce their hours below what is considered full-time. Marjorie Honig, "Partial Retirement in the Labor Market Behavior of Older Women" (unpublished paper, November 1983).

**TABLE 6.12   Median Income of Women Working Year-Round, Full-Time
as a Percent of Men's Income, by Age, Selected Years, 1967-83**

AGE	1967	1973	1983
25–34	62.2	62.6	73.3
35–44	55.1	52.5	61.3
45–54	54.0	52.3	56.2

Source: Bureau of the Census: Current Population Reports, Money Income of Households,
Families and Persons in the United States, various issues.

as men at that time. The data for one point in time do not enable us to answer
this question. Information in Table 6.12, however, does help to shed some
light on this subject.

If young women's incomes were a higher percentage of men's than that
of older women, but the income ratio of women in each age group were the
same in each year, no improvement would be taking place over time. Older
women would fare less well than younger ones only because of the life-cycle effect. If, on the other hand, young women's income were a higher pecentage of
men's than that of older women in the first year, and remained just as high as
they aged, there would be no evidence of life-cycle effects, but rather of an upward trend. Members of the younger cohort would do better throughout their
life cycle.

Our data, which focus on adults in their prime working years, conform
to neither of these two extremes. Women's incomes were a larger percent of
men's for each age group in 1983 than in 1967 and 1973, suggesting clear improvement in their relative status over time. The gains were most pronounced
for the 25 to 34 year age group whose relative income increased by almost 11
percentage points between 1973 and 1983. While the income of the 35 to 44 age
group was a smaller percent of men's in 1983 than that of the 25 to 34 age
group in either of the previous years, the difference was quite modest. Further,
the fact that the income of the 45 to 54 age group was actually a slightly larger
percent of men's income than that of the 35 to 44 group in either of the prior
years is most encouraging. These data suggest that younger women are likely
to retain a substantial amount of the improvement in their relative earnings as
they age. Moreover, the observation that young women are now entering less
traditional occupations and are spending more time in the labor market reinforces our conclusion that they are likely to continue faring better than their
predecessors at each point of the life cycle. As this occurs, the overall sex gap
in earnings and income should decline considerably more as earlier cohorts of
women with relatively low earnings are replaced increasingly by the more recent cohorts with higher earnings.

BUSINESS SCHOOL DEAN
ELIZABETH E. BAILEY*

Elizabeth E. Bailey is a woman who gets things done.

She couldn't find a special school for a physically handicapped son—so she founded one herself.

She hates cigarette smoke—so, during a term on the Civil Aeronautics Board [C.A.B.], she pushed through rules guaranteeing non-smokers a smoke-free seat on airplanes.

She has little patience with academics or businessmen who do not integrate computers into their daily routines. And now, 15 months after becoming dean of Carnegie-Mellon University's Graduate School of Industrial Management, Mrs. Bailey, a short, stocky, 45-year-old woman with a firm chin and a determined expression, is pushing the Pittsburgh-based school into the middle of the computer age. "My thrust is on integrating computers into the curriculum a lot better than has been done in the past," she said.

The National Academy of Sciences says that Carnegie-Mellon's computer science department is one of the nation's leaders, but Mrs. Bailey says she is not satisfied with the graduate school's degree of computerization. Since . . . [becoming] dean in May 1983, she has insisted that each student use a personal computer, and has set up a computer "network" that enables students and faculty members to communicate electronically. She has hired 10 new faculty members, 4 of them specialists in information systems. And she has revised the school's research agenda to emphasize studies of how businesses deal with information.

That seems a lot to accomplish in one year, even for an energetic woman who schedules her first appointments before 8:30 A.M. and goes to lunch-hour exercise classes three days a week. And indeed, many of the activities traditionally handled by deans have taken a back seat. For example, Mrs. Bailey has limited fund raising to just four or five days a month . . . Mrs. Bailey even delegates some internal duties. She appointed a deputy dean to serve as liaison with the faculty on routine matters. But, associates say, she does plumb faculty members' views on technology and business . . .

Mrs. Bailey, meanwhile, describes her main priority in one sentence. "I want our students to feel as though they are on the threshold of a revolution," she said, her eyes, although masked by large glasses, lighting up at the thought.

Mrs. Bailey herself has been a trail-blazer in a revolution of sorts—the push of women into management positions. She was the first woman to receive a doctorate in economics from Princeton University. She was the first woman to head a department at Bell Laboratories (in her case, the economic research

*Kirk Johnson, "Technology's Dean: Elizabeth E. Bailey—A Computer Whiz at the Helm of Carnegie-Mellon," *New York Times* (August 26, 1984), Sect. III: p. 5. Copyright ©1984 by The New York Times Company. Reprinted by permission.

section). In 1977 President Jimmy Carter, at the recommendation of his domestic policy staff, made her the first woman C.A.B. commissioner, and in 1981, President Reagan named her the agency's first woman vice chairman.

Although there are seven women deans among the country's 617 accredited business schools, Mrs. Bailey is the first to head a Top 10 graduate business school. Of her first 10 faculty appointments, only one was a woman, giving the school a total of five women teachers in a faculty of 70—a still small 7 percent. But her associates say that more women teachers are likely to be appointed soon.

The hurtful comments, intentional or unintentional, that Mrs. Bailey says she has run into during her career—she still feels anger when she recalls a male colleague asking if she was at Bell Lab management meetings to take notes—have given her such a strong antipathy to sexism that, by her own admission, she will sometimes spot sexist slights when none exist. When Carnegie-Mellon officials first tried to interest her in the deanship, she refused to return their calls for three months. "I thought they wanted to interview some woman to show they had done their affirmative action process," she said.

It was not until Allan H. Meltzer, head of the university's selection committee, flew to Washington to personally reassure her that the school meant business that she started taking her candidacy seriously. "We were looking for someone who valued research and would direct the effort toward forthcoming problems," said Professor Meltzer, who insists that the fact that Mrs. Bailey was a woman was a monumental non-issue. "We realize we have to keep moving to stay relevant to problems as they emerge."

Mrs. Bailey has built her career around "relevant" research. While compiling her doctoral dissertation, entitled "Economic Theory of Regulatory Constraint," she became a staunch supporter of government deregulation of the airline industry, a theme that pervaded her five years on the C.A.B. . . .

Mrs. Bailey's career at first centered on immediate applications of technology, rather than policy issues. From 1960 through 1972, she worked in the technical programming department at Bell Labs. She developed a hands-on knowledge of computers, but had little chance to work through her ideas about their relationship to management.

But then, armed with a newly earned Ph.D., Mrs. Bailey transferred in 1972 to the economics department, and spent the next five years focusing on the changes that technology and impending deregulation might bring to the economy in general and to her company specifically. Her economic analysis group at Bell Laboratories is credited with making one of the first hard examinations of where technology was taking the Bell System. The report concluded—somewhat controversially, although prophetically for the mid-1970s—that A.T.&T.'s insistence that it was a "natural monopoly" would not be an economically convincing defense against a breakup.

"We said, 'look, if the government is going to bust you up, there are some ways that are going to be a lot less costly and a lot more efficient than others,'" Mrs. Bailey said. Many of her team's conclusions—for example, that local telephone company operations would not be opened to competition—were realized in the A.T.&T. breakup.

Now Mrs. Bailey says she is trying to infuse Carnegie-Mellon's graduate business school, which produces about 125 M.B.A.'s a year, with the same sort of spirit that she brought to the Bell Labs economic research team . . .

So far, Mrs. Bailey has had fairly smooth sailing in getting her ideas listened to and acted on at Carnegie Mellon. People who have known her in former jobs predict that, should she run into obstacles in the future, her academic colleagues will see a side of her they may not have seen yet: that of a scrapper who will not budge an inch when she believes she is right . . .

Once, while she was a member of the C.A.B., a flight attendant for Eastern Airlines told Mrs. Bailey that she had shown up too late to reserve a seat in the non-smoking section of her flight. Mrs. Bailey, who knew full well that the rules at that time guaranteed a smoke-free seat to anyone who desired one, held her ground. In the loud argument that followed she was called, among other things, a "witch."

Mrs. Bailey got her seat, but she also filed a C.A.B. complaint against Eastern the next day. Frank Borman, Eastern's chairman, showed up at Mrs. Bailey's Washington office a few weeks later to offer her [a] personal apology, and to assure the commissioner that the offending flight attendant would be reprimanded.

. . . Mrs. Bailey is quite open when it comes to her views about business issues, she is far more reticent about her personal life. Born in New York City, the daughter of a professor of medieval history, she has four sisters, most of them still living in the New York area.

Today, Mrs. Bailey, who has been divorced for seven years, lives in what she described as a "Washington D.C.-style townhouse" in the Squirrel Hill section of Pittsburgh with her two sons, James Jr., 20, and William, 18. She divides her time between the university and her hobby of wood-carving.

She resists being characterized by any of her activities. When asked how she would describe herself—an economist? a feminist? a mother? a dean?—she shrugged her shoulders, drew an imaginary line along the edge of her desk with her finger, and thought long and hard before answering. The finally response? "All those things, I guess."

CONCLUSION

In this chapter, we presented data on occupations and earnings of women as compared to men in general, as well as for various subgroups, and briefly discussed the nature of the differences between them. While occupational segregation by sex remains substantial, it has been declining slowly but steadily since the 1960s. The overall gap in the earnings of male and female full-time workers appears to have started to narrow in the late 1970s or early 1980s, although the differential remains quite large. Perhaps most importantly, occupation and earnings differentials have declined significantly for younger cohorts, and an analysis of trends suggests that they are likely to retain at least some of the relative improvement in their earnings position as they age. Further, racial differences in occupations and earnings have declined for both sexes, and black women have posted particularly large relative increases. The next two chapters will thoroughly investigate the possible explanations for the sex differences described here.

Chapter 7

DIFFERENCES IN OCCUPATIONS AND EARNINGS: THE HUMAN CAPITAL MODEL

In this chapter, we present supply-side explanations for the sex differences in earnings and occupations described in Chapter 6. Initially, we simply summarize the arguments of scholars who emphasize this point of view and leave the evaluation of their contributions and the exposition of alternative interpretations for later. In addition, to the extent that supply-side factors are important in causing sex differences in market outcomes, we review government and employer policies that may help to increase women's human capital investments and labor force attachment.

Supply-side explanations focus on the observation that men and women may come to the labor market with different tastes and with different qualifications, such as education, formal training, and experience, or other productivity-related characteristics. Sex differences in tastes might mean, for example, that one group or the other has greater tolerance for an unpleasant, unhealthy, or dangerous environment, for mental or physical strain, boredom, etc. and is more willing to accept these in return for higher wages. Many examples could be offered of sex differences in qualifications related to job performance. A woman may have a college degree in English while a man may have a college degree in Engineering. Or again, while in the labor market, a woman may make different decisions, even when faced with the same economic incentives as a man. For example, a woman may move in and out of the labor force as her family situation changes, while a man's attachment may be more continuous.

Such differences in men's and women's tastes for different types of work, education, and experience could cause women to earn less and to be concentrated in different occupations. Little is known about tastes and their effects on occupational choices and rewards, while there has been a great deal of research on job-related qualifications. Hence, we too shall concentrate on the latter.

Before considering the effects of sex differences in qualifications on earnings and occupations, one issue that arises is whether they should be viewed as the result of the voluntary choices men and women make or as the outcome of what has been termed prelabor market or *societal discrimination*. Societal discrimination denotes the multitude of social influences that cause women to make decisions that adversely influence their status in the labor market. Since we are all products of our environments to a greater or lesser extent, it is often difficult to draw the line between voluntary choice, and this type of discrimination.

This distinction may reflect disciplinary boundaries. The discipline of economics tends to view individual decision-making as determined by economic incentives and individual preferences (or tastes). It does not analyze the formation of preferences and choices are generally viewed as being at least to some extent voluntary. In contrast, sociologists and social psychologists are more apt to examine the role of socialization and social-structural factors in producing what economists classify as individual preferences.[1] Thus, within the context of sociology or social psychology, individual choices are more likely to be seen as stemming from social conditioning or constraints rather than as voluntary.

The tendency to emphasize the role of choice vs. societal discrimination may also reflect an implicit value judgment. Those who are reasonably content with the *status quo* of gender differences in economic outcomes tend to speak mainly of voluntary choices whereas those who decry sex inequality in pay and occupations are more likely to focus on societal discrimination.

We tend towards the view that at least some of the sex differences in qualifications that currently exist stem from undesirable societal discrimination although we acknowledge that, particularly in the past and to a lesser extent today, this type of gender differentiation has been regarded as perfectly appropriate. The most important point is that even if societal discrimination is a problem, it is essentially different from *labor market discrimination* (which is

---

[1]Sociologists might question the appropriateness of the term "discrimination" in the context of gender socialization. We use it here only to the extent that the socialization process adversely affects the labor market success of young women.

discussed in Chapter 8), and a different set of policies is required to deal with it.

A second issue that deserves attention is that distinguishing between supply and demand side factors is not as easy as it may at first appear. Labor market discrimination may affect women's economic status *indirectly* by lowering their incentives to invest in themselves and acquire particular job qualifications. Thus, sex differences in productivity-related characteristics may reflect not only the voluntary choices of men and women and the impact of societal discrimination but also the indirect effects of labor market discrimination. This latter point will be developed further in Chapter 8.

HUMAN CAPITAL

Within the economics literature, the major supply-side explanation for sex differentials in economic outcomes has been developed within the context of the human capital model. Most of us are familiar with the notion of investments in **physical capital.** For example, business people expend resources today to build new plants or to purchase new machinery. This augments their firms' productive capabilities and increases their output in future years. They make such decisions based upon a comparison of the expected costs and benefits of these investments. Economists like Theodore Schultz, Gary Becker, and Jacob Mincer have pointed out that individuals and their families make analogous decisions regarding **human capital** investments.[2] In this case, resources are invested in an individual today in order to increase his or her future productivity and earnings. Examples of human capital investments include expenditures on formal education, on-the-job training, job search, and geographic migration.

While the analogy between physical and human capital is compelling, there are some important differences between the two. Chiefly, an individual's human capital investment decisions will be influenced to a greater extent by nonpecuniary (nonmonetary) considerations than is typically the case for physical capital investment decisions. Some people enjoy going to school while others do not. Some find indoor, white collar work attractive, others would prefer to do manual work in the fresh air. This difference between physical and human capital illustrates the general point that while labor markets are similar to other markets, they are not identical to them—in large part because labor services cannot be separated from the individuals who provide them. This does not invalidate the use of economic analysis in the study of labor markets but does require us to be more aware of the impact of nonpecuniary factors, which can be very important.

[2]See, for example, Theodore W. Schultz, "Investment in Human Capital," *American Economic Review* 51, no. 1 (March 1960): 1–17; Gary S. Becker, *Human Capital: A Theoretical and Empirical Analysis, With Special Reference to Education,* 2nd ed., (Chicago: University of Chicago Press, 1975); Jacob Mincer; "On-the-Job Training: Costs, Returns and Some Implications," *Journal of Political Economy* 70, no. 5, pt. 2, (Oct. 1962), S50–S79.

We first focus upon the pecuniary aspects of the human capital investment decision and then consider how nonpecuniary factors might influence the analysis. We emphasize two major kinds of human capital investments—formal schooling and on-the-job training. According to the work of Jacob Mincer and Solomon Polachek, and other human capital theorists, sex differences in these areas—in both the amount and type of investments to make—can produce substantial differences in the pay and occupations of men and women in the labor market.[3]

SEX DIFFERENCES IN EDUCATIONAL ATTAINMENT

Sex differences in the educational attainment of men and women in the labor force are shown in Table 7.1 for 1962 and 1983.[4] The table shows that the median years of schooling of women workers were the same as that of men in 1983 and actually slightly higher in 1962. However, this overall similarity concealed some significant sex differences in the *pattern* of educational attainment of men and women.

Historically, women have been more likely to complete high school than men, but a higher proportion of men than women have completed college and gone on to post-graduate education. This is reflected in the data for both years shown in the table. For example, in 1983, 20.0 percent of the men, compared to 15.2 percent of the women, had completed less than four years of high school. On the other hand, a higher proportion of men (23.1 percent) than women (18.4 percent) in the labor force had four or more years of college. Among younger male and female workers, however, patterns of educational attainment are more similar than for the labor force as a whole. Among workers aged 25 to 34, 12.7 percent of the men, compared to 9.4 percent of the women, had not completed high school, while 26.5 percent of the women in comparison to 27.2 percent of the men had four or more years of college.

Educational attainment is shown separately by race and Hispanic origin in Table 7.2. We see that, in 1983, both blacks and Hispanics in the labor force had lower educational attainment than whites. The racial differential, however, was fairly small and reflected a considerable increase in the relative

---

[3]See, for example, Jacob Mincer and Solomon Polachek, "Family Investments in Human Capital: Earnings of Women," *Journal of Political Economy* 82, no. 2, pt. 2 (March/April 1974), S76–S108; Elizabeth M. Landes, "Sex Differences in Wages and Employment: A Test of the Specific Capital Hypothesis," *Economic Inquiry* 15, no. 4 (Oct. 1977): 523–38; Harriet Zellner, "The Determinants of Occupational Segregation," ed. Cynthia B. Lloyd, *Sex Discrimination and the Division of Labor* (New York: Columbia University Press, 1975), pp. 125–45.

[4]The patterns of sex differences are similar for the male and female population as a whole. We present data for the labor force because we are interested in education as a potential explanation for sex differences in labor market outcomes.

TABLE 7.1   Educational Attainment of the Labor Force by Sex, 1962, 1983[a]

YEARS OF SCHOOL COMPLETED	1962		1983	
	MALES (%)	FEMALES (%)	MALES (%)	FEMALES (%)
Total	100.0	100.0	100.0	100.0
Less than 4 years of high school	48.0	39.4	20.0	15.2
4 years of high school only	29.6	39.7	38.6	45.8
1 to 3 years of college	10.5	11.2	18.4	20.6
4 or more years of college	11.9	9.7	23.1	18.4
Median school years completed	12.1	12.3	12.8	12.8

[a]Data are for workers aged 18 to 64 in March of each year.

Source: U.S. Department of Labor, Bureau of Labor Statistics, Special Labor Force Report Bulletin #2191 (April 1984), Table B-1, p. 10.

educational attainment of blacks, particularly since the 1960s. For example, in 1962, the median years of school completed by black males were 3.1 years less than that of white males, but the gap was only 0.4 years in 1983. Among females, the racial difference in median educational attainment declined from 1.8 years in 1962 to 0.2 years in 1983. The Hispanic-white differential was larger than the racial difference in 1983 but had declined slightly since statistics began to be collected separately for Hispanics in 1974.

Among minority workers, women actually had higher educational attainment than men. In the case of blacks, this reflects the higher educational attainment of women in the population as a whole (including non-labor force participants). Among the Hispanic population, however, the educational attainment of women was not higher than men's. Females in the labor force had more years of schooling than males because of the tendency of more highly educated women to be more inclined to participate in the labor force.

The trends in higher education by sex, shown in greater detail in Table 7.3, reinforce our impression of declining sex differences among younger cohorts. As may be seen in the table, the proportion of Bachelor's and Master's degrees awarded to women was about 50 percent in 1981. While women received a substantially smaller proportion of doctorates and first-professional degrees than men in 1981, this represented a substantial increase of the female share since the mid-1960s.

The figures on educational attainment reveal only part of the story of sex differences in formal schooling, however. For at each level of education, men and women differ substantially in the types of courses they take and their fields of specialization. For example, data for the early 1970s show that at the secondary level, women took fewer courses in natural sciences and

TABLE 7.2   Educational Attainment of the Labor Force by Sex, Race and Hispanic Origin, 1983[a]

YEARS OF SCHOOL COMPLETED	WHITES		BLACKS		HISPANICS	
	MALES (%)	FEMALES (%)	MALES (%)	FEMALES (%)	MALES (%)	FEMALES (%)
Less than 4 years of high school	21.1	16.9	34.0	25.3	48.1	41.0
4 years of high school only	37.6	44.9	39.8	43.5	30.4	35.9
1 to 3 years of college	17.9	20.0	15.9	19.5	13.5	14.5
4 or more years of college	23.4	18.2	10.3	11.7	8.0	8.6
Median school years completed	12.8	12.7	12.4	12.6	12.1	12.3

[a]Data are for workers aged 16 and over.

Source: U.S. Department of Labor, Bureau of Labor Statistics, *Special Labor Force Report*, Bulletin 2191 (April 1984), Table B-2, pp. 12–14.

TABLE 7.3   Percentage of Degrees Awarded to Women, by Level of Degree, 1930–1981 (Selected Years)

YEAR	BACHELOR'S (%)	MASTER'S (%)	DOCTOR'S (%)	FIRST PROFESSIONAL (%)
1930	39.9[a]	40.4	15.4	n.a.
1966	42.6	33.8	11.6	4.5
1971	43.4	40.1	14.3	6.3
1975	45.3	44.8	21.3	12.4
1981	49.8	50.3	31.1	26.6

[a]Includes first professional degrees.

Sources: U.S. Department of Labor, Women's Bureau, *Trends in Educational Attainment of Women,* October 1969, Table 5, p. 16; Curtis O. Baker, *Earned Degrees Conferred: An Examination of Recent Trends,* National Center for Educational Statistics, undated, Table 3, p. 10; U.S. Department of Health Education and Welfare, Office of Education, "Earned Degrees Conferred, 1965–66;" U.S. Department of Education, National Center for Educational Statistics, "Earned Degrees Conferred, 1980–81."

mathematics than men. In terms of vocational courses, they were more likely to take commercial (including secretarial) training and home economics and less likely to take trade or industrial arts.[5] Table 7.4 shows that there were also substantial differences between men and women in fields of specialization at the college level in 1981, but that they had narrowed considerably over the preceding 15 years. Women also posted large gains in the proportion of first professional degrees awarded to them in traditionally male professions (Table 7.5).

In summary, we find that the equality between men and women in median educational attainment conceals some important sex differences that may have an impact on women's earnings and occupational attainment in the labor market. Historically, women have been more likely than men to complete high school, but a higher proportion of men than of women have completed four or more years of college. Further, at both the level of secondary and higher education, men and women tend to differ in their fields of specialization. However, all these differences have been narrowing in recent years.

We now turn to a consideration of the human capital theorists' explanation for the historical tendency of men and women to acquire different

[5]Robert H. Meyer, *An Economic Analysis of High School Voational Education: I. Vocational Education: How Should it be Measured?* Project Report, The Urban Institute, 1981, cited in June O'Neill, "Women and the Labor Market: A Survey of Issues and Policies in the United States" (mimeo, The Urban Institute, November 1981); and Carol Ireson, "Girls' Socialization for Work," eds. Ann H. Stromberg and Shirley Harkess, *Women Working: Theories and Facts in Perspective,* (Palo Alto: Mayfield, 1978), pp. 176–200.

TABLE 7.4 **Percentage of Bachelor's Degrees Awarded to Women by Discipline, 1966 and 1981 (Selected Fields)**

DISCIPLINE	1966 (%)	1981 (%)
Agriculture	2.7	30.8
Architecture	4.0	18.3
Biological sciences	28.2	44.1
Business	8.5	36.7
Computer and information science	13.0[a]	32.5
Education	75.3	75.0
Engineering	0.4	10.3
English and English literature	66.2	66.5
Foreign languages	70.7	75.6
Health	76.9	83.5
Home economics	97.5	95.0
Mathematics	33.3	42.8
Physical sciences	13.6	24.6
Psychology	41.0	65.0
Social sciences	35.0	44.2
Economics	9.8	30.5
History	34.6	37.9
Sociology	59.6	69.6

[a]Data are for 1969, the earliest year available.

Source: U.S. Department of Health, Education and Welfare, Office of Education, "Earned Degrees Conferred: 1965–66;" U.S. Department of Education, National Center for Education Statistics, "Earned Degrees Conferred, 1980–81."

TABLE 7.5 **Percentage of First Professional Degrees Awarded to Women by Discipline, 1966 and 1981 (Selected Fields)**

FIELD	1966 (%)	1981 (%)
Dentistry	1.1	14.4
Medicine	6.7	24.7
Pharmacy	16.4	42.6
Veterinary Medicine	8.0[a]	35.2
Law	3.8	32.4
Theological professions	4.1	14.0

[a]Data are for 1968, the earliest year available.

Source: U.S. Department of Health, Education and Welfare, Office of Education, "Earned Degrees Conferred, 1965–66;" U.S. Department of Education, National Center for Educational Statistics, "Earned Degrees Conferred, 1980–81."

amounts of education and to specialize in different fields. We then consider the consequences of these decisions for sex differentials in labor market outcomes according to this model.

THE EDUCATIONAL INVESTMENT
DECISON

We begin by considering an individual's decision whether or not to invest in formal education as illustrated in Figure 7.1. Here we consider Daniel's choice between going to college and ending his formal education with high school. Initially, we focus solely upon the pecuniary costs and benefits of investing in education, although later we consider psychic (nonpecuniary) costs and benefits as well. This decision entails a comparison of the expected **experience-earnings profile,** which shows the annual earnings associated with each level of labor market experience, for each type of schooling.

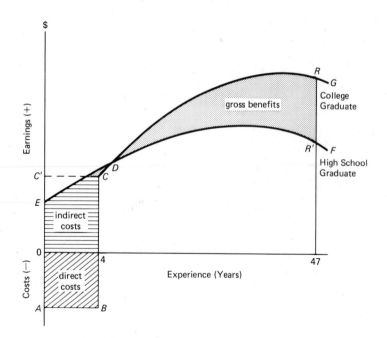

FIGURE 7.1   The Educational Investment Decision

In this case, Daniel expects his profile to be *EF* if he enters the labor market after completing high school. Alternatively, if he goes on to college, he will incur out-of-pocket expenses on tuition and books of *OA* dollars per year (negative "earnings") for the four year period. (He does not anticipate working during school.) Upon graduation, he expects to earn *OC'* dollars. The investment in a college education is believed to increase his productivity and, hence, his earnings above what he could have earned entering the labor force directly after high school (*OE*). While he initially earns less than he could have if he had worked for four years rather than going to college, over his work life his expected earnings are higher. His experience-earnings profile, if he goes to college, is *ABCG*.

As indicated in Figure 7.1, the earnings of both high school and college graduates are expected to increase with labor market experience over much of the individual's work life. Human capital theorists attribute this to the productivity enhancing effects of on-the-job training, which we discuss later in this chapter. Note that Figure 7.1 shows the college graduate's profile as rising more steeply than that of the high school graduate. This has indeed been found to be the case empirically and suggests that college graduates acquire more training informally on-the-job as well as formally in school.

Now let us consider how Daniel can use the information in Figure 7.1 to make his investment decision. To do so he considers both the incremental costs and the incremental benefits associated with graduating from college. There are two types of costs of schooling that he must take into account. **Direct costs** are expenditures on such items as tuition and fees and books. Less obvious, but no less important than direct costs, are the earnings foregone during the time an individual is in school. These **indirect costs** correspond to the opportunity costs of schooling. We have assumed that Daniel does not work while attending college, but even if he did work, his foregone earnings are still likely to be substantial—college students seldom work as many hours or for as high a wage as workers who are not enrolled in school. The full costs of a college education are equal to the sum of the direct and indirect costs or area *EABCD*.

The gross benefits of a college education are given by the excess of the expected earnings of a college graduate over those of a high school graduate over the work life. The size of these benefits depends on the length of the expected work life. If Daniel expects to work 43 years after college until retirement at age 65, his benefits are equal to the shaded area *DRR'*.

For Daniel to decide in favor of a college education (on an economic basis) , the *gross benefits* of this investment must exceed the costs, i.e., the *net benefits* must be positive. Further, gross benefits must exceed costs by an amount sufficient to give him an adequate return on his investment. Individuals may differ on the rate of return required to induce them to undertake this investment, but all are likely to require a positive rate of return.

For one thing, instead of investing resources in human capital, Daniel could have put his money into a savings bank or invested it in other assets. Those alternatives provide a positive rate of return and, thus, his human capital investment must also do so in order to be competitive. More fundamentally, Daniel, like most people, prefers income (and the opportunity to spend it) now to income (and the opportunity to spend it) later. To induce him to delay his gratification and receive his income later rather than sooner, the market has to offer him (and others like him) an inducement in the form of a positive rate of return. In Daniel's case, the investment does appear profitable, and he is likely to decide to go on to college. Actual estimates of the average private rate of return to a college education range from 10 to 15 percent.[6] Numerous studies have confirmed that earnings rise with additional education for both men and women, although not necessarily to the same extent (this is illustrated in Table 6.8 of Chapter 6).

EDUCATION AND PRODUCTIVITY

Human capital theorists believe that earnings rise with additional education because of the productivity-enhancing effects of education. Intuitively, it seems reasonable that education imparts a variety of skills and knowledge that would potentially be useful on the job, ranging from specific skills like computer programming and accounting to general skills like reasoning ability, writing skills, and proficiency in solving mathematical problems. Educational institutions may also teach certain behaviors that are valued on the job like punctuality, following instructions and habits of predictability and dependability.[7]

Others have suggested an alternative interpretation of the positive relationship between education and earnings in which education functions solely as a **screening device** or a signal.[8] In this view, employers have imperfect infor-

[6]See, for example, Walter W. McMahon and Alan P. Wagner, "The Monetary Returns to Education as Partial Social Efficiency Criteria," *Financing Education, Overcoming Inefficiency and Inequity* (Urbana: University of Illinois Press, 1982), pp. 150–87; George Psacharopoulos, "Returns to Education: An Updated International Comparison," *Comparative Education* 17, no. 3 (1981): 337–28. Calculating the rate of return involves estimating the increase in earnings attributable to additional education as well as all the costs involved in acquiring it, including both foregone earnings and out-of-pocket expenses, then relating the former to the latter. For a critical review of the empirical literature testing the human capital approach, see Mark Blaug, "The Empirical Status of Human Capital Theory: A Slightly Jaundiced Survey," *Journal of Economic Literature* 14, no. 3 (September 1976): 827–55.

[7]The importance of such behavioral traits has been particularly emphasized by radical economists, see, for example, Richard C. Edwards, "Individual Traits and Organizational Incentives: What Makes a 'Good' Worker?" *The Journal of Human Resources* 11, no. 1 (Winter 1976): 51–68.

[8]See, especially, Michael Spence, *Market Signalling* (Cambridge, Mass.: Harvard University Press, 1974).

mation on worker productivity and, thus, seek ways to distinguish more productive applicants from less productive applicants before hiring them. At the same time, it is assumed that more able (productive) individuals find the (psychic and monetary) costs of acquiring additional schooling lower than the less able (say because they find their studies less arduous or because they are awarded scholarships). Having lower costs, an educational investment may be profitable for the more able when it would not be for the less able. In an extreme version of the signalling model, education is rewarded *solely* because it *signals* higher productivity to the employer and *not* because of any skills it imparts.

Unfortunately, this theoretical disagreement between the human capital and signalling models has proved difficult to resolve empirically. This is the case because the issue is a particularly thorny one—not whether more education is correlated with higher productivity and earnings, but *why*.[9] From the individual's perspective, however, it does not matter whether education raises earnings by increasing productivity or by signalling greater ability. Thus, the decision-making process illustrated in Figure 7.1 would be unaffected.

Nonetheless, there is one potential consequence of the signalling model for sex differences in labor market outcomes that is worth noting. If employers believe that a given level of education signals lower productivity for a woman than for a man, women may have to have higher educational credentials than men to obtain the same job. So, for example, suppose an employer who is hiring for entry-level management positions believes that a college education signals a lower commitment to the labor market for women than for men. He or she may require a woman to have an MBA degree in order to obtain employment, while being perfectly willing to hire a man with only a college degree.[10] This is quite similar to the notion of **statistical discrimination** to be discussed in Chapter 8.

SEX DIFFERENCES IN EDUCATIONAL
INVESTMENT DECISIONS

Does this analysis suggest that men and women may decide to acquire different amounts and/or types of formal education? According to the analysis we have presented, the major factors to consider are the expected costs and benefits of

[9]For a summary of this literature, see Blaug, "The Empirical Status of Human Capital Theory;" see also, John Riley, "Testing the Educational Screening Hypothesis," *Journal of Political Economy* 87, no. 5, pt. 2 (October 1979): S227–S252.

[10]Such "qualifications" discrimination has been emphasized by Dolores A. Conway and Harry V. Roberts, "Reverse Regression, Fairness and Employment Discrimination," *Journal of Business and Economic Statistics* 1, no. 1 (January 1983): 75–85; and Richard F. Kamelich and Solomon W. Polachek, "Discrimination: Fact or Fiction? An Examination Using an Alternative Approach," *Southern Economic Journal* 49, no. 2 (October 1982): 450–61.

the investment. Realistically, the definitions of costs and benefits may be extended to include psychic (nonpecuniary), as well as pecuniary, costs and benefits, and we do so below. In addition, since individuals may find it hard to borrow to finance their human capital investments, access to funds is a further consideration of some importance. Thus, we will want to consider why men and women might differ in these respects.

Expected Work Life

The major factor emphasized by human capital theorists, as producing sex differences in human capital investments, is that, given traditional roles in the family, many women anticipate shorter, more disrupted work lives than men. Such women will reach the point sooner when additional investment is no longer worthwhile. Further, it will not pay for them to make the types of human capital investments that require sustained, high-level commitment to the labor force to make them profitable and that depreciate rapidly during periods of work interruptions.

The impact of these factors is illustrated in Figure 7.2 where we have reproduced the earnings profiles shown in Figure 7.1. Note that the horizontal

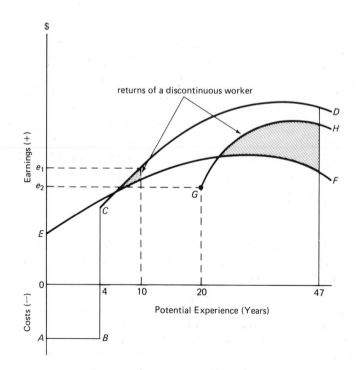

FIGURE 7.2   **The Impact of Expected Work Life on the Education Investment Decision**

axis now refers to potential experience or the total time elapsed. We have done this in order to be able to represent periods of time out of the labor force on this diagram.

A career-oriented woman who anticipates working the same number of years as Daniel will find it equally profitable to invest in a college education, assuming she faces similar costs and has the opportunity to reap the same returns. However, a woman who expects to spend fewer years in the labor market will find her benefits correspondingly reduced.

For example, suppose Adele plans to work for a time—6 years—after college and then to drop out of the labor force for 10 years, say for childrearing. If she, like Daniel, expects to retire at age 65, her expected work life is 33 years in comparison to his 43 years. Her shorter work life reduces the benefits of her human capital investment because she does not earn income during the time she spends out of the labor force. Further, human capital theorists believe that skills depreciate during time spent out of the labor force—that is, when they are not used. They expect that upon her return to the labor force after an interruption of 10 years, Adele's earnings of e_2 will be less than she was making when she left (e_1) and that she will be faced with profile *GH* rather than profile *CD*. We have shown profile *GH* as approaching *CD* over time as Adele retools or becomes less rusty.[11] Nonetheless, the time out of the labor force has cost her a reduction in earnings over the remainder of her working life. In this particular example, the benefits of the investment in a college education, the sum of the two shaded areas, may not be large enough to make it worthwhile.

Thus, the human capital model shows how an adherence to traditional sex roles in the family can explain why women have been less likely than men to pursue college and graduate study. It also suggests one reason why sex differences in college attendance have been declining. As we saw in Chapter 4, women have increased their labor force participation. As young women anticipate longer and more continuous working lives, it will be more profitable for them to increase their investment in formal education. Further, Figure 7.2 suggests that once women have decided to acquire higher education, for whatever reason, their attachment to the labor force is reinforced since the opportunity cost of time spent out of the labor force is increased.

Although the human capital model suggests a plausible explanation for the historical tendency of men to be more likely to pursue college and graduate study, it does not explain why women have tended in the past to be *more* likely than men to complete high school. The sex disparity was quite sizable at one

---

[11]For empirical evidence that earnings tend to "rebound" after work force interruptions, see Mary Corcoran, "Work Experience, Labor Force Withdrawals and Women's Earnings: Empirical Results Using the 1976 Panel Survey of Income Dynamics," eds. Cynthia B. Lloyd, Emily Andrews, and Curtis L. Gilroy, *Women in the Labor University* (New York: Columbia University Press, 1979), pp. 216–245; Jacob Mincer and Hiram Ofek, "Interrupted Work Careers: Depreciation and Restoration of Human Capital," *Journal of Human Resources* 17, no. 1 (Winter 1982): 3–24 and Mary Corcoran, Greg J. Duncan, and Michael Ponza, "Longitudinal Analysis of White Women's Wages," *Journal of Human Resources* 18, no. 4 (Fall 1983): 497–520.

time. For example, in the year 1900, 56,808 young women graduated from high school in comparison to 38,075 young men. One possible explanation for this difference is that the opportunity cost of remaining in high school was lower for young women than for young men, since their potential labor market earnings were less. As job opportunities for young men who have not finished high school have declined, so too has the sex differential in high school completion.

Human capital theorists believe that discontinuity of expected labor force participation also helps to explain sex differences in fields of specialization. In some fields, as in science and engineering, technological change progresses rapidly. A woman returning from a labor force interruption will not only have to contend with her depreciation of skills over the interim but also with the advancement of the field during her absence. On the other hand, in such other fields as teaching history or English, the pace of technological progress is slower. A woman returning from a work force interruption is likely to find that her earnings fall less steeply. Women anticipating traditional roles are, therefore, expected to avoid fields where the rate of technological change is rapid and to concentrate in fields where the cost of work force interruptions is lower. [12] Again, women's increasing labor force attachment may partially explain their increased representation in traditionally male fields of study.

Societal Discrimination

While expected working life is a factor that has been particularly emphasized by human capital theorists, societal discrimination may also cause sex differences in educational attainment and field of specialization. To see this we must consider the psychic as well as the pecuniary costs and benefits of human capital investments. Societal influences may raise the costs of and/or lower the returns to specific types or levels of education for women relative to men. At these higher costs, and/or lower returns, the investment in education may not prove profitable for many women.

This situation is particularly apt to arise in fields that have traditionally been predominantly male. Moreover, it is important to bear in mind that social pressures also help to cause the sex differences in labor force participation emphasized by the human capital theorists. In addition, to some extent it is the lower labor market earnings available to women (due to labor market discrimination) that cause their lower labor force participation, not only *vice versa* (feedback effects of labor market discrimination are considered in greater detail in Chapter 8).

---

[12]For evidence in support of lifetime work commitment as a factor causing sex differences in college major, see Solomon W. Polachek, "Sex Differences in College Major," *Industrial and Labor Relations Review* 31, no. 4 (July 1978): 498–508.

Socialization. At the most basic level, the socialization process influences the occupational orientation of men and women, as well as the role they expect work to occupy in their lives.[13] The socialization process is the name given to the way in which individuals' attitudes and behaviors are shaped by the influence of their family, friends, teachers, and the media. We have already shown in the preceding section how sex differences in the expected importance of market work in their lives may influence men's and women's human capital investment decisions.

The consequences of sex differences in occupational orientation are also important. From an early age, boys and girls are taught to aspire to and train for sex appropriate lines of work. This tends to result in sex differences in fields of specialization. Further, even if, despite these influences, a young woman does form a desire to enter a traditionally male field, the disapproval of her family, teachers, or friends is a psychic cost for her that lowers her subjective evaluation of the net value of this investment.[14] Familial disapproval may also pose practical problems for a young woman, if her family is more reluctant to finance her education than her brother's.

Gender appropriate traits and competencies. Social influences may operate in other ways that are less direct but no less influential. For example, women may be socialized to emphasize appropriate "feminine" personality traits like being subordinate, nurturant, and emotional. Traditionally male fields may be stereotyped as requiring "masculine" personality traits like dominance, competitiveness, and rationality. Having internalized the idea of what is properly female, women may then avoid male fields because they perceive a psychic cost in acting in an "unfeminine" manner or simply because they feel unequipped to do so. In the latter case, they might expect to be less successful in the field, thus lowering their expected returns. Similarly, if women are reared to believe they lack competence in "masculine" subjects like math and science, this would raise their perceived costs and lower their

---

[13]For descriptions of the impact of the socialization process on the occupations and economic success of men and women, see, for example, Margaret M. Marini and Mary C. Brinton, "Sex Stereotyping in Occupational Socialization," ed. Barbara Reskin, *Sex Segregation in the Work Place: Trends, Explanations, and Remedies* (Washington, D.C.: National Academy Press, 1984); Ireson, "Girls Socialization for Work;" and Lenore J. Weitzman, "Sex-Role Socialization: A Focus on Women," ed. Jo Freeman, *Women: A Feminist Perspective,* 3rd. ed., pp. 157–237.

[14]One study found that women graduate students in the biological and physical sciences received less moral support from their mothers than either the male students in their own field or students of either sex in education. See Helen M. Berg and Marianne A. Ferber, "Men and Women Graduate Students: Who Succeeds and Why?" *Journal of Higher Education* 54, no. 6 (November/December 1983): 629–48.

perceived returns to entry into fields emphasizing this knowledge.[15] Men may see traditionally female fields as inappropriate for similar reasons.

Fear of success. There has been concern that given traditional sex roles, even academic or career success itself may bring with it psychic costs for women. Experiments originally conducted by psychologist Matina Horner in the mid-1960s were interpreted as showing that college women were ambivalent about the desire or need to achieve and what she termed the "motive to avoid success."[16] She suggested that the latter stemmed from the fear of many women that *professional* success would be accompanied by negative *social* consequences. In other words, they feared that men would be less interested in a woman who did extremely well in her studies or career, particularly in a "male" field. Men did not face a similar problem in that, given their provider role, academic and career success would be viewed as enhancing their attractiveness to women.

While Horner's work received a great deal of popular attention, efforts to replicate this research were often unsuccessful. Further, to the extent that this conflict exists or did exist for women, it has not been shown that it necessarily affects their performance. Indeed, at each educational level, young women regularly receive higher grades,[17] although the sex gap narrows with adolescence and presumably greater awareness of social pressures.[18]

Biased evaluations. Even women's possession of "male" traits or competencies and their willingness to display them may not guarantee them an equal amount of success. Studies have found that, among both female and male college students, identical papers were given higher ratings on such dimensions as value, persuasiveness, profundity, writing style, and competence when respondents believed the author to be male rather than female. Similar findings have been obtained in studies requiring both women and men to evaluate the qualifications of applicants for employment.[19] The expectation

[15]For analyses of gender differences in attitudes towards, and competence in, mathematics see Weitzman, "Sex-Role Socialization;" and Sheila Tobias, *Overcoming Math Anxiety* (New York: W. W. Norton, 1978), Ch. 3.

[16]Matina S. Horner, "Fail: Bright Women," *Psychology Today* 3, no. 6 (November 1969): 36, 38, 69. For a review of the results of later studies, see Martha Mednick, Sandra Tangri, and Lois Hoffman, eds., *Women and Achievement* (New York: John Wiley and Sons, 1975).

[17]*Climbing the Academic Ladder: Doctoral Women Scientists in Academe,* National Academy of Sciences, The National Research Council Committee on the Education and Employment of Women in Science and Engineering, Commission on Human Resources (Washington, D.C.: 1979).

[18]The decline in mathematical performance is particularly pronounced, see Weitzman, "Sex-Role Socialization."

[19]See the studies cited in Virginia E. O'Leary and Ranald D. Hansen, "Trying Hurts Women, Helps Men: The Meaning of Effort," ed. H. John Bernardin, *Women in the Work Force* (New York: Praeger, 1982), pp. 102–4.

of inferior performance may eventually cause that inferior performance. Even if it does not, it would lower the expected return to investments in educational credentials.

Discrimination by educational institutions. Discrimination against women in the course of their studies, particularly in male fields, may increase the psychic costs of obtaining the education and/or lower the returns to their investment. It is well to remember that overt discrimination against women in admission to college and professional school was pervasive in the not too distant past. In America, women were not admitted to higher education until 1837 when Oberlin College opened its doors.[20] Women did not gain entrance to medical school until 1847, and it was not until 1915 that the American Medical Association accepted women members. As late as 1869, the U.S. Supreme Court upheld the refusal of the Illinois State Bar to admit a woman. One of the justices declared that "the natural and proper timidity and delicacy which belongs to the female sex evidently unfit it for many of the occupations of civil life."[21] Nonetheless, a year later, in 1870, the first woman did succeed in graduating from an American law school.

Even after these "firsts," women were not universally admitted to all institutions of higher education in all fields for a very long time. The prestigious Harvard Medical School did not admit women until 1945 while the Harvard Law School excluded women until 1950. Similarly, many highly respected undergraduate institutions, like Princeton and Yale, remained male-only until the late 1960s or early 1970s. Others, like Harvard and Columbia, granted women access to classes and some facilities but officially restricted them to a separate college.

Moreover, the opening of doors to women did not necessarily mean that the doors opened as widely for them as for men. Women continued in many cases to be discriminated against in admissions and financial aid policies long after they gained formal admittance. In some cases, women were held to higher standards than men; in others, overt or informal quotas limited the number of places available to them.[22] Often course requirements for male and female high school students were different, and at all levels, sex-based counseling was prevalent.

Policy issue: The role of government in combatting discrimination. These were the types of policies that Title IX of the Education Amendments (to the Civil Rights Act of 1964), passed by Congress in 1972, was intended to

[20]The information on admission of women is from Michelle Patterson and Laurie Engleberg, "Women in Male-Dominated Professions," eds. Stromberg and Harkness, *Women Working*, pp. 266–292.

[21]Cited in Patterson and Engleberg, "Women in Male-Dominated Professions," p. 277.

[22]See, for example, Ann Sutherland Harris, "The Second Sex in Academe," *AAUP Bulletin* 56, no. 3 (Fall 1970): pp. 283–95 and references therein.

remedy. It prohibits discrimination on the basis of sex in any educational program or activity receiving federal financial assistance and covers admissions, financial aid, access to programs and activities, as well as employment of teachers and other personnel.

The main provisions relevant at the high school level are that all courses and programs except sex instruction, chorus, and contact sports must be available to both males and females. At the university level, the most important provisions probably are for equal availability of scholarships and fellowships, assistantships, research opportunities, and housing.

Even though a variety of schools are exempt from these provisions,[23] and enforcement has not been rigorous, there can be no doubt that this legislation has contributed to the substantial changes in the extent and type of participation of women in the educational system that we have noted. A 1984 Supreme Court decision restricting the application of Title IX only to the specific program receiving federal funds may, however, reduce future effects of this law in providing equal educational opportunities for women.[24]

Subtle barriers. While most of these overt barriers have been removed, it is important to bear in mind that they did place serious limits on the educational options of older women. Thus, their impact continues to be reflected in the *current* occupational distribution of women. Further, subtle barriers to women's success in the study of traditionally male fields remain a problem.[25]

Just the male dominance of a given field itself can discourage young women from attempting to enter. In this way, past discrimination continues to have an impact on younger women. Lacking contact with or first-hand knowledge of successful women, they may assume (quite possibly erroneously) that they too would not be able to succeed. Even if they believe that times have changed and that their prospects for success are greater than indicated by the present low representation of women, the scarcity of women may still pose problems for them, limiting their eventual success and lowering the returns to entering predominantly male fields. For example, without older women to serve as **role models**, female entrants face more confusion about acceptable (or

[23]Among those that may be exempt are single-sex, private, undergraduate schools and public undergraduate schools that have been segregated since their inception, as well as religious and military schools.

[24]In the specific case, the Supreme Court upheld the Reagan Administration's contention that only the financial aid office at Grove City College was subject to Title IX regulations, even though the federal funds going to the students eventually reach the general operating budget of the college.

[25]These types of subtle barriers are well-described in Cynthia Fuchs Epstein, *Women's Place: Options and Limits in Professional Careers* (Berkeley: University of California Press, 1970); Mary Frank Fox, "Women and Higher Education: Sex Differentials in the Status of Students and Scholars," ed. Freeman, *Women: A Feminist Perspective*; and Rosabeth Kanter, *Men and Women of the Corporation* (New York: Basic Books, 1977).

successful) modes of dress and behavior than do young men. They also lack access to the knowledge that older women have acquired about successful strategies for combining work roles and family responsibilities. Thus, they are forced to be pioneers, and blazing a new trail is undoubtedly more difficult than following along a well-established path.

Women students may also be excluded from the informal relationships desirable for eventual career success. Older individuals who are well-established in the field (mentors) often take promising young students (proteges) under their wing—informally socializing them into the norms of the field, giving them access to the latest research in the area, and tying them into their network of professional contacts.

The **mentor-protege system** is generally the result of the older individual identifying with the younger person. Male mentors may simply not identify with young women. They may possibly fear that the development of a close relationship with a young woman would be misunderstood by their colleagues and/or their wives.[26] Thus, women students are likely to be at a disadvantage in a predominantly male field. Their problems will be aggravated if male students neglect to include them in their **informal network.** Such informal contacts among students include study groups and discussions over lunches, sports, coffee breaks, or a Friday afternoon beer, where important information about the field and career opportunities are exchanged.

Thus, women often lack the support, encouragement, and access to information and job opportunities provided by informal contacts between teachers and students and among students, as well as female role models to emulate. This raises the psychic costs for them in comparison to otherwise similar male students, lowering their incentives to enter traditionally male fields. It also may result in their being less successful than comparable men in the field when they complete their studies. To the extent that they foresee this, their entry into predominantly male fields is further discouraged. Finally, labor market discrimination itself can adversely affect the incentives of women to invest in formal schooling insofar as it results in a lower return on their investment. We shall consider this possibility in greater detail in the next chapter.

ON-THE-JOB TRAINING

One of the major insights of human capital theory is the observation that individuals can increase their productivity not only through their investment in formal education but also by learning important work skills while they are ac-

---

[26]For evidence that lack of mentors is a problem for female graduate students, see, Berg and Ferber, ''Men and Women Graduate Students.''

tually on the job.[27] Sometimes they participate in formal training programs sponsored by their employers. More often they benefit from the informal instruction of their supervisors or coworkers and grow proficient at their jobs through repetition and trial-and-error. Human capital theorists argue that women's weaker attachment to the labor force, and their resulting lesser amount of labor market experience, means that they will acquire less of this valuable on-the-job training. Further, their expectation of spending fewer years in the labor market could result in their making smaller investments in this type of training than men during each year they spend on the job. As will be discussed in Chapter 8, women may also be denied equal access to on-the-job training.

SEX DIFFERENCES IN LABOR MARKET EXPERIENCE

Before developing these ideas further, let us look at the actual extent of sex differences in work experience and labor force attachment. Unfortunately, this information is not routinely collected by the government on a regular basis but must be pieced together from various special surveys.

The data in Table 7.6 illustrate average sex differences in work history and labor force attachment in 1975 among employed workers, aged 18 to 64. The difference column shows the male mean minus the female mean. Thus, a positive number indicates that the male mean is larger than the female mean and a negative number indicates that the female mean is larger than the male mean. Among both whites and blacks, women had, on the average, less work experience and more labor force interruptions than men. On average, women spent three to five more years out of the labor force than men since completing their formal schooling. They averaged one to three years less work experience prior to their present job and two to three years less tenure with their current employer. They also completed fewer years of training on their job than men and spent a smaller proportion of their years in the labor market engaged in full-time (as opposed to part-time) work.

Table 7.6 also shows that differentials in work histories are larger among whites than among blacks. This reflects, in part, the smaller amount of work experience of black men than of white men, perhaps in part due to their higher unemployment rates. It also reflects the higher labor force participation rates of black women than of white women over their work lives—counterbalancing the effect of black women's higher unemployment rates. Black women's labor

---

[27]See, for example, Becker, *Human Capital*; Mincer, "On-the-Job Training: Cost, Returns and Some Implications;" and Walter Oi, "Labor as a Quasi-Fixed Factor," *Journal of Policital Economy* 70, no. 6 (December 1962): 538–55.

TABLE 7.6 Means of Variables Indicating Work History and Labor Force Attachment of Employed Workers, Aged 18 to 64, 1975

VARIABLES	WHITES			BLACKS		
	MEN	WOMEN	DIFFERENCE[a]	MEN	WOMEN	DIFFERENCE[a]
Work History						
Years out of labor force since completing school	0.51	5.75	−5.24	0.63	4.03	−3.40
Years of work experience before present employer	11.27	8.05	3.22	10.44	9.27	1.17
Years of tenure with current employer[b]	8.78	5.79	2.99	8.06	6.47	1.59
Years of training completed on current job	1.69	0.72	0.97	0.79	0.70	0.09
Proportion of total working years that were full-time	0.91	0.79	0.12	0.91	0.83	0.08
Formal education (in years)	12.85	12.73	0.12	10.96	11.75	−0.79
Labor Force Attachment						
Hours of work missed due to own illness	36.5	43.0	−6.5	50.4	58.0	−7.6
Hours of work missed due to illnesses of others	4.0	12.5	−8.5	8.1	25.7	−17.6
Percent who place limits on job hours or location	14.5	34.2	−19.7	12.2	21.6	−9.4
Percent who plan to stop work for nontraining reasons	3.0	8.6	−5.6	1.7	6.8	5.1

[a]Computed as the male mean minus the female mean.
[b]Calculated as the sum of the mean lengths of the various tenure segments reported by Corcoran and Duncan.

Source: Mary Corcoran and Greg J. Duncan, "Work History, Labor Force Attachment, and Earnings Differences Between the Races and Sexes," *The Journal of Human Resources* 14 (Winter 1979), Table 1, pp. 8–10. Reprinted by permission of the publisher.

force interruptions averaged two years less than those of white women, and their total years of work experience (prior to and on the current job) averaged two years more.

Sex differences in the priority placed on market work are also suggested by the differences between men and women in the means of the variables listed under the heading Labor Force Attachment. For both race groups, the average hours missed from work over the past year due to their own illness or the illnesses of others was higher for women than for men. Women were also more likely than men to place limits on the hours or location of their jobs (possibly to facilitate the meshing of work and family responsibilities) and to plan to stop working at some point for nontraining reasons. On the average, black women were less likely than white women to place limits on their jobs or to plan to stop working. They did, however, miss more hours from work due to illnesses of themselves or others. Of course, this is not solely a measure of work commitment. Black families are less healthy, on the average, due in part to their lower incomes.[28] They also tend to have a larger number of children.

The data presented in Table 7.6 suggest that women in the labor market,

TABLE 7.7   Average Proportion of Years Worked by Employed Women Since Leaving School, for Various Age Groups and Years

AGE GROUP AND YEAR	WHITES	BLACKS
25–29 years		
1973	.67	.56
1978	.79	.70
30–34 years		
1967	.63	.63
1978	.67	.63
35–39 years		
1967	.59	.63
1972	.63	.66
40–44 years		
1967	.57	.67
1972	.59	.68
1977	.62	.68
45–49 years		
1972	.59	.72
1977	.61	.68

Source: June O'Neill, "The Trend in the Male-Female Wage Gap in the United States," *Journal of Labor Economics* 2, no. 4 (Jan. 1985 Supp.), Table 7. Copyright ©1984 by the University of Chicago. All rights reserved. Reprinted by permission of the publisher.

[28]According to a report released by the Department of Human Services, blacks and other minorities have persistently suffered higher rates of death, illness, and disability than whites, *New York Times,* January 18, 1984.

TABLE 7.8 Tenure on Current Job of Employed Men and Women by Race and Age, 1968 and 1981[a]

MEDIAN YEARS ON THE JOB

	1968			1981		
	MALES	FEMALES	DIFFERENCE	MALES	FEMALES	DIFFERENCE
Whites						
Total 16 and over	5.0	2.4	2.6	4.0	2.4	1.6
16 to 24 years	0.8	0.8	0.0	0.9	0.8	0.1
25 to 34 years	2.8	1.6	1.2	2.9	2.0	0.9
35 to 44 years	7.2	2.8	4.4	6.7	3.3	3.4
45 to 54 years	11.6	5.2	6.4	11.2	5.7	5.5
55 to 64 years	15.1	8.8	6.3	14.9	9.1	5.8
65 years and over	13.7	9.8	3.9	10.1	9.8	0.3
Blacks[b]						
Total 16 and over	3.3	2.0	1.3	4.0	3.3	0.7
16 to 24 years	0.7	0.6	0.1	0.7	0.8	−0.1
25 to 34 years	2.4	1.5	0.9	3.0	2.7	0.3
35 to 44 years	4.6	3.3	1.3	6.2	5.2	1.0
45 to 54 years	9.2	4.9	4.3	10.0	8.1	1.9
55 to 64 years	11.8	7.8	4.0	14.4	10.3	4.1
65 years and over	11.6	11.1	0.5	12.0	11.9	0.1

[a]Data are from January of each year.
[b]The data for 1968 include nonwhites.

Sources: U.S. Department of Labor, Bureau of Labor Statistics, *Job Tenure of Workers, January 1968*, Special Labor Free Report, no. 112 (undated); U.S. Department of Labor, Bureau of Labor Statistics, *Job Tenure and Occupational Change, 1981*, Special Labor Force Report, no. 2162 (January 1983).

on the average, have less work experience and labor force attachment than men. On the other hand, the somewhat sketchy information available on recent trends in work experience presented in Tables 7.7 and 7.8 suggest that sex differences have been narrowing in recent years. Table 7.7 shows the mean proportion of years worked by employed women since leaving school for various age groups and years. Among white women, all age groups show a tendency to work an increasing proportion of time. This is particularly true of the younger (25 to 29 year) age group. Among black women, this trend is also evident but less consistent across age groups. It should be noted, however, that the figures for blacks are based on relatively small sample sizes and, thus, should be interpreted with some caution.[29]

Data are more readily available on average tenure on current job (Table 7.8). Here we see that the sex difference in job tenure unambiguously declined between 1968 and 1981, from 2.6 to 1.6 years among whites and from 1.3 to 0.7 years among blacks. Over that time, there was an increase in the size of the two youngest cohorts, 16 to 24-year-olds and 25-to-34-year-olds, as the baby boom cohort entered the job market. This exerted downward pressure on the average tenure of all race-sex groups, since younger workers generally have less tenure. Indeed, among white males, average tenure fell by a year during this period, primarily due to this factor, although there was also a decline in average tenure within some of the age categories. However, among both white and black females and among black males, average years of tenure increased within almost all age categories.

To summarize, the view that women have on average less work experience and labor market attachment than men appears to be borne out by the evidence. However, the differences between men and women in the extent of involvement in work outside the home seem to be narrowing over time. We examine below how, according to the human capital model, such differences could result in lower pay and differences in occupational choices between men and women.

THE ON-THE-JOB TRAINING INVESTMENT DECISION

Again we begin with a general analysis on the training investment decision. On-the-job training may be divided into two types:

1. General training
2. Firm-specific training.

---

[29]Using an entirely different approach and source of data, another study also found evidence of increases in the average level of experience of employed women, particularly in the younger age groups, over the 1970s. See, James P. Smith and Michael P. Ward, *Women's Wages and Work in the Twentieth Century* (Santa Monica, CA: Rand Corporation, October 1984), p. 71.

General training increases the individual's productivity to the same extent in all (or a large number of) firms. For example, an individual may learn to operate an office machine that is widely used by other firms in the labor market. On the other hand, **firm-specific** training, as its name implies, increases the individual's productivity only at the firm that provides the training. For example, one may learn how to operate and get things done within a particular bureaucracy or to deal with the idiosyncracies of a particular piece of equipment. Most training probably combines elements of both. However, for simplicity we assume that training may be classified as being entirely general or entirely firm-specific.

General Training

General training is, by definition, completely transferable from the firm providing the training to other firms. The employer would presumably not be willing to foot any part of the bill for such training, since, in a competitive labor market, there is no way for the employer to collect any of the returns. The worker could simply leave the firm after obtaining the training and be paid what he or she is worth elsewhere. Thus, if general training is to occur, the employee must be willing to bear all the costs, since he or she will reap all the returns. As in the case of formal education, an individual decides whether or not to invest in general training by comparing the costs and benefits.

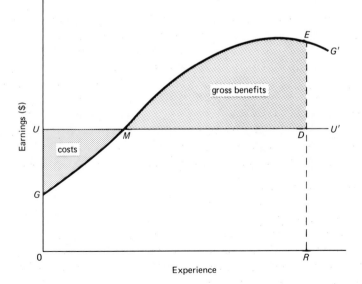

FIGURE 7.3   The On-the-job Training Investment Decision: General Training

Let us consider Lisa's investment decision, illustrated in Figure 7.3. She will contrast the experience-earnings profile she can expect if she takes a job with no training (*UU'*) to the profile she can expect if she receives general training (*GG'*). On-the-job training, although often informal, still entails costs just as does formal schooling. Some of these costs may be direct, such as for materials used in the training. Another portion of the costs is indirect as the worker and his or her coworkers or supervisor transfer their attention from daily production to training activities. The resulting decline in output represents the opportunity cost to the firm of the training activity.

How does Lisa go about "paying" such costs if she decides to invest in general training? She does so by accepting a wage below what she could obtain elsewhere. This lower wage corresponds to her productivity (net of training costs) to the firm during the training period. The costs of the investment in general training are given by the area *UGM*. As Lisa becomes more skilled, her earnings catch up to and eventually surpass what she could have earned without training. Assuming a total of *OR* years of labor market experience, over her work life, her gross benefits will be equal to the area *MED*. As in the case of formal schooling, she is likely to undertake the investment if gross benefits exceed costs by a sufficient amount to yield the desired rate of return (as appears to be the case in Figure 7.3).

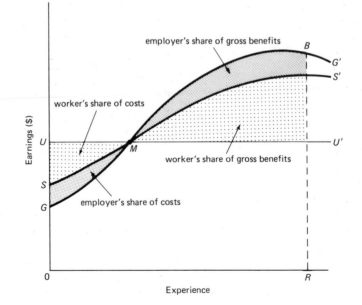

FIGURE 7.4   The On-the-job Training Investment Decision: Firm-Specific Training

Firm-Specific Training

Figure 7.4 illustrates Don's decision of whether or not to invest in firm-specific training. His productivity on the job is shown by the profile *GG'*. This is what his earnings profile would be also, if the training were general. However, since firm-specific training is not transferable, Don will not be willing to bear all the costs of the training since his ability to reap the returns depends upon continued employment at the firm that initially provided the training. Were he to lose his job, his investment would be wiped out (the earnings profile available to him at another firm is *UU'*). While Don would have a strong incentive to remain at the firm, the firm would have no particular reason to accord him any special protection from layoffs.

Similarly, the firm is unwilling to shoulder all the costs of firm-specific training since if Don were to quit, the firm would lose its investment. If the firm were to pay all the costs and receive all the returns, Don's profile would be *UU'*. He would have no special incentive to remain with the firm since he would be earning no more than he could get elsewhere. A temporary shift in demand that resulted in higher wages in another industry or even just more favorable working conditions at another firm might be sufficient to lure him away.

The solution is for the worker and the firm to share the costs of, and returns to, firm-specific training, in which case, the specifically trained worker's profile would be *SS'*. The worker (Don) has an incentive to remain with the firm after completing training because he earns more there than he can get elsewhere (given by profile *UU'*). The firm also has an incentive to retain a worker who has completed specific training, even say in the face of a dip in the demand for the firm's product. This is because the specifically trained worker, again, Don in this case, is actually being paid less than his productivity—after point *M, SS'* lies below *GG'*.

There are two important implications of this analysis of firm-specific training. First, a relatively permanent attachment is likely to develop between the firm and the specifically trained worker. Such workers are less likely either to quit or to be laid off their jobs than untrained or generally trained workers. Second, since employers pay part of the costs of firm-specific training, they will be concerned about the expected employment stability of workers hired into jobs where such training is important. (We develop this point further below.)

As Figures 7.3 and 7.4 suggest, earnings will increase with experience for workers who have invested in training. Considerable empirical evidence does indeed exist of a positive relationship between labor market experience and earnings for workers of both sexes, although the return to experience has been found to be less for women than for men.[30]

[30]See, for example, Mincer and Polachek, "Family Investments in Human Capital;" and Mary Corcoran and Greg J. Duncan, "Work History Labor Force Attachment, and Earnings Differences Between Races and Sex," *Journal of Human Resources* 14, no. 1 (Winter 1979): 3–20.

EXPERIENCE AND PRODUCTIVITY

Human capital theory suggests that the reason why earnings tend to increase with experience in the labor market is that a worker's productivity is augmented by on-the-job training. However, critics of the human capital explanation have argued that it has not been proven that the productivity enhancing effects of on-the-job training have actually *caused* the higher earnings.[31]

For example, the rise in earnings with experience may simply reflect the widespread use of seniority arrangements which appear to govern wage setting to some extent in the nonunion as well as the union sector. Of course, this does not explain why firms would adhere to this practice, if more senior workers were not also generally more able.

One interesting suggestion is that upward sloping earnings profiles, which reward experience with the firm (tenure), raise workers' productivity, because employees are motivated to work hard so as to remain with the firm until retirement and, thus, reap the higher earnings that come with longer tenure.[32] This is in the interest of both workers and firms because the increased productivity makes possible both higher earnings and higher profits. Note that while workers are induced to put forth extra effort and be more productive, higher productivity is *not* due to training and productivity does *not* rise with experience. It should be noted that these alternative explanations focus on the return to tenure (experience with a particular employer) and, thus, do not necessarily challenge the human capital explanation for the return associated with *general* labor market experience.

It is particularly difficult to obtain empirical data to shed light on this controversy since information on actual productivity of workers is seldom available. Thus far, the empirical evidence on the relationship between tenure and productivity is mixed, with some studies supporting the human capital explanation and others refuting it.[33]

---

[31]See especially, James L. Medoff and Katherine G. Abraham, "Experience, Performance, and Earnings," *Quarterly Journal of Economics* 95, no. 4 (December 1980): 703–36; and James L. Medoff and Katherine G. Abraham, "Are Those Paid More Really More Productive? The Case of Experience," *Journal of Human Resources* 16, no. 2 (Spring 1981): pp. 186–216.

[32]Edward P. Lazear, "Why Is There Mandatory Retirement?" *Journal of Political Economy* 87 (December 1979): 1261–84; and Edward P. Lazear, "Agency, Earnings Profiles, Productivity and Hours Restrictions," *American Economic Review* 71, no. 4 (September 1981): 606–20. See also Joseph E. Stiglitz, "Incentives, Risk and Information: Notes Toward a Theory of Hierarchy," *Bell Journal of Economics* 6, no. 2 (Autumn 1975): 552–79.

[33]Negative studies include, Medoff and Abraham, "Experience, Performance, and Earnings," and Medoff and Abraham, "Are Those Paid More Really More Productive?" Those providing more support for the training hypothesis include Cheryl L. Maranto and Robert C. Rodgers, "Does Work Experience Increase Productivity? A Test of the On-the-Job Training Hypothesis," *Journal of Human Resources* 19, no. 3 (Summer 1984): 341–57; and Stanley A. Horowitz and Allan Sherman, "A Direct Measure of the Relationship Between Human Capital and Productivity," *Journal of Human Resources* 15, no. 1 (Winter 1980): 67–76. Also, using

From our perspective, the factors influencing an individual's investment decision are not affected by the reasons for the upward sloping experience-earnings profile. However, if training were not a factor influencing the shape of the profile, the rationale for some jobs providing such opportunities (for earnings increases and higher lifetime earnings), and other jobs not providing them, becomes shakier, especially if it is the case that women tend to be excluded from the former.

SEX DIFFERENCES IN TRAINING INVESTMENT DECISIONS

Expected Work Life

Does our analysis of the training investment decision suggest that women will be less likely to invest in on-the-job training than men? Putting this somewhat differently, would they be less willing to spend time say as poorly paid apprentices, medical residents, or academic "post-docs," in order to reap a later return in terms of higher earnings? Again, human capital theorists argue that adherence to traditional sex roles does indeed lower women's incentives to invest.

The impact of women's shorter work lives is illustrated in Figure 7.5. Let us assume TT' represents the earnings profile of a generally trained worker. Here we see that, just as in the case of formal education, the gross return to on-the-job training depends upon the number of years over which the return is earned. Jane, who plans to be in the labor market for a shorter period of time than Lisa, will find the investment in on-the-job training less profitable. For example, suppose she expects to work R' years, then return after an interruption of $R''-R'$ years. Her benefits are reduced by the time spent out of the labor force when her earnings are zero. Further, human capital theorists believe that the work force interrruption after R' years will lower her earnings profile from TT' to II', resulting in a further loss of benefits. While we have again shown the post-interruption profile (II') as approaching the profile of a continuous worker (TT'),[34] a lifetime loss in earnings still occurs.

Jane's return to her investment in general training is equal to the sum of the two shaded areas, considerably less than Lisa's return shown in Figure 7.3. As we noted in our discussion of field of educational specialization, if occupa-

---

direct information on training (although not on productivity), one study concludes that on-the-job training appears to explain a substantial share of the total wage growth experienced in a given job. See James N. Brown, "Are Those Paid More Really No More Productive? Measuring the Relative Importance of Tenure Versus On-the-Job Training in Explaining Wage Growth," Industrial Relations Section, Princeton University, Working Paper #169 (October 1983).

[34]See footnote 11 for evidence that earnings tend to "rebound" after work force interruptions.

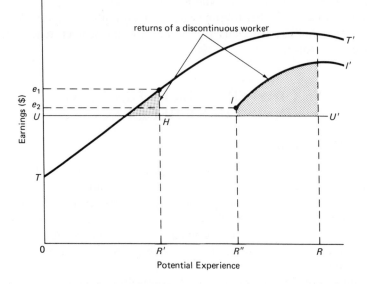

FIGURE 7.5   The Impact of Expected Work Life on the Training Investment Decision

tions differ in the amount of depreciation associated with them, women who anticipate discontinuous work careers are likely to be attracted to fields in which such depreciation is relatively small.[35] Given these reductions in benefits, women following traditional roles are likely to find it profitable to make smaller investments in general training than will career-oriented men. On the other hand, as women's labor force attachment increases, the profitability of such investments for them is also likely to increase. Moreover, we may note that as more women are employed in jobs with general training opportunities (profile TT'), the opportunity cost of work force interruptions is increased, and their labor force attachment is reinforced.

The consequences of women's shorter, and more discontinuous, labor force participation for their incentives to invest in firm-specific training may also be illustrated by Figure 7.5. Assume TT' is now the earnings profile of a specifically trained worker. The impact of work interruptions is potentially even more serious in this case, depending crucially on whether or not a woman is able to return to her initial employer.

[35]See, especially, Solomon W. Polachek, "Occupational Self-Selection: A Human Capital Approach to Sex Differences in Occupational Structure," *The Review of Economics and Statistics* 63, no. 1 (February 1981): 60–69.

Suppose Jennifer has been out of the labor force for a substantial period of time and is unable to get her old job back. Since she has acquired specific training, her skills are useless in other firms. Her earnings upon her return to the labor force will be only *U dollars (the earnings of an untrained individual), and her new earnings profile will be UU'* (the profile of an untrained individual). The returns to Jennifer's investment in firm-specific training have been completely wiped out by her withdrawal from the labor force! That is, the second shaded area shown in Figure 7.5 is eliminated, although she will still receive some return for the brief period before she leaves the labor force. Of course, this conclusion depends on our assumption that she could not return to her original employer. But unless a woman is guaranteed re-employment, she must always face this risk. Thus, human capital theorists believe that women who anticipate work force interruptions of a long and/or an uncertain duration[36] will particularly avoid jobs where firm-specific training is important.

As women increase their labor force attachment, their representation in jobs requiring firm-specific training should increase. The most important factor in this case, however, is attachment to a particular firm. This most probably requires that women keep any work force interruptions within the limits of their employer's leave policy and also raises the question of what such policies should be. We consider this matter briefly later. Figure 7.5 makes clear that, as in the case of the other human capital investments we have discussed, as women take jobs in which they obtain firm-specific training, their incentives to remain in the labor market (and with the firm) are correspondingly increased.

Discrimination

The explanation for sex differences in on-the-job training investment decisions emphasized by human capital theorists stresses differences between men and women in planned labor force participation over the life cycle. However, it is important to point out that, just as in the case of men's and women's formal education decisions, societal discrimination may be a factor increasing the (pecuniary and psychic) costs and/or lowering the (pecuniary and psychic) returns to entry into traditionally male fields. Further, labor market discrimination, which is discussed in greater detail in Chapter 8, may also play a part in reducing women's representation in jobs where training is important. That is, overt or subtle discrimination on the part of employers, coworkers, or customers may prove an obstacle to women seeking access to jobs in such areas.

Consideration of firm-specific training introduces a particular rationale

[36]Shorter, fixed duration interruptions may be covered by an employer's leave policy. Thus, a woman who seeks three months of unpaid leave after the birth of a child is in a very different position from one who quits her job and withdraws form the labor force for an indefinite period.

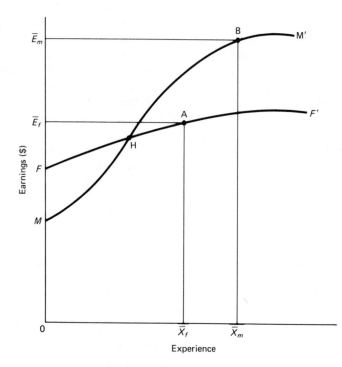

FIGURE 7.6 On-the-job Training and Sex Differences in Occupations and Earnings

for employer discrimination that may be important in the labor market. As illustrated in Figure 7.4, the employer is expected to share some of the costs of firm-specific training. The returns to the firm's (as well as to the worker's) investment depend on how long the individual remains with the firm. Thus, if an employer believes that women are less likely to remain with the firm, on average, than men, he or she may prefer men for jobs that require specific training. This has been termed **statistical discrimination.** Such behavior on the part of employers can restrict opportunities for career-oriented as well as noncareer-oriented women, if employers cannot easily distinguish between them. Finally, labor market discrimination may indirectly lower women's incentives to invest in themselves by lowering the rewards for doing so.

OCCUPATIONS AND EARNINGS

The consequences predicted by the human capital analysis for sex differences in earnings and employment are fairly straightforward. Human capital theorists argue that most women do indeed anticipate shorter and less continuous work careers than men. Thus, women are expected to select occupations requiring less investment in on-the-job training than those chosen by men. They will particularly avoid jobs in which firm-specific training is important, and employers will be reluctant to hire them for such jobs. Further, they will seek jobs where depreciation of earnings for time spent out of the labor force is minimized.

Hypothetical earnings profiles for predominantly male and predominantly female jobs are shown in Figure 7.6. For simplicity, we assume all workers have the same amount of formal schooling. Earnings profiles in predominantly male jobs are expected to slope steeply upward as does profile *MM'*, since men are expected to undertake substantial investments in on-the-job training. Women, on the other hand, are expected to choose the flatter profile *FF'*, representing smaller amounts of investment in on-the-job training. The existence of the crossover point, *H,* is crucial to this argument. Before *H,* profile *FF'* lies above profile *MM'*. It is argued that women choose higher earnings now in preference to greater earnings in the future because they do not expect to be in the labor market long enough for the larger human capital investment to pay off. Thus, we see that the human capital analysis of on-the-job training decisions, in conjunction with our previous discussion of formal education, provides an explanation for the occupational segregation by sex detailed in Chapter 6.

The human capital analysis also provides an explanation for sex differences in earnings. We have already seen why human capital theorists believe women are less likely to make large investments in formal schooling. To the extent that women in the labor force have been less likely than men to obtain a college or graduate education their earnings would be lowered relative to men's. In terms of median educational attainment, however, this is counterbalanced by their greater likelihood of completing high school. Of potentially more importance in explaining sex differences in earnings would be differences between men and women in fields of specialization if men are more likely to enter the more lucrative areas.

For given levels of formal education, our consideration of on-the-job training investments also gives us reasons to expect women to earn less as illustrated in Figure 7.6. Mean female earnings are $\bar{E}_f$ dollars and are less than male mean earnings of $\bar{E}_m$ dollars. Why do women earn less? First, on average they have less labor market experience than men—$\bar{X}_f$ is less than $\bar{X}_m$. Since earnings tend to increase with experience, this lowers their earnings relative to men's. Second, for reasons given earlier, males experience larger increases in earnings for additional years of experience (have steeper profiles). After crossover point *H,* this produces a widening gap between male and female earnings with increasing labor market experience.

OTHER SUPPLY-SIDE FACTORS

Traditional gender roles may work to produce sex differences in economic outcomes in a variety of other ways. To the extent that families place priority on the husband's, rather than the wife's, career in determining the location of the family, her earnings are likely to be lowered, since the best job for both is not necessarily to be found in the same labor market.[37] Anticipation of lesser ability to determine the geographic location of the family may also lead women to select occupations in which jobs are likely to be readily found in any labor market. Further, if women tend to give greater priority than men to family concerns, they may restrict the amount of daily commuting they are willing to do,[38] their hours or work schedules, as well as their availability for work-related travel. Such constraints may also reduce women's earnings relative to men's and adversely influence their occupational choices. Finally, if women anticipate a shorter work life than men, they may invest less time in searching out the best possible job and, as a consequence, receive lower earnings.[39]

As with the other supply-side influences we have discussed, it is important to bear in mind that such decisions may reflect social pressures as well as the voluntary choices of women. Further, labor market discrimination, to the extent it exists, reinforces traditional gender roles in the family by lowering the wife's opportunity cost (relative to the husband's) of sacrificing her career objectives to family demands.

THE HUMAN CAPITAL EXPLANATION: AN ASSESSMENT

The human capital model can provide a clear, consistent theoretical explanation for sex differences in earnings and occupations in terms of the voluntary

---

[37]See Robert H. Frank, "Why Women Earn Less: The Theory and Estimation of Differential Qualification," *American Economic Review* 68, no. 3 (June 1978): 360–73; Steven H. Sandell, "Women and the Economics of Family Migration," *The Review of Economics and Statistics,* (November 1977): 406–14; and Jacob Mincer, "Family Migration Decisions," *Journal of Political Economy* 86, no. 5 (October 1978): 749–73.

[38]See Victor Fuchs, "Differences in Hourly Earnings Between Men and Women," *Monthly Labor Review* 94, no. 5 (May 1971); Albert Rees and George P. Shultz, *Workers and Wages in an Urban Labor Market* (Chicago: University of Chicago Press, 1970). Janice Madden has suggested that the lesser willingness of women to commute increases the monopsony power of firms over their wages, thus lowering their wages relative to men's. See her "A Spatial Theory of Sex Discrimination," *Journal of Regional Science* 17, no. 3 (December 1977): 369–80. The monopsony model is discussed further in Chapter 8.

[39]Some evidence consistent with this possibility is found in Steven H. Sandell, "Is the Unemployment Rate of Women Too Low? A Direct Test of the Economic Theory of Job Search," *The Review of Economics and Statistics* 62, no. 4 (November 1980): 634–38.

choices women and men make. If it is believed that this model provides the *sole* explanation for sex differences in economic outcomes, economic inequality between men and women in the labor market would perhaps not be considered a serious social problem. Certainly, it would not require policy intervention to combat sex discrimination in employment. We have already pointed out that even to the extent that sex inequality in the labor market is caused by such supply-side factors as emphasized by human capital theorists, societal discrimination against women as well as their own voluntary choices may be an important explanatory factor. Further, women's anticipation of and experience with labor market discrimination can also lower their human capital investments. This latter process will be described in greater detail in the following chapter. We now consider two more straightforward issues. Do the factors emphasized by human capital theorists help to explain sex differences in labor market outcomes? If so, do they provide the *full* explanation?

A crude test of explanatory power of the human capital explanation for sex differences in earnings is provided by an examination of the trends in the sex-pay differential. As discussed in Chapter 6, virtually no progress was made in closing the overall male-female pay gap during the 1960s and 1970s. Beginning in the late 1970s or ealy 1980s, there were some signs that the ratio of female to male earnings was beginning to turn up. Yet, the data presented in this chapter suggest that women workers' qualifications have been increasing relative to men's at least since the mid-1960s. Though women's median educational attainment, which used to be somewhat greater than men's, is now only equal, their fields of study and propensity to pursue college and graduate education have become more similar to male's. Although women on average have less labor force experience than men for the most part, the sex differential appeared to decline here as well, particularly during the 1970s. Thus, if human capital factors were the *sole* explanation for the male-female pay gap, one would have expected to see a narrowing of the aggregate pay gap throughout the 1970s, and perhaps a greater overall reduction achieved by the early 1980s.

A more detailed examination of earnings trends is, however, more consistent with the human capital model. Younger women have been most rapidly approaching males in terms of their college-going behavior and fields of study. They have also exhibited the largest increases in labor force attachment in recent years as growing proportions of them have continued to work during the prime childbearing years. And we did indeed find in Chapter 6 that younger women (those under 35) have experienced a substantial increase in their earnings relative to younger males. This finding is consistent with the human capital explanation for women's lower earnings. However, the earnings of younger women still lag considerably behind those of younger men. It has not been determined whether their relative earnings have increased by the full amount that would be expected on the basis of their improved average qualifications.[40]

We now turn to a more detailed examination of the explanatory power of the human capital model, focusing upon data on sex differences in earnings at a point in time. Figure 7.7 shows the **age-earnings profiles** of individuals by sex for those with four years of high school and four years of college, respectively, in 1983. An age-earnings profile shows how earnings vary with age or potential rather than actual experience. As we saw in Figures 7.2 and 7.5, women's greater likelihood of work force interruptions means that, at any given age, they tend to average less actual labor market experience than men. It is important to bear this in mind in comparing the profiles for males and females shown in Figure 7.7.

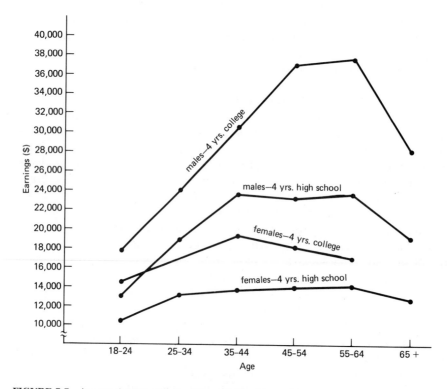

FIGURE 7.7   Age-earnings Profiles by Sex and Education, 1983

[40]Some evidence suggests that their earnings have not kept pace with their greater qualifications, see Gordon W. Green, Jr., "Wage Differentials for Job Entrants, by Race and Sex," unpublished doctoral dissertation, George Washington University (December 1983). On the other hand, another study found evidence consistent with a lessening of discrimination against younger women workers over the 1970s. See Francine D. Blau and Andrea H. Beller, "Trends in Sex and Race Earnings Differential: 1971–1981," paper presented at the American Economic Association meetings in Dallas, Texas (December 1984).

The figure suggests that sex differences in earnings are not fully explained by differences in educational attainment of men and women, since within each educational category women earn less. Indeed, except in the youngest group, women college graduates earn considerably less than men who have only completed high school. Of course, sex differences in labor market experience and investments in on-the-job training may also be a factor.

To consider this issue, let us compare Figure 7.7 to Figure 7.6. We see that, as predicted by human capital theorists, women's age-earnings profiles tend to be flatter than men's. This is consistent with less investment in on-the-job training for women than for men. Note, however, that in the hypothetical diagram, Figure 7.6, there is a crossover point *H* between the male and female profiles. This implies that during their early years in the labor market, women should actually earn more than men (with the same education), since the men are investing in on-the-job training and the women are not or are doing so to a lesser extent. However, the actual data shown in Figure 7.7 do not show such a crossover point. On the contrary, within educational categories, men earn more than women at every age, even among the youngest workers who are recent entrants to the labor force. This suggests that sex differences in years of formal education and on-the-job training do not fully explain sex differences in earnings.[41]

Is it possible to determine exactly what proportion of the sex gap in pay is due to differences in qualifications, especially human capital investments? Economists and other social scientists have studied this question extensively. Actual estimates vary depending on the sources of the data used and the types of qualifications examined. While most studies do find that human capital factors, particularly women's lesser labor market experience, do contribute to the sex differential, they also find that a substantial portion of the pay gap cannot be explained by sex differences in qualifications.[42] The portion of the pay gap that is not due to sex differences in qualifications is presumed to be due to labor market discrimination. We discuss this evidence at greater length in Chapter 8.

As suggested by our discussion of Figure 7.6, the human capital model

---

[41]Among young women, it has been found that those who expect to work at age 35 have experience-wage profiles that ". . . begin at a lower point and have a steeper (initial) slope than those of their no-work-plans counterparts" (Steven H. Sandell and David Shapiro, "Work Expectations, Human Capital Accumulation, and the Wages of Young Women," *Journal of Human Resources* 15, no. 3 [Summer 1980]:343). That is, the women who were more committed to the labor market were moving along an earnings profile like *MM'* in Figure 7.6, while the less committed women were moving along a profile like *FF'*. However, the data presented in Figure 7.7 (as well as other evidence of labor market discrimination reviewed in Chapter 8) suggests that *both* groups of women earn less than comparable men. That is, again, that human capital factors do not fully account for the sex pay gap.

[42]For summaries of this literature, see Francine Blau, "Discrimination Against Women: Theory and Evidence," ed. William A. Darity, Jr., *Labor Economics: Modern Views* (Boston: Kluwer-Nijhoff, 1984); Cynthia Lloyd and Beth Niemi, *Economics of Sex Differentials*; and Donald J. Treiman and Heidi I. Hartmann, eds., *Women, Work and Wages: Equal Pay for Jobs of Equal Value* (Washington, D.C.: National Academy Press, 1981).

also provides an explanation for occupational segregation by sex in terms of women's optimizing behavior, given the traditional division of labor by sex within the family. Women are believed to choose occupations characterized by flatter experience-earnings profiles—illustrated by FF' in Figure 7.6. Men, on the other hand, are willing to undertake the larger human capital investments represented by profile MM'. This implies that women who do enter predominantly male occupations should be those who anticipate more continuous labor force participation and are willing to undertake the larger investments in on-the-job training required in male jobs. In return, they should reap higher returns to each year of their labor market experience. In other words, women in predominantly male jobs should be moving along profile MM', while women in predominantly female jobs should be moving along profile FF'. Further, women who anticipate more work interruptions should enter predominantly female jobs where depreciation of earnings due to time spent out of the labor force is less than in predominalty male jobs.

In fact, most of the research in this area does not support the human capital explanation for sex differences in occupations.[43] Women in predominantly male jobs do not earn greater returns to each year of experience than women in predominantly female occupations. Nor is it the case that the earnings of women in predominantly female jobs depreciate less during periods of time spent out of the labor force than do the earnings of women in predominantly male jobs. Finally, women who have discontinuous work histories are not more likely to be in a predominantly female occupation than are women who have been employed more continuously. While some other researchers have obtained findings that are more consistent with the human capital explanation for occupational segregation, it appears that this view is not strongly supported by the evidence at this point. However, it is possible that further study will reveal greater support for this view, at least as a partial explanation. Moreover, it should be borne in mind that the available evidence does not rule out the importance of other supply-side factors which may encourage men and women to aspire to and train for "sex appropriate" lines of work.

POLICY ISSUES: INCREASING WOMEN'S HUMAN CAPITAL AND LABOR FORCE ATTACHMENT

While the human capital model does not appear to fully explain sex differences in labor market outcomes, human capital factors undoubtedly contribute to the pay gap. In this section, we consider policies that government or private

---

[43]See Paula England, "The Failure of Human Capital Theory to Explain Occupational Sex Segregation," *Journal of Human Resources* 17, no. 3 (Summer 1982): 358–370; Mary Corcoran,

employers have pursued, or might consider adopting, in order to increase women's human capital and labor force attachment.

Government Training Programs

Particularly since the 1960s, the federal government has been active in providing training and employment programs for disadvantaged or unemployed workers. The most important initial program in this area was the Manpower Development and Training Act (MDTA) of 1962, which emphasized a fairly centralized approach to these problems. It was replaced by the Comprehensive Employment and Training Act (CETA) of 1973, which gave a greater role in decision-making and program implementation to local governments. Under the Reagan Administration, the Job Training Partnership Act (JTPA), passed in 1982, placed greater reliance on the private sector.

While the strategies and emphases of these programs have varied, their goal has been the provision of skills to workers to enhance their employability and earnings. The programs provided the government with an excellent opportunity for intervention to reduce occupational segregation by offering women training in traditionally male jobs. Such a strategy would have helped to reduce the male-female pay gap directly since predominantly male jobs are generally higher paying than predominantly female jobs. Further, training for male-dominated occupations would therefore have increased the opportunity cost of labor withdrawals to a greater extent than training for female-dominated occupations. It could, thus, be expected to increase the labor force attachment of those receiving the training to a greater extent.

While the evidence available on this topic is sparse, what there is suggests that the training and employment opportunities associated with these training programs have been predominantly sex segregated. Indeed, one study of CETA found that even female participants who had previously worked in a predominantly male job or expressed a preference for being trained for such a job, were very likely to be placed in sex-typical occupations. Yet it was found that those women training for or working in male-dominated occupations as part of the program received higher wages than those training for or working in female-dominated jobs.[44] Thus, it is indeed unfortunate that, as of the early 1980s, the opportunity that government training programs offered for reducing occupational segregation and the male-female pay gap does not appear to

---

Greg J. Duncan, and Michael Ponza, "Work Experience, Job Segregation and Wages," ed. Reskin, *Sex Segregation in the Workplace*; and John Abowd and Mark P. Killingsworth, "Sex Discrimination, Atrophy and the Male-Female Wage Differential," *Industrial Relations* 22, no. 3 (Fall 1983): 387–402; On the other hand, results more consistent with the human capital model are obtained by Polachek, "Occupational Self-Selection" and Landes, "A Test of the Specific Capital Hypothesis."

[44]Linda J. Waite and Sue E. Berryman, "Occupational Desegregation in CETA Programs," ed. Reskin, *Sex Segregation in the Workplace,* pp. 292–307.

have been realized.[45] It is to be hoped that a greater priority will be placed on achieving these goals in the future.

The Role of Employers

In Chapter 5, we discussed the possibility of businesses participating in the provision of child care and that they themselves, as well as workers, might benefit. In this section, we consider a variety of policies to facilitate the meshing of work and family responsibilities for workers of both sexes, such as flexible work schedules, parental leave, and others. Since, at present, women most often bear the major responsibility for housework and child care, they would be the primary beneficiaries of such policies. Not only would it become easier for women to meet their "home obligations" and succeed on the job but also to remain more permanently attached to the labor force. This would increase the incentives of both women themselves and of their employers to invest in the human capital of women workers.

The existence of such policies would also make it easier for men to undertake a larger share of the homemaking chores, promoting a more equal division of labor in the home. Men who have already made a commitment to sharing the housework would also benefit.

For the most part in this section we consider policies which employers might adopt voluntarily, rather than as a consequence of legal requirements. Profit-maximizing employers would be motivated to institute such changes, possibly to some extent in lieu of other worker benefits, only to the extent that the resulting benefits are expected to exceed the costs. For the individual employer, possible benefits include greater ease in recruiting workers and reductions in turnover, absenteeism, and tardiness. Morale and effort of workers may also be increased. These are among the factors that are likely to raise productivity. Costs, of course, depend on the specific policy under consideration but could include scheduling problems, hiring of replacements and adjustment costs of reformulating existing practices.

Total benefits to the employer increase as the number of workers potentially positively affected by the policies rises. On the other hand, the costs of some policies, for example parental leaves, will also rise as more workers take advantage of them. On balance, however, it is highly likely that employers' incentives to adopt policies of this type will increase as a larger portion of the work force attempts to cope with the difficulties of successfully combining market careers with homemaking responsibilities. As more women take

---

[45]On the other hand, government training programs appear to have been moderately successful in increasing the earnings of program participants over their counterparts of the same sex who did not participate. See, for example, Nicholas M. Kiefer, "The Economic Benefits from Four Government Training Programs," ed. Farrell E. Bloch, *Evaluating Manpower Training Programs, Research in Labor Economics,* Supp. 1 (1979), pp. 159–86.

market jobs, and particularly as they move into higher level positions, employers' concern over the retention and job performance of women should become more urgent. Further, as men do a greater share of housework, the pool of potential beneficiaries of these policies will be further increased. Thus, it seems reasonable to expect growing interest on the part of employers in such policies.

Work schedules. A decrease in the standard work week of full-time workers would clearly be advantageous to those with time-consuming household responsibilities. As mentioned in Chapter 4, there has been a sizable decline in weekly hours since the turn of the century. However, most of this decrease was accomplished by the 1940s, and little further reduction has occurred since that time.[46] Thus, further reductions in the standard work week do not appear likely in the near future.

More attention has been focued on alternative work schedules that can permit workers to utilize their off-job time more efficiently or enjoyably, as well as to do some tasks they could not otherwise accomplish, for example, picking a child up from school. *Flextime* permits workers to select the beginning and ending time of their work day, within certain limits, provided they work a specified total number of hours over a given period. An additional advantage of flextime is a reduction in commuting time since workers are able to avoid rush hour traffic. In 1980, 12 percent of full-time workers in this country had flexible schedules, including 13 percent of male and 10 percent of female full-time workers. In addition, some 3 percent of male and female full-time workers worked schedules of 4½ days or less, the so-called *four-day week.* No data are available on the prevalence of flexible work schedules in earlier years, but the incidence of the four-day week increased from less than 2 percent of workers in 1973, suggesting that there had been some moderate growth in alternative schedules over the 1970s.[47]

A third alternative, part-time employment (less than 35 hours per week), is already quite common, especially among women. For example, in 1984, 28 percent of employed women and 12 percent of employed men were on part-

[46]As noted in Chapter 4, some decline in *annual* hours has continued to occur with greater provisions for paid holidays, vacations, and sick days.

[47]These data are from U.S. Department of Labor, press release (February 24, 1981), Tables 1 and 3. Flextime is considerably more widespread in some Western European countries. Estimates range up to 40 percent of workers covered by such arrangements in Switzerland. (Sheila B. Kamerman and Paul W. Kingston, "Employer Responses to the Family Responsibilities of Employers," eds. Sheila B. Kamerman and Cheryl D. Hayes, *Families That Work: Children in a Changing World,* [Washington, DC: National Academy Press, 1982], pp.144–208.) An Israeli study of flexible schedules found that it reduced absenteeism, especially among married women and mothers. See Moshe Krausz and Nechama Freiback, "Effects of Flexible Working Time for Employed Women Upon Satisfaction, Strains, and Absenteeism," *Journal of Occupational Psychology* 58, no. 2 (June 1983): 155–59.

time schedules, in comparison to 26 percent and 8 percent, respectively, in 1968. The main problem with part-time employment as a solution to women's problems in combining job and family responsibilities is the quality of opportunities offered. Part-time workers frequently receive lower fringe benefits and often are excluded from opportunities to be hired for or promoted into high-level jobs. Thus, emphasis needs to be placed on improving the long-term career opportunities associated with part-time jobs. One innovative approach to opening more challenging positions to part-time workers is job-sharing, where two individuals share one position.[48]

Parental leave time. Under the Pregnancy Discrimination Act of 1978 (an amendment to Title VII of the Civil Rights Act of 1964), employers are prohibited from discriminating against workers on the basis of pregnancy. An employer may not, for example, refuse to hire or terminate a woman because she is pregnant. Further, employers must provide paid disability leave for pregnancy and childbirth on the same basis as for other medical disabilities.[49] A 1984 study of major corporations found that 95 percent offered short-term disability leave for pregnancy. The length of the disability leave varied, with 63 percent of firms reporting between five to eight weeks.[50]

Paid leaves for child care are not required by law. And, in 1984, only 7.4 percent of major corporations offered paid maternity or parental leaves.[51] However, a major development of the 1970s was that unpaid maternity leaves, for a relatively short period after childbirth, became available to most female workers. According to studies conducted in the early 1980s, approximately 90 percent of firms provided unpaid maternity leave to female employees, most commonly for a period of three to six months. The majority of firms surveyed guaranteed the same or a comparable job upon return from the leave, although two studies found that a significant minority of 14 and 28 percent, respectively, did not. Far fewer firms, approximately 40 percent, made provision for child care leave for male workers.[52]

---

[48]For a discussion of the positive and negative features of this arrangement, see, for example, Glenn Collins, "Lawyers Share Jobs for More Family Time," *The New York Times* (July 9, 1984).

[49]Employers with no medical disability program are not required to provide paid disability for pregnancy and childbirth.

[50]The study was conducted by Catalyst, a national organization established to promote productivity in the workplace and to resolve career and family issues. It was reported in the Bureau of National Affairs, *Daily Labor Report,* no. 163 (August 22, 1984), pp. A-6–A-8.

[51]See footnote 50.

[52]Bureau of National Affairs, "Employers and Child Care: Development of a New Employee Benefit," BNA Special Report (Washington, DC: Bureau of National Affairs, Inc., 1984), p. 45. In 1984, Congress passed legislation guaranteeing that workers who take up to one year of employer-approved parental leave will not lose previously earned credit toward a pension, provided that they return to their jobs after the leave.

The provision of parental leaves, even relatively short and unpaid ones, is significant in that they allow women to maintain their tie to the firm. This is particularly important for increasing women's incentives to invest in firm-specific training, as well as for making employers more willing to provide them with such training opportunities.

It might be desirable if longer leaves were available, perhaps with pay for at least some portion of the time. However, few employers are likely to voluntarily provide such benefits, given their costs. Laws mandating paid maternity leaves would be one way to achieve this outcome, but potentially raising the costs of hiring women could increase employer's preferences for hiring men. Making parental leave available to fathers as well as mothers might mitigate this problem, if men actually availed themselves of this opportunity. The evidence from Sweden, one country that has such provisions, is that so far men do not do so to any significant degree. Nonetheless, whether the parental leave policy is legislated or voluntary, it is highly desirable that it be made available to both men and women so as to encourage men to take on a greater share of parental responsibilities.

A constructive employer response to the situation of new parents also involves assistance to the employee in adjusting to work upon return from the parental leave. For example, a period of part-time employment or flextime scheduling might be helpful, as might a short- or long-term transfer to a position that required less travel. One company has a maternity leave coordinator in its personnel department who helps employees both in obtaining the leave and in making the post-leave arrangements.[53]

While only women become pregnant and bear children, either parent can take care of a sick child. With no provisions for such emergencies, women tend to take time from work, if need be by subterfuge, and help to earn a reputation for excessive absenteeism. Once more, the most useful solution would be to make available some leave for this purpose to both parents. This would encourage the father to take his turn in caring for the child, at least after the mother has used up her time allowance, and would tend to reduce the differences in days absent from work between men and women.

Managing two careers. As we have noted, frequently in the past when the career demands of the members of a couple have conflicted, women have tended to sacrifice their own career advancement for their husband's. While it is to be hoped that couples will share these adjustment costs more equally in the future, employers can assist two-career couples by reducing the sacrifices that need to be made. For example, 15 of the largest firms in Chicago have

[53]Eleanor Byrnes, "Dual Career Couples: How the Company can Help," ed. Jennie Farley, *The Woman in Management: Career and Family Issues* (Ithaca, N.Y.: ILR Press, 1983), pp. 49–53. See also, *The New York Times* (August 4, 1985) pp. F1, F6.

formed a spouse employment network. If one of the firms hires a person who is married to a professional, it helps the spouse find work by referring his or her resumé to the network. Participating firms are committed to seriously considering the spouse for employment. Firms can also assist two-career couples by helping the spouse of an employee that is transferred to locate a new job. One firm, for example, hires an outside consultant to do this.[54] Firms can also assist couples by realizing that an employee who declines a transfer or promotion, say because of particularly heavy family responsibilities or difficulties finding employment for a spouse, need not be consigned to the "slow track" forever. When the situation changes, the individual may make an excellent candidate for advancement.

Firms need to scrutinize their internal policies regarding the employment of members of a couple. In the past, anti-nepotism rules often simply forbade the hiring or retaining of a relative of a current employee. If two employees married, usually it turned out to be the wife who would have to go. Today, many firms have gotten rid of such rules. Some, however, retain restrictions on the employment of two family members, for example, prohibiting them from working in the same department. Concern has also been focused on the situation in which two workers form a romantic attachment. In either case, it is feared that if one partner is powerful he or she will exert influence to have the other hired or promoted and that the couple may form a working alliance that will be resented by their coworkers.[55]

Such abuses undoubtedly take place, but there is no evidence that they are any greater than when people simply are or become close friends. In fact, one might expect couples to be somewhat more circumspect, because favoritism would be so obvious. Reducing what risk there is of problems by placing restrictions on the employment of couples must in any case be weighed against the disadvantages of not being able to hire the best qualified people regardless of marital status or other relationships and of not being able to offer a job to a spouse when the firm wants to hire or relocate the other partner. In addition, as long as men are typically the ones in a higher job category, if one member of a couple is asked to leave, the woman will probably be viewed as the most expendable. Thus, any such policy is likely to result in de facto discrimination against women. Further, employment of one member of the couple at another firm may create its own set of problems if that firm turns out to be a competitor.[56] These are probably some of the reasons why a 1984

[54]Byrnes, "Dual Career Couples."

[55]A particularly negative view on a firm's employment of individuals who are romantically involved is put forth by Eliza G. C. Collins in the September 1983 issue of the *Harvard Business Review* (as reported in *Newsweek,* September 5, 1983, p. 60).

[56]In December 1984, "a California state appeals court affirmed a $300,000 verdict against IBM for wrongfully discharging a female manager because she was dating an employee from a rival office products firm." See Bureau of National Affairs, *Daily Labor Report,* no. 237, December 12, 1984, pp. 2–3.

survey found that 58 percent of firms were relaxing their rules on the hiring and placement of close relatives. Also, in dealing with the growing number of couples who were simply living together, 48 percent of the firms ". . . said they would rather 'pretend such things don't go on' than be charged with violating rights of privacy."[57]

CONCLUSION

In this chapter, we have examined supply-side explanations for sex differences in occupations and earnings, chiefly focusing upon the human capital model. We also reviewed government and employer policies that could increase women's human capital investments and promote greater labor force attachment among them. While the evidence suggests that such factors are undoubtedly important, they explain only part of the story. Discrimination against women in the labor market is also an important factor to which we turn in the next chapter.

SUGGESTED READINGS

BECKER, GARY S., *Human Capital,* 2nd ed. Chicago: University of Chicago Press, 1975.

CORCORAN, MARY AND GREG J. DUNCAN, "Work History, Labor Force Attachment, and Earnings Differences Between the Races and Sexes." *Journal of Human Resources* 14, no. 1 (Winter 1979): 3–20.

ENGLAND, PAULA, "The Failure of Human Capital Theory to Explain Occupational Sex Segregation," *Journal of Human Resources* 17, no. 3 (Summer 1982): 358–70.

KANTER, ROSABETH, *Men and Women of the Corporation.* New York: Basic Books, 1977.

LLOYD, CYNTHIA B. AND BETH T. NIEMI, *The Economics of Sex Differentials.* New York: Columbia University Press, 1979, chs. 3 and 4.

MINCER, JACOB AND SOLOMON POLACHEK, "Family Investments in Human Capital: Earnings of Women," *Journal of Political Economy* 82, no. 2, pt. 2 (March/April 1974): S76–S108.

TOBIAS, SHEILA, *Overcoming Math Anxiety.* New York: W. W. Norton, 1978.

WEITZMAN, LENORE J., "Sex-Role Socialization: A Focus on Women," ed. Jo Freeman, *Women: A Feminist Perspective,* 3rd. ed. (Palo Alto: Mayfield, 1984), pp. 157–237.

[57]*New York Times,* June 17, 1985, p. 20. The survey was conducted by the American Society for Personnel Administration.

Chapter 8

DIFFERENCES IN OCCUPATIONS AND EARNINGS: THE ROLE OF LABOR MARKET DISCRIMINATION

In the preceding chapter, we examined the role of supply-side factors in producing the gender inequality in earnings and occupational attainment that we observe in the labor market (Chapter 6). We now focus upon the demand-side, specifically the role of labor market discrimination. As we explained at the end of Chapter 7, the available evidence suggests that both supply- and demand-side influences are responsible for sex differences in economic outcomes.

In this chapter, we begin by providing a definition of labor market discrimination and then examine the empirical evidence on the extent of sex discrimination in the labor market, first with respect to earnings, then with respect to occupations. We then consider the various explanations that economists have offered for the existence and persistence of such discrimination. While our focus is on sex discrimination, much of the analysis is equally applicable to discrimination based on race, age, disability, etc. In fact, most of the models of discrimination that we discuss were initially developed to explain racial discrimination.

Our primary concerns here are to what extent discrimination may exist and its possible effects on the groups directly involved. However, the issue of misallocation of resources is also potentially serious when workers are not hired, promoted, or rewarded equally when they are equally qualified. This, in addition to considerations of equity or fairness, provides an important rationale for government intervention to combat labor market discrimination. In this chapter, we also review the government's anti-discrimination policies and examine their possible effects.

LABOR MARKET DISCRIMINATION: A DEFINITION

Labor market discrimination exists when *two equally qualified individuals are treated differently solely on the basis of their sex* (race, age, disability, etc.).[1] As we saw in Chapter 1, in the absence of discrimination, profit-maximizing employers in a competitive labor market will pay workers in accordance with their productivity. For similar reasons, they will also find it in their economic self-interest to make other personnel decisions, such as hiring, placement or promotion decisions, on the same objective basis. An individual's sex (or race, age, disability, etc.) itself would be an irrelevant consideration.

If labor market discrimination nonetheless exists, it is expected to adversely affect the economic status of women *directly* by producing differences in economic outcomes between men and women that are *not* accounted for by differences in productivity-related characteristics or qualifications. That is, men and women who, in the absence of discrimination, would be equally productive and would receive the same pay (or be in the same occupation) do not receive equal rewards. As we shall see, in some economic models of discrimination this inequality occurs because women are paid less than their marginal products due to discrimination. In other views of this process, labor market discrimination *directly* lowers women's productivity as well as their pay, as for instance, when a woman is denied access to an employer-sponsored training program or when customers are reluctant to patronize a female sales person.

If such sex differences in *treatment* of equally qualified men and women are widespread and persistent, the behavior of women themselves may be adversely affected. As we saw in the preceding chapter, productivity differences among workers reflect, in part, the decisions they make whether or not to continue their schooling, participate in a training program, remain continuously in the labor market, etc. Faced with discrimination against them in the labor market, women may have less incentive to undertake such human capital investments. If such indirect or **feedback effects** of labor market discrimination exist, they are also expected to lower the economic status of women relative to men.

---

[1] This definition is derived from the work of Gary S. Becker, *The Economics of Discrimination,* 2nd ed. (Chicago: University of Chicago Press, 1971).

Much of the theoretical and virtually all of the empirical work on labor market discrimination has focused on its more readily measured *direct* effects; that is, on pay or occupational differences between equally well-qualified (potentially equally productive) men and women. We shall follow that emphasis in this chapter. However, it is important to recognize that the *full* impact of discrimination also includes any feedback effects on women's behavior that result in their being less well-qualified than men.[2] Thus, we also discuss such feedback effects.

One of the major difficulties in determining the existence of discrimination is that it may take very subtle forms. One of these is that men and women behaving in similar ways may, nonetheless, be perceived quite differently. Such attitudes are almost impossible to document, let alone measure, but that does not mean they do not exist. Here are some examples of typical reactions.*

The family picture is on HIS desk:
Ah, a solid, responsible family man.

The family picture is on HER desk:
Hmm, her family will come before her career.

HIS desk is cluttered:
He's obviously a hard worker and a busy man.

HER desk is cluttered:
She's obviously a disorganized scatter-brain.

HE'S talking with co-workers:
He must be discussing the latest deal.

SHE'S talking with co-workers:
She must be gossiping.

HE'S not at his desk:
He must be at a meeting.

SHE's not at her desk:
She must be in the ladies' room.

HE's not in the office:
He's meeting customers.

SHE'S not in the office:
She must be out shopping.

HE's having lunch with the boss:
He's on his way up.

SHE's having lunch with the boss:
They must be having an affair.

The boss criticized HIM:
He'll improve his performance.

The boss criticized HER:
She'll be very upset.

HE got an unfair deal:
Did he get angry?

SHE got an unfair deal:
Did she cry?

HE'S getting married:
He'll get more settled.

SHE'S getting married:
She'll get pregnant and leave.

[2]Note that the argument is *not* that *all* differences in qualifications between men and women are due to the indirect effects of discrimination, but, rather, that *some* of these differences may be a response to such discrimination.

*From Natasha Josefowitz, *Paths to Power* (Reading, MA: Addison-Wesley Publishing Co., ©1980): p. 60. Reprinted with permission.

HE'S having a baby:
He'll need a raise.

SHE'S having a baby:
She'll cost the company money in
maternity benefits.

HE'S going on a business trip:
It's good for his career.

SHE's going on a business trip:
What does her husband say?

HE'S leaving for a better job:
He recognizes a good opportunity.

SHE's leaving for a better job:
Women are undependable.

EMPIRICAL EVIDENCE

Having defined labor market discrimination we now consider the empirical
evidence as to the existence and extent of such discrimination. We restrict
ourselves entirely to the direct effects of such discrimination and, thus, take as
given any sex differences in qualifications. We seek to address more fully the
two relatively straightforward questions considered in Chapter 7. Are sex differences in labor market outcomes *fully* explained by sex differences in
qualifications or (potential) productivity? If not, how large is the unexplained
portion of the sex differential? It is this differential that is commonly used as
an estimate of the impact of labor market discrimination. Unfortunately, as
we shall see, while the questions are fairly simple, the answers are not so easily
obtained. We turn first to a consideration of sex differences in earnings and
then to an examination of sex differences in occupations.

Earnings Differences

Economists and other social scientists have studied the earnings gap between men and women workers extensively. Actual estimates vary depending
on the sources of the data used and the types of qualifications examined.
However, virtually all studies find that a substantial portion of the pay gap
cannot be explained by sex differences in qualifications.[3] For example, in

[3]See, for example, Ronald Oaxaca, "Sex Discrimination in Wages," eds. Orley Ashenfelter and Albert Rees, *Discrimination in Labor Markets* (Princeton, New Jersey: Princeton
University Press, 1973), pp. 124–51; Isabel V. Sawhill, "The Economics of Discrimination
Against Women: Some New Findings," *Journal of Human Resources* 8, no. 3 (Summer 1973):
335–53; Jacob Mincer and Solomon Polachek, "Family Investments in Human Capital: Earnings
of Women," *Journal of Political Economy* 82, no. 2, Part 2 (March/April 1974): S76–S108; and
Mary Corcoran and Greg J. Duncan, "Work History, Labor Force Attachment, and Earnings
Differences Between Races and Sexes," *The Journal of Human Resources* 14, no. 1 (Winter 1979):
3–20. For summaries of this literature, see Francine D. Blau, "Discrimination Against Women:
Theory and Evidence," ed. William A. Darity, Jr., *Labor Economics: Modern Views* (Boston:
Kluwer-Nijhoff, 1984): pp. 53–89; Cynthia Lloyd and Beth Niemi, *Economics of Sex Differen-
tials*; and Donald J. Treiman and Heidi I. Hartmann, eds., *Women, Work and Wages: Equal Pay
for Jobs of Equal Value* (Washington, D.C.: National Academy Press, 1981).

Table 8.1 we show the proportions of the male-female wage differentials that are explained by the sex differences in work history, formal education, and labor force attachment shown in Table 7.5 of Chapter 7.

Differences in work history (labor market experience) were relatively more important in explaining wage differences between white men and black and white women, while differences in formal education were relatively more important in explaining racial wage differences. Less on-the-job training was a significant factor lowering the wages of both blacks and women in comparison to white men. Perhaps, surprisingly, indicators of labor force attachment, like absenteeism and placing constraints on job location or hours, did not play an important role in explaining wage differences between white men and black and white women. Though, as we have seen, there were substantial sex differences in attachment, this factor was not very strongly related to the wages of either men or women.

Table 8.1 indicates that while such qualifications are indeed important determinants of sex and race wage differentials, they are only part of the story. Together, differences in qualifications are estimated to explain the following:

- 44 percent of the wage differential between white women and white men
- 32 percent of the (larger) wage differential between black women and white men
- 53 percent of the wage differential between black and white men.

The proportion of the pay differential that is not explained by productivity-related characteristics (which serves as an estimate of the impact of labor market discrimination on earnings differential by sex or race) is roughly half or more of the pay gap in each case. This is particularly striking in light of the many job-related qualifications taken into account in this particular study.[4]

We saw in Chapter 6 that the relative earnings of younger women have been increasing in comparison to those of younger men in recent years. Does that mean that labor market discrimination against that group has been declining? Not necessarily, for their relative qualifications have also been rising. In particular, women have increased their receipt of higher degrees and their representation in traditionally male fields of study. A recent study that focused on new entrants (workers who had completed their schooling one to two years previously) found that the estimate of labor market discrimination against white females (relative to white males) actually increased between 1970 and

---

[4]A more recent study using data collected by the Bureau of the Census in 1979 found that labor market experience, work interruptions, and education explained only 15 percent of the male-female earnings gap. (Joseph J. Salvo and John M. McNeil, *Lifetime Work Experience and Its Effect on Earnings: Retrospective Data from the 1979 Income Survey Developmennt Program,* U.S. Bureau of the Census, Current Population Reports, Series P-23, no. 136, [June 1984]. The estimate of discrimination in the study by Salvo and McNeil (85 recent) is considerably higher than that from the Corcoran and Duncan study reported in the text. This is probably because Salvo and McNeil lacked information on job tenure and on-the-job training and, thus, were not able to include them in their analysis.

TABLE 8.1   Percentages of the Wage Gap Between White Men and Other Groups of Workers Explained by Differences in Qualifications 1975[a]

	BLACK MEN (%)	WHITE WOMEN (%)	BLACK WOMEN (%)
Formal education	38	2	11
Years of training completed on current job	15	11	8
Other work history	3	28	14
Indicators of labor force attachment	−3	3	−1
Unexplained	47	56	68
Total	100	100	100
Wage Differential (%)[b]	23	36	43

[a]Includes workers aged 18 to 64.
[b]This is computed on the basis of the geometric means of the hourly wage for each group.
Source: Mary Corcoran and Greg J. Duncan, "Work History, Labor Force Attachment, and Earnings Differences Between Races and Sexes," *The Journal of Human Resources* 14, no. 1 (Winter 1979): 8, 18. Reprinted by permission of the publisher.

1980, while the estimate of labor market discrimination against black males and black females (vis-a-vis their white male counterparts) remained about the same.[5]

How conclusive are such estimates? Certainly not entirely so because there are a number of problems with these types of analyses that may result in either upward or downward biases in the estimate of discrimination. One difficulty is that we do not have information on all the qualifications of individuals that are associated with their (potential) productivity. Some of the factors that affect earnings, like motivation or work effort, cannot easily be quantified. Others, for example, field of specialization in school, may simply be unavailable in any particular data set.[6] Thus, it is not possible to include all

[5]Gordon W. Green, Jr., "Wage Differentials for Job Entrants, by Race and Sex," unpublished doctoral dissertation, George Washington University (December 1983). Since data on actual labor market experience and work force interruptions are not available in the census data used in this study, their effects are not controlled in the estimate of discrimination. However, since the results cited in the text refer to recent entrants, this omission is not likely to be too serious. On the other hand, another study that considered male and female workers of all ages did find evidence of reduced discrimination against the younger cohorts. See Francine D. Blau and Andrea H. Beller, "Trends in Sex and Race Differentials: 1971–1981," paper presented at the American Economic Association Meetings, Dallas (December 1984).

[6]In a rare study that did include information on college major, it was found that, in 1979, differences in college major explained almost half of the earnings differential between recent male and female college graduates. See Thomas N. Daymont and Paul J. Andrisani, "Why Women Earn Less than Men: The Case of Recent College Graduates," Industrial Relations Research Association, *Proceedings of the Thirty-Sixth Annual Meetings* (December 1982), pp. 425–35. While these results suggest the importance of this factor, it is not necessarily the case that field of study would account for such a high proportion of the larger pay differential between male and female workers as a whole (in contrast to new entrants). In any case, disentangling the effects of field of study from sex composition of the occupation is no easy matter.

relevant job qualifications in an analysis, and the impact of labor market discrimination may be misestimated. If men are more qualified with respect to the factors that are not included in the analysis, the extent of labor market discrimination is likely to be *overestimated*. For instance, some of the portion of the sex differential, which is found to be "unexplained," may, in fact, be due to males being more highly motivated or concentrating in more lucrative fields of study. On the other hand, women may be more highly qualified in some respects not taken account of, in which case discrimination may be underestimated. In general, the concern is that discrimination is likely to be overestimated due to omitted factors.[7]

On the other hand, as noted above, some of the lower qualifications of women may be directly the result of labor market discrimination against them. For example, qualified women may be excluded from training programs or denied promotion to higher-level jobs. While the resulting sex differences in qualifications could accurately reflect productivity differences, these differences in productivity (and the consequent differences in pay) would be due to labor market discrimination. To the extent that studies of discrimination control for qualifications that themselves reflect the direct effects of labor market discrimination, the impact of discrimination on the pay gap will be *underestimated*.[8] Further, the feedback effects of labor market discrimination on the behavior and choices of women themselves are also neglected by such analyses. For example, the lesser amount of work experience obtained by women in comparison to men may be due in part to the lower economic incentives they face to accumulate such experience.

Where does this leave us? It suggests that pinpointing the exact portion of the pay gap that is due to labor market discrimination is difficult. Nonetheless, the findings of most studies provide strong evidence of pay differences between men and women that are *not* accounted for by sex differences in qualifications, even when the list of qualifications is quite extensive. Further evidence that labor market discrimination exists is provided by the many employment discrimination cases in which employers have been found guilty

[7]This problem is a bit less serious than it appears at first glance in that the included factors most likely capture some of the effects of those that cannot be controlled for due to lack of information. For example, it is likely that more-educated individuals are also more intelligent and more able, on the average, than the less-educated. For an interesting explication of the statistical issues raised by imperfect measures of productivity in empirical analyses, see Arthur Goldberger, "Reverse Regression and Salary Discrimination," *Journal of Human Resources* 19, no. 3 (Summer 1984): 293–318.

[8]This point is made by Alan Blinder, "Wage Discrimination: Reduced Form and Structured Estimates," *Journal of Human Resources* 8, no. 4 (Fall 1973): 436–55. For evidence consistent with discrimination against women in access to on-the-job training, see Greg J. Duncan and Saul Hoffman, "On-the-Job Training and Earnings Differences by Race and Sex," *Review of Economics and Statistics* 61, no. 4 (Nov. 1979): 594–603.

of discrimination in pay or have reached out-of-court settlements with the plaintiffs.[9] Finally, it is suggestive that the American public believes there is such discrimination. In a Louis Harris National Survey conducted in 1984, over 70 percent of black and white women and over 55 percent of black and white men agreed that "Women often do not receive the same pay as men for doing comparable jobs with similar skill and training."[10] We conclude that sex discrimination does indeed exist. While precisely estimating its magnitude is difficult, the evidence suggests that the *direct* effects of labor market discrimination may explain half or more of the pay differential between men and women.

Occupational Differences

As we saw in Chapter 6, not only do women earn less than men, they also tend to be concentrated in different occupations. In this section, we address two questions.

1. What are the *consequences* for women of such occupational segregation? In particular, what is its relationship to the pay gap between men and women?
2. What are the *causes* of these sex differences in occupational distributions? Specifically, what role does labor market discrimination play?

From a policy perspective, an understanding of the consequences of segregation is crucial for assessing how important a problem it is, while an analysis of its causes helps us to determine the most effective tools for attacking it.

Consequences of occupational segregation. Table 8.2 shows median weekly earnings of full-time workers in detailed occupational categories with the highest and lowest pay. The occupations were ranked on the basis of the median earnings of *all* (male and female) employees. However, where data are available, it may be seen that the same occupation tends to provide relatively

---

[9]For example, in an out-of-court settlement announced in October 1983, General Motors Corporation agreed to pay $42.5 million to settle a suit charging employment discrimination against women, blacks, and Hispanics. Some indication of the volume of complaints alleging sex discrimination is provided in the Annual Reports of the Equal Employment Oportunity Commission (the federal agency that enforces the Equal Pay Act and Title VII of the Civil Rights Act). In fiscal year 1981, approximately half of the 94,460 charges received by the Commission alleged sex discrimination. A review of the provisions of the employment discrimination laws and regulations is provided later in this chapter.

[10]*Ms. Magazine,* July 1984, p. 59. A Gallup survey of women executives with the title of vice president or higher found that 70 percent answered yes to the question, "Have you ever felt that you were being paid less than a man of equal ability?" *The Wall Street Journal,* October 29, 1984, p. 31.

TABLE 8.2 Median Weekly Earnings of Full-Time Workers by Sex and Selected Occupation, 1983 Annual Averages[a]

OCCUPATION	EARNINGS			RATIO FEMALE TO MALE EARNINGS (PERCENT)	PERCENT FEMALE IN OCCUPATION
	TOTAL	MEN	WOMEN		
Total	$309	$379	$252	66.6	40.4
Occupations with Highest Earnings					
Administrators, protective services	509	—	—	—	11.3
Personnel and labor relations managers	502	605	—	—	44.1
Purchasing managers	557	625	—	—	22.5
Managers, marketing, advertising, and public relations	559	614	367	59.8	21.0
Administrators, education and related areas	505	557	401	69.5	35.8

236

Management analysts	556	—	—	—	42.6
Architects	502	507	—	—	13.3
Engineers	603	604	500	82.8	5.9
Mathematical and computer scientists	546	602	448	74.4	29.7
Natural scientists	508	538	409	76.0	19.2
Physicians	504	508	421	82.9	22.8
Pharmacists	509	529	—	—	27.8
Teachers, college and university	502	508	403	79.3	28.5
Economists	600	703	—	—	36.5
Lawyers and judges	650	670	575	85.8	19.6
Securities and financial services sales	508	607	—	—	26.8
Supervisors, protective service	500	501	—	—	4.2
Supervisors, mechanics, and repairers	501	501	—	—	7.2
Structural metal workers, construction trades	513	514	—	—	0.0
Rail transportation occupations	506	506	—	—	0.7

TABLE 8.2 Median Weekly Earnings of Full-Time Workers by Sex and Selected Occupation, 1983 Annual Averages[a] (Continued)

OCCUPATION	EARNINGS			RATIO FEMALE TO MALE EARNINGS (PERCENT)	PERCENT FEMALE IN OCCUPATION
	TOTAL	MEN	WOMEN		
Occupations with Lowest Earnings					
Salesworkers, apparel	166	—	157	—	77.8
Sales counter clerks	184	—	—	—	66.2
Cashiers	168	201	164	81.6	80.9
Teachers' aides	173	—	174	—	94.6
Child care workers, private household	69	—	69	—	98.4
Cleaners and servants, private household	135	—	135	—	95.2
Waiters and waitresses	157	210	152	72.4	82.8
Cooks, except short-order	172	197	162	82.2	47.8
Food counter, fountain and related occupations	142	—	—	—	73.0

238

Kitchen workers, food preparation	176	—	—	—	75.9
Waiters' and waitresses' assistants	162	158	—	—	36.9
Nurses' aides, orderlies, and attendants	191	231	186	80.5	86.8
Attendants, amusement and recreation facilities	199	—	—	—	37.9
Child-care workers	158	—	164	—	88.8
Textile sewing machine operators	166	—	164	—	94.0
Shoe machine operators	173	—	—	—	72.2
Pressing machine operators	196	—	—	—	60.7
Laundry and dry cleaning machine operators	176	—	164	—	62.4
Garage- and service station related occupations	168	169	—	—	2.8
Farm workers	179	182	153	84.1	12.7

[a]Earnings are not shown where base is less than 50,000 workers. Occupational categories are not all at the same level of aggregation.

Source: Earl F. Mellor, "Weekly Earnings in 1983: A Look at More than 200 Occupations," *Monthly Labor Review* 188, no. 1 (January 1985): 54–59.

high or low earnings for both sexes (in comparison to the median earnings for the group as a whole). The percentage female in the full time work force of each occupation is shown in the last column of the table. In 18 out of the 20 highest paying jobs, the representation of women is smaller than their share of the employed full-time labor force as a whole, often considerably so. On the other hand, 16 out of the 20 lowest paying jobs are predominantly female, and in 10 of these, the female share exceeds 70 percent.

Thus, the data in Table 8.2 suggest that women are concentrated in relatively low-paying occupations. At the same time, where information on the pay of both men and women is available, we see that the ratio of female to male earnings within detailed occupations is generally higher than the overall ratio of female to male earnings of 66.6 percent. (This appears to be less true of the managerial categories than of the others, possibly because of the recency of women's entry into these jobs, as well as the greater scope for hierarchical differentiation within them.) These two observations taken together suggest that occupational segregation and the concentration of women in low-paying occupations help to explain the male-female earnings gaps.

When this question is examined more systematically with data from the 1980 Census, it is found that 35 to 39 percent of the earnings difference between men and women is associated with sex differences in the distribution of employment among 479 detailed occupational categories.[11] While the number of occupational categories available in the Census is impressive, employers use even finer breakdowns. It is very likely that were such extremely detailed categories available for the economy as a whole, an even higher proportion of the pay gap would be attributed to occupational segregation.[12] Moreover, such aggregate analyses do not take into account the tendency of women to be employed in low-wage firms and of men to be employed in high-wage firms within the same occupational category.[13] Also, when only earnings are examined, the full difference in rewards is often underestimated, for women are considerably more likely to be in positions that have fewer fringe benefits, such as insurance and pension plans.

On the other hand, there are factors other than the sex composition of these occupations that help to account for the pay differences among them. For example, male jobs may tend to require more education and training than female jobs or call for the exercise of skills, like supervisory responsibility,

---

[11]Treiman and Hartmann, eds., *Women, Work, and Wages.*

[12]As an example of the imporance of these factors, in one large fiduciary institution, it was found that 76 percent of the pay gap between equally qualified men and women was due to sex differences in occupational distributions (see Francine D. Blau, "Occupational Segregation and Labor Market Discrimination," ed. Barbara Reskin, *Sex Segregation in the Workplace: Trends, Explanations, Remedies* (Washington, D.C.: National Academy Press, 1984), pp. 117–143.

[13]For documentation of this employment pattern, see Francine D. Blau, *Equal Pay in the Office* (Lexington, MA: Lexington Books, 1977).

that are more valuable to the employer. Also, some require more physical strength, inconvenient hours, etc. Such characteristics are important, but occupational differences do appear to be a significant factor in explaining the earnings gap, even when other productivity-related factors are controlled for. A variety of researchers have found that, all else equal, employment in a predominately female occupation is significantly negatively related to female earnings. Male workers are often found to earn less in female jobs as well.[14]

In evaluating the negative consequences of occupational segregation on women, it is important to bear in mind that the focus upon earnings does not take into account any adverse nonpecuniary consequences of such segregation for women. For one, it is likely that occupational segregation reinforces cultural notions that there are fundamental differences between men and women in capabilities, preferences, and social and economic roles.

Causes of occupational segregation. As with earnings differences, the causes of occupational segregation may be classified into supply-side vs demand-side factors. It is only the latter—differences in treatment—that represents *direct* labor market discrimination. Of course, the anticipation of or experience with labor market discrimination may indirectly influence women's choices via feedback effects.

In the preceding chapter, we considered a variety of supply-side factors that would influence women's occupational choices, including the socialization process and various barriers to their obtaining training in traditionally male fields. Human capital theorists also argue that since women generally anticipate shorter and less continuous work lives than men, it will be in their economic self-interest to choose female occupations, which presumably require smaller human capital investments and have lower wage penalties for time spent out of the labor market. On the demand side, employers may contribute to occupational segregation by discriminating against equally qualified women in hiring, placement, access to training programs, and promotion for traditionally male jobs.

While it is not possible to ascribe a specific portion of sex differences in occupations to supply-side vs. demand-side factors, the evidence suggests that both are important. As in the case of pay differences, evidence of discrimination may be found in both academic studies and the many discrimination cases

---

[14]See, for example, Andrea Beller, "Occupational Segregation by Sex: Determinants and Changes," *Journal of Human Resources* 17, no. 3 (Summer 1982): 317–92; Paula England, "The Failure of the Human Capital Theory to Explain Occupational Sex Segregation," *Journal of Human Resources* 17, no. 3 (Summer 1982): 358–70; Paula England, Marilyn Chassie, and Linda McCormack, "Skill Demands and Earnings in Female and Male Occupations," *Sociology and Social Research* 66, no. 2 (Jan. 1982): 147–68; and June O'Neill, "The Determinants and Wage Effects of Occupational Segregation," The Urban Institute (unpublished paper, March 1983). For a more extensive consideration of this issue, see Blau, "Occupational Segregation and Labor Market Discrimination."

in which employers have been found guilty of such sex discrimination or have settled the cases out of court.[15] As in the case of pay discrimination, most Americans believe such occupational discrimination does exist. In a national poll conducted in 1984, 75 percent of black women and 62 percent of white women agreed that "Women are often discriminated against in being promoted to supervisory and executive jobs;" 55 percent of men of both races also thought this was the case. Similarly, half or more of the men and women surveyed believed that "Women are discriminated against in getting skilled labor jobs."[16]

THE SUBTLE BARRIERS: SEX DIFFERENCES IN SPEECH PATTERNS

Women in the workplace are less often confronted with conscious, overt discrimination today than they were in the past. However, subtle barriers continue to hamper their progress. As the excerpt below suggests, even sex differences in speech patterns may create problems for women.*

One of the funniest moments in the movie "Tootsie" is the bar scene in which Dustin Hoffman bats a pair of six-inch eyelashes and, with a perky smile, tells the waiter, "I'll have a Dubonnet on the rocks with a twist, please?"

The actor's questioning intonation at the end of a declarative sentence did more for his characterization of a woman than any number of false eyelashes. This is the way women have been socialized to speak, according to Dr. Lillian Glass, a speech pathologist who coached Mr. Hoffman for his role in "Tootsie" . . . "many casualties in the war between the sexes result from a failure to realize that men and women actually speak different languages" [she said].

The communication gap widens when the scene shifts to the workplace. There, a woman who doesn't understand male shoptalk, with all its sports and military references may find herself at a disadvantage. At a business meeting

---

[15]See, for example, Rosabeth Kanter, *Men and Women of the Corporation* (New York: Basic Books, 1977); Greg J. Duncan and Saul Hoffman, "On-the-Job Training and Earnings Differences;" Craig A. Olson and Brian E. Becker, "Sex Discrimination in the Promotion Process," *Industrial and Labor Relations Review* 36, no. 4 (July 1983): 624–41; and Robert Cabral, Marianne A. Ferber, and Carole A. Green, "Men and Women in Fiduciary Institutions: A Study of Sex Differences in Career Development," *Review of Economics and Statistics* 63, no. 4 (November 1981): 573–80. For reviews of the literature on this topic, see Paula England, "Socioeconomic Explanations of Job Segregation," ed. Helen Remick, *Comparable Worth and Wage Discrimination: Technical Possibilities and Political Realities* (Philadelphia: Temple University Press, 1984), pp. 28–46; and Patricia A. Roos and Barbara R. Reskin, "Institutional Factors Contributing to Occupational Sex Segregation," ed. Reskin, *Sex Segregation in the Workplace,* pp. 235–60. See, also, footnote 9.

[16]*Ms. Magazine,* July 1984, pp. 56, 59.

*Georgia Dullea, "Relationships, The Sexes: Differences in Speech," *New York Times,* March 19, 1984, p. C-10. Copyright © 1984 by The New York Times Company, Reprinted by permission.

last week, for example, a male colleague nudged Dr. Jerie McArthur and said, "that looks like a panic pass."

Dr. McArthur, a communications instructor at the University of Minnesota, got the message. She has taken a cram course in football jargon, and she encourages women in her management education seminars to do likewise. Since women tend to be task-oriented, she says, they may not realize what sports metaphors mean to men and even belittle such language. As a result, the men may feel uncomfortable around women.

"In the workplace," Dr. McArthur said, "the male culture is the dominant culture, and women need to understand it if both sexes are going to work together effectively. Coming in and telling men that they have to change is just not very adaptive."

But even women who know the language may not get much chance to use it in mixed company. Recent research on sex differences in male-female conversations suggests that the stereotypical wife who keeps butting in on her husband's jokes was probably never that real. Men interrupt women much more often than they do other men, according to one study, while women are less likely to interrupt either men or women.

At business meetings, Dr. McArthur said, men typically engage in "competitive turn-taking," or grabbing the floor by interrupting another speaker. Women have been conditioned from childhood to believe that to interrupt is impolite. Instead, they will sit for hours waiting for a turn to speak, she said, "while their male colleagues wonder if they'll ever have anything to say."

A woman who does speak up may undermine her credibility in other ways—by using tentative phrases such as "I guess," by turning statements into questions or by making indirect statements. In a typical scenario, a woman might say at a meeting, "Don't you think it would be better to send them that report first?" A man could then agree, saying, "Yes, it would be better to send that report first." Others at the meeting will come away with the impression that it was the man's idea because, in Dr. McArthur's words, "the woman never really claimed it."

Still another problem for women in the workplace is the use of off-color language by male colleagues. Echoing the view of several female executives interviewed, Ravelle Brickman, vice president at Richard Weiner Inc., a public-relations concern, said that the woman is then faced with a double-edged sword.

"Men in meetings routinely use four-letter words, almost as a way of establishing fraternity," she said. "When a woman is present, the man will often apologize. If the woman wants to be accepted into the fraternity, she cannot accept the apology but must, in fact, respond in kind."

MODELS OF LABOR MARKET
DISCRIMINATION

The empirical evidence suggests that there are indeed pay and occupational differences between men and women that are not accounted for by (potential) productivity differences. We now turn to an examination of how discrimination produces such sex differences in economic outcomes and why this inequality has persisted over time. Economists have developed a variety of models that may be used to analyze these issues. Unfortunately, empirical research in this area has not yet established which of these approaches most accurately describes the labor market. Indeed, for the most part, these explanations are *not* mutually exclusive and each may shed light on part of the impact of labor market discrimination on women's economic status.

Unless otherwise indicated, the analyses presented here assume that male and female labor are perfect substitutes in production. That is, it is assumed that male and female workers are equally well qualified and, in the absence of discrimination, would be equally productive and receive the same pay. Of course, we know that this assumption is not an accurate description of reality—that is, there are sex differences in qualifications that explain some of the pay gap. However, this assumption is appropriate in that models of discrimination are efforts to explain the portion of the pay gap that is *not* due to differences in qualifications. That is, to explain pay differences between men and women who are (potentially) equally productive.

Tastes for Discrimination

The foundation for the modern neoclassical analysis of labor market discrimination was laid by Gary Becker.[17] Becker conceptualized discrimination as a personal prejudice or what he termed a taste against associating with a particular group. In his model, employers, co-workers, and/or customers may all potentially have such discriminatory tastes. In contrast to the case of racial discrimination that Becker initially analyzed, it may at first seem odd to hypothesize that men would not like to associate with women when, in fact, they generally live together in families. The issue here may be more one of socially appropriate roles than of the desire to maintain social distance as Becker postulated was the case with race.[18]

Employers may have no compunctions about hiring women as secretaries but may be reluctant to employ them as pipefitters. Men may be willing to work with women who are in complementary or subordinate positions but dislike interacting with them as equals or superiors. Customers may be delighted to purchase nylons from female clerks but avoid women who sell cars or are attorneys. These discriminatory tastes may be held whether or not it is believed that women are less qualified than men for nontraditional

---

[17]Gary S. Becker, *The Economics of Discrimination.* In our presentation of the tastes for discrimination model, we incorporate some of the insights of Kenneth Arrow. See, for example, his "The Theory of Discrimination," eds. Orley Ashenfelter and Albert Rees, *Discrimination in Labor Markets* (Princeton, New Jersey: Princeton University Press, 1973), pp. 3–33.

[18]Indeed, the notion of socially appropriate roles may also be a factor in racial discrimination, as when blacks have little difficulty in gaining access to menial jobs but encounter discrimination in obtaining higher level positions.

pursuits.[19] This latter possibility is considered under notions of statistical discrimination (see below).

In order for such discriminatory tastes to have important consequences for women's earnings and employment, they must actually influence people's behavior. According to Becker, individuals with tastes for discrimination against women act as if there were nonpecuniary costs of associating with women—say in what is viewed as a socially inappropriate role.[20] The strength of the individual's discriminatory taste is measured by his or her **discrimination coefficient** (that is, the size of these costs in money terms). We now examine the consequences of discrimination based on employer, employee, and customer preferences, respectively.

Employer discrimination. If an employer has tastes for discrimination against women, he or she will act as if there were a nonpecuniary cost of employing women equal in dollar terms to d_r (the discrimination coefficient). To this employer, the costs of employing a man will be his wage, w_m, but the *full* costs of employing a woman will be her wage *plus* the discrimination coefficient ($w_f + d_r$). This means that discriminating employers will hire women only at a lower wage than men ($w_m - d_r = w_f$). Further, if we assume that men are paid in accordance with their productivity, women will be hired only if they may be paid less than their productivity.

The consequences of this situation for female workers depend on the prevalence and size of discriminatory tastes among employers, as well as on the number of women seeking employment. Nondiscriminatory employers are willing to hire men and women at the same wage rate (i.e., their discrimination coefficient equals 0). If there are a relatively large number of such nondiscriminatory employers and/or there are relatively few women seeking employment, they may all be absorbed by the nondiscriminatory firms. In this case, there will be no discriminatory pay differential based on sex, even though some employers have tastes for discrimination against women.

However, if discriminatory tastes are widespread and/or there are relatively many women seeking employment, some women will have to find jobs at discriminatory firms. As we have seen, the women obtain such employment only if w_f is less than w_m. If we assume that the labor market is competitive, all employers will pay the (same) going rate for labor of a particular sex. This means that in equilibrium the market wage differential between men and

[19]It should be noted, however, that such preferences on the part of workers or customers for men will cause women to be less productive from the point of view of the employer.

[20]Throughout, we assume that employers, co-workers, or customers have tastes for discrimination against women. It is also possible that they have positive preferences for employing, working with, or buying from men. This may be termed a kind of *nepotism*. See Matthew Goldberg, "Discrimination, Nepotism, and Long-Run Wage Differentials," *Quarterly Journal of Economics* 97, no. 2 (May 1982): 307–19 for an interesting analysis of the consequences of nepotism for the persistence of discrimination in the long run.

women must be large enough so that all the women find employment—including those who must find work at the discriminatory firms. Thus, the more prevalent and the stronger are employers' discriminatory tastes against women and/or the larger the number of women seeking employment, the larger will be the aggregate wage gap ($w_m - w_f$) between men and women.

The model of employer tastes for discrimination is consistent with the inequalities between men and women that we observe in the labor market. There may be a wage differential between equally qualified male and female workers because discriminatory employers will hire women workers only at a wage discount.[21] Further, since less discriminatory employers will hire more women workers than more discriminatory employers, male and female workers may be segregated by firm—as also appears to be the case. Finally, if, as seems likely, employer tastes for discrimination vary across occupations, occupational segregation by sex can also occur.

However, one problem that economists have identified with this model is that discrimination here is not costless to the employer who foregoes the opportunity to hire more of the lower-priced female labor and less of the higher-priced male labor. Therefore, less discriminatory firms should have lower costs of production. Such a competitive advantage would enable them to expand and drive the more discriminatory firms out of business in the long run. As the less discriminatory firms expand, the demand for female labor would be increased and the male-female pay gap would be reduced. If there were enough *entirely* nondiscriminatory firms to absorb all the women workers, the pay gap would be eliminated. Hence, the question is how discrimination, which represents a departure from profit-maximizing behavior, can withstand the impact of competitive pressures.

One answer to this question is that discrimination is likely to be related to lack of competitive pressures in the economy. Becker hypothesized that, on average, employer discrimination would be less severe in competitive than in monopolistic industries and some support has been obtained for this prediction.[22] As we shall see, it is also true that women are less highly represented in

---

[21]Some have proposed testing the employer discrimination model by comparing the sex pay gap among self-employed workers and employees. The claim is that if *employer* discrimination is responsible for the pay differential, female self-employed workers should fare relatively better than female employees, all else equal. See Victor R. Fuchs, "Differences in Hourly Earnings Between Men and Women," *Monthly Labor Review* 94, no. 5 (May 1971): 9–15; and Robert L. Moore, "Employer Discrimination: Evidence from Self-Employed Workers," *Review of Economics and Statistics* 65, no. 3 (August 1983): 496–501. While such studies have not supported the employer discrimination model, they do not provide an ideal test. If there are important economies of scale in self-employment, women's lesser endowment of capital, relative to men, could lower their returns. Also, there may be discrimination against women by lenders, suppliers, customers, etc.

[22]See, for example, William A. Luksetich, "Market Power and Sex Discrimination in White-Collar Employment," *Review of Social Economy* 37, no. 2 (October 1979): 211–24; and Timothy H. Hannan and Orley Ashenfelter, "Sex Discrimination and Market Concentration: The Case of the Banking Industry," paper presented at the American Economic Association Meetings, December 1983.

unionized employment and, thus, do not benefit from the monopoly wage advantage of unionism to the same extent as men.[23]

It has also been suggested that *monopsony* power by employers in the labor market may play a role in producing and perpetuating the sex pay differential.[24] A firm has monopsony power when it is a large buyer of labor relative to the size of the particular market.

To see how this can adversely affect women consider the not uncommon case of a one-university town. In the past, when the husband's job prospects usually determined the location of the family, the faculty wife with a Ph.D. had little choice but to take whatever the university offered her—most considered themselves fortunate if they were able to obtain employment at all. Even the growing numbers of egalitarian Ph.D. couples cannot entirely avoid this problem. In order to change jobs, they must find *two* acceptable alternatives in a single location.[25] This will obviously be harder to do than to find *one* desirable alternative. Thus, the Ph.D. couple will have fewer options than those with only one Ph.D. in the family. (Similar problems can arise for two-career couples in other fields.)

This situation gives the employer a degree of monopsony power and is likely to lower the pay of both members of the couple relative to Ph.D.s who can relocate more easily. Note that among Ph.D. couples, both the husband's *and* the wife's salary may be adversely affected. However, since women with Ph.D.s are more likely than men Ph.D.s to have a Ph.D. spouse, this factor will probably have a larger adverse effect on academic women as a group than on academic men.[26]

Another reason for the persistence of discrimination in the labor market

---

[23]For an analysis of the contribution of this factor to the pay gap, see Orley Ashenfelter, "Discrimination and Trade Unions," eds. Ashenfelter and Rees, *Discrimination in Labor Markets.*

[24]Janice F. Madden, *The Economics of Sex Discrimination* (Lexington, MA: Lexington Books, 1973).

[25]Unless, of course, they adopt the solution of the growing number of two-career couples who work in different locations and see each other, say, on weekends. It is estimated that in 1985 about one million married couples lived apart in order to keep their jobs or advance their careers (*Wall Street Journal,* June 24, 1985), p. 17.

[26]There is evidence, at least for one institution, that both men and women with a spouse who was also a faculty member were paid less. (Marianne A. Ferber and Jane W. Loeb, "Professors, Performance and Rewards," *Industrial Relations* 13, no. 1 [February 1974]: 67–77.) Madden offers the monopsony model as a general explanation for the sex pay gap. She argues that such factors as occupational segregation and the power of male unions may limit women's options and, thus, decrease their wage elasticity of supply to the firm, all else equal. Further, women tend to engage in less job search than men and to seek jobs that are closer to home. However, as Francine Blau and Carol Jusenius ("Economists' Approaches to Sex Segregation in the Labor Market: An Appraisal," *Signs: Journal of Women in Culture and Society* 1, no. 3, Pt. 2 [Spring 1976]: 181–99) point out, women's wage elasticity of supply to the firm is increased by the fact that home work provides a viable alternative for those at the margin of labor force participation. Furthermore, if men are more likely than women to acquire firm-specific training that would also lower their mobility relative to women. It seems likely, as suggested by the example we present in the text, that the monopsony explanation is more applicable to specific occupations and specific labor markets than to the aggregate sex pay differential.

is the possibility (not originally considered by Becker) that the employers' motivation for discriminating against women is not simply personal prejudice but is related to actual or perceived differences between male and female workers in productivity or behavior. We consider such models of "statistical discrimination" later in this chapter. A major contribution of Becker's, however, is the realization that, even if employers themselves have no taste for discrimination against women, their profit-maximizing behavior may result in sex discrimination in the labor market if employees or customers have such tastes. There is no conflict here with the profit maximization of employers. Hence, there is no economic reason why this type of discrimination cannot continue. We now consider the possibility of discriminating employees and customers.

Employee discrimination. If a male employee has tastes for discrimination against women, he will act as if there were nonpecuniary costs of working with women equal to his discrimination coefficient, d_e. This is the premium he must be paid to induce him to work with women.[27] This is analogous to the compensating wage differential which economists expect workers to be offered for unpleasant or unsafe working conditions.

What will be the profit-maximizing employer's response to this situation? One solution would be for the employer to hire a sex-segregated work force. This would eliminate the necessity of paying a premium to male workers for associating with female wokers. If all employers responded in this way (but had no taste for discrimination themselves), male and female workers would be paid the same wage rate, although they would work in segregated settings.

However, complete segregation may not be profitable where there are substantial costs of adjustment from the previous situation.[28] For example, the hiring of new workers entails recruitment and screening costs for the firm. Further, for jobs in which firm-specific training is important, the firm must incur the costs of these investments as well. Where there are such costs to change, history matters. Given rising female participation rates over time, women, as relatively new entrants, will find men already in place in many sectors. Further, as we saw in Chapter 2, women were heavily concentrated in a few female-dominated activities even when they constituted a small proportion of the labor force. Regardless of the various factors initially causing this segregation, adjustment costs in conjunction with employee tastes for discrimination could help to perpetuate it.

Given employee tastes for discrimination and adjustment costs, market-wide wage differences between male and female workers may result. Again, the size of the wage differential depends on the distribution and intensity of

---

[27]Male workers may also require higher pay to induce them to work with women to satisfy their need to establish their superiority.

[28]Arrow, "The Theory of Discrimination."

employees' discriminatory tastes, as well as the relative number of women seeking employment. If there is a large proportion of employees with no taste for discrimination against women and/or relatively few women seeking jobs, then it may be possible for all the women to work with nondiscriminatory men. In this case no pay differential would occur.

However, if discriminatory tastes are widespread and/or there is a relatively large number of women seeking jobs, some of the women will have to work with discriminating male workers. Those males will require higher compensation to induce them to work with women. The result will be a wage differential between male and female workers, on the average, since some males will receive this higher pay, and women may be paid less to compensate for this. There also will be more variation in male workers' wage rates than would otherwise be the case. Discriminating male workers who do not work with women do not need to be paid a wage premium, nor do non-discriminating males, regardless of whether or not they are employed with women.

In an empirical test of this prediction, one study compared the wages of men and women (within the same narrowly defined white-collar occupations) in sex-integrated and sex-segregated firms. It was found that, contrary to what was expected on the basis of the employee discrimination model, men earned *more* in sex-segregated than in integrated firms, and women earned *more* when they worked with men than when they worked only with other women. These findings are more consistent with a situation in which high wage (for example, monopolistic, unionized) employers are better able to indulge their preferences for hiring men than one in which the pay differential is due to employee discrimination.[29] There may, however, be other areas in which employee discrimination has played an important role.

If, as we speculated earlier, employee tastes for discrimination do exist, and, if they vary by occupation, employee discrimination may be a factor causing occupational segregation as well as pay differentials. For example, one reason why women are often not hired for supervisory and managerial positions may be that male employees who do not mind working with women, nonetheless, do not like being supervised by them. Female as well as male employees may not like to have women supervisors.[30] This could also create a barrier to the employment of women in such jobs.

As Barbara Bergmann and William Darity have pointed out, employee

---

[29]Blau, *Equal Pay in the Office.*

[30]In a 1984 poll of women executives with the title of vice president or higher, 41 percent answered yes to the question, "Have you ever felt that a male subordinate resisted taking orders from you because he felt threatened by a female boss?" (*The Wall Street Journal,* October 29, 1984, p. 31). It is not clear how persistent such attitudes are in the face of actual experience with a female superior. For example, one study found that while both men and women, on the average, expressed a preference for a male boss, both rated women more highly than men among the bosses they ever had. See Marianne A. Ferber, Joan A. Huber, and Glenna Spitze, "Preferences for Men as Bosses and Professionals," *Social Forces* 58, no. 2 (December 1979): 466–76.

discrimination may also adversely affect the morale and productivity of discriminating male workers who are forced to work with women, a possibility not initially considered by Becker.[31] This would make employers reluctant to hire women, especially when their male employees have considerable firm-specific training and are hard to replace. Further, if employers did hire women under such circumstances, they would pay them less to compensate for the reduction in the productivity of the discriminating male employees. In a sense, a woman's marginal productivity is lower than a man's because adding her to the work force causes a decline in the productivity of previously employed male workers. Adding an additional male worker causes no such decline in output.

Another way in which employee discrimination could affect worker productivity, which was also not initially considered by Becker, is to directly reduce the productivity of women in comparison to men. This is most likely to be a problem in traditionally male fields where the majority of workers are male. For example, on-the-job training frequently occurs informally as supervisors and/or co-workers demonstrate how things are done and give advice and assistance. When male employees have tastes for discrimination against women, they are likely to be unwilling or reluctant to teach them these important skills, and, as a result, women may learn less and be less productive.

The informal barriers we discussed in Chapter 7 with respect to women's acquisition of formal schooling are also relevant here. Women may participate less in the beneficial *mentor-protégé* relationships that often develop between senior and junior workers and may be excluded from the *informal networks* that tend to arise among peers at the workplace. As a result, they will be denied access to important job-related information, skills, and contacts, as well as the informal support systems that male workers generally enjoy. In these cases, although women are *potentially* equally productive, discrimination has the effect of reducing both their productivity and pay.

It is important to recognize that discrimination against women by fellow employees or by employers is not always conscious and overt. As a female management consultant comments:

> Men I talk to would like to see more women in senior management... But they don't recognize the subtle barriers that stand in the way... At senior management levels, competence is assumed... What you're looking for is someone who fits, someone who gets along, someone you trust. Now that's subtle stuff. How does a group of men feel that a woman is going to fit?

A female vice president of a large bank echoes these sentiments. She believes it will be many years before a woman is appointed to the higher position of executive vice president in her organization because:

[31]Barbara R. Bergmann and William A. Darity, Jr., "Social Relations in the Workplace and Employer Discrimination," *Proceedings of the Thirty-Third Annual Meetings of the Industrial Relations Research Association* (University of Wisconsin, Madison, 1981), pp. 155–62.

...the men just don't feel comfortable... They make all sorts of excuses —that I'm not a banker [she worked as a consultant originally], that I don't know the culture. There's a smokescreen four miles thick. I attribute it to being a woman.

In general, as Rosabeth Kanter has pointed out, women's position as "tokens" in male-dominated fields subjects them to special pressures and difficulties with which their male peers do not have to contend.[32]

Customer discrimination. Customers or clients who have tastes for discrimination against women will act as if there were a nonpecuniary cost associated with purchasing a good or a service from a woman, equal to their discrimination coefficient, d_c. In order to sell as much as a comparable male, a woman would have to charge a lower price. Again, discrimination, this time on the part of possible customers or clients, may result in potentially equally productive women being less productive (in terms of revenue brought in) than comparable males. They are, thus, less desirable employees and receive lower pay. If, as we speculated earlier, such customer discrimination exists in some areas but not in others, occupational segregation may also result.

As in the case of employee discrimination, women as well as men may have these prejudices. A national poll conducted in 1983 found that half of the women surveyed preferred men as doctors and bus drivers, and 36 percent said they would prefer a male accountant. There was also evidence of some intriguing conflicts which suggest that these views may change as more women (and men) have firsthand experience with women in nontraditional areas. For example, a woman accountant claimed that women made better accountants than men but that men were better doctors and bus drivers than women. On the other hand, a woman bus driver preferred women as bus drivers but said, "men are more shrewd about accounting."[33]

Statistical Discrimination

As noted earlier, models of statistical discrimination developed by Edmund Phelps and others[34] attribute a different motivation to employers for discrimination, one that is consistent with profit maximization and, thus, with

[32]See Kanter, *Men and Women of the Corporation*. The quotations in the text are from Susan Fraker, "Why Women Aren't Getting to the Top," *Fortune Magazine* 109, no. 8 (April 16, 1984): 40.

[33]*New York Times* (December 4, 1983): pp. 1, 36. Also Ferber, Huber, and Spitze, "Preferences for Men as Bosses and Professionals," found that both men and women who had ever known any women in a particular profession were less likely to prefer a man in that profession.

[34]See, for example, Edmund S. Phelps, "The Statistical Theory of Racism and Sexism," *American Economic Review* 62, no. 4, September 1972: 659–61; Arrow, "The Theory of Discrimination;" Dennis J. Aigner and Glen C. Cain, "Statistical Theories of Discrimination in Labor Markets," *Industrial and Labor Relations Review* 30, no. 2, (January 1977): 175–87; and Peter Lewin and Paula England, "Reconceptualizing Statistical Discrimination," paper presented at the annual meeting of the Southwest Social Science Association, San Antonio, Texas (March 1982).

the persistence of discrimination in the long run. In this view, employers are constantly faced with the need for decision-making under conditions of incomplete information or uncertainty. Even if they carefully study qualifications of applicants, they never know for certain how individuals will perform on the job or how long they will stay with the firm after being hired. Mistakes can be costly, especially where there are substantial hiring and training costs. Promotion decisions entail similar risks, although in this case employers have additional firsthand information on past job performance with the firm.

In light of these uncertainties, it is not surprising that employers often use any readily accessible information that may be correlated with productivity or job stability in making difficult personnel decisions. If they believe that, *on average,* women are less productive or less stable employees, *statistical discrimination* against *individual* women may result. That is, employers may judge the individual woman on the basis of their beliefs about group averages. The result is discrimination against women in pay and/or hiring and promotion.

For example, suppose an employer is screening applicants for an entry-level managerial position and that the two major qualifications considered are level of education and grades. Assume further that the employer believes that at the same level of qualifications (say, an MBA with an A- average), women as a group will be less likely to remain with the firm than men. Then, for a given level of qualifications, the employer would hire a woman only at a lower wage or, perhaps, simply hire a man rather than a woman for the job. More careful screening of applicants might enable the employer to distinguish more from less career-oriented women (for example, a consideration of the candidate's employment record while a student or of extracurricular activities while in school), but it may not be cost-effective for the employer to invest the additional resources necessary to do this.

Judged on the basis of statements employers themselves make, such beliefs regarding differences in average ability or behavior by sex are quite common. For example, in one study male managers and administrators compared men and women with respect to a variety of traits that are likely to be related to productivity. Men as a group were rated more highly on understanding the "big picture" of the organization; aproaching problems rationally; getting people to work together; understanding financial matters; sizing up situations accurately; administrative capability; leadership potential; setting long-range goals and working toward them; wanting to get ahead; standing up under fire; keeping cool in emergencies; independence and self-sufficiency; and aggressiveness. Women scored more highly on clerical aptitude; being good at detail work; and enjoyment of routine tasks. They were also perceived as crying easily; being sensitive to criticism; timid; jealous; being excessively emotional regarding their jobs; being more likely to be absent and to quit; and putting family matters ahead of their job.[35]

Interviews with male executives generally reveal the recurrent concern that women do not take their careers as seriously as men and the fear that they will quit their jobs when they have children. "For years, women managers say, the feeling was that mothers shouldn't work; now it's that workers shouldn't be mothers." This is the case, even though a 1980 study of women managers found that median maternity leave after the birth of the baby was only three months.[36]

If such employer beliefs are simply incorrect or exaggerated or reflect time lags in adjusting to a new reality, actions based on them are clearly unfair and constitute labor market discrimination as we have defined it. That is, they generate wage and occupation differences between men and women that are not accounted for by (potential) productivity differences. If such views are not simply rationalizations for personal prejudice, it might be expected that over time they will yield to new information. However, this process may be more sluggish than one would like and, meantime, employers make less than optimal choices.

The situation is different, and a bit more complicated, if the employer views *are* indeed correct *on the average.* Employers make the best choices possible with imperfect knowledge, and, in a sense, labor market discrimination, as we have defined it, does not exist in this case—any resulting wage and employment differences between men and women would be accounted for by *average* productivity differences.

Yet, the consequences for *individual* women are far from satisfactory. A particular woman who would be as productive and as stable an employee as her male counterpart is denied employment or paid a lower wage. It seems fairly clear from a *normative* perspective that basing employment decisions on a characteristic like sex—a characteristic that the individual cannot change—is unfair. Indeed, the practice of judging an *individual* on the basis of *group* characteristics rather than upon his or her own merits seems the very essence of stereotyping and discrimination. Such behavior is certainly not legal under the antidiscrimination laws and regulations that we discuss later in this chapter. Yet, it most likely still plays a role in employer thinking. Moreover, statistical discrimination, which is based on employers' *correct* assessment of average sex differences, is not likely to be eroded by the forces of competition.

[35]Benson, Rosen and T. H. Jerdee, "Perceived Sex Differences in Managerially Relevant Behavior," *Sex Roles* 4, no. 6 (December 1978): 837–43.

[36]Barbara Tolman, "Maternity Costs: Parenthood and Career Overtax Some Women Despite Best Intentions," *Wall Street Journal* (September 7, 1983): pp. 1, 21; see, also, Susan Fraker, "Why Women Aren't Getting to the Top."

As Kenneth Arrow has pointed out, the consequences of statistical discrimination are particularly pernicious where there are *feedback effects*.[37] For example, if employers' views of female job instability lead them to give women less firm-specific training and to assign them to jobs where the costs of turnover are minimized, women have little incentive to stay and may respond by exhibiting exactly the unstable behavior that employers expect. Employers' perceptions are confirmed, and they see no reason to change their discriminatory behavior. Yet, if employers had believed women to be stable workers and had hired them into positions that rewarded such stability, they might well have been stable workers! Hence, where statistical discrimination is accompanied by feedback effects, even employer behavior that is based on *initially* incorrect assessments of average sex differences may persist in the long run and be fairly impervious to competitive pressures.

Some indication that such feedback effects, essentially self-fulfilling prophecies, are important is provided by studies of male and female "quit" behavior.[38] On average women are indeed more likley to quit their jobs than men. However, most of this difference is explained by the types of jobs women are in. The evidence suggests that among both blacks and whites when a woman worker is confronted with the same incentives to remain on the job in terms of wages, advancement opportunities, etc., she is no more likely to quit than a comparable male worker. Similarly, it is often thought that blacks are less stable workers than whites. Yet, their quit rates appear to be no higher than those of whites on the average. Indeed, given the same job characteristics as whites, they are found to be *less* likely to quit than otherwise similar white workers.

THE SUBTLE BARRIERS:
THE ROLE OF MALE CLUBS*

There are factors influencing women's careers that may at first appear to be only tangentially related to the labor market. For instance, recent research suggests that being denied admittance to prestigious all-male private clubs can impede the progress of

[37]Arrow, "The Theory of Discrimination." The example in the text is from Kenneth Arrow, "Economic Dimensions of Occupational Segregation: Comment I," *Signs: Journal of Women in Culture and Society* 1, no. 3, Pt. 2 (Spring 1976): 233–37.

[38]See Francine D. Blau and Lawrence M. Kahn, "Race and Sex Differences in Quits by Young Workers," *Industrial and Labor Relations Review* 34, no. 4 (July 1981): 563–77; and W. Kip Viscusi, "Sex Differences in Worker Quitting," *Review of Economics and Statistics* 62, no. 3 (August 1980): 388–98. For similar findings with respect to sex differences in absenteeism, see Paul Osterman, "Sex Discrimination in Professional Employment: A Case Study," *Industrial and Labor Relations Review* 32, no. 4 (July 1979): 451–64.

*Adapted from Robin L. Bartlett, "Clubs that Exclude Women: 'Who You Know' vs.

career women. These "social" clubs are, in fact, places where influential people meet, relationships are developed, and deals are made and not simply places where weary businessmen go to relax and socialize. Moreover, court testimony demonstrates that membership in these clubs is often a prerequisite for corporate promotions.

Studies have shown that most people find their jobs through whom they know or by word of mouth. Club affiliations give those in executive positions information and contacts that allow them to reap benefits not accessible to those who are excluded. Thus, women's under-representation in high-level jobs, and their flatter experience-earnings profiles, may be traced in part to their exclusion from the networks that insiders enjoy.

Male executives also participate in other associations and activities in which women are substantially under-represented. Female executives do not belong to as many Boards of Directors, are conspicuously absent from the lay governing bodies of religious institutions, and, as students, generally missed out on the bonding provided by participation in team sports. But exclusion from important all-male clubs is an additional serious barrier because important business and professional meetings often take place there. It is, to say the least, very awkward for a young professional when a prospective employer schedules a luncheon interview at a club where women are only permitted to enter the lobby or for a female executive who arrives at a club to meet a group of peers only to be denied entry.

The Overcrowding Model

In the models we have previously discussed, sex segregation in employment (by firm or occupation) is a possible consequence of discrimination against women in hiring and job assignments, as are pay differentials. Both wage and employment differences are believed to result either from tastes for discrimination against women (among employers, employees, and/or customers) or from (real or perceived) sex differences in average productivity or job stability. Barbara Bergmann[39] has developed an analysis of the pay gap that gives a more central role to employment segregation.

While it sheds no new light on the *causes* of segregation, Bergmann's "overcrowding" model demonstrates that, regardless of the reason for segregation (for example, socialization, labor market discrimination), the consequence may be a male-female pay differential. This will occur if job opportunities (demand) in the female sector are small relative to the supply of

'What You Know,' " *Committee on the Status of Women in the Economics Profession (CSWEP) Newsletter* (Spring 1984), pp. 11–14. Adapted by permission. See also, Robin L. Bartlett and Timothy I. Miller, "Executive Compensation," paper presented at the American Economic Association Meetings, Dallas (December 1984); and Michael M. Burns, "The Exclusion of Women from Influential Men's Clubs: The Inner Sanctum and the Myth of Full Equality," *Harvard Civil Rights/Civil Liberties Law Review* 18, no. 2 (Summer 1983): 322–407.

[39]Barbara R. Bergmann, "Occupational Segregation, Wages and Profits When Employers Discriminate by Race or Sex," *Eastern Economic Journal* 1, nos. 1–2 (April–July 1974): 103–10.

women available for such work. The overcrowding model is consistent with the evidence presented earlier that, all else equal, earnings tend to be lower in predominantly female than in predominantly male jobs. The fact that men in predominantly female occupations also receive low wages is not necessarily inconsistent with the overcrowding hypothesis. Although men as a group are obviously not excluded from the male sector, some of them may, nonetheless, enter female occupations because they have a strong preference or particular skills for this type of work. Or they may be simply unlucky or poorly informed about alternative opportunities. They will accept the lower wages paid in female jobs. However, this lower pay is primarily caused by the many women who enter these jobs for lack of alternative opportunities.

This model is illustrated in Figure 8.1. "F" jobs and "M" jobs are considered. As in the previous models of discrimination, it is assumed that male and female workers are perfect substitutes for each other (that is they are potentially equally productive). The hypothetical situation in which there is no discrimination is represented by demand curves D_f and D_m and supply curves S_{fo} and S_{mo}. The nondiscriminatory equilibrium points in the two markets (E_{fo} and E_{mo}) are determined so that the wage rate (w_0) is the same for both types of jobs.

To see why this is the case, recall that we have assumed that all workers are equally well-qualified for F and M jobs and that employers are indifferent between hiring male and female workers. Suppose that, by chance, the wage in

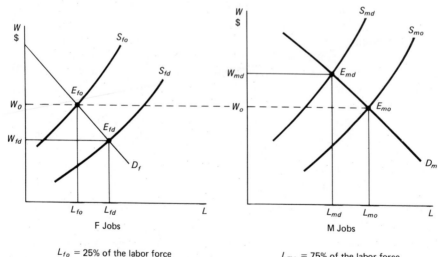

$$L_{fo} = 25\% \text{ of the labor force}$$
$$L_{fd} = 40\% \text{ of the labor force}$$

$$L_{mo} = 75\% \text{ of the labor force}$$
$$L_{md} = 60\% \text{ of the labor force}$$

FIGURE 8.1 An Illustration of the Overcrowding Model

F jobs is set higher than the wage in M jobs. Then, workers attracted by the higher wage rates would transfer from M jobs to F jobs. This process would continue until wages in F jobs were bid down to the level of wages in M jobs. Similarly, if, by chance, wages in M jobs were set above those in F jobs, workers would move from F jobs to M jobs until the differential was eliminated. Thus, in the absence of discrimination, worker mobility ensures that the wages paid for both types of work are the same, at least after there has been time to make adjustments.[40]

In the hypothetical example given in Figure 8.1, it is assumed that demand conditions are such that, in equilibrium, L_{fo} workers (25 percent of the labor force) are employed in F jobs and L_{mo} workers (75 percent of the labor force) work in M jobs. F and M jobs have no sex labels associated with them and both women and men are randomly divided between the two sectors.

How does the situation differ when there is discrimination against women in some occupations or when, for a variety of reasons, women choose to concentrate in typically female jobs? The consequences of such segregation may be ascertained by comparing the hypothetical situation in which there is no segregation to one in which M jobs are restricted to men (or women avoid such jobs). In our example, this results in an inward shift of the supply curve to male jobs from S_{mo} to S_{md}, causing wages to be bid up to w_{md}. At this higher wage only L_{md} workers (60 percent of the labor force) are employed in M jobs. The exclusion of women from M jobs means that all the women must (or choose to) "crowd" into the F jobs. The expanded supply of labor in F jobs, represented by an outward shift of the supply curve from S_{fo} to S_{fd}, depresses wages there to w_{fd}. Now L_{fd} workers (40 percent of the labor force) are employed in F occupations.

The overcrowding model shows how sex segregation in employment may cause a wage differential between otherwise equally productive male and female workers. This occurs if the supply of women seeking employment is large relative to the demand for labor in the F jobs. This may well be what actually occurs in the labor market. Nevertheless, the analysis also shows that sex segregation in employment need not always result in a wage differential between men and women. If it so happens that the wage rate that equates supply and demand in the F sector is the same as the wage that equates supply and demand in the M sector, no wage differential will result, that is, if the female sector is not overcrowded. However, this will happen only by chance. Labor market discrimination (or some other barrier) has eliminated the free mobility of labor between the two sectors that would otherwise ensure wage equality between M and F jobs.

---

[40]This also assumes that there are no *nonpecuniary* differences in the relative attractiveness of the two jobs that would result in a compensating wage differential.

Returning to the more likely situation illustrated in Figure 8.1 in which segregation does lower women's pay, we may examine its impact on the *productivity* of women relative to men. Employers of women in F jobs accommodate a larger number of workers (L_{fd} rather than L_{fo}) by substituting labor for capital. The relatively low wages of the women, w_{fd}, make it profitable to use such labor-intensive production methods. On the other hand, the higher wage in the male sector, w_{md}, encourages employers to substitute capital for labor to economize on relatively high-priced labor. In the overcrowding model, women earn less than men, but both are paid in accordance with their productivity. Discrimination causes both wage and productivity differentials between *potentially* equally productive male and female labor—women are less productive than men because, due to segregation and crowding, they have less capital to work with.

The claim that the supply of labor to a particular occupation (or industry) helps to determine the wage rate is relatively noncontroversial. But the crowding hypothesis, in and of itself, does not explain why so many women are employed in typically female sectors. Controversy has centered on the question of whether this is because men and women have inherently different talents and/or preferences for different types of work; because, due to differences in socialization and/or in household responsibilities, women are willing to trade higher wages and steeper lifetime earnings profiles for more favorable job conditions and lower penalties for discontinuous labor force participation; or because employers, co-workers, and/or customers discriminate against women in some occupations but not in others.

Institutional Models

The theme that the male-female pay gap is closely related to employment segregation is echoed in institutional models of discrimination.[41] Such explanations emphasize that labor markets may not be as flexible as the simple competitive model assumes. Rigidities are introduced both by the institutional arrangements found in many firms and by various barriers to competition introduced by the monopoly power of firms in the product market or of unions in the labor market.

[41]See, for example, Peter B. Doeringer and Michael J. Piore, *Internal Labor Markets and Manpower Analysis* (Lexington, MA: D. C. Heath and Co., 1971); Michael J. Piore, "The Dual Labor Market: Theory and Implications," ed. D. M. Gordon, *Problems in Political Economy: An Urban Perspective* (Lexington, MA: D. C. Heath and Co., 1971), pp. 90–94; Blau and Jusenius, "Economists' Approaches to Sex Segregation in the Labor Market;" Glen Cain, "The Challenge of Segmented Labor Market Theories to Orthodox Theory: A Survey," *Journal of Economic Literature* 14, 4 (Dec. 1976): 1215–57; David M. Gordon, Richard Edwards, and Michael Reich, *Segmented Work, Divided Workers: The Historical Transformation of Labor in the United States* (Cambridge: Cambridge University Press, 1982); and Michael Wachter, "Primary and Secondary Labor Markets: A Critique of the Dual Aproach," *Brookings Papers on Economic Activity,* no. 3 (1974): 637–94.

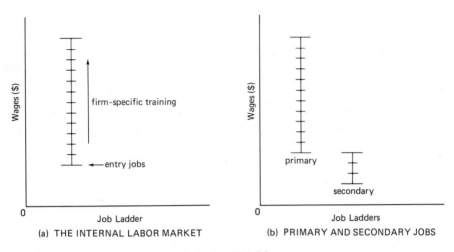

FIGURE 8.2   An Illustration of the Institutional Model

The internal labor market. Institutionalists point out that the job struc-ture of many large firms looks like the illustration in Figure 8.2(a). Firms hire workers from the outside labor market for so-called "entry jobs." The re-mainder of the jobs are internally allocated by the firm as workers progress along well-defined promotion ladders by acquiring job-related skills, many of which are firm-specific in nature. When firm-specific skills are emphasized and a high proportion of jobs are filled from internal sources, the firm has an *internal labor market.* That is, it determines wages for each job category and the allocation of workers among categories and is insulated to some extent (although not entirely) from the impact of market forces.

To administer their personnel systems, larger firms often take the oc-cupational category as the decision unit, establishing pay rates for each category (with some allowance for seniority and merit considerations), and linking jobs together into promotion ladders. Thus, group treatment of in-dividuals is the norm, and it will be to the employer's advantage to make sure that workers within each job category are as similar as possible. If it is believed that men and women (as well as, say, whites and nonwhites) differ in their productivity-related characteristics (like quit and absenteeism rates), statistical discrimination is likely to result in their being channeled into different jobs.

Primary and secondary jobs. The dual labor market model developed by Peter Doeringer and Michael Piore takes this analysis a step further and emphasizes the distinction between primary and secondary jobs.[42] **Primary**

---

[42]Doeringer and Piore, *Internal Labor Markets*; and Piore, "The Dual Labor Market."

jobs emphasize high levels of firm-specific skills and, thus, pay high wages, have good promotion opportunities, and emphasize long-term attachment between workers and firms. In **secondary jobs,** firm-specific skills are not as important. Such jobs will pay less, offer relatively fewer promotion opportunities, and have fairly high rates of labor turnover. This situation is depicted in Figure 8.2(b). Applying the dual labor market model to sex discrimination leads us to expect that men would be more likely to be in primary jobs, women in secondary jobs.

The distinction between primary and secondary jobs may occur within the same firm—say between the managerial and clerical categories. In addition, it is believed that primary jobs are more likely to be located in monopolistic, unionized industries and that secondary jobs are more likely to be found in competitive industries. This is an additional reason for expecting women to be more concentrated in the competitive sector.

Radical economists further argue that employers as a group benefit from such segmentation of the labor force by sex and race because it prevents workers from seeing their common interests. That is, capitalists (employers) practice "divide and rule" tactics to thwart unionization and other attempts by workers to share power. Radical feminists add another element to this analysis. In their view, one must take into account the effects not only of capitalism, but also of patriarchy, which is defined as a system of male oppression of women. Thus, they point to the role of male workers and of their unions, as well as of employers, in maintaining occupational segregation.[43]

Segmentation of male and female workers into primary and secondary jobs is likely to produce both pay and productivity differences between them due to unequal access to on-the-job training. Institutionalists also argue that feedback effects are likely to magnify any initial productivity differences there are, as women respond to the lower incentives for worker stability in the secondary sector.

The institutional analysis also reinforces the point made earlier that labor market discrimination against women is not necessarily the outcome of conscious, overt acts by employers. Once men and women are channeled into different types of entry jobs, the normal, everyday operation of the firm—"business as usual"—will virtually ensure sex differences in productivity, promotion opportunities, and pay. This is termed *institutional discrimination.*[44] Even sex differences in initial occupational assignment may be in part due to adherence to traditional policies that tend to work against women. For example:

[43]See Gordon, Edwards, and Reich, *Segmented Work, Divided Workers* for the radical view, and, for the radical feminist analysis, Heidi I. Hartmann, "Capitalism, Patriarchy, and Job Segregation by Sex," *Signs: Journal of Women in Culture and Society* 1, no. 3, Pt. 2 (Spring 1976): 137–69.

[44]See Roos and Reskin, "Institutional Factors Contributing to Occupational Sex Segregation," for a description of business practices that tend to adversely affect women.

- Referrals from current male employees or an informal network of male colleagues at other firms
- Sexist recruitment materials picturing women in traditionally female and men in traditionally male jobs
- Lack of encouragement of female applicants to broaden their sights from traditional areas.

Feedback Effects

As we have noted several times, labor market discrimination or unequal treatment of women in the labor market may adversely affect women's own decisions and behavior.[45] This is illustrated in Figure 8.3. Human capital theory and other supply-side explanations for gender differences in economic outcomes tend to emphasize the role of the sexual division of labor in the family in causing differences between men and women in labor market outcomes. This is indicated by the arrow pointing to the right in the figure.

While this relationship undoubtedly exists, such explanations tend to neglect the impact of labor market discrimination in reinforcing the traditional division of labor (shown by the arrow pointing to the left). Even a relatively small amount of initial labor market discrimination can have greatly magnified effects if it discourages women from making human capital investments, weakens their attachment to the labor force, and provides economic incentives for the family to place priority on the husband's career. While it is unlikely that labor market discrimination is responsible for initially having caused the traditional division of labor in the family, which clearly predates modern labor markets, it may well help to perpetuate it by inhibiting more rapid movement toward egalitarian sharing of household responsibilities today.

The net result is what might be termed a "vicious circle." Discrimination against women in the labor market reinforces traditional gender roles in the family while adherence to traditional roles by women provides a rationale for labor market discrimination. However, this also means that effective policies to end labor-market discrimination can have far-reaching effects, particularly when combined with simultaneous changes in social attitudes towards women's roles.

[45]A number of authors have emphasized the importance of feedback effects in analyzing discrimination in pay and employment. See, for example, Arrow, "Theories of Discrimination;" Barbara R. Bergmann, "Reducing the Pervasiveness of Discrimination," ed. Eli Ginzberg, *Jobs for Americans,* (Englewood Cliffs, N.J.: Prentice-Hall, 1976), pp. 120–41; Blau, *Equal Pay in the Office*; Ferber and Lowry, "The Sex Differential in Earnings;" Shelly J. Lundberg and Richard Startz, "Private Discrimination and Social Intervention in Competitive Labor Markets," *American Economic Review* 73, no. 3 (June 1983): 340–47; Myra H. Strober, "Toward Dimorphics: A Summary Statement to the Conference on Occupational Segregation," *Signs: Journal of Women in Culture and Society* 1, no. 3, Pt. 2 (Spring 1976): 293–302; and Yoram Weiss and Reuben Gronau, "Expected Interruptions in Labour Force Participation and Sex-Related Differenes in Earnings Growth," *Review of Economic Studies* 48, no. 4 (October 1981): 607–19.

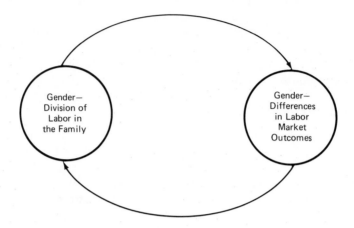

FIGURE 8.3   An Illustration of Feedback Effects

A decrease in labor market discrimination will have feedback effects as the equalization of market incentives between men and women induces further changes in women's supply-side behavior. In addition, as more women enter previously male-dominated fields, the larger number of female role models for younger women is likely to induce still further increases in the availability of women for such jobs. Thus, demand-side policies can be expected to play an important role in sustaining a process of cumulative change in women's economic status.

POLICY ISSUE: THE GOVERNMENT AND EQUAL EMPLOYMENT OPPORTUNITY

Government policies to combat labor market discrimination against women can be justified on two grounds. One is equity or fairness—"a matter of simple justice."[46] Thus, government intervention may be rationalized to assure equal treatment for all participants in the labor market, regardless of sex (or race, ethnic origin, etc.).

As well as being unfair, unequal treatment on the basis of sex may result in an inefficient allocation of resources. This provides the second rationale for government intervention. To see this, consider the case where equally productive men and women are hired for different jobs and women's jobs are lower

---

[46]This was the title of the Report of the President's Task Force on Women's Rights and Responsibilities (Washington, D.C.: U.S. Government Printing Office, April 1970).

paid (as in the overcrowding model). Under these circumstances, prices do not serve as accurate indicators of social costs. In comparison to the non-discriminatory situation, society produces "too little" of the outputs that use "overpriced" male labor, given that equally productive female labor is available at a lower price to expand production. Society produces "too much" of the outputs that use "underpriced" female labor, given that the contribution of equally productive labor is valued more highly in the male sector (as measured by its price).

The inefficiency caused by discrimination is even greater when we take into account feedback effects. If women are deterred from investing in their human capital because of discrimination, society loses a valuable resource. Thus, opening doors to women that were previously closed (or only slightly ajar) benefits society as well as individual women by bringing their talents and abilities to bear in new areas. As Nobel laureate Paul A. Samuelson commented about the gains achieved through the mid-1980s, "To the degree that women are getting an opportunity they didn't have in the past, the economy is tapping an important and previously wasted resource."[47]

Weighed against these potential gains are the costs of the increased government intervention in society that may be necessary to produce this result. Some may also fear what they regard as the possible excesses of such policies in the form of "reverse discrimination" or preferential treatment for women and minorities. However, research to date provides no evidence that the increased employment of women and minorities encouraged by legislation has entailed such efficiency costs.[48] We examine the record of government intervention in this area below.[49]

Equal Employment Opportunity Laws and Regulations

Government has long been involved in shaping conditions encountered by women in the labor market. During the period following the Civil War, in response to concern and agitation by workers and their sympathizers, a number of states passed protective labor laws limiting hours and regulating other terms of employment. At first, the Supreme Court struck these laws

---

[47]*Business Week,* January 28, 1985, p. 80.

[48]Jonathan S. Leonard, "Antidiscrimination or Reverse Discrimination: The Impact of Changing Demographics, Title VII and Affirmative Action on Productivity," *Journal of Human Resources* 19, no. 2 (Spring 1984): 145–74. Similarly, Marianne A. Ferber and Carole A. Green, "Traditional or Reverse Sex Discrimination? A Case Study of a Large Public University," *Industrial and Labor Relations Review* 35, no. 4 (July 1982): 550–64 found concern with possible reverse discrimination to be misplaced.

[49]For excellent summaries of the current legal situation, see Susan Deller Ross and Ann Barcher, *The Rights of Women: The Basic ACLU Guide to a Woman's Rights,* revised edition (Toronto: Bantam Books, 1983); and Claire Sherman Thomas, *Sex Discrimination,* Pt. 4 (St. Paul: West Publishing Co., 1982).

down as unconstitutional. The justification was that they interfered with the freedom of workers to enter contracts. Subsequently, the Court upheld such laws when they were confined to women alone, arguing that individual rights may be abridged because the state has a legitimate interest in the possible social effects of women's work. In the decision handed down in Muller v. Oregon in 1890 Supreme Court Justice Brandeis said:

> The two sexes differ in structure of body, in the functions performed by each, in the amount of physical strength, in the capacity for long-continued labor, particularly when done standing, the influence of vigorous health upon the future well-being of the race, the self-reliance which enables one to assert full rights, and in the capacity to maintain the struggle for subsistence. The difference justifies a difference in legislation, and upholds that which is designed to compensate for some of the burdens which rest upon her.

In time, however, the concern shifted from protection to equal opportunity. Indeed, protective laws came eventually to be viewed as undesirable impediments to the advancement of women.[50]

As early as 1961, President Kennedy issued an Executive Order calling for a Presidential Commission on the Status of Women. Two years later, the **Equal Pay Act** of 1963 was passed, which requires employers to pay the same wages to men and women who do substantially equal work, involving equal skill, effort and responsibility, and performed under similar conditions in the same establishment. By 1964, **Title VII** of the Civil Rights Act, which was originally to prohibit discrimination in employment on the basis of race, religion, and national origin was changed to include the word "sex."[51] Title VII prohibits sex discrimination in virtually all aspects of employment, including hiring and firing, training, promotions, wages, fringe benefits, or other terms and conditions of employment. As amended, it covers all businesses employing 15 or more workers including federal, state and local governments and educational institutions. It also prohibits discrimination by employment agencies and labor organizations. The **Equal Employment Opportunity Commission** (EEOC) is the federal agency charged with enforcing the Equal Pay Act and Title VII.

Exceptions to Title VII's prohibition of discrimination may be permitted when sex is found to be a *bona fide* occupational qualification. However, both the EEOC and the courts have taken the position that this exception should be

---

[50]Supreme Court Justice Brennan expressed this view very well in Frontiero v. Richardson, "Traditionally, discrimination was rationalized by an attitude of romantic paternalism which in practical effect put women not on a pedestal but in a cage."

[51]Since it was Howard Smith, a conservative Congressman from Virginia who proposed this amendment, it is widely believed that the purpose of doing so was to increase opposition to the bill, and reduce the chances of its passage. While the Act was passed with the word "sex" in it, the application of this law to lesbians and homosexuals has consistently been rejected by the Courts.

interpreted narrowly. That is, men and women are entitled to consideration on the basis of their individual capabilities, rather than on the basis of characteristics generally attributed to the group.[52] Nor can sex in combination with some other factor be used as a legal basis for discrimination under Title VII. The court has held, for example, that an employer cannot refuse to hire women with preschool age children while men with preschool age children are hired.[53] Sexual harrassment, including "unwanted sexual advances, employment decisions based on acceptance or rejection of sexual favors, and offensive remarks and pictures in the workplace . . .," has also been found to be illegal under Title VII.[54] Further, it is illegal to pay women lower monthly pension benefits than men.[55] In the past this practice had been justified on the basis that, on average, women live longer and, thus, it would be more costly to provide them with the same monthly benefit. Nonetheless, the courts have ruled that each woman is entitled to be treated as an individual, rather than as a group member.

The **Executive Order** 11246 issued in 1965, and amended by Executive Order 11375 in 1967 to include sex, bars discrimination in employment by all employers with federal contracts and subcontracts. It also requires affirmative action for classes of workers disadvantaged by past discrimination. Such contractors are required to analyze their own employment patterns to determine where women and minorities are under-represented. Whenever such deficiencies are found, they are to set up goals and timetables for the hiring of women and minorities and to make good faith efforts to reach their goals in the specified period. The Executive Order is enforced by the Office of Federal Contract Compliance. Violators face possible loss of their government contracts, although this sanction has been very seldom invoked.

[52]Major cases include *Weeks v. Southern Bell Telephone and Telegraph*, 408 F.2d 228 (5th Cir. 1969); *Rosenfeld v. Southern Pacific Company*, 444 F.2d 1219 (9th Cir. 1971); and *Diaz v. Pan American World Airways, Inc.*, 444 F.2d 385 (5th Cir.). In the only major case to date in which sex was found to be a bona fide occupational qualification (BFOQ), *Dothard v. Rawlinson* 433 U.S. 321 (1977), the Supreme Court allowed the hiring of males only for the position of guard in Alabama's maximum security prisons. The court reasoned that due to the nature of the prison population, as well as the atmosphere of the prison, women would be particularly subject to sexual assault, which would interfere with their job performance. Regardless of whether or not one agrees with this reasoning, this case is not likely to result in substantially greater acceptance by the courts of the BFOQ exception, since the circumstances of the case are so unique. See Ross and Barcher, *The Rights of Women*, p. 222.

[53]Philips v. Martin Marietta Corp., 400 U.S. 542 (1971).

[54]Ross and Barcher, *The Rights of Women*, p. 43. Major cases cited by them include *Barnes v. Castle*, 561 F.2d 983 (D.C. Cir. 1977); *Tomkins v. Public Service Electric and Gas Co.*, 568 F.2d 1044 (3d Cir. 1977); and *Garber v. Saxon Business Products, Inc.*, 552 F.2d 1032 (4th Cir. 1977).

[55]Relevant cases include *EEOC v. Colby College*, 589 F.2d 1139 (1st. Cir. 1978); *Peters v. Wayne State University*, 476 F. Supp. 1343 (E. D. Mich, 1979); *Spirt v. Teachers Insurance & Annuity Assn.*, 475 F. Supp. 1298 (S. D. N.Y. 1979), cited in Ross and Barcher, *The Rights of Women*, p. 92.

Effectiveness of the Government's
Anti-Discrimination Effort

Much remains to be learned about the functioning of these laws and regulations. Questions have been raised both about their effectiveness in improving opportunities for the protected categories and about the possibility noted above that they might result in "reverse discrimination" against groups that are not covered.

It is highly likely that the Equal Pay Act has had relatively little impact. The major reason is that men and women rarely do exactly the same kind of work in the same firm. However, the protection offered by this law may become more important as occupational segregation declines.

Considerably less agreement exists on the effects of Title VII and the Executive Order. While some empirical work has been done examining their effectiveness, the results have not been entirely conclusive, in large part because it is difficult to isolate the effect of legislation from other changes that have been occurring.

A review of the trends in the male-female pay gap was presented in Chapter 6. It gave no indication of a notable increase in women's economic status in the post-1964 period that might be attributable to the effects of the government's anti-discrimination effort, at least through the late 1970s or early 1980s. At the same time, blacks experienced considerable increases in their earnings relative to whites, which have been ascribed by many in part to the impact of the anti-discrimination laws.[56]

On the other hand, some more detailed studies do find positive effects of the government's policies on women's earnings and occupations.[57] Moreover, the improvement in women's economic position that began around 1980, should it prove to be the beginning of a long-term trend, could be due in part

---

[56]See Charles Brown, "The Federal Attack on Labor Market Discrimination The Mouse that Roared?" ed. Ronald Ehrenberg, *Research in Labor Economics,* (Greenwich, CN: JAI Press, 1982): 33–68.

[57]For example, one study suggests that the trend toward larger male-female earnings differentials was reversed in the middle 1960s, about the time the effect of the government legislation would be expected to become apparent. See Ronald Oaxaca, "The Persistence of Male-Female Earnings Differentials" ed. Thomas F. Juster, *The Distribution of Economic Well-Being,* (Cambridge, MA: Ballinger Publishing Company, 1977), pp. 303–44. Two other studies that also obtained positive findings attempted to measure the impact of Title VII through regional differences in its enforcement. They report that, between 1967 and 1974, enforcement of Title VII narrowed the sex differential in earnings by about 7 percentage points and sex differences in the probability of being employed in a male occupation by about 6 percentage points, all else equal. See Andrea H. Beller, "The Impact of Equal Employment Opportunity Laws on the Male/Female Earnings Differential," eds. Cynthia B. Lloyd, Emily Andrews, and Curtis L. Gilroy, *Women in the Labor Market,* (New York: Columbia University Press, 1979), pp. 304–30; and Andrea H. Beller, "Occupational Segregation by Sex: Determinants and Changes," *Journal of Human Resources* 17, no. 3 (Summer 1982): 371–92.

to the opportunities created by the government's anti-discrimination laws and regulations. This would potentially include both the direct effect of improving the treatment of women in the labor market and, in response to that, the indirect effect of increasing the incentive for women to train for nontraditional jobs.

Affirmative Action

Just as there is disagreement on the effectiveness of the government's anti-discrimination effort, so there is controversy about the form it should take. Debate has particularly centered on the desirability of affirmative action to remedy past under-representation of women (or minorities). Affirmative action plans are legally mandated only by the Executive Order or, in some instances, by court orders or out-of-court settlements of discrimination suits. But some employers have adopted such programs voluntarily.

A variety of different views are held about affirmative action. First, there are those who argue that there is no conclusive evidence that there has been serious discrimination in the past and that even if there had been, removing it would be sufficient and affirmative action is not needed. Second, there are others who accept the need for some form of affirmative action but oppose the use of goals and timetables for fear that they will be too rigidly enforced and become de-facto quotas. There is a difference of opinion, even among strong proponents of affirmative action, whether it should take the form of sincere efforts to find and encourage fully qualified candiates from the protected groups or go so far as to hire them preferentially. Some believe that preferential treatment may at times be needed to overcome the effects of past discrimination.

While employment preferences are controversial, the Supreme Court has found that they are legal under certain circumstances. Specifically, employers can voluntarily give employment preferences to minorities (and also presumably to women) as a temporary measure to remedy manifest imbalances in traditionally segregated job categories.[58] It is important to recognize, however, that most affirmative action programs do not require such preferences. For example, virtually all the employers included in a sample of government contractors stated that no lowering of employment standards was

---

[58]*Steelworkers v. Weber,* 443 U.S. 193 (1979). In June 1984, the Supreme Court ruled in the Stotts case that judges could not interfere with a *bona fide* seniority system so as to protect minority workers from layoffs. Some claimed that this decision marked a retreat from the principles of Weber, and courts could not order preferential treatment on the basis of race (sex, etc.), except to actual victims of illegal discrimination. However, in the cases decided afterwards, federal judges appeared to be narrowly interpreting the Stotts case and concluding that under most circumstances ". . . it did not prohibit the use of numerical goals to correct patterns of job discrimination," (*The New York Times,* February 10, 1985, p. 18).

necessary to achieve the company's affirmative action objectives.[59] Interestingly enough, it was found that, in most companies, affirmative action programs had brought about an improvement in personnel management systems. This may be because, in the face of affirmative action pressures, many companies implemented wider and more systematic search procedures and developed more objective criteria and procedures for hiring and promotion. Further evidence that such policies are widely regarded as advantageous comes from a 1984 survey of the chief executive officers of large corporations. More than 90 percent claimed they had established numerical objectives for affirmative action at least in part to satisfy corporate objectives unrelated to government regulations. Even more impressive is that 95 percent stated that they planned to continue to use numerical objectives regardless of government requirements.[60]

Comparable Worth

In the latter half of the 1970s, impatience with the slow progress in closing the male-female earnings gap, as well as some reluctance to accept the movement of women into different occupations as a necessary component of the solution, led to great interest in a possible alternative approach to increasing women's wages. The new idea, in simple terms, amounts to extending the notion of equal pay for equal work to the broader concept of equal pay for work of comparable worth within the firm.[61] Proponents argue this is a reasonable interpretation of Title VII and a feasible way of achieving a more rapid reduction of the male-female pay gap. Opponents point to the dif-

---

[59]The survey was conducted for the Center for National Policy Review and reported in the *BNA's Employee Relations Weekly* 1, no. 2 (September 12, 1983), p. 45. Similarly, a recent analysis of firms' employment patterns found that goals were not fulfilled with the rigidity one might expect of quotas. However, the goals did appear to be effective in that firms that promised to employ more women and minorities did actually do so in subsequent years. See Jonathan S. Leonard, "What Promises Are Worth: The Impact of Affirmative Action Goals," *Journal of Human Resources* 20, no. 1 (Winter 1985): 1–20. See also the references cited in footnote 48.

[60]The survey was conducted by Organization Resources Counselors and reported in Anne B. Fisher, "Businessmen Like to Hire by the Numbers," *Fortune* 112, no. 6 (September 1985): 26–30. The article also reports that in May 1985, the directors of the National Association of Manufacturers adopted a policy statement supporting affirmative action as "good business policy," also stating, however, that "goals, not quotas, are.the standards to be followed in the implementation of such programs."

[61]For an early article articulating the legal basis for this approach, see Ruth G. Blumrosen, "Wage Discrimination, Job Segregation, and Title VII of the Civil Rights Act of 1964", *University of Michigan Journal of Law Reform* 12, no. 3 (Spring 1979). The issues involved are thoroughly discussed in Treiman and Hartmann, *Women, Work and Wages*; E. Robert Livernash, ed., *Comparable Worth: Issues and Alternatives* (Washington, D.C.: Equal Opportunity Council, 1980); and Helen Remick, ed., *Comparable Worth and Wage Discrimination* (Philadelphia: Temple University Press, 1984).

ficulties involved in determining exactly what comparable worth means in functional terms. They are also concerned about interfering with the working of the free market and the possibility of bringing about a substantial imbalance in the supply of and demand for female workers. Both of these problems deserve serious attention.

Comparing the value to the firm of workers employed in different jobs is a difficult task involving the establishment of equivalences for various fields of education, different types of skill, and varying work environments. Nonetheless, job evaluation is used to determine pay scales, not only by governments, but also by many businesses. This certainly shows that the approach is feasible. However, it should be noted that such a procedure is generally used in conjunction with information about market wage rates, rather than as a completely separate alternative to the market. Further, existing job evaluation schemes have been criticized for undervaluing the skills and abilities that are emphasized in female jobs.

Turning to the issue of setting wages at a level other than that determined by the market, the strongest opposition to such a policy comes primarily from those who believe that the existing labor market substantially resembles the neoclassical competitive model. In such a market, only the person's qualifications and tastes limit access to jobs, and all workers are rewarded according to their productivity. In this view, raising women's wages is not only unnecessary but would lead to excess supply, hence unemployment and misallocation of resources.

On the other hand, many of those in favor of the comparable worth approach begin with a view of a segmented labor market, where workers' access to highly paid positions is often limited by discriminating employers, restrictive labor organizations, entrenched internal labor markets, and differences in the prelabor market socialization of men and women. Under such circumstances, the crowding of women into traditional occupations is believed to represent a misallocation of resources, which is permitted to continue, by societal and labor market discrimination against women. Mandating higher wages would bring the earnings of those who remain in women's jobs closer to the level of comparably qualified men.

However, raising women's wages without changing the underlying conditions that produced them could still result in job loss. This is illustrated in Figure 8.1 on page 256. Suppose we begin with the discriminatory situation. The relevant supply curves are S_{fd} and S_{md}, and wages are w_{fd} and w_{md}, in the female and male sectors, respectively. Suppose further that a comparable worth system set wages in female jobs at w_o, the rate that would prevail in the absence of discrimination. At that wage, only L_{fo}, rather than L_{fd} workers, would be demanded by employers. The remainder, $L_{fd} - L_{fo}$, would be displaced from their jobs.

If such shifts were major and abrupt (which, of course, need not be the case), the transition period might be quite protracted. To the extent that not only new entrants but experienced workers were involved, it would be disruptive and painful. Female unemployment rates might well be increased. The costs associated with this policy depend crucially on how many workers are displaced, how quickly, and what happens to them. At present, we simply do not know how severe these problems would be.

It is worth noting that the traditional approach to raising women's pay through the principles of equal pay for equal work and equal employment opportunity also has the potential of increasing the wages even of women who remain in female jobs. This may also be illustrated in Figure 8.1. Suppose that we again begin with the discriminatory situation. If the barriers to entry into the male jobs are reduced, women will transfer from F jobs to M jobs. The supply curve in F jobs will shift inward towards S_{fo} while the supply curve in M jobs shifts outward towards S_{mo}. Wages in the female sector are increased by the reduction of overcrowding there. A completely successful anti-discrimination policy would result in a wage of w_o being established for both types of jobs. Proponents of comparable worth contend, however, that existing policies have not achieved notable success as yet and that a new strategy is called for.

We have emphasized the economic issues relevant to the subject of comparable worth—issues that are paramount in concluding whether, and for whom, such a policy would be beneficial. Meantime, however, the courts are making decisions concerning the issue on purely legal grounds, and it may be largely settled in those terms, unless Congress decides to take action on the matter.[62] In addition, many state and local governments have commissioned pay equity studies that could form the basis for wage realignments, and some unions, most notably The American Federation of State, County and Municipal Employees, have pressed for pay equity as a collective bargaining demand.

---

[62]In the widely publicized case of *County of Washington v. Gunther,* 452 U.S. 161 (1981), the Supreme Court removed a major legal stumbling block to the comparable worth doctrine by ruling that it is not required that a man and woman do "equal work" in order to establish pay discrimination under Title VII. However, many other issues remain unsolved and the Court stopped short of endorsing the comparable worth approach. See Ross and Barcher, *The Rights of Women,* pp. 23-24. A major legal victory for proponents of comparable worth was attained in September 1983 when a federal court ruled in favor of the American Federation of State, County, and Municipal Employees (AFSCME) and found that the State of Washington had violated Title VII by paying employees in traditionally female job classifications less than employees in traditionally male occupations. A 1974 comparable worth study, commissioned by the state, found that women received 20 percent lower pay than men for jobs requiring equal skill and responsibility. When Washington failed to eliminate the disparity, AFSCME filed suit (Bureau of National Affairs, *Daily Labor Report,* no. 181 [September 16, 1983]). The case is under appeal.

JOB EVALUATION*

The implementation of comparable worth requires an evaluation of the contribution of the many different jobs within an enterprise. At present, formal job evaluation procedures are already used by the federal government, a number of state governments and many large private firms as an aid in determining pay rates. Among the reasons for this policy is, first, that many positions are filled entirely from within the units themselves through promotion and upgrading of the existing work force; and second, that, because some jobs are unique to a particular firm, "going rates" for all jobs are not always available in local labor markets. This puts employers in a position of having to establish wages, rather than simply to accept those determined by the market. This does not mean that market forces are ignored. In setting wages, most firms and governmental units try to take into account whatever information is available on prevailing wages for different types of labor. At the same time, the existence of job evaluation and other procedures for setting wages, tend to make wages less responsive to short-term shifts in market conditions than they would otherwise be.

The actual methods used differ in detail, but share the same basic rationale and approach. The first step is always a description of all the jobs within the given organization. The next step is to rate each according to all the various features which it is believed determine pay differentials. Last, these ratings are combined to create a score for each job, which may then be used to help determine wages.

Among the factors used to construct job scores are such characteristics as level of education, skills, and responsibility, as well as the environment in which the work is performed. Commonly, multiple regression is used to link these to the existing pay structure. At other times, weights are assigned according to the judgment of the experts constructing the scale. In theory, various jobs can be assigned values objectively, presumably not influenced by irrelevant factors, such as say, the sex and race of the incumbent, and quite different jobs may be assigned equal values, if warranted.

It would be a mistake, however, to take the objectivity of such procedures for granted. Both prevailing wage structures and the judgments of individuals may be tainted by existing inequalities in the economy and in society, although efforts are under way to develop unbiased compensation schemes.** All one can, at this point, conclude is that the use of job evaluation to determine pay rates is neither an impractical pipedream, nor a sure-fire cure for discrimination.

---

*Job evaluation is discussed in Donald J. Treiman and Heidi I. Hartmann, eds. *Women, Work and Wages: Equal Pay for Jobs of Equal Value* (Washington, D.C.: National Academy Press, 1981), pp. 71-4. Institutional models, discussed earlier, emphasize the importance of job evaluation and other administrative procedures for determining wages. See Peter B. Doeringer and Michael J. Piore, *Internal Labor Markets and Manpower Analysis* (Lexington, Mass.: D.C. Heath and Co., 1971).

**See Ronnie Steinberg and Lois Haignere, "Equitable Compensation: Methodological Criteria for Comparable Worth," paper presented at a conference on "Ingredients for Women's Employment Policy," State University of New York at Albany, April 19-20, 1985.

POLICY ISSUE:
WOMEN AND UNIONS

As discussed above, one of the reasons for the lower wages of women is their relatively low representation in unions. Therefore, in this section we take a closer look at this issue.

Representation of Women in Labor Organizations

As may be seen in Table 8.3, women are under-represented in labor unions in comparison to their share of the labor force as a whole. Between 1956 and 1984, labor organizations accounted for a shrinking proportion of both male and female workers. In relative terms, however, the under-representation of women in unions decreased, as women's share of labor union membership increased more rapidly than their share of total employment. Table 8.3 also shows that blacks are more likely to be members of labor organizations than whites and Hispanics and that sex differences in membership are smaller among blacks than among either of the other two groups.

Benefits of Union Membership

The under-representation of women in unions is a cause for concern to some because unions confer benefits on their members that women, thus, enjoy to a lesser extent than men. Unions have been found to increase the wages of their members, although there is some disagreement over the magnitude of the union wage gain. One recent review of the evidence estimated the union impact to be on the order of 20 to 30 percent in the 1970s.[63] Not all workers gain to the same extent by unionization, since the monopoly power of unions differs among different industries and groups of workers. Moreover, the union wage premium appears to have been at historically high levels during the late 1970s when most of the relevant studies were done. Nonetheless, there is little doubt that unions do increase the wages of their members, and the under-representation of women in unions lowers their wages relative to men's, all else equal. At the same time, the higher participation of blacks than of whites in labor organizations raises the relative earnings of blacks somewhat, all else equal.[64]

[63]Richard B. Freeman and James L. Medoff, *What Do Unions Do?* (New York: Basic Books, 1984). The evidence on fringe benefits discussed below is also from this source. The evidence suggests that, for the most part, the relative wage gains to union members are about as large for women as for men and, in the public sector, possibly higher for women. See Richard B. Freeman and Jonathan S. Leonard, "Union Maids: Unions and the Female Workforce." Paper presented at the "Conference on Gender in the Workplace," The Brookings Institution, November 15–16, 1984.

[64]Ashenfelter, "Discrimination and Trade Unions."

TABLE 8.3   The Representation of Women in Labor Organizations Selected Years, 1956-1984

YEAR	WOMEN AS A PERCENTAGE OF		UNION MEMBERSHIP AS A PERCENTAGE OF ALL EMPLOYED WORKERS		
	ALL EMPLOYED WORKERS	MEMBERSHIP OF LABOR ORGANIZATIONS	MEN	WOMEN	TOTAL
Unions only:					
1956	32.0	18.5	32.3	15.7	27.0
1966	35.6	19.3	30.7	13.1	24.4
Unions and associations:					
1970	37.7	23.9	32.9	16.9	26.8
1976	40.1	26.8	31.9	17.4	26.1
1980					
All	42.4	30.1	25.1	14.7	20.7
Whites	41.7	28.3	24.4	13.4	19.8
Blacks[a]	48.1	40.7	31.5	23.2	27.5
1984					
All	43.7	33.6	19.5	12.7	16.5
Whites	43.1	31.8	18.7	11.5	15.6
Blacks	49.4	42.1	28.4	21.2	24.8
Hispanics	40.9	32.1	21.6	14.8	18.8

[a]Includes other nonwhites.

Sources: U.S. Department of Labor, Bureau of Labor Statistics, "Earnings and Other Characteristics of Organized Workers," Bulletin 2105 (May 1980), Table 2, p. 2; Linda H. LeGrande, "Women in Labor Organizations: Their Ranks are Increasing," *Monthly Labor Review* 101, no. 8 (August 1978), Table 1, p. 9; *Employment and Training Report of the President* (1981), Table A-16, pp. 144–6; and *Employment and Earnings* 32, no. 1 (January 1985), pp. 154–5, 157–8, 198, 208.

Unions have also been found to increase the fringe benefits of union workers relative to their nonunion counterparts. Indeed, the union fringe effect has been found to be greater (in percentage terms) than the union wage effect. Finally, unions impart nonpecuniary benefits to their members, chiefly by giving them a greater opportunity to shape their work environment by directly communicating with employers in the collective bargaining process and by providing for grievance procedures. Richard Freeman has termed this the "voice effect" of unions.[65]

[65]Richard B. Freeman, "Individual Mobility and Union Voice in the Labor Market," *American Economic Review* 66, no. 2 (May 1976): 361–68.

On the other hand, to the extent that the demand for labor is responsive to its cost, the advantages of higher wages and greater fringe benefits brought about by unionization would also be associated with lower employment. Hence, the gains of those who get greater rewards are in part at the expense of those who are not hired, or are displaced, due to unionization.

Reasons for the Under-representation of Women in Unions

In light of the advantages of union membership, how do we explain the under-representation of women in unions? It is commmonly believed that women are less interested in unionism than men because of their lesser attachment to the labor force. This appears not to be the case, however. In 1977, among private sector workers who were not represented by labor organizations, women were considerably more likely than men to respond that they would vote in favor of union representation if an election were held—41 percent of women gave this response in comparison to 27 percent of men. Interestingly, nonrepresented blacks also were more likely than nonrepresented whites to indicate that they would vote for union repesentation—69 percent of blacks in comparison to 29 percent of whites.[66]

The primary reason for the under-representation of women in labor organizations is that they tend to be concentrated in industries and occupations where, for whatever reason, unionization is below average. Traditionally, unionization has been highest among blue-collar workers in manufacturing, while women have been concentrated in clerical and service occupations and in the service industries. Within the manufacturing sector, women are more likely than men to be employed in the more competitive industries, while unionization has been higher in monopolistic industries. Blacks, on the other hand, are more likely than whites to be in blue-collar jobs, and this helps to explain their higher rates of unionization. In 1979, differences in industry and occupation accounted for 60 percent of the lower unionization rate of women (in comparison to men) and 50 percent of the higher unionization rate of blacks (in comparison to whites).[67]

The policies of unions themselves have no doubt also contributed to the under-representation of women among their members. Male craft unions did not begin to admit women to their ranks until the late 1800s.[68] Even after unions began to officially open their doors to women, they have been criticized for their less than vigorous efforts to organize women workers and lack of sup-

---

[66]Freeman and Medoff, *What Do Unions Do?*

[67]Freeman and Medoff, *What Do Unions Do?*

[68]Barbara M. Wertheimer,"'Union is Power': Sketches from Women's Labor History," ed. Jo. Freeman, *Women: A Feminist Perspective,* 3rd ed. (Palo Alto: Mayfield, 1984), pp. 337–52.

port for women's own efforts to unionize. Moreover, it is claimed that unions have emphasized issues of concern to male workers at the bargaining table and neglected female concerns. This lowers the appeal of unions for women. For example, the emphasis of unions on fringe benefits like health insurance would be of less value to women than to men, because many women, as members of two-earner families, are already covered under their husband's plans.[69] On the other hand, given the traditional division of labor in the family, provision of such benefits as parental leaves and day care is likely to be of greater interest to women than to men.

Part of the reason for the lesser attention of unions to women's issues may be the low participation of women in national union leadership positions. This is dramatically illustrated in Table 8.4, which gives this information for most large unions where women comprised 30 percent or more of the membership in 1980. In only one case, the Retail, Wholesale, and Department Store Workers, does the representation of women among national officers and officials approximate their share of the membership. The reasons for this low representation of women in union leadership positions are complex, but most likely reflect the same types of barriers to participation as in other traditionally male high-level pursuits. The situation is not unlike that in national elective office. In the 99th Congress (which took office in January 1985), only 2 percent of senators (2 out of 100) and 5 percent of representatives (22 out of 435) were female. And, it was not until 1984 that Geraldine Ferraro, the defeated Democratic candidate, became the first woman to be nominated for Vice President of the United States by a major political party.[70] Both within unions and in politics, women are making progress at the local level that should eventually be reflected in greater representation at the national level.

Prospects for the Future

Unions have a strong interest in organizing female workers because unions must make inroads into traditionally female occupations and industries if they are to reverse the decline in the share of the labor force that is organized and begin, once again, to expand. High-level union leadership has recognized this and is placing greater priority on efforts to organize women and giving more support to women's issues. The Coalition of Labor Union Women was founded in 1974 to increase the number of women in union leadership positions and to help organize women workers. Thus, the relative participation of women in unions, at all levels, may well increase in the future.

[69]Freeman and Medoff, *What Do Unions Do?* Adoption of so-called cafeteria benefit programs where workers can select benefit packages that meet their needs would be more desirable to two-earner families.

[70]For an analysis of women's political attitudes and behavior, see Virginia Sapiro, *The Political Integration of Women* (Urbana, IL: University of Illinois Press, 1983).

TABLE 8.4 Representation of Women Among National Officers, Officials and Governing Boards, Selected Labor Organizations 1980

UNION	WOMEN AS A PERCENTAGE OF MEMBERSHIP	OFFICERS AND OFFICIALS			GOVERNING BOARD		
		TOTAL NUMBER	WOMEN NUMBER	WOMEN PERCENT	TOTAL NUMBER	WOMEN NUMBER	WOMEN PERCENT
Bakery, confectionary and tobacco workers	33.5	7	1	14.3	35	0	0.0
Clothing and textile workers	71.0	10	3	30.0	50	0	0.0
Communications workers	52.0	11	0	0.0	22	0	0.0
Electrical workers (IBEW)	30.0	4	0	0.0	9	0	0.0
Electrical radio and machine workers (IUE)	40.0	9	2	22.2	28	2	7.1
Glass bottle blowers	33.0	8	0	0.0	16	0	0.0
Glass workers, flint	35.0	6	0	0.0	104	12	11.5
Government employees (AFGE)	45.0	10	2	20.0	19	1	5.3
Graphic arts	33.3	11	1	9.1	33	4	12.1
Hotel, restaurant	n.a.	8	0	0.0	21	1	4.8
Industrial workers	38.0	7	0	0.0	9	0	0.0

Ladies garment workers	80.0	9	1	11.1	26	0	0.0
Laundry, dry-cleaning workers	90.0	4	0	0.0	9	2	22.2
Newspaper guild	34.0	8	0	0.0	16	3	18.8
Postal workers	40.0	6	0	0.0	14	0	0.0
Pottery and allied labor	40.0	7	0	0.0	12	0	0.0
Retail clerks	51.0[a]	8[a]	0[a]	0.0	27[a]	1[a]	3.7
Retail, wholesale and department store workers	40.0	5	2	40.0	34	3	8.8
Service employees	45.0	8	2	25.0	48	7	14.6
State, county, and municipal employees	40.0[a]	8	1	12.5	27	1	3.7
Teachers	60.0[a]	8	2	25.0	34	11	32.4
Telegraph workers	50.0	2	0	0.0	11	2	18.2
Textile, united	40.0	4	0	0.0	20	1	5.0
Upholsterers	30.0	5	0	0.0	11	0	0.0

[a]Data are for 1978 (not available in 1980).

Sources: Unpublished Bureau of Labor Statistics data for 1980; and, for 1978, U.S. Department of Labor, Bureau of Labor Statistics, "Directory of National Unions and Employees Associations, 1979," Bulletin 2079, Tables D–1, E–1 and F–1, pp. 91–92, 93–94, 96.

CONCLUSION

Economists define labor market discrimination as a situation where two equally qualified individuals are treated differently on the basis of sex (race, age, etc.). Such discrimination against a particular group is likely to be detrimental, both directly and indirectly, through feedback effects on their accumulation of human capital. Empirical studies have used available evidence on differences in the characteristics of male and female workers to explain the pay gap and the differences in occupational distributions between the two groups. Productivity-related factors have not been able to account for all of the sex differences in economic outcomes, suggesting that discrimination does play a part, accounting for perhaps half of the male-female earnings differential.

As much attention as has been focused on the issue of whether discrimination exists, there has been almost equal interest in the question who discriminates, why, and how. We reviewed theories suggesting that:

- Employers, co-workers, or customers have tastes for discrimination against women
- Employers judge individual women in terms of the characteristics of the group (statistical discrimination)
- Women's wages are depressed because they are crowded into a few sectors
- Women are concentrated in dead-end jobs with few opportunities for on-the-job training and promotion

Last, we examined the government's equal employment opportunity policy and considered the role that unions have played in women's failure to achieve equal economic outcomes to men.

There is good reason to believe that each of these explanations contributes to our understanding of a complex reality, where factors keeping women in segregated and poorly paid jobs, rather than being mutually exclusive, are far more likely to have reinforced each other. By the same token, however, we pointed out that any reduction in one of the negative factors is likely to have feedback effects. By rewarding women more highly for their human capital, they are encouraged to accumulate more human capital on which they can gather rewards.

SUGGESTED READINGS

ARROW, KENNETH, "The Theory of Discrimination." In *Discrimination in Labor Markets,* eds. Orley Ashenfelter and Albert Rees. Princeton, N.J.: Princeton University, 1973, pp. 3–33.

BECKER, GARY S., *The Economics of Discrimination,* 2nd ed. Chicago: University of Chicago Press, 1971.

BERGMANN, BARBARA R., "Occupational Segregation, Wages and Profits When Employers Discriminate by Race or Sex," *Eastern Economic Journal,* nos. 1-2 (April–July 1974): 103-10.

BLAU, FRANCINE D., "Discrimination Against Women: Theory and Evidence." In *Labor Economics: Modern Views,* ed. William A. Darity, Jr., Boston: Kluwer-Nijhoff, 1984, pp. 53-89.

CAIN, GLEN G., "The Economic Analysis of Labor Market Discrimination: A Survey." In *Handbook of Labor Economics,* eds. Orley Ashenfelter and Richard Layard, Amsterdam: North Holland Press, forthcoming.

CORCORAN, MARY AND GREG J. DUNCAN, "Work History, Labor Force Attachment and Earnings Differences Between the Races and the Sexes." *Journal of Human Resources* 14, no. 1 (Winter 1977), 3-20.

DOERINGER, PETER B. AND MICHAEL J. PIORE, *Internal Labor Markets and Manpower Analysis,* Lexington, MA: D. C. Heath, 1971.

FREEMAN, RICHARD B. AND JAMES L. MEDOFF, *What Do Unions Do?* New York: Basic Books, 1984.

GORDON, DAVID M., RICHARD EDWARDS AND MICHAEL REICH, *Segmented Work, Divided Workers: The Historical Transformation of Labor in the United States.* Cambridge: Cambridge University Press, 1982.

MADDEN, JANICE F., *The Economics of Sex Discrimination.* Lexington, MA: Lexington Books, 1973.

RESKIN, BARBARA, ed., *Sex Segregation in the Workplace: Trends, Explanations and Remedies.* Washington, D.C.: National Academy Press, 1984.

TREIMAN, DONALD J. AND HEIDI I. HARTMANN, eds., *Women, Work, and Wages: Equal Pay for Jobs of Equal Value.* Washington, D.C.: National Academy Press, 1981.

WEITHEIMER, BARBARA M., *We Were There: The Story of Working Women in America.* New York: Pantheon, 1977.

Chapter 9

DIFFERENCES IN JOBLESSNESS: DISCOURAGEMENT, FRICTIONAL AND STRUCTURAL UNEMPLOYMENT

In preceding chapters, we have dealt with decisions about the allocation of time as though individuals could choose freely according to their preferences. In reality, employment necessarily involves not only the willingness to do a job but also the ability to find one. Thus, at any given time there are some people who are looking for work but are unemployed. Traditionally, this has been considered to be a situation when a person is unable to find work and, hence, would be a serious constraint on the individual's ability to maximize utility as our models suggest.

We begin this chapter by defining unemployment and distinguishing between various types of unemployment. We then discuss the concept of full employment and the cost to the economy of not achieving it. Subsequent sections deal with the incidence of joblessness among various segments of the population, with emphasis on sex differences. Because the seriousness of the problem of unemployment for women has at times been questioned, we close by considering sex differences in the burden of unemployment.

DEFINITION OF UNEMPLOYMENT

The official definition of **unemployment** includes all individuals not currently working for pay but actively looking for work or persons temporarily laid off from a job to which they expect to return. This includes the **seasonally unemployed,** such as construction workers in the snow belt during the winter or ski instructors in the summer. Also, in a dynamic economy, there will always be new entrants and re-entrants as well as job quitters and job losers looking for jobs.[1] Given imperfect information it will take them some time to find jobs, even when enough appropriate job openings are available. This is referred to as **frictional unemployment.** Or there may be more serious **structural unemployment** when those looking for work do not have the right skills or are not in the right location to fill the vacancies that exist. Such unemployment is likely to be more persistent, because these difficulties are not easily or quickly remedied.

The type of unemployment that causes the most serious concern, however, is that associated with an overall deficiency in demand, when there is an excess of workers in relation to unfilled positions. This is most commonly referred to as demand-deficient or **cyclical unemployment,** because in advanced industrialized economies such insufficient demand for labor tends to recur in cycles.

In addition to unemployment, there is also the problem of **underemployment,** when workers take jobs for which they are clearly overqualified, or when they work less than they would prefer to. Examples of the former would be a Ph.D. taking a job house cleaning or a skilled automobile worker harvesting fruit. Examples of the latter are persons who work only part-time when they would prefer to work full-time. These situations tend to arise more often in a slack labor market, when the recorded unemployment rate is also high.

Last but not least, individuals who have searched for employment for some time without success may eventually stop looking. Others who would like a job may postpone their entry into the labor force until economic conditions improve. These individuals are generally referred to as **discouraged workers.**

---

[1]This is so even though the majority of those who change jobs actually experience no unemployment because most workers search while holding on to the old job until they have found a new one. See J. Peter Mattila, "Job Quitting and Frictional Unemployment," *American Economic Review* 64, no. 1 (March 1974): 235–9. Recent evidence also indicates that many labor market entrants never experience a period of unemployment. See Ethel B. Jones, *Determinants of Female Reentrant Unemployment* (the W. E. Upjohn Institute for Employment Research, 1983); and Ronald G. Ehrenberg, "The Demographic Structure of Unemployment Rates and Labor Market Transition Probabilities," ed. Ronald G. Ehrenberg, *Research in Labor Economics* 3 (Greenwich, Conn.: JAI Press, Inc., 1980): 253.

Relatively few men of prime working age fall into this category, because giving up on the labor market is not an acceptable option for them. It does, however, include many young people who often postpone entry into the labor market or return to school, older people who retire, and women who remain in or return to the household full-time. Such discouraged workers are considered to be out of the labor force rather than unemployed and, thus, are not included in the official estimates of the unemployment rate.[2] As we saw in Chapter 4, their numbers increase during recessions and decline during upswings.

COST OF UNEMPLOYMENT
TO THE ECONOMY

Unemployment involves a loss for the economy because a larger output could be achieved with a better allocation of resources. One widely cited study found that for every additional 1 percentage point of unemployment, GNP declined

TABLE 9.1 Unemployment Rates of Men and Women 16 Years and Older, Selected High and Low Years 1948–1984

YEAR	TOTAL	MEN	WOMEN	SEX DIFFERENCE[a]
1948	3.8	3.6	4.1	0.5
1949	5.9	5.9	6.0	0.1
1953	2.9	2.8	3.3	0.5
1954	5.5	5.3	6.0	0.7
1956	4.1	3.8	4.8	1.0
1958	6.8	6.8	6.8	0.0
1959	5.5	5.2	5.9	0.7
1961	6.7	6.4	7.2	0.8
1969	3.5	2.8	4.7	1.9
1971	5.9	5.3	6.9	1.6
1973	4.9	4.2	6.0	1.8
1975	8.5	7.9	9.3	1.4
1979	5.8	5.1	6.8	1.7
1982	9.7	9.9	9.4	−0.5
1983	9.6	9.9	9.2	−0.7
1984	7.5	7.4	7.6	0.2

[a]The female unemployment rate minus the male unemployment rate.

Source: *Employment and Training Report of the President,* Washington, D.C.: U.S. Government Printing Office, 1982 (for 1948–1979); *Monthly Labor Review* 107, no. 12 (December 1984) (for 1982–1983); *Employment and Earnings* 32, no. 1 (January 1985) (for 1984).

[2]However, Christopher J. Flinn and James J. Heckman, "Are Unemployment and 'Out of the Labor Force' Behaviorally Distinct Labor Force States?" *Journal of Economics* 1, no. 1 (January 1983): 28–42, report that while the unemployed receive more job offers than those who are not in the labor force, some individuals go directly from being out of the labor force to a job. They conclude that the difference between the unemployed and "discouraged workers" is one of degree only.

by about 3 percentage points,[3] though more recently it has been suggested that the figure may now be closer to 2 percentage points.[4] This loss may, in part, be caused by the underemployment of some of the workers who do have jobs, as well as the idleness of those entirely without work. Excess capacity in plant and equipment is also likely to be a contributing factor.

Table 9.1 shows unemployment rates of men and women in the United States for years of relatively high and low unemployment between 1948 and 1984. While the unemployment rates never approach the more than 1 in 4 rates reached during the Great Depression of the 1930s, they are substantially higher than the 2 percent unemployment rate achieved in the wartime period of the early 1940s. Further, there is a clear upward trend, and the unemployment rates in 1982 and 1983 were higher than in any of the previous 40 years. The shortfall of GNP below its potential was obviously substantial.

THE BURDEN OF UNEMPLOYMENT FOR INDIVIDUALS

More controversial than the loss to the economy is the extent of the burden that falls upon the unemployed themselves. This is because the measured unemployment rate is not a perfect indicator of the degree of economic hardship for individuals.[5] How this is viewed depends in part on the reason why the person is out of work.

Though the very definition of unemployment appears to imply that it is involuntary, this is not necessarily the case. An individual who turns down a job and continues to search for a more attractive offer is making a voluntary decision, yet will be counted as unemployed. Indeed, the very notion of voluntariness is difficult to define and still harder to measure empirically. Is a Ph.D. who turns down a job doing house cleaning voluntarily unemployed? One common-sense definition of involuntary unemployment to which many economists would subscribe is the inability to find a position at the prevailing market wage for one's skills.[6] This would exclude persons who have received a reasonable offer but are holding out for higher rewards.

Unfortunately, no data are available to determine exactly what proportion of the unemployed would be classified as involuntary on the basis of this definition. It would, in any case be a mistake to assume that a large proportion

[3]Arthur M. Okun, *The Political Economy of Prosperity,* Washington, D.C.: Brookings Institution (1970), Appendix, pp. 132–46.

[4]Robert J. Gordon and Robert E. Hall, "Arthur M. Okun, 1928–1980," *Brookings Papers on Economic Activity,* no. 1 (1980): 1–5.

[5]For a more extensive treatment of this issue, see National Commission on Employment and Unemployment Statistics, *Counting the Labor Force* (Washington, D.C.: U.S. Government Printing Office, 1979).

[6]See Orley Ashenfelter, "What is Involuntary Unemployment?" *Proceedings of the American Philosophical Society* 122, no. 3 (June 1978): 135–38.

of the unemployment rate, particularly during times when it is high, can be ascribed to individuals simply holding out for better offers. There is evidence that many of the unemployed never reject any offer at all.[7]

There are other reasons as well why the official unemployment rate does not perfectly measure the economic hardship of unemployment. For one, to the extent that the unemployed person uses some of the now available time to increase household production, or to invest in human capital by getting education or training, the decline in money earnings would overestimate the decrease in economic welfare caused by the spell of unemployment.[8] On the other hand, no on-the-job training is acquired during a period of unemployment, and if the spell is prolonged, skills may depreciate. Hence, there may be a negative effect on future as well as on present earnings.[9] It has also been pointed out that the current loss of earnings will be cushioned for some individuals by unemployment insurance[10] or the earnings of other family members. Moreover, workers in seasonal or cyclically sensitive jobs probably receive higher wages to compensate for the irregularity of their work.[11]

Nonetheless, the figures in Table 9.2 make clear that considerable economic hardship is caused by unemployment. In 1983, a year of relatively high unemployment (9.6 percent), the median incomes of married couple families that experienced some unemployment were 25 percent lower than families with no member unemployed. Only 4 percent of the latter in comparison to 13 percent of the former had incomes below the poverty line. The economic hardship

---

[7]See, for example, U.S. Bureau of Labor Statistics, Bulletin 1886, *Job Seeking Methods Used by American Workers* (Washington, D.C.: U.S. Government Printing Office, 1975), cited in Ronald G. Ehrenberg and Robert S. Smith, *Modern Labor Economics* (Glenview, IL: Scott Foresman and Co., 1982), p. 447; and Stanley P. Stephenson, Jr., "The Economics of Youth Job Search Behavior," *The Review of Economics and Statistics* 58, no. 1 (February 1976): 104–11. It must be noted, however, that an individual who is not interested in a job may not pursue it to the point of obtaining an offer.

[8]This implies that the welfare loss due to unemployment is smaller for groups whose members have a high value of nonmarket time relative to market earnings. This would include youth, who may return to school or devote full-time (rather than part-time) to their studies, older workers who are on the verge of retirement, and married women who, given the traditional division of labor in many families, are more likely to devote their time to household chores. The latter point has been used as an argument for considering female unemployment a less serious problem than male unemployment. We examine this viewpoint later in this chapter.

[9]See, for instance, Mary Corcoran, "The Employment and Wage Consequences of Teenage Women's Non-Employment," eds. Richard B. Freeman and David A. Wise, *The Youth Labor Market Problem: Its Nature, Causes and Consequences,* (Chicago: University of Chicago Press, 1982) pp. 391–425; and David T. Ellwood, "Teenage Unemployment: Permanent Scars or Temporary Blemishes," eds. Freeman and Wise, *The Youth Labor Market Problem,* pp. 349–90.

[10]Unemployment insurance, even for those who are eligible, is always less than the regular wage. Further, in 1983, a year of serious recession, only about 40 percent of the unemployed were covered by unemployment insurance (Statistical Abstract, 1984).

[11]For evidence of such a compensating differential, see John M. Abowd and Orley Ashenfelter, "Anticipated Unemployment, Temporary Layoffs and Compensating Wage Differentials," ed. Sherwin Rosen, *Studies in Labor Markets* (Chicago: University of Chicago Press, 1981), pp. 141–70.

TABLE 9.2 Income by Family Type, Unemployment Status, and Incidence of Poverty, 1983

| | WITH NO MEMBER UNEMPLOYED | | WITH AT LEAST ONE MEMBER UNEMPLOYED | | DIFFERENCE IN MEDIAN INCOMES |
	MEDIAN FAMILY INCOME	PERCENT IN POVERTY	MEDIAN FAMILY INCOME	PERCENT IN POVERTY	%
All families					
Married couple families	$31,495	4.3	$23,592	13.2	25.1
Families maintained by women	16,116	17.0	9,860	44.5	38.8
Families maintained by men	25,950	6.4	17,309	19.2	33.3
Persons not living in families	15,538	10.2	7,238	38.0	53.4

Source: Ellen Sehgal, "Work Experience in 1983 Reflects the Effects of the Recovery," *Monthly Labor Review* 107, no. 12 (December 1984): 18–24.

of families maintained by women was particularly serious. Their income declined by 39 percent with unemployment, and the percentage of such families in poverty increased from 17 to 45 percent when a family member was unemployed. While these data were not broken down by race, it should be noted that the incidence of unemployment and the corresponding poverty is particularly severe among nonwhites, and especially so among women in this group.

These data suggest that the impact of unemployment on family income and poverty status is likely to be serious. Moreover, it has been found to be quite similar even in times of lower unemployment rates.[12] Since searching for a job is likely to involve many expenses usually related to working, such as travel, clothing, etc., as well as a good deal of time away from home, this income loss may not be mitigated very much by declining job expenses and additional home production.

Individuals who are out of work not only fail to gain valuable labor market experience but may also lose tenure on the job, as well as insurance and pension benefits. Further, the unemployed suffer psychologically as well as economically by losing the feeling of dignity associated with being a productive member of society.[13] Beyond that, a high unemployment rate slows the progress of disadvantaged groups. In occupations that have traditionally been restricted to white males, layoffs fall disproportionately on women and minorities, who tend to be more recently hired. The failure of new jobs to open up also reduces opportunities for hiring women and minorities to only those jobs that open up through attrition.

Finally, it should be pointed out that the official unemployment rate provides only incomplete information on joblessness in other respects as well. First, it tells us only the percentage of people who are unemployed at any one point in time. In order to learn how many people have been unemployed at some point during the year, and how long they were unemployed, we need to look at Table 9.3. In 1983, a year of recovery from the 1981–82 recession, but of continued high unemployment, 21 percent of men and 18 percent of women in the labor force were out of work at some time; and 54 percent of the

---

[12]See, for example, Sylvia L. Terry, "Unemployment and Its Effect on Family Income in 1980," *Monthly Labor Review* 105, no. 4 (April 1982): 40.

[13]A study by Jeanne Prial Gordus and Sean P. McAlinden of the University of Michigan found that job loss was associated with depression, anxiety, aggression, insomnia, loss of self-esteem, and marital problems. The spouse of the unemployed worker also suffered psychological problems. In work settings where many have been laid off, even those who remain employed are negatively affected due to their need to cope with a highly stressful situation. Another study by Harvey Brenner of Johns Hopkins University found that the 14.3 percent increase in the unemployment rate during the 1973–74 recession was associated with a 7.3 percent increase in total mortality from all causes and a 2.8 percent increase in deaths by heart attacks. These studies are reported in the Bureau of National Affair's *Daily Labor Report,* no. 128 (July 3, 1984): A-13 to A-15.

TABLE 9.3   Extent of Unemployment by Sex, 1979 and 1983

	1979		1983	
	MEN	WOMEN	MEN	WOMEN
Unemployment rate	5.1	6.8	9.9	9.2
Percent of labor force with unemployment at some time during the year	15.5	16.1	21.0	17.8
Percent of unemployed with				
1 to 14 weeks	65.5	69.0	46.5	56.7
15 weeks or more	35.5	31.0	53.5	43.3
Median weeks of unemployment	11.0	9.0	15.2	12.3

Sources: Ellen Seghal, "Work Experience in 1983 Reflects the Effects of the Recovery," *Monthly Labor Review* 107, no. 12 (December 1984): 18–24; Sylvia Lazos Terry, "Unemployment and its Effect on Family Income in 1980," *Monthly Labor Review* 105, no. 4 (April 1982): 35–43.

unemployed men and 43 percent of the unemployed women were out of work for 15 weeks or more. Even in 1979, a relatively good year, a substantially higher proportion of individuals were out of work at some time in the year than were unemployed at any point in time. However, the incidence of long-term unemployment (15 weeks or more) was lower, as was the duration of spells of unemployment. In both years, the median length of time unemployed was shorter for women than for men, quite possibly because they were more inclined to drop out of the labor force if unsuccessful in locating a job.

Second, as was pointed out earlier, the official definition of unemployment does not include a number of categories that could reasonably be viewed as representing joblessness. The data in Table 9.4 indicate the consequences of including two of these—discouraged workers and involuntary part-time workers. (Only one-half of the latter are included in the index of joblessness to reflect that they are only partially unemployed.) As may be seen in the table, even in 1979, a year of relatively low unemployment, inclusion of these categories would raise the estimate of joblessness a not inconsiderable 2.3 percentage points, from 5.8 to 8.1 percent. In 1983, a year marked by the beginnings of recovery from a serious recession, the estimate of joblessness would be raised by 4 percentage points using the expanded definition; even in 1984, with the recovery in full swing, the estimate would be increased 3.6 percentage points.

Table 9.4 also illustrates that women are more likely to be discouraged workers or involuntarily employed part-time than are men. There is, thus, a larger disparity between the official unemployment rate and the jobless rate for women than for men. Indeed, although in 1983 the measured unemploy-

TABLE 9.4 Jobless Rates of Men and Women in 1979, 1983, and 1984[a]

YEAR AND GROUP	OFFICIAL UNEMPLOYMENT RATE (%)	EXPANDED LABOR FORCE DEFINITION[b]			
		UNEMPLOYED (%)	DISCOURAGED WORKERS (%)	1/2 INVOLUNTARY PART-TIME (%)	JOBLESS[c] (%)
	(1)	(2)	(3)	(4)	(5)
1979					
Total	5.8	5.8	0.7	1.6	8.1
Men	5.1	5.1	0.5	1.2	6.8
Women	6.8	6.7	1.1	2.1	9.9
1983					
Total	9.6	9.5	1.4	2.6	13.6
Men	9.9	9.8	1.0	2.2	13.0
Women	9.2	9.0	2.0	3.3	14.3
1984					
Total	7.5	7.4	1.1	2.5	11.1
Men	7.4	7.4	.8	.4	8.5
Women	7.6	7.5	1.6	2.9	12.0

[a]Data refer to civilians 16 years of age and over.
[b]The expanded labor force definition includes discouraged workers. It is the denominator in columns (2) through (5).
[c]The jobless include the unemployed, discouraged workers and one-half of the involuntary part-time. Column (5) may not exactly equal the sum of columns (2) through (4) due to rounding.

Sources: Computed from data published in the *Employment and Training Report of the President* (1982), *Employment and Earnings* 31, no. 1 (January 1984), and *Employment and Earnings* 32, no. 1 (January 1985).

ment rate was lower for women than for men, the jobless index was 1.3 percentage points higher for women.[14]

FULL EMPLOYMENT

It is clear from the above that the official unemployment data are not necessarily a fully accurate measure either of the waste of resources for the economy or the degree of hardship for individuals brought about by unemployment. Nonetheless, the unemployment rate undoubtedly reflects, to a considerable extent, both the degree of misallocation of resources and the economic and psychological difficulties for many of the jobless workers and their families.

At the same time, there is agreement that even an economy that has achieved full employment in the sense that demand for labor is not deficient must expect to have an unemployment rate higher than zero. There is, however, considerable disagreement about how much higher it needs to be.

Traditionally, the approach was to attempt to estimate the amount of unemployment that was seasonal and frictional and add the portion of structural unemployment that was considered inevitable. This would presumably result in the **full employment unemployment rate.** However, as the preceding discussion shows, it is both conceptually and practically difficult to draw a precise line between frictional and structural unemployment or to establish exactly how much of the latter is inevitable. Furthermore, all other types of unemployment tend to go up as cyclical unemployment increases. Hence, it is not surprising that not everyone agreed on a single figure, but for some time, there appeared to be a substantial consensus on 3 to 4 percent. When unemployment grew higher, many viewed it as the responsibility of government to implement measures that would increase the overall demand for labor.

As inflation became an increasingly serious problem in the late 1960s, the emphasis shifted increasingly toward controlling it, if need be, by permitting a higher rate of unemployment. In addition, opposition to government intervention also came from economists who subscribed to the new theory that traditional fiscal and monetary policy cannot be successful in the long run in reducing unemployment below its **natural rate** or can only do so at the expense of ever-accelerating inflation.[15] Accordingly, there was increasing opposition to government efforts to bring down unemployment rates.

[14]Lest anyone be tempted to think it is not worth quibbling over such small differences, it should be noted that in the early 1980s each percentage point of female (or male) unemployment represented about one-half million people.

[15]This theory was proposed by Milton Friedman, "The Role of Monetary Policy," *American Economic Review* 58, no. 1 (March 1968): 1–17.

Not all economists subscribe to these new views. Some suggest that they hark back to the beliefs of theorists who, in the early part of the century, had complete confidence in markets and complacently argued that full employment is whatever volume of employment the economy is moving toward and that its achievement "requires of the government nothing more than neutrality, and nothing less."[16] Nevertheless, for the most part there has been a drift toward accepting a 5 to 6 percent rate of unemployment as an acceptable target for full employment, even among advocates of government action. They too tend to believe that the realistic full-employment target has risen.[17]

INCIDENCE OF UNEMPLOYMENT

While the unemployment rates of all groups in the labor market tend to move up and down with the business cycle, at any point in time, there tend to be considerable differences among demographic groups in the incidence of unemployment. Table 9.1 and Figure 9.1 show the unemployment rates of men and women over the 1948 to 1984 period. Three important points regarding sex differences in unemployment experience emerge from an examination of these data.

First, women's unemployment rates have been higher than men's throughout the period, except for the years of extremely high unemployment, 1982–83. As we have seen, the sex gap would have existed even during those years and would have been wider in others, if a more comprehensive measure of joblessness were used. Second, the sex differential in unemployment rates follows a cyclical pattern. Women's unemployment rates are *lowest* relative to men's during *recessions* and *highest* relative to men's during *prosperous times*. Third, abstracting from cyclical variations, an examination of Figure 9.1 reveals that the size of the gap between men's and women's unemployment rates appears to have risen from the early 1960s to the late 1970s.[18] Prior to

---

[16]James Tobin, "Inflation and Unemployment," *American Economic Review* 62, no. 1 (March 1972): 1–18.

[17]The persistent problem of unemployment is viewed differently by radical economists. They argue that, in a capitalist economy, periodic recessions discipline the work force and, thus, are in the interest of capitalists. See, for instance, Raford Boddy and James R. Crotty, "Class Conflict and Macro-Policy: The Political Business Cycle," *Review of Radical Political Economy* 7, no. 1 (Spring 1975): 1–19; Michele I. Naples, "Industrial Conflict and its Implications for Productivity Growth," *American Economic Review* 71, no. 2 (May 1981): 36–41. It should also be noted that unemployment rates in quite a few other countries have been substantially lower than in the United States, particularly prior to the serious recession of the early 1980s. Relevant data are shown in Chapter 10.

[18]This overall pattern appears to particularly reflect the trends among whites. See, Ehrenberg, "The Demographic Structure of Unemployment Rates."

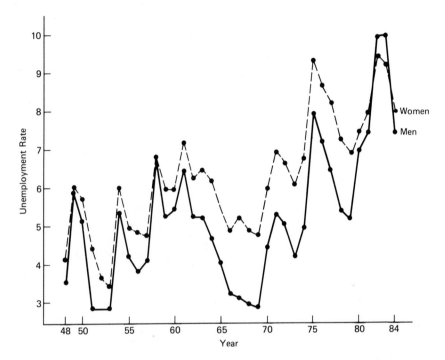

FIGURE 9.1   Unemployment Rates of Men and Women Age 16 and Over 1948–84

1963, the unemployment rate of women never exceeded men's by more than one percentage point, while the differential was never smaller than that from then until 1980.

In the next section, we examine the reasons for these sex differences in unemployment experience in detail. However, before turning to that subject, we briefly consider the overall pattern of demographic differences in unemployment rates to place the sex differences in a larger context.

Table 9.5 shows unemployment rates by race, Hispanic origin, and age, as well as sex for 1979, 1983, and 1984. In all years, unemployment rates are substantially higher for teenagers than for adults. Members of minority groups are also seen to have a considerably higher incidence of unemployment than whites. Even in 1979, a nonrecessionary year, the Hispanic rates are about one-and-a-half times greater than those of whites, while black rates are over twice as high. The data also show that in 1979 the female rate exceeded the male rate for each category of workers, and, in 1984, this was true for whites and Hispanics.

TABLE 9.5   Unemployment Rates by Sex, Age, Race and Hispanic Origin, 1979, 1983 and 1984[a]

	1979	1983	1984
Age 16–19			
Men	15.9	23.3	19.6
Women	16.4	21.3	18.0
Age 20 and over			
Men	4.2	8.9	6.6
Women	5.7	8.1	6.8
Whites (age 16 and over)			
Men	4.5	8.8	6.4
Women	5.9	7.9	6.5
Blacks (age 16 and over)			
Men	11.4	20.3	16.4
Women	13.8	18.6	15.4
Hispanics (age 16 and over)			
Men	7.0	13.5	10.4
Women	10.3	13.8	11.0

[a]Civilian labor force.

Sources: *Employment and Training Report of the President* (1982); *Employment and Earnings* 31, no. 1 (January 1984); and *Employment and Earnings* 32, no. 1 (January 1985).

EXPLANATIONS
OF SEX DIFFERENCES[19]

As discussed in Chapter 4, on average, women are less firmly attached to the labor force than men, although sex differences have been declining. The *higher labor force turnover* of women in comparison to men has an ambiguous effect on their relative unemployment rates.

On the one hand, it contributes to the relatively larger proportion of entrants and re-entrants among female labor force participants. According to one study, 1.2 percent of men but 2.7 percent of women labor force participants were re-entrants in 1982, and 0.2 percent of men but 0.5 percent of

[19]For interesting discussions of these issues see Beth Niemi, "Recent Changes in Differential Unemployment," *Growth and Change* 8, no. 3 (July 1977): 22–30; Clair (Vickery) Brown, Barbara Bergmann, and Katherine Swartz, "Unemployment Rate Targets and Anti-Inflation Policy as More Women Enter the Workforce," *American Economic Review* 68, no. 2 (May 1978): 90–94; Ehrenberg, "The Demographic Structure of Unemployment Rates;" and Janet L. Johnson, "Sex Differentials in Unemployment Rates: A Case for No Concern," *Journal of Political Economy* 91, no. 2 (April 1983): 293–303.

women were new entrants.[20] The majority of women (65 percent) enter the labor force without experiencing any unemployment, [21] and sex differences in the probability of such successful labor force entry are small.[22] Nonetheless, the higher proportion of women than men in the labor force who are entrants or re-entrants contributes to the women's higher unemployment rates. This is illustrated in Table 9.6 where we see that entrants and re-entrants constituted a far larger proportion of the unemployed among women than among men. The large flow of labor force entrants among teenagers also contributes to their higher unemployment rates.

On the other hand, as we have seen, women, and particularly married women, are considerably more likely to become discouraged workers, rather than to continue looking as men would tend to do. This is still true, even though with the growing proportion of two-earner couples there are increasingly more men who could possibly drop out of the labor market. Since discouraged workers are not counted as unemployed, such behavior causes measured unemployment of women to be lower than would otherwise be the case. For the 1967 to 1977 period, the average proportion of adult, unemployed workers who left the labor force was 27 percent for white women and 32 percent for black women. Among males, however, only 10 percent of white and 13 percent of black unemployed workers left the labor force.[23]

It appears that, on balance, the weaker labor force attachment of women does raise their unemployed rates relative to men but less so in recessions when the number of discouraged workers is larger. This helps to explain why the gap between female and male unemployment rates narrows during economic downturns. As conditions improve, previously discouraged workers enter the labor force and the sex differential in unemployment rates widens. To the extent that women's weaker labor force attachment does raise their unemployment rate relative to men's, it is important to bear in mind that, as discussed in Chapter 8, labor market discrimination may to some extent cause such differences between men and women in commitment to market work. Discrimination against women in earnings or occupations can lower the opportunity cost to women of work force interruptions.

Ironically, the growing labor force attachment of women may have contributed to the widening male-female unemployment differential during the

[20]Jones, "Determinants of Female Reentry Unemployment.'

[21]Jones, "Determinants of Female Reentry Unemployment."

[22]Sex differences were greater among blacks than whites, however. Over the 1967 to 1977 period, the average probability that a labor force entry would be successful was about 10 percentage points lower for black women than for black men. See, Ehrenberg, "The Demographic Structure of Unemployment Rates," p. 253.

[23]The figures in the text are for workers aged 25 to 59. See Ehrenberg, "The Demographic Structure of Unemployment Rates," p. 251.

TABLE 9.6 Percent of Unemployed Workers by Reasons for Unemployment: Men, Women, and Teenagers, 1979, 1983

	1979			1983			1984		
	AGE 20 YEARS AND OVER		AGE 16-19 BOTH SEXES	AGE 20 YEARS AND OVER		AGE 16-19 BOTH SEXES	AGE 20 YEARS AND OVER		AGE 16-19 BOTH SEXES
	MEN	WOMEN		MEN	WOMEN		MEN	WOMEN	
Lost last job	63.6	37.4	20.5	77.7	49.5	20.2	71.2	43.5	18.1
Left last job	14.1	16.3	11.8	6.4	10.6	6.0	8.2	12.4	7.6
Re-entered labor force	19.3	40.0	29.0	13.2	34.0	26.4	16.9	37.0	24.7
Never worked before	3.0	6.3	38.6	2.6	5.8	47.4	3.7	7.1	49.7
Total[a]	100.0	100.0	100.0	100.0	100.0	100.0	100.0	100.0	100.0

[a]May not add up precisely because of rounding.

Source: *Employment and Training Report of the President*, 1982 (Washington D.C.; U.S. Government Printing Office); *Employment and Earnings* 31, no. 1 (January 1984); and *Employment and Earnings* 32, no. 1 (January 1985).

1960s and 1970s, since their probability of leaving unemployment to exit from the labor force declined during that time.[24] This (and other factors to be discussed below) appears to have counterbalanced the improvement in women's unemployment experience that would otherwise have been expected to result from their growing labor force attachment.[25]

The data in Table 9.6 also suggest that women's lesser commitment to a particular job is another reason for their higher unemployment rate. A higher proportion of female than of male unemployed workers have left (quit) their last job. This may in part be caused by the lack of substantial rewards for stable employment associated with the scarcity of career ladders in women's jobs. It has, in fact, been noted that holding everything else, including occupations, constant, there is no difference in male and female quit rates.[26] Thus, women do have higher quit rates than men, but primarily because they are concentrated in occupations where both men and women have few incentives for job continuity, not necessarily because they tend to place their family responsibilities before their careers.

There is also the question of to what extent the higher quit rate among women contributes to the higher overall female unemployment rate. The results of at least one study suggest that when there are as many people looking for work as has generally been the case in this country, this effect is small. The person who quits a job increases the number of unemployed, but the vacancy created will be quickly filled by someone who had been searching for a position. This will reduce the rate to its previous level.[27] Female unemployment might nonetheless be adversely affected if most of the quitters were women and most of the replacements were men. But this could only happen to the extent that the groups are competing for the same jobs, which is, as discussed in Chapter 6, not generally the case because of occupational segregation.[28]

[24]Ehrenberg, "The Demographic Structure of Unemployment Rates," p. 262. See, also Niemi, "Recent Changes in Differential Unemployment," and Marianne A. Ferber and Helen M. Lowry, "Women—The New Reserve Army the Unemployed," *Signs: The Journal of Women in Culture and Society* 1, no. 3, pt. 2 (Spring 1976): 213-32.

[25]Specifically, over the same time period, women were found to have a declining probability of leaving the labor force from employment. All else equal, this aspect of their rising labor force attachment would *lower* their unemployment rates (Ehrenberg, "The Demographic Structure of Unemployment Rates," pp 257-8).

[26]See Francine D. Blau and Lawrence M. Kahn, "Race and Sex Differences in Quits by Young Workers," *Industrial and Labor Relations Review* 34, no. 4 (July 1981): 563-77; and W. Kip Viscusi, "Sex Differences in Worker Quitting," *The Review of Economics and Statistics* 62, no. 3 (August 1980): 388-98.

[27]Barbara Bergmann, "Labor Turnover, Segmentation and Rates of Unemployment: A Simulation-Theoretic Approach," (mimeo: Project on the Economics of Discrimination, University of Maryland, Mar. 1973). In a very tight labor market, it will take longer to fill the job so that the net effect will be to increase unemployment while the quitter is looking. But in such a situation, a new job should also be easy to find, reducing the search time.

[28]Evidence indicating that men do not have a lower unemployment rate in occupations with a larger proportion of women, where they would presumably gain from the higher quit rate of women, bears out this point. See Ferber and Lowry, "Women: The New Reserve Army of the Unemployed."

Differences in job search behavior may also contribute to the sex differential in unemployment rates. As has been pointed out, "Most unemployed women do not devote the entire typical work week to job search; they instead spend some of their time in activities outside the labor market."[29] To the extent that the additional hours men spend on search are effective, rather than merely a way to keep occupied, women may be at a disadvantage. More serious may be the common reluctance of married women to move in order to find a job for themselves,[30] and their frequent willingness to relocate to advance their husband's careers. Their unwillingness to work long or irregular hours or to travel very far to work may also be an obstacle to their finding a job.

The shorter duration of women's unemployment spells, seen in Table 9.3, does not suggest that unemployed women have more difficulty locating work than men, but it should be recalled that unemployed women drop out of the labor force to a greater extent than unemployed men. Thus, the factors discussed above may contribute to women's greater tendency to become discouraged workers rather than to their unemployment rate. Additional evidence that women's search behavior does not contribute to their higher unemployment rates is the finding that unemployed women tend to set their sights too low. That is, they may take a job even when the benefits (in terms of higher wages) of additional search would have outweighed the costs.[31] Such behavior is likely to lower their wages, all else equal, but certainly should not raise their unemployment rate.

In contrast to most of the factors we have considered thus far, sex differences in the distribution of employment by occupation and industry do not appear to *directly* contribute to the higher unemployment rate of women.[32] Men are more heavily represented in blue-collar jobs and durable manufacturing where layoff and unemployment rates are above average. Women are more likely to be employed in white-collar jobs where layoff and unemployment rates are lower, although they are also disproportionately represented in service jobs

---

[29]Steven H. Sandell, "Job Search by Unemployed Women: Determinants of the Asking Wage," *Industrial and Labor Relations Review* 33, no. 3 (April 1980): 368–78.

[30]Evidence of this was found, even for very highly educated women, by Marianne A. Ferber and Betty Kordick, "Sex Differentials in the Earnings of Ph.D.'s," *Industrial and Labor Relations Review* 31, no. 2 (January 1978): 227–38.

[31]Steven H. Sandell, "Is the Unemployment Rate of Women Too Low? A Direct Test of the Economic Theory of Job Search," *The Review of Economic and Statistics* 62, no. 4 (November 1980): 634–38. See, also, Lawrence M. Kahn, "The Returns to Job Search: A Test of Two Models," *The Review of Economics and Statistics* 60, no. 4 (November 1978): 496–503. Kahn finds evidence consistent with the view that women do not start their job search by sampling high-wage employers to the same extent as men do. Rather, they appear to set their sights lower and begin with firms that pay lower wages but have a higher probability of making them an offer.

[32]One study found that if women (with work experience) had the same occupational distribution as experienced male workers in 1969, their unemployment rate would have *increased* by 5 percent. See Nancy Barret and Richard D. Morgenstern, "Why do Blacks and Women Have High Unemployment Rates?" *Journal of Human Resources* 9, no. 4 (Fall 1974): 452–64.

where unemployment rates are above average. These sex differences in occupational distributions are one reason that a higher proportion of men than of women are unemployed because they lost their last job (Table 9.6).[33]

As discussed avove, however, the characteristics of women's jobs (including the occupations and industries in which they tend to be employed) may *indirectly* raise women's unemployment by increasing their propensity to quit their jobs. In contrast, the tendency of blacks to be heavily represented in poorly paid blue-collar and service jobs does contribute, both directly and indirectly, to their higher unemployment rates relative to whites.[34]

Sex differences in distribution by occupation and industry also help to explain why unemployment rates for men tend to be high relative to those of women at times when cyclical unemployment is high. The blue-collar jobs and durable goods manufacturing industries where a larger proportion of men is employed are subject to greater cyclical variations in employment.

As noted earlier, not only are women's unemployment rates generally higher than men's and relatively higher during periods of prosperity, the sex gap in unemployment rates widened during the 1960s and 1970s. We have already mentioned one factor that may help to account for this, namely a decline in women's propensity to drop out of the labor force when confronted with problems in finding jobs. An additional factor is that women appeared to be having, on average, growing difficulty in finding jobs during this period. Between 1966 and 1976, an unemployed woman's probability of leaving unemployment by finding a job declined. Similarly, for a woman who was out of the labor force, the probability of entering the labor force without having a job lined up (that is, the probability of experiencing some unemployment) increased.[35] The reasons for this are not clear. One factor may be the persistence of occupational segregation by sex, in the presence of increasing female labor force participation rates. Further, women may also have faced increasing competition for some of the same jobs from the growing number of teenagers who were seeking employment at the same time.[36]

---

[33]Among young workers, women were found to have lower layoff probabilities than men, on average. This remained the case even after controlling for a variety of personal and job-related characteristics. However, the occupational and industrial variables were quite aggregated, and, thus, it is still possible that sex differences in detailed distributions are responsible for the observed layoff difference. See Francine D. Blau and Lawrence M. Kahn, "Causes and Consequences of Layoffs," *Economic Inquiry* 19, no. 2 (April 1981): 270–96.

[34]Barret and Morganstern, "Why Do Blacks and Women Have High Unemployment Rates?" Blau and Kahn ("Causes and Consequences of Layoffs") found that in contrast to the case for sex differences, black workers had higher average layoff rates than whites. This racial differential remained even after adjusting for their personal and job characteristics.

[35]Ehrenberg, "The Demographic Structure of Unemployment," pp. 255–81. Ehrenberg argues that a variety of government policies may have contributed to these trends.

[36]For evidence that employers treat women and youths as substitutes in production, see James Grant and Daniel Hamermesh, "Labor-Market Competition among Youths, White Women and Others," *Review of Economics and Statistics* 63, no. 3 (August 1981): 354–60.

The complex set of factors that has influenced unemployment rates of women as compared to those of men all have been closely linked to the particular conditions during the period examined. As women's labor force participation, attachment to the labor force, occupational distribution, and position in the family continue to change, the sex gap in unemployment may be expected to change also and most likely to decline.[37]

To the extent that men and women remain employed in different sectors, there is some reason to believe that the relatively higher unemployment rate of men as compared to women since the late 1970s is not just a cyclical phenomenon but may rather turn out to be a trend. The main reason for this expectation is that several of the predominantly male sectors of the economy—particularly farming and mining, but also manufacturing as well as transportation and public utilities—are expected to grow more slowly in the future than most of the sectors that are more heavily female.[38]

WOMEN AND THE FULL EMPLOYMENT TARGET

The fact that women's unemployment rates have generally been higher than men's coupled with the increasing representation of women in the labor force has been used to explain the increase in recent decades both in the actual total unemployment rate and also in the full employment unemployment rate. This cannot, however, be the sole or even the main explanation for these increases. As Figure 9.1 shows, the male rate itself has also been higher. Indeed, rough calculations suggest that the increase in women's share of the labor force accounts for little of the rise in the actual unemployment rate.

---

[37]Different definitions of the official unemployment rate can also play a role. The new way the rate was calculated from 1967 on may have contributed to the upward shift in women's, relative to men's, reported unemployment, though the evidence on this point is not very strong. The definition was changed as follows: (1) Prior to 1967, the period of active job search (in order to qualify as being unemployed rather than out of the labor force) was not specified. Since then, it has been specified as the four-week period preceding the survey. (2) Persons absent from work because of a vacation or labor dispute, who were at the same time looking for work, had been counted as unemployed. Since 1967, they were counted as employed. (3) Persons stating that they had given up the search for work were counted as unemployed before, but not after, 1967. It is not clear how these changes would affect women's, as compared to men's, unemployment. Barnes and Jones, "Differences in Male and Female Quitting," found that when the 1967 definition was applied to the 1966 data, the unemployment rate for women became 0.4 percent higher and for men 0.3 percent lower. Given, however, the sampling error for these data, evidence for only one year is not very convincing, especially since 1966 had an unusually low unemployment rate as compared to the whole post-World War II period.

[38]Larry DeBoer and Michael Seeborg, "The Female-Male Unemployment Differential: Effects of Changes in Industry Employment," *Monthly Labor Review* 107, no. 11 (November 1984): 8–15.

In 1957, for instance, the unemployment rate was 4.3 percent, while in 1979 the rate was 5.8 percent. If the female share of the labor force had remained at its 1957 level, the 1979 unemployment rate would have been 5.65 percent. That is, by this measure, the increase in female labor force participation accounted for less than two-tenths of a percentage point of the 1.5 percentage point increase in the unemployment rate over the period.[39] Both 1957 and 1979 have been regarded by many economists as years of full employment. Hence, it is also clear that the shift in what is considered the full employment unemployment rate cannot be explained merely in terms of the rising representation of women in the labor force either.

SEX DIFFERENCES IN THE BURDEN OF UNEMPLOYMENT

The relative seriousness of women's unemployment as a public policy concern has at times been downgraded for a variety of reasons. We consider some of the major ones in turn. We conclude that sex is too imprecise a measure of economic hardship to dismiss women's unemployment problems as less important or serious than men's.

One argument for viewing women's higher unemployment rate as less cause for concern is that it is primarily due to frictional factors, related to their higher rates of labor force and job turnover.[40] The fact that women's median weeks of unemployment are shorter than men's appears to suggest that they do not experience undue difficulty in finding a job. Since frictional unemployment is viewed as being voluntary and of short duration, it is not generally perceived to be a serious problem.

But this characterization of female unemployment is not entirely accurate.[41] First, as we have previously observed, unemployed women are more likely to become discouraged and drop out of the labor force. Therefore, unemployment duration is not as reliable an indicator of their difficulty in obtaining employment as it is for men. Further, the "reason" given for a woman's unemployment may be misleading. For example, a woman may be

---

[39]When changes in the age composition of the labor force are also included, demographic factors are found to explain about half of the rise in the unemployment rate (Daniel S. Hamermesh and Albert Rees, *The Economics of Work and Pay,* 3rd. ed. (New York: Harper & Row, 1984), p. 194. For further evidence that rising female labor force participation does not explain very much of the trend towards higher unemployment rates, see Michael Podgursky, "Sources of Secular Increase in the Unemployment Rate, 1969–82," *Monthly Labor Review* 107, no. 7 (July 1984): 19–25.

[40]Ehrenberg and Smith, *Modern Labor Economics,* pp. 450–52.

[41]See Nancy S. Barrett, "Women in the Job Market: Unemployment and Work Schedules," ed. Ralph E. Smith, *The Subtle Revolution: Women at Work* (Washington, D.C.: The Urban Institute, 1979) pp. 63–98, for a good discussion of this issue.

fired from her job, become discouraged, and leave the labor force. If she returns to look for work, the reason for her unemployment is "re-entry" rather than "lay off." Indeed, entrants or re-entrants may be "job losers" in another sense; marital breakup has been found to be highly correlated with labor force entry for women who have become "displaced homemakers."[42]

Second, there is no direct evidence that women's higher unemployment is voluntary in the sense that we have defined—that is, that they decline offers at the prevailing market rate for their skills to a greater extent than men do. On the contrary, they appear, if anything, to be too willing to curtail their search and accept a lower paying job. Finally, women's weaker labor force attachment may reflect not only their own voluntary choices but the indirect effects of labor market discrimination as well.

A second reason why women's unemployment problems are often viewed as less serious is because they supposedly do not need income as much as men do.[43] This attitude is essentially based on the assumption that even when a woman is employed she is only an auxiliary wage earner.

It is true that in families where husband and wife are both employed she tends to earn considerably less, only somewhat more than half as much as he does. This is not an insignificant contribution though. In a good many cases, it is the wife's earnings that bring the family over the poverty line; in many more cases, they make the difference between mere adequacy and comfort. Accordingly, the loss of the woman's income results in a substantial reduction in the family's standard of living. In cases where the family has made substantial long-run commitments by buying on credit, the unanticipated loss of earnings can result in especially great hardship.

Even when the wife is a new entrant or re-entrant, the family has made the decision that her labor market earnings would be more valuable than her full-time household production. Her inability to find work, thus, entails a decline in her family's welfare below what it would have been if she were employed. This is particularly serious when her labor force entry was prompted by a change in family circumstances that increased the need for her market income.

There is also a large number of women whose contribution to family income is absolutely pivotal, because they are the sole family head. Approximately 14 percent of all women in the labor market in 1984 fell into this category. They are likely to be more dependent on continuous employment than either spouse in a two-earner family.

While the reasons for women's lesser need for income readily spring to

[42]Francine D. Blau, "The Impact of the Unemployment Rate on Labor Force Entries and Exits," *Women's Changing Roles at Home and in the Job,* National Commission for Manpower Policy, Special Report No. 26 (September 1978), pp. 262–86.

[43]See, for instance, Bettina Berch, *The Endless Day: The Political Economy of Women and Work* (N.Y.: Harcourt, Brace, Jovanovich, Inc., 1982), ". . . during most economic downturns the myth that women do not 'need' to work is usually revived as a justification for laying off women first" p. 18.

mind, it is less often recognized that in some respects men's unemployment is less likely to cause economic hardship than women's. Since men are job losers to a greater extent than women, they are more likely to be covered by unemployment insurance which replaces at least part of their lost income. Moreover, since they are more highly unionized, they are more likely to receive supplemental unemployment benefits from their employer. (These are provided under many collective bargaining agreements.) Further, the wages of many male workers may already reflect a compensating differential due to their employment in seasonal or cyclically sensitive industries. Finally, today many men are members of two-earner families and can, thus, like many women, rely on the incomes of other family members during spells of unemployment.

On balance, it is not clear that women need income less than men. While we have left behind the now thoroughly outdated view that women always have men to support them, and men's families are entirely composed of dependents, it will take longer to dispell the notion that women are only secondary workers. Meanwhile, the perception that women's inability to find market work is not so much of a problem is also likely to persist.

One reason for this is the assumption that a woman can always fall back on household work. Further, it has been pointed out that women's unemployment is exaggerated because those who search while working as homemakers are counted as unemployed, whereas men who search for a better job while employed are not counted.[44] Here again, however, this depiction is not likely to be entirely correct. As we pointed out earlier, the majority of women (and men) who enter the labor force experience no unemployment, just as the majority of individuals who change jobs move directly from one to the other without experiencing unemployment. While the line between "employed" and "unemployed" search may be difficult to draw for married women who do some housework, the proportions suggest that women generally do not report themselves as unemployed until job search becomes a primary activity. Unemployed married women (like their employed counterparts) may do most of the housework in their families, but this does not seem adequate reason to consider their unemployment any less of a problem than their husband's.

In conclusion, a larger question needs to be raised about the fundamental assumption that the unemployment of men and women may be viewed differently because women are not dependent on their own income and because they can be productive in the household when they cannot find employment in the market. Not only was this view based on the premise that every woman was a member of a family that also included an adult male but also that the division of responsibilities was necessarily a traditional one. The man needed to be employed because he had dependents; the woman did not need to be employed because she had a man to support her. The woman who was unemployed had

[44]Janet L. Johnson, "Sex Differentials in Unemployment Rates: A Case for No Concern," *Journal of Political Economy* 91, no. 2 (April 1983): 293–303.

the opportunity to take care of her household responsibilities, but a man had no such alternative. Gradual recognition that these views are no longer appropriate, and are likely to become increasingly less so, is a welcome development.

CONCLUSION

We began this chapter by defining unemployment, and explaining the difference between seasonal, frictional, structural, and cyclical, or demand-deficient unemployment, as well as the related concepts of underemployment and discouraged workers. This was followed by a brief indication of the costs of unemployment for the economy and for the persons who are unemployed, and a discussion of the lowest level of unemployment an economy could expect to achieve and sustain. The last three sections dealt with the varying incidence of unemployment in different population groups, examined the reasons for the higher rate of women than men, and, finally, considered the question to what extent unemployment is a burden for women.

We have seen that the issue of unemployment is one about which it is far easier to raise questions than to find definitive answers. There is not even agreement on the correct definition, let alone the causes of and solutions for unemployment. It is to be hoped that economists will make some progress in all these respects. Even with improved knowledge, however, the potentially divergent interests of different groups will make solutions difficult.

SUGGESTED READINGS

BLAU, FRANCINE D., "The Impact of the Unemployment Rate on Labor Entries and Exits:" In *Women's Changing Roles at Home and on the Job,* National Commission for Manpower Policy, Special Report No. 26, September 1978.

EHRENBERG, RONALD G., "The Demographic Structure of Unemployment Rates and Labor Market Transition Probabilities" ed. Ronald G. Ehrenberg, *Research in Labor Economics* 3 (Greenwich, Conn.: JAI Press, Inc., 1980): 241-91.

JOHNSON, JANET L., "Sex Differentials in Unemployment Rates: A Case for No Concern," *Journal of Political Economy* 91, no. 2 (April 1983): 293-303.

NATIONAL COMMISSION ON EMPLOYMENT AND UNEMPLOYMENT STATISTICS, *Counting the Labor Force,* Washington, D.C., Government Printing Office, 1979.

NIEMI, BETH, "Recent Changes in Differential Unemployment," *Growth and Change* 8, no. 3 (July 1977): 22-30.

SANDELL, STEVEN H., "Is the Unemployment Rate of Women Too Low? A Direct Test of the Economic Theory of Job Search," *The Review of Economics and Statistics* 62, no. 4 (November 1980): 634-38.

(VICKERY) CLAIR BROWN, BARBARA BERGMANN, AND KATHERINE SWARTZ, "Unemployment Rate Targets and Anti-Inflation Policy as More Women Enter the Workforce," *American Economic Review* 68, no. 2 (May 1978): 90-94.

Chapter 10

SEX DIFFERENCES IN OTHER COUNTRIES: WHAT CAN WE LEARN FROM INTERNATIONAL COMPARISONS?

So far in this book, except for the discussion in Chapter 2 of the changing roles of women and men in the course of economic development, we have focused entirely on the situation in the United States. Throughout, we emphasized the influence of economic factors in determining the status of women. This is not to suggest that nothing else matters, but, rather, that, everything being the same, economic considerations play an important role. Of course, in the real world everything else is generally not the same. Societies differ in their political systems, in their cultures, in their religions. In this chapter, we turn to a consideration of women in other countries in order, on the one hand, to shed light on the causes of the substantial diversity in their status, and, on the other hand, to see what we can learn about institutions and policies that have retarded or enhanced improvements in the position of women.

We begin by presenting information on various indicators of the economic status of women as compared to men and discussing regularities as well as diversity among various countries and regions. Because of serious limitations in terms of availability, accuracy, and comparability of data, particularly for developing countries, evidence is often limited to only selected countries

and must be interpreted with great caution. We go on to present a brief interpretation of the findings, acknowledging that we have much to learn about the
determinants of existing differences. Last, we briefly examine some of the
issues of special concern in developing countries, with their serious problem of
low per capita income, and in two advanced industrialized countries, the
Union of Soviet Socialist Republics (USSR) and Sweden, which, each in its
own way, have an explicit commitment to equality for women.

INDICATORS OF WOMEN'S
ECONOMIC STATUS

There are a number of measures that, by general agreement, would be regarded as useful indicators of women's economic status. We consider labor
force participation first. Unless women participate in production beyond
homemaking, few can expect to have their own income, or to achieve status in
their own right. In other words, they will be restricted to the role of economic
dependent, even if they are fortunate enough to obtain a relatively high standard of living. Many will not be that fortunate. For this reason, the labor force
participation rate is an important indicator of women's progress toward
equality.

The second criterion to be discussed is the degree of occupational segregation, which is often viewed as representing the exclusion of women from
rewarding and challenging jobs. The third item to be addressed is the male-
female earnings gap, obviously an issue of great relevance to women's
economic status. Fourth, we compare the unemployment rates of women and
men, because they represent significant hardships for those unable to find
jobs. Last, we present the scant evidence that is available on the amount of
housework done by women and men, which is likely to affect women's relative
status in and out of the work force.

Labor Force Participation

Labor force participation is determined by demand and supply factors
that vary from place to place, as well as over time, depending in part on the
level of economic development and the industry mix of each economy. The
nature of the jobs available in the labor market influences the demand for
women workers. Both the availability of goods and services for purchase, and
the relative value of market earnings as compared to time spent in household
production, influence the supply of female labor.

Demographic factors also play an important role. An unusually high
proportion of women in the population necessarily means a large number of
them will be unmarried, at least in countries where monogamy is the rule, and

will have little incentive or opportunity to become full-time homemakers. An unusually high birthrate necessarily means families with large numbers of children, giving women more incentive to become full-time homemakers.

It would, however, be a mistake to overlook the importance of such other factors as the preferences of employers for male workers rather than female workers, perceptions of what type of work is appropriate for each sex, general attitudes toward the appropriate roles for women and men, and tastes for market goods as compared to commodities mainly produced at home. A comparison of varying labor force participation rates sheds some light on these issues.

Most countries provide data on the number of economically active males and females in the adult population, which enable us to calculate the labor force participation rates for men and women. The information provided must, however, be interpreted with great caution, for there are a number of factors that can produce misleading results.

First, when two otherwise similar countries include populations from a different minimum age, the one that uses a higher cutoff will appear to have a higher labor force participation rate. This is so because younger individuals are more likely to be in school. Second, when there is a larger proportion of the population in the age groups that still tend to be in school, or that are already retired, there will be a lower labor force participation rate. Third, the number of years young people generally spend in school and the typical retirement age obviously influence the proportion of those who are economically active.

Insofar as these variables influence the proportion of men and women who are economically active in the same way, their effect can be neutralized by computing the ratio of female to male labor force participation rates in each country. For this reason, and because we are in any case primarily concerned with the relative status of women, we mainly rely on this ratio in our discussion.

Even these data, however, have substantial limitations. Serious issues arise because of problems that do not affect men and women to the same extent. As was explained in Chapter 4, in the United States, all individuals 16 years of age and over who are employed or self-employed for at least one hour per week are included in the labor force; among unpaid family workers, only those working at least 15 hours a week are counted. Similar definitions are used by many, though not all, other countries. Since it is predominantly women who are considered to be unpaid family workers, while men in the same family enterprise are most often considered to be self-employed, such a distinction causes women's labor force participation to be relatively low both as compared to men in the same country and as compared to women in those countries where all family workers are treated as self-employed.

Distortions are greatest in the Third World, where a substantial part of the population continues to be occupied in family establishments, most often subsistence agriculture, and are aggrevated by the inevitable inaccuracy of estimates of hours worked in such an informal setting. Hence, there are serious questions about comparability. This is especially true since those countries where women's labor force participation is genuinely low also appear to be most likely to undercount marginal female workers, thus exaggerating sex differences in labor force participation across countries.[1]

Last, one additional problem deserves mention. As in the United States, those who work only in the household are not counted as members of the labor force. This omission is far more serious in developing countries where water and fuel are often carried by women for long distances; clothes are washed in the river for lack of running water; food must be procured and prepared on a daily basis for lack of refrigeration; and where many goods and services generally purchased in economically advanced countries are produced at home.

For all these reasons, cross-country comparisons of labor force participation are, at best, only rough indications of actual differences in the extent to which men and women participate in productive work. In spite of these shortcomings, the data are instructive.

Table 10.1 shows male and female labor force participation rates and the ratio between the two, as well as per capita income, for selected countries arranged in relatively homogeneous groups.[2] The ratios of female to male labor force participation for the regions, computed as the mean (giving each country equal weight) are also shown. The order is from highest to lowest average ratio of women's to men's labor force participation rate. The very large country-by-country variation in the ratio, from 99 percent to a mere 11 percent, can only partly be explained in terms of the differences in economic development that were emphasized in Chapter 2.[3]

---

[1] "In cultures where women's role in productive activity is not readily acknowledged and valued, there is likely to be a tendency to undercount the number of women who are working," United Nations, *The Economic Role of Women in the ECE Region,* (New York, 1980), p. 3.

[2] Countries were chosen for which the necessary data were available for 1975 or later, so that they would be fairly comparable, and which as far as possible, also provided the information for an earlier period so that changes over time could be determined. Regrettably, here as elsewhere, China had to be omitted for lack of adequate information. Since it is the most populous country in the world, this is a great loss. Inevitably, the grouping is, to some extent, judgmental, as for instance in drawing the line between North Africa and the remainder of that continent and between South Central and East Asia.

[3] We would not, however, go as far as some other authors, in arguing that economic development has little or no uniform effect on female labor force participation. For that point of view, see for instance, Nadja Youssef, *Women and Work in Developing Societies,* (Berkeley: University of California Press, 1974); and Guy Standing, *Labour Force Participation and Development,* 2nd ed., (Geneva: International Labour Office, 1981). At the same time, substantial variations among regions and among individual countries within regions suggest that differences in the form that economic development takes, as well as many other factors, influence female labor force participation.

The least economically developed countries, those with the lowest per capita income,[4] mainly in the Sub-Saharan African countries (group III), only recently moved from the horticultural to the agricultural stage. As would be expected, they have a relatively high ratio of economically active women relative to men, many of whom continue to grow, sometimes process, and sell food. The ratio of women's to men's labor force participation in the Latin American countries (group VI), most of them countries solidly in the agricultural phase, is considerably lower. With further development and growth of the service and industrial sectors, the trend is reversed and increasing numbers of women enter the labor market, as seen, for instance, in Eastern Europe and the Western advanced industrialized countries (groups I and V).

The interpretation that women's labor force participation declines, relative to men's, at least as measured by official statistics, during the early stages of development and then increases again is also supported by changes over time in labor force participation observed in these same regions. The ratio of economically active women to men has been declining in all but one of the Sub-Saharan African countries (group III) for which data over time are available. Here urbanization, especially in the early stages, appears to confine women to the household to a greater extent than was the case in rural areas.[5] During this same period, the ratio has been increasing for the vast majority of countries in groups I, II, IV, V, and VI.[6]

There are, however, serious complications that should not be overlooked. It is not possible to explain the very substantial difference in the ratio of female to male participation between the Caribbean and Latin American regions (groups II and VI) in these terms. The former is not much more economically advanced (in terms of per capita income) than the latter nor, for that matter, are those in East Asia (group IV), which also have relatively high participation rates of women relative to men.

A second incongruity is that Eastern Europe (group I), with the highest participation ratio, consists of countries that are, on the average, not as ad-

---

[4]Income data for various countries expressed in a single currency inevitably depend for their comparability on the exchange values used, which are at best approximations of their respective purchasing power. In addition, it will be noted that the data in our table come from years ranging between 1975 and 1982. The differences in per capita income between the various groups of countries are, however, so great in a number of instances that they tend to dwarf any possible inaccuracies caused by these deficiencies.

[5]Lourdes Beneria, ed., *Women and Development. The Sexual Division of Labor in Rural Societies* (N.Y.: Praeger, 1982).

[6]Data, once again, are provided for different years in various countries and range from the late 1950s to the middle 1960s. The means for the earlier, as compared to the later, sets of years were 63.4 and 57.9 for the five countries in group III for which earlier data are available (Congo-Kinshasa, Ivory Coast. Malawi, Liberia and Seychelles); but 60.8 and 74.6 for I; 63.2 and 74.0 for II; 43.0 and 61.1 for IV; 38.4 and 58.3 for V; 23.4 and 33.7 for VI; and 10.3 and 18.3 for group VII.

TABLE 10.1   Labor Force Participation in Selected Countries, by Region[a]

I	YEAR[d]	MEN	WOMEN	RATIO OF WOMEN'S TO MEN'S LABOR FORCE PARTICIPATION RATE	YEAR[d]	PER CAPITA INCOME
Eastern Europe				74.6		n.a.
Czechoslovakia	1980	75.5	60.8	80.5		n.a.
Hungary	1980	71.9	50.2	69.8		n.a.
Poland	1978	76.6	69.1	90.2		n.a.
Rumania	1977	75.0	59.6	79.5		n.a.
Yugoslavia	1978	73.6	39.1	53.2		n.a.
II						
Caribbean				74.0		1433
Bermuda[b]	1976	90.5	69.3	76.6		n.a.
French Guyana	1977	75.1	56.4	75.1		n.a.
Haiti	1980	87.8	68.9	78.5	1975	219
Jamaica	1980	67.5	40.4	59.9	1975	1259
Martinique	1980	61.2	48.8	79.7	1975	2604

III

Sub-Saharan Africa

	Year				Year	
Sub-Saharan Africa				64.7		350
Congo-Kinshasa	1974	81.7	56.2	68.8	1978	453
Ethiopia	1978	90.1	57.4	63.7	1975	91
Ivory Coast	1975	91.1	44.9	49.3	1978	906
Liberia	1974	70.0	24.8	35.4	1975	333
Malawi	1977	81.6	62.1	76.0	1975	119
Rwanda	1978	92.9	91.8	98.9	1978	174
Seychelles	1977	85.0	51.0	60.0		n.a.
Togo	1980	83.5	54.7	65.5	1979	375

IV

East Asia

	Year				Year	
East Asia				61.1		1089
Hong Kong	1981	82.5	49.5	60.0	1975	1740
Indonesia	1978	86.9	45.3	52.2	1979	299
Korea, Rep.	1981	71.6	42.3	59.1	1979	1481
Malaysia	1979	79.0	44.7	56.6	1975	714
Philippines	1978	81.4	46.8	57.5	1979	576
Singapore	1981	80.9	44.3	54.8	1975	2279
Thailand	1980	87.8	76.6	87.2	1979	536

TABLE 10.1 Labor Force Participation in Selected Countries, by Region[a] (*Continued*)

	YEAR[d]	MEN	WOMEN	RATIO OF WOMEN'S TO MEN'S LABOR FORCE PARTICIPATION RATE	YEAR[d]	PER CAPITA INCOME
V						
Advanced Industrialized Nations				58.3		8102
Australia	1981	79.3	43.8	55.3	1979	8110
Austria	1980	69.1	37.4	54.0	1979	7988
Canada	1980	74.5	48.4	64.9	1979	8318
Denmark	1981	74.7	57.0	76.3	1979	11570
Finland	1981	69.6	55.6	79.0	1979	7399
France	1981	69.1	41.3	59.7	1979	9562
German Fed. Rep.	1981	72.3	39.8	55.0	1979	11029
Iceland	1981	82.9	59.2	71.4	1979	9021
Ireland	1977	76.8	28.2	36.7	1979	4149
Israel	1981	63.8	36.2	56.6	1979	4049

Italy	1980	70.0	32.3	46.1	1979	5133
Japan	1981	81.3	46.9	57.6	1979	7421
Luxembourg	1979	72.0	30.8	42.8	1978	10014
Netherlands	1981	68.7	30.6	44.6	1979	9568
New Zealand	1981	76.5	38.6	50.4	1979	6259
Norway[c]	1981	77.2	51.9	67.2	1979	9239
Portugal	1981	78.8	46.9	59.5	1978	1701
Spain	1979	70.2	27.3	38.9	1979	4796
Sweden	1982	77.0	66.3	86.1	1979	11416
Switzerland	1980	79.4	42.3	53.3	1979	13978
United States	1982	74.7	51.0	68.3	1979	9429

VI

Latin America | | | | 33.7 | | 1182 |

Argentina	1980	76.6	29.8	38.9	1975	1388
Chile	1980	70.3	27.6	39.3	1975	423
Columbia	1980	78.4	22.4	28.5	1979	949
Costa Rica	1980	82.1	26.4	32.1	1979	1692
Ecuador	1981	84.8	30.2	35.6	1975	561

TABLE 10.1 Labor Force Participation in Selected Countries, by Region[a] (*Continued*)

VI	YEAR[d]	MEN	WOMEN	RATIO OF WOMEN'S TO MEN'S LABOR FORCE PARTICIPATION RATE	YEAR[d]	PER CAPITA INCOME
El Salvador	1980	82.8	40.2	48.5	1979	755
Guatemala	1980	89.5	14.3	16.0	1979	855
Honduras	1981	87.7	17.5	20.0	1979	551
Panama	1980	69.2	27.3	39.4	1978	322
Paraguay	1980	94.6	24.7	26.1	1979	1005
Peru	1982	79.0	31.5	39.9	1979	742
Uruguay	1975	78.4	29.3	37.4	1979	2267
Venezuela	1981	80.4	29.6	36.9	1979	3362

VII

North Africa, Middle East
South Central Asia

				18.3		3847
Bahrain	1981	86.1	18.2	21.2	1975	2746
Egypt	1980	73.6	7.8	10.6	1975	343
Iran	1976	83.2	13.4	16.1	1975	1583
Kuwait	1980	84.5	19.8	23.5	1979	20172
Pakistan	1982	86.6	12.6	14.8	1979	296
Syria	1979	76.3	13.4	17.5	1975	735
Tunisia	1980	79.2	19.5	24.6	1979	1055

[a]For population 15 years of age and older, unless otherwise noted.
[b]16 years of age and older.
[c]20 years of age and older.
[d]Year in which the data were collected.
n.a. Not available.

Sources: Labor force participation, International Labour Office, Yearbook of Labour Statistics, various years. Per capita income, United Nations Statistical Yearbook, 1981.

313

vanced as the Western industrialized countries. While Eastern European countries do not provide official information on the subject, there is universal agreement that their per capita income is lower than for Western advanced industrialized countries (group V).

Last, but not least, we have so far ignored group VII, comprised of North Africa, the Middle East, and South Central Asia, which has a female to male labor force participation ratio far below that of any of the others. It includes countries at various stages of economic development, from Pakistan (one of the poorest countries in the world) to Bahrain and Kuwait (among the wealthiest, if not necessarily the most highly developed).

There are, no doubt, many factors that play a part in determining female labor force participation. As we saw in Chapter 2, women's roles varied during the pre-agricultural period, and traditions tend to linger well beyond the era during which they are shaped. The fact that the peoples of North Africa and the Middle East were often pastoral, rather than horticultural, may help to explain why women's role is so heavily centered in the household. The importance of the nature of economic development in different countries is well illustrated by the high labor force participation of women in the Caribbean, where tourism is a major industry, and the low participation in such countries as Iran and Kuwait, whose economies are dominated by oil production. There is reason to believe that guest workers (foreigners temporarily working in a country but not expected to remain there) may to some extent be substitutes for female workers, and that the presence of a large number of guest workers has a depressing effect on the employment of women.[7] Last, the negative effect of large numbers of children helps to explain the situation in Latin America, North Africa, the Middle East, and South Central Asia (groups VI and VII).

It is, however, clear that such factors as ideology and religion also play an important part. For one, fertility is, to a greater or lesser degree, influenced by governmental policies and religious doctrines. In numerous countries, there have at one time or another been laws which prohibited various types of family planning, on the one hand, and severe penalties for having more than a specified number of children on the other. Divine sanctions have frequently been invoked against those who chose not to follow the command to "be fruitful and multiply." Second, beliefs in what are appropriate roles for women and men, whether shaped by the dogma of philosophers, church, or state, appear to have considerable direct influence on the extent to which women's activities are confined to the home.

In general, universalistic egalitarian standards tend to be related positively to the role women play in the economy. It has been found, for instance, that a more equal distribution of income is associated with higher female labor

---

[7]Patricia Roos, *Gender and Work: A Comparative Analysis of Industrial Societies* (Albany, NY: SUNY Press, 1985) suggests that the sharp increase in women's labor force participation in Sweden coincided with a substantial cutback in use of workers from abroad.

force participation,[8] as is a larger share of resources allocated to social welfare.[9] Marxist ideology, which strongly advocates women's entry into the work force, surely helps to explain the situation in Eastern Europe.

It is also interesting to note that the Latin American countries (group VI) are predominantly Catholic. Similarly, within group V, the ratio of women's to men's labor force participation rate tends to be lower in the predominantly Catholic countries (for example, Austria, the German Federal Republic, Ireland, Luxembourg, and Spain). Further, the highest ratios are found in the Scandinavian countries which are not predominantly Catholic and where there is also a notable dedication to an egalitarian ideology. Group VII, on the other hand, consists entirely of Moslem countries, which have emphasized women's roles as wives and mothers to the virtual exclusion of activities outside the home.[10] Even here, however, women carry on income-earning activities in the home, which are not taken into account as labor force participation.

An inspection of labor force data also reveals that the changes in women's work roles, which we have seen in the United States in recent decades, are reasonably representative of other advanced industrialized countries in general, as may be seen in Figure 10.1. There are, however, some exceptions. Three of these can also be seen in the Figure. Labor force participation of women in Italy and Japan declined somewhat in the 1960s as the agricultural sectors, where women were heavily represented, were shrinking. More recently, women's influx into the modern sector has halted the downward trend.[11]

Another interesting case is Germany (the German Federal Republic) where labor force participation of women appears not to have risen in the 1970s. In fact, when Figure 10.2 is examined, we see a substantial increase for each age group. This does not show up for the population as a whole because during the same period the growth in the proportion of older women, less likely to be in the labor force, offset this shift.

Figure 10.2 also shows the consistent decline in the tendency of women to drop out during the childbearing years. Nonetheless, the lifetime participation pattern continues to vary across countries. In Germany and especially in

---

[8]Moshe Semyanov, "The Social Context of Women's Labor Force Participation: A Comparative Analysis," *American Journal of Sociology* 86, no. 3 (November, 1980): 534–50, using a regression with industrialization, fertility, and the divorce rate as additional variables, finds a higher degree of inequality leads to a lower labor force participation rate. The measure of inequality used is the percentage of income going to the top 5 percent of the population.

[9]Jane Weiss, Francisco Ramirez, and Terry Tracy, "Female Participation in the Occupational System: A Comparative Institutional Analysis," *Social Problems* 23 no. 5 (June, 1976): 593–608.

[10]A substantial proportion of the small minority of women who do work outside their home have jobs that involve working with girls and women, most notably as teachers, nurses, and servants.

[11]Constance Sorrentino, "International Comparisons of Labor Force Participation, 1960–81," *Monthly Labor Review* 106, no. 2 (February 1983): 23–36.

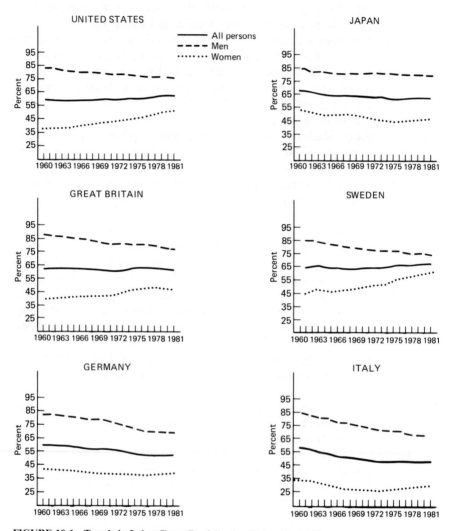

FIGURE 10.1 Trends in Labor Force Participation Rates, for All Persons and by Sex, Selected Countries, 1960–81

Source: Constance Sorrentino, "International Comparisons of Labor Force Participation, 1960–81," *Monthly Labor Review,* 106, no. 2 (February 1983), p. 26.

Italy, female labor force participation tends to decline after an early peak. As we have seen, this pattern was characteristic of the situation in the United States before World War II. In Japan and Britain, there is an M-shaped pattern—labor force participation decreases during the childbearing years but increases to a second peak later. This pattern prevailed in the United States after World War II until the early 1970s. Only the United States and Sweden show an inverted U pattern, where labor force participation increases in the early years, followed by a plateau, and an eventual decline as retirement age is reached. It may be noted that these patterns are associated with a progression from lower to higher overall labor force participation rates for women and that Sweden as well as the United States went through each of the earlier stages.

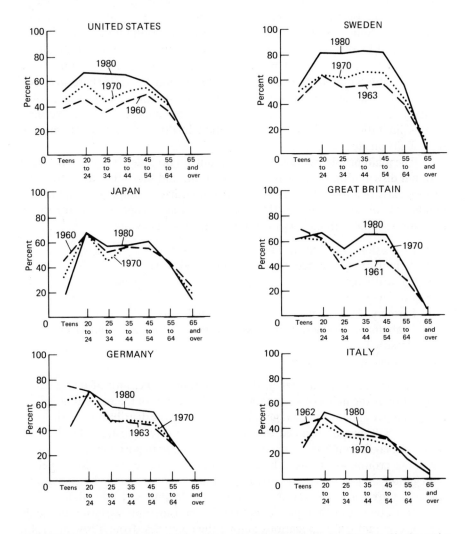

FIGURE 10.2   Age Structue of Labor Force Participation Rates for Women, Six Countries, Selected Years

Source: Constance Sorrentino, ''International Comparisons of Labor Force Participation, 1960–81,'' *Monthly Labor Review,* 106, no. 2 (February 1983), p. 33

Occupational Segregation

Just as there are substantial differences in women's labor force participation, so there are in the degree of occupational segregation. There are a number of reasons why occupational segregation is a matter of concern. Jobs vary in terms of the skills, effort, and preparation they require, as well as the challenges, rewards, and opportunities for power and influence they offer. There may be differences between men and women in the assortment of characteristics they typically prefer. Since, however, not everyone is "typical," but on the contrary, there is considerable variation within each group, sex-typing to the point that particular occupations are virtually monopolized by one sex, unnecessarily reduces options for many individuals.

As we have seen, in the United States there has been, and continues to be, a considerable amount of occupational segregation by sex. There also continues to be a great deal of disagreement as to why this is the case. Though available data are far from ideal for this purpose and, as we shall see, have serious limitations, comparing the situation in different countries can shed some light on this question.

The main problems are that many countries provide no data on the occupational distribution of men and women at all, and those that do tend to use various classification schemes. The only standardized grouping available for a number of countries is that of the seven very broad occupational categories in the International Labour Organization Yearbook. They are:

- Professional, technical, and kindred workers
- Administrative, executive, and managerial workers
- Clerical workers
- Sales workers
- Farmers, fishermen, loggers, and related workers
- Craftsmen, production process workers, and laborers not elsewhere classified
- Service, sports, and recreation workers.

As discussed in Chapter 6, the most common measure of occupational segregation is the index of segregation, which is equal to the percentage of one group that would have to change jobs to duplicate the distribution of the other group. It will also be recalled that this measure gives substantially different results depending on how detailed the occupational categories are. Since only a few large groupings are used here, we would expect relatively low levels of segregation as compared to those found when more detailed occupational categories are used. The results are shown in Column 1, Table 10.2.

It is obvious at first glance that there is considerable variation in the degree of occupational segregations among the countries, from a low of 11.4 in Bangladesh to a high of 64.4 in the United Arab Emirates. It is not obvious

TABLE 10.2 Occupational Segregation, Ratio of Women's to Men's Hourly Earnings in Manufacturing, and Ratio of Women's to Men's Labor Force Participation Rate, by Region[a]

	OCCUPATIONAL SEGREGATION		RATIO OF WOMEN'S TO MEN'S EARNINGS		RATIO OF WOMEN'S TO MEN'S LABOR FORCE PARTICIPATION RATE	
Eastern Europe						
Hungary	(1980)	34.3	n.a.		(1980)	72.2
Caribbean						
Barbados	(1970)	32.4	n.a.		(1980)	77.7
Sub-Saharan Africa						
Ghana	(1970)	12.2	n.a.		(1970)	77.9
East Asia						
Indonesia	(1978)	11.6	n.a.		(1980)	48.6
Korea, Rep.	(1981)	19.2	n.a.		(1982)	63.5
Philippines	(1980)	28.6	n.a.		(1978)	59.4
Singapore		n.a.	(1982)	63.2	(1982)	56.6
Sri Lanka	(1981)	14.4	(1982)	80.1	(1980)	39.9

TABLE 10.2 Occupational Segregation, Ratio of Women's to Men's Hourly Earnings in Manufacturing, and Ratio of Men's and Women's Labor Force Participation Rate, by Region[a] (*Continued*)

	OCCUPATIONAL SEGREGATION		RATIO OF WOMEN'S TO MEN'S EARNINGS		RATIO OF WOMEN'S TO MEN'S LABOR FORCE PARTICIPATION RATE	
Advanced Industrialized Countries						
Australia	(1982)	47.9	(1982)	82.9	(1981)	60.1
Belgium		n.a.	(1982)	73.5	(1980)	56.7
Canada	(1982)	42.0	(1981)	71.2[c]	(1981)	67.3
Denmark		n.a.	(1982)	85.1	(1981)	77.9
Finland		n.a.	(1982)	77.2	(1982)	83.3
France		n.a.	(1981)	78.1	(1982)	62.3
Germany, Fed. Rep.	(1980)	36.4	(1982)	73.0	(1982)	57.4
Greece		n.a.	(1982)	73.1	(1981)	45.2
Ireland	(1979)	48.2	(1982)	68.5	(1977)	37.4
Israel	(1981)	44.6		n.a.	(1982)	58.6
Japan	(1981)	22.8		n.a.	(1982)	61.9
Luxembourg		n.a.	(1981)	60.0	(1979)	43.7
Netherlands	(1979)	43.2	(1982)	74.0	(1982)	49.3
New Zealand	(1981)	42.1	(1982)	77.6	(1981)	51.4
Norway	(1981)	49.0	(1982)	83.2	(1981)	70.1
Portugal	(1981)	29.4		n.a.	(1981)	63.7
Sweden	(1981)	43.2	(1982)	90.3	(1980)	80.9
Switzerland		n.a.	(1982)	67.5	(1980)	54.6
United Kingdom		n.a.	(1982)	68.8	(1980)	61.1
United States	(1981)	40.7	(1982)	71.0[b]	(1982)	70.3

Latin America

El Salvador	(1980)	40.9	n.a.	(1980)	50.5
Panama	(1980)	58.6	n.a.	(1980)	39.3
Venezuela	(1981)	50.4	n.a.	(1982)	37.0

North Africa, Middle East, South Central Asia

Bahrain	(1981)	57.8	n.a.	(1981)	18.0
Bangladesh	(1974)	11.4	n.a.	(1974)	37.0
Kuwait	(1980)	51.2	n.a.	(1980)	19.7
United Arab Emirates	(1975)	64.4	n.a.	(1975)	7.8

[a]The year in which the data were collected is shown in parentheses.
[b]Hours adjusted weekly earnings for all workers, from June O'Neill, "The Trend in the Male-Female Wage Gap in the United States," *Journal of Labor Economics* (January 1985, Supplement).
[c]All full-time, year-round workers. Source: Labour and Household Surveys Analysis Division, Statistics Canada (unpublished data).
n.a. Not available.

Source: Calculated from data in International Labour Office, *Yearbook of Labour Statistics*, various years.

what causes these differences. If it were primarily the requirement for physical strength that keeps women out of some jobs, segregation would be expected to decline as economies become more sophisticated. If women chose different occupations because they did not expect to spend much time in the labor market, segregation would be expected to be lower where women's labor force attachment is greater. If men and women are better suited to, or prefer different types of work, the degree of segregation would be expected to be fairly similar across countries. The existing situation does not conform to any of these hypotheses.

Clearly, the occupational structure of an economy can have a considerable effect on the degree of occupational segregation. Take the extreme case where agriculture, possibly subsistence farming, is the only way of making a living. There may well be a substantial division of labor within that sector, but, obviously, all men and women will be in the same "occupation," using the definitions employed in Table 10.2. While this is not true for any of the countries shown in the table, agriculture is the dominant sector in several instances. For example, of the economically active population the following percentages were employed in agriculture: 71 percent in Bangladesh; 61 percent in Indonesia; 54 percent in Ghana; and 38 in Sri Lanka. These are also countries with the lowest levels of the index of occupational segregation.

Two other countries where agriculture employs a relatively large share of the labor force should be noted—Panama with 29 percent and El Salvador with 27 percent. Nonetheless, occupational segregation in both these countries is very high. The reason for the striking difference is that in the first four countries, women constitute virtually the same proportion in agriculture as they do in the remainder of the economy, while the participation of women in agriculture (again, according to official statistics) in the latter two is extremely low.

It is this type of incongruity that raises real questions about explaining occupational segregation in rational, economic terms. When women do much of the agricultural work in the underdeveloped African countries, and very little in North America, it is easy to point to the differences in what such workers do. But when we find that women are also very heavily represented in the increasingly mechanized agricultural sectors of Eastern Europe, but are virtually excluded in the developing countries of Latin America, North Africa, and the Middle East, it becomes obvious that very similar work is considered appropriate only for men in some countries but viewed as equally or even more appropriate for women in others.

There are also other intriguing differences in the occupational distribution among the countries in our set. The proportion of each occupational category that is female varies widely for different countries, as seen in Table 10.3. Though several of these categories are predominantly male or female in most countries, and especially so in the advanced industrialized countries, this

TABLE 10.3 Percent of Workers Who Are Women by Occupational Category

	HIGHEST PERCENT		LOWEST PERCENT	
Professional, technical, and kindred workers	Venezuela (1981)	55.1	Bangladesh (1975)	5.9
Administrative, executive, and managerial workers	Canada (1982)	29.2	Un. Arab. Emir. (1975)	0.7
Clerical workers	United States (1981)	80.6	Bangladesh (1974)	1.1
Sales workers	El Salvador (1980)	70.9	Un. Arab. Emir. (1975)	0.8
Farmers, fishermen, loggers, and related workers	Korea, Rep. (1981)	37.5	Un. Arab. Emir. (1975)	0.1
Craftsmen, production process workers, and laborers not elsewhere classified	Japan (1981)	48.2	Bangladesh (1974)	0.2
Service, sports, and recreation	Norway (1981)	77.6	Un. Arab. Emir. (1975)	6.2

Source: Calculated from data in International Labour Office, Yearbook of Labour Statistics, various years.

does not tend to hold uniformly when a broader range of nations is considered. Six of the seven occupational categories have a higher proportion of women than the economy as a whole in some countries and a lower proportion in others. Only among administrative, executive, and managerial workers are women regularly under-represented.

The data we have used have serious limitations beyond the fact that they are only available for a handful of countries. As previously mentioned, they represent broad categories and provide no information about the extent of segregation by more detailed occupations, which may be substantial. Second, they do not tell us to what extent women are distributed throughout the hierarchy within each group. Third, the nature of particular occupations may vary radically from one economy to another, particularly when they are at very different levels of economic development. Secretaries may copy letters longhand or operate sophisticated word processing machinery. Agricultural workers may till the land with a hoe or use complex farm equipment. Transport workers may lift heavy boxes or push buttons.

Even with all the shortcomings and limitations the picture that emerges is instructive. An examination of Table 10.3 must dispel the view that most clerical and service work is always done by women or that only an extremely small proportion of women is capable of doing managerial or blue-collar work. We, therefore, conclude that the substantial degree of occupational segregation found in many countries cannot be explained by inherent differences between women and men alone. On the contrary, both economic factors and such considerations as social norms, traditions, religious beliefs, and other noneconomic considerations appear to play an important part in the varied pattern of distribution of men and women by occupation.

The Male-Female Earnings Gap

As we have seen, the patterns of labor force participation and occupational segregation in various countries are anything but simple. The same is no less true of the earnings gap and its relation to labor force participation and occupational distribution. As we shall see, though the difference between men's and women's earnings has declined in most countries for which data are available, this is not universally true, and the rate of change varies substantially. Nor is there any discernable relationship between the size of the earnings gap and the degree of occupational segregation.

Table 10.2 provides data on the ratio of women's to men's labor force participation, occupational segregation, and the ratio of women's to men's earnings in manufacturing.[12] The question may be raised to what extent the earnings in manufacturing are representative for the whole economy. However, of the 11 advanced, industrialized countries that provide information for both, the mean difference in the female-male ratio between the two is only 2.6 percentage points. The greatest discrepancies are in Australia, where the gap for wages in manufacturing is 7.7 percentage points greater than for earnings in all nonagricultural sectors, and in New Zealand, where it is 6.2 percentage points smaller. Most important, the trend for the two series has been very similar in each of the countries.

Among the countries with the smallest earnings gap, Sri Lanka has an extremely low index of occupational segregation. The other three, Sweden, Norway, and Australia, do not. Indeed, sex segregation by occupation in the latter three countries is greater than in the United States and Germany, but the ratios of women's to men's manufacturing wages are 90.3, 83.2, and 82.9, respectively, in comparison to 71.0 percent in the United States and 73.0 in Germany. (The U.S. figure is not strictly comparable; this is discussed below.)

Given the degree of aggregation in the measure of occupation, as well as the large number of cases for which earnings data are not available, it is not possible to reach firm conclusions based on the information presented here. Nonetheless, the data do point to the importance of the size of pay differentials within and among different occupations as well as simply sex differences

---

[12]Hourly earnings in manufacturing were used because these were available for the largest number of countries. Others provide daily, weekly, or monthly earnings, all of which are influenced considerably more by the worker's full-time or part-time status.

in occupational distributions.[13] Until we learn more about this intriguing issue we shall not be able to answer the puzzling questions raised by the existing relationships between occupations and earnings in various countries. The overcrowding model presented in Chapter 8 suggests that relative supply and demand conditions in female and male jobs would be an important factor. Further, government policies, which set a floor on wages or limit pay differentials among occupations, could also play a role.

The complexities of supply and demand considerations also make it difficult to predict what the relationship between female labor force participation and the male-female pay gap will be. On the one hand, a large influx of women into the labor market could tend to depress their earnings as compared to those of men. On the other hand, women's greater labor force participation may be associated with greater demand for female-type jobs and possibly with more egalitarian wage policies, which would tend to have the opposite effect. In light of these conflicting forces it is, perhaps, not surprising that there does not appear to be a relationship between the ratio of women to men in the labor force and the ratio of their earnings.

Thus, no uniform patterns emerge from an examination of the data in Table 10.2, except that women are always paid less than men. Scholars who have examined this situation have tended to put far more emphasis on this fact than on the very substantial extent to which the size of the earnings gap differs, even among advanced industrailized countries.[14] Similarly, though the earnings gap has been declining in all the countries in our sample, the rate of change has varied considerably, as can be seen in Table 10.4.[15]

Data for manufacturing only are not available for the United States, but, as noted earlier, evidence from countries that provide these as well as data for all nonagricultural sectors combined, suggests the difference between them is

[13]Similar conclusions were reached by Donald J. Treiman and Patricia A. Roos, "Sex and Earnings in Industrial Society: A Nine-Nation Comparison," *American Journal of Sociology* 89, no. 3 (April 1984): 612–46. They found there was almost no effect of occupational distribution on earnings but quite substantial and complicated effects of rates of return for men and women within major occupational groups. The suggested explanation is that the observed differences reflect the legacy of traditional patterns of disadvantages and discrimination (p. 643).

[14]Examples include Marjorie Galenson, *Women and Work: An International Comparison,* (N.Y. State School of Industrial and Labor Relations, 1973) and Treiman and Roos, "Sex and Earnings in Industrial Society." This is somewhat less true of Jacob Mincer, "Inter-Country Comparisons of Labor Force Trends and of Related Developments: An Overview" in *Growth of Women's Labor Force: Causes and Consequences,* eds. Richard Layard and Jacob Mincer, Special Volume of *Journal of Labor Economics* (Chicago: University of Chicago Press, 1985).

[15]Two interesting, but conflicting, interpretations of the situation in Great Britain are B. Chiplin, M. M. Curran, and C. J. Parsley, "Relative Female Earnings in Great Britain and the Impact of Legislation," ed. P. J. Sloane, *Women and Low Pay,* (London: Macmillan, 1980) and A. Zabalza and Z. Tzannatos, "The Effect of Britain's Anti-Discriminatory Legislation on Relative Pay and Employment," *Economic Journal* 95, no. 379 (September 1985): 679–99.

TABLE 10.4   Ratio of Women's to Men's Hourly Earnings in Manufacturing, Selected Years 1955–1982

	1955	1973	1982
Australia[4]	n.a.	76.5	82.9
Belgium	n.a.	68.7	73.5
Denmark[5]	65.3	82.3	85.1
Finland[6]	67.6	71.7	77.2
France	n.a.	76.8	78.1[1]
Germany, Fed. Rep.[7]	62.8	70.9	73.0
Greece	64.7[2]	65.5	73.1
Ireland	36.4	59.9	68.5
Luxembourg	n.a.	55.3	60.0[1]
Netherlands	58.8	72.6	74.0
New Zealand	62.5	71.8[3]	77.6
Norway[4]	67.4	76.2	83.2
Sweden[8]	69.2	84.1	90.3
Switzerland[7]	n.a.	67.7	67.5
United Kingdom	42.3	60.7	68.8
United States[9]	n.a.	68.0	71.0

(1) 1981; (2) 1961; (3) 1974; (4) Employees; (5) Excludes vacation pay; (6) Includes mining and quarrying, electricity; (7) Includes family allowances paid by employers; (8) Includes holiday and sick pay, and value of payments in kind; (9) Weekly, adjusted for hours, for all full-time employees.
n.a. Not available.

Sources: International Labour Office, Yearbook of Labour Statistics, various years. U.S. data from June O'Neill, "The Trend in the Male-Female Wage Gap in the United States," *Journal of Labor Economics* (January 1985, supplement).

not great and could go in either direction. To the extent that the data are comparable, the earnings gap was greater in the United States than in 10 of the 16 other countries in 1973 and 11 out of the 16 in 1982. In addition, between 1973 and 1982 (for two countries it is 1981), the earnings gap declined more slowly in the United States than in 10 of the 16 countries. It should be noted, however, that most of the change in the other countries came during the earlier part of this decade, while the opposite is true here. If recent trends continue, there is reason to expect that the United States would rank higher on both counts by the 1990s.

Unemployment Rates

Among the 10 advanced, industrialized countries for which data are shown in Table 10.5, unemployment rates are generally higher for women than for men.[16] This has also been the case in the United States, except for the high

---

[16]Data on unemployment in other countries are available in the International Labour Office Statistical Yearbook. However, they are based on different definitions of the concept and, hence, are not necessarily comparable to the data in Table 10.5 or to each other.

TABLE 10.5 Unemployment Rates by Sex, Approximating U.S. Concepts, Selected Countries, 1970–82

	AUSTRALIA	CANADA	FRANCE	GERMANY	ITALY	JAPAN	NETHERLANDS	SWEDEN	U.K.	U.S.
Men										
1970	1.1	5.6	1.5	.5	2.2	1.1	n.a.	1.4	3.4	4.4
1971	1.3	6.0	1.7	.5	2.2	1.2	n.a.	2.4	4.2	5.3
1972	2.0	5.8	1.7	.7	2.6	1.4	n.a.	2.5	4.7	5.0
1973	1.6	4.9	1.6	.6	2.4	1.3	2.8	2.2	3.5	4.2
1974	1.9	4.8	1.8	1.5	2.0	1.3	n.a.	1.7	3.1	4.9
1975	3.8	6.2	2.9	3.3	2.2	1.9	3.8	1.4	4.9	7.9
1976	3.9	6.3	3.0	3.1	2.4	2.1	n.a.	1.3	6.3	7.1
1977	4.6	7.3	3.3	2.9	2.5	2.0	4.0	1.5	6.6	6.3
1978	5.4	7.6	3.7	2.7	2.6	2.2	n.a.	2.1	6.2	5.3
1979	5.2	6.6	4.3	2.3	2.7	1.9	3.7	1.9	5.5	5.1
1980	5.1	6.9	4.3	2.3	2.6	1.7	n.a.	1.7	7.3	6.9
1981	4.8	7.1	5.4	3.4	2.9	1.9	6.3	2.4	11.4	7.4
1982	6.3	11.1	n.a.	5.2[1]	3.4	1.9	n.a.	3.0	13.3	9.9

TABLE 10.5 Unemployment Rates by Sex, Approximating U.S. Concepts, Selected Countries, 1970–82 *(Continued)*

	AUSTRALIA	CANADA	FRANCE	GERMANY	ITALY	JAPAN	NETHERLANDS	SWEDEN	U.K.	U.S.
Women										
1970	2.8	5.8	4.1	.6	4.5	2.5	n.a.	1.7	2.5	5.9
1971	3.1	6.6	4.6	.8	4.5	2.7	n.a.	2.8	3.3	6.9
1972	3.9	7.0	4.7	.8	5.2	2.9	n.a.	3.0	3.4	6.6
1973	3.6	6.7	4.5	.9	5.4	2.7	4.2	2.8	2.7	6.0
1974	4.1	6.4	4.8	1.8	4.5	2.9	n.a.	2.4	3.0	6.7
1975	7.0	8.1	6.3	3.6	5.0	3.8	6.9	2.0	4.1	9.3
1976	6.4	8.4	7.2	4.0	5.8	3.8	n.a.	2.0	5.4	8.6
1977	7.5	9.4	7.6	4.5	6.0	4.3	6.7	2.2	5.9	8.2
1978	7.9	9.6	8.0	4.4	6.1	4.3	n.a.	2.4	6.3	7.2
1979	8.2	8.8	9.0	4.1	6.4	4.1	8.1	2.3	5.6	6.8
1980	7.9	8.4	9.8	3.8	6.6	3.3	n.a.	2.3	6.6	7.4
1981	7.4	8.3	11.1	5.1	7.2	3.6	11.1	2.7	9.4	7.9
1982	8.5	10.8	n.a.	6.9	7.6	4.0	n.a.	3.4	10.8	9.4

[1]Preliminary estimates.
n.a. Not available.

Sources: Joyanna Moy, "Recent Labor Market Developments in the U.S. and Nine Other Countries," *Monthly Labor Review* 107, no. 1 (January, 1984): 4–51.

unemployment years of 1982–83, as discussed in Chapter 9. In spite of this similarity, there are also some intriguing differences. First, while the unemployment rate in the United States rose with the influx of women into the labor market, this has not been the case in Sweden where women's labor force participation has been increasing even more rapidly. Second, in Japan, in Sweden, and in Germany before 1981, women's unemployment rates were consistently lower than the estimates for minimal frictional unemployment in the United States. Third, in the United Kingdom, the unemployment rate has consistently been higher for men than for women.

In addition to the above, it is particularly interesting to note that the unemployment rate for women is not very high in Sweden either in absolute terms or as compared to that for men, even though the ratio of women's to men's earnings is, as we have seen, exceptionally high. This suggests that measures to raise the earnings of women by, say, raising the minimum wage or broadening the scope of equal pay for comparable work may not have large detrimental effects on their employment. However, a more detailed analysis of the Swedish experience would be necessary to verify this conclusion.

Thus, the information presented here sheds some light on the issues discussed in Chapter 9. It is to be hoped that further research on other countries will help us learn more about solving the substantial unemployment problems women and other disadvantaged groups have experienced in the United States.

Household Work

As was discussed at some length in earlier chapters, the roles of women and men in the labor market are closely inter-related with their roles in the household. We found that in the United States, while women's participation in the labor market has been increasing rapidly for some time, participation of men in housework began to increase only far more recently. Such an unequal division of responsibilities influences both the amount of leisure men and women have and their achievements on the job. Hence, inevitably, it also influences the quality of their lives.

It would be most interesting to be able to compare how men and women spend their time in different countries, most particularly between advanced, industrialized vs. developing countries, as well as between private enterprise and Soviet-type economies. Unfortunately, virtually no data are available that would enable us to do the former. Therefore, we cannot provide evidence on whether more time is spent on the labor-intensive chores of the large families crowded into the huts of the poor countries of the world or on managing a modern household, full of appliances and purchased goods, but aspiring to a higher standard of living not dreamt of by others. Nor do we have any information whether men participate more in one or the other.

TABLE 10.6   Number of Hours Spent on Household Care Per Day 1965

	EMPLOYED MEN		EMPLOYED WOMEN		NON-EMPLOYED WOMEN	
	Single	*Married*	*Single*	*Married*	*Single*	*Married*
Belgium	.2	.3	1.9	3.7	5.6	6.6
Bulgaria	.2	.8	2.5	3.4	4.8	7.4
Czechoslovakia	.7	.9	3.6	3.8	5.9	7.3
France	.5	.5	2.7	4.0	5.6	6.9
Germany, Federal Rep.	.2	.3	2.5	5.1	5.8	7.0
Germany, Democratic Rep.	1.1	1.0	4.0	4.8	n.a.	7.4
Hungary	.3	.5	2.7	4.7	7.8	8.6
Poland	.3	.7	2.5	4.1	5.9	7.4
United States of America	.5	.5	2.7	3.7	5.5	5.9

Union of Soviet Socialist Republics	.8	1.4	2.8	4.0	6.7	7.4
Yugoslavia	.3	.4	3.0	4.6	7.0	8.2
Mean: Belgium, France, Germany (F.R.), U.S.A.	.4	.4	2.5	4.1	5.6	6.6
Mean: Bulgaria, Czechoslovakia Germany (D.R.), Hungary, Poland USSR, Yugoslavia	.5	.8	3.0	4.2	6.4	7.7

n.a. Not available.

Source: John P. Robinson, Philip E. Converse, and Alexander Szalai, "Everyday Life in Twelve Countries," ed. Alexander Szalai, *The Use of Time: Daily Activities of Urban and Suburban Populations in Twelve Countries*, Hawthorne, N.Y.: Moutan Publishers, 1972, Table 5, p. 126. Reprinted with permission.

Even for the Western advanced industrialized countries, data are quite sparse and somewhat out-of-date. This needs to be kept in mind because in the United States it was only by the 1980s that there were any significant changes in males' participation in household work. The available information, shown in Table 10.6, is nonetheless worth examining. There can be no doubt that the similarities between the countries are far more striking than the differences. Even single, employed women do considerably more housework than single men, but the difference is substantially greater for married women and men. (Information for husbands of employed and non-employed women separately is not available.) Not surprisingly, nonemployed, married women put in more hours on housework than any other group. These patterns hold uniformly.

When examining the differences between Western and Eastern countries, the mean number of hours of housework is higher for the latter in each category. It would appear that whatever progress there has been in the Soviet-type countries toward "socializing housework" is more than offset by the greater availability of appliances and convenience goods in the others. The other difference between the two groups is not as clear-cut. Employed, married men in the Eastern countries spent 19 percent as much time on housework as employed, married women, compared to 10 percent in the West, but the hours differential was quite large in both cases. Employed, married women spent 3.7 hours more on housework per day than employed, married men in the West, and 3.4 hours more in the East.

PATTERNS
AND INTERPRETATIONS

One fact that clearly emerges from the evidence presented in the previous sections is that there is substantial variation in the status of women between different countries for which data are available, as measured by any of the indicators used. Labor force participation of women, as presented in official statistics, varies from negligible to a level almost equal to that of men. Segregation, with respect to major occupational categories, is so low in some countries that scarcely more than one in ten women workers would have to change jobs to duplicate the male pattern of distribution, while in at least one country it would involve over six out of ten women making such a change. Women in manufacturing earn between 60 and 90 percent as much per hour as men. Furthermore, the rate of change in the male-female earnings ratio has varied considerably. Only when it comes to housework did we not find great differences, at least for the advanced industrialized countries.

We began with the hypothesis that economic factors influence the status of women as compared to men, and our data provide some clues what a few of these might be. They also show, however, that for the most part, the situation is very complex and that noneconomic factors can also play an important role. Further, we see that women may be doing well in a country in terms of some criteria but not in terms of others.[17] It appears that we shall have to wait for more and better data before we can learn more from international comparisons. Meantime, we may be able to gain some insights from examining, on the one hand, developing countries, where there are especially serious problems, and two countries, the USSR and Sweden, where women appear to have made considerable progress.

WOMEN IN DEVELOPING COUNTRIES

In our examination of the status of women, we have been emphasizing how they are doing as compared to men, whether it be in terms of labor force participation, occupational distribution, or earnings. The justification for this is obvious. For instance, women in one country may have high earnings compared with the inhabitants of a much poorer nation, but this tells us nothing about the degree of equality they have achieved with men. It is, nonetheless, clear that the absolute level of well-being is hardly a matter of indifference. Even a cursory examination of the lives of women in developing countries will dispel any doubts one might have on that score.

To provide anything like an adequate coverage of the situation of women in the Third World would require a book larger than this one.[18] One reason for this is the tremendous variation in many respects among individual countries. Included are some that can only euphemistically be called "developing," others that are soon likely to join the ranks of the "advanced industrialized" nations. Some are rich in resources only waiting to be exploited, others have almost none. Among many additional issues that might be mentioned, there are also substantial differences in the extent and the way that women participate in productive labor, and, as previously mentioned, differences in statistical reporting. We cannot even begin to give proper attention to all such complex topics, but these diverse countries do share one characteristic—low per capita income. Consequently, they also share problems that are somewhat

---

[17]A similar conclusion, that the relation of economic development and women's status is erratic and not readily explainable, was reached by Shirley Nuss and Larraine Majka, "The Economic Integration of Women: A Cross National Investigation," *Work and Occupations* 10, no. 1 (February 1983): 29–48.

[18]A number of very useful books on women in developing countries have been written since 1970. The pioneering work among these was Ester Boserup, *Women's Role in Economic Development* (New York: St. Martin's Press, 1970), followed by Nadja Youssef, *Women and Work in Developing Societies* (Berkeley, University of California Press, 1974), and the more recent Lourdes Beneria, ed., *Women and Development. The Sexual Division of Labor in Rural Societies* (NY: Praeger, 1982).

different from those in more affluent nations. One of these is particularly ominous and deserves to be at least mentioned here.

Not only do women and men share in scant education, hard labor, general deprivation and, as a result, a short life, but there is reason to believe that women carry a disproportionate part of this burden. Further, this appears to be particularly true where women's productive contribution outside the household is small. Among the 13 countries where per capita income in the late 1970s was less than $500 per year, and where the labor force participation of women was less than one-fourth that of men, the average number of women was only 98 for 100 men, while it was 105 in the other 39 countries at the same low level of income. One need not go so far as to suspect female infanticide, though that has not been unknown historically.[19] An unequal allocation of food and medicine, under conditions when both are scarce, would be quite sufficient to explain this situation.

WOMEN IN THE UNION OF SOVIET SOCIALIST REPUBLICS: MARXIST IDEOLOGY AND SOVIET PRACTICE[20]

Though other Soviet-type countries hold the same views about the role of women, and have, in general, pursued similar policies, we focus on the situation in the Union of Soviet Socialist Republics. It is not only the largest of these countries, and the one that has had the most time to implement its ideas, but is also the one that set the example the others have tended to follow.

The leaders who successfully carried out the revolution and shaped the ideas that dominated the country during the early years saw the relationship between men and women as inextricably entwined with the revolutionary reconstruction of society. They essentially espoused the view that the abolition of private property and class structure is both necessary and sufficient for achieving equality between women and men. They struck down all legal discrimination against women. Equal treatment in the educational system and

[19]The existence of such practices in the past appears to be well-established. See, for instance, Elisabeth Croll, *Feminism and Socialism in China* (London: Routledge and Kegan Paul, 1978) with reference to China before the revolution, "Girls were the main, if not exclusive, victims of infanticide and tended to have a higher infant mortality rate in times of poverty and famine. In a nineteenth century survey the 160 women over 50 years of age who were interviewed, and who between them had borne a total of 631 sons and 538 daughters, admitted to destroying 158 of their daughters; none had destroyed a boy. As only four of the women had reared more than three girls, the field workers felt that the number of infanticides confessed to was considerably below the truth" (p. 24).

[20]The source of data on the USSR is Gail Warshafsky Lapidus, *Women in Soviety Society* (Berkeley, CA: University of California Press, 1978). An interesting discussion of the issues considered here is also found in Hilda Scott, *Does Socialism Liberate Women? Experiences from Eastern Europe* (Boston: Beacon Press, 1974).

in the labor market were mandated. Liberal family laws were introduced, making the marriage contract egalitarian and legalized abortion readily available, though some of this legislation was later modified.[21]

Because there was, generally, not only full employment but often a labor shortage, doctrinal belief in labor force participation of women was reinforced by the need for them to help with the rapid industrialization that was the main goal of the regime. But for the very same reason little progress was made in "socializing housework," the Soviet solution for women's double burden. Such work was to be made unnecessary by the provision of public services, from communal dining rooms to day-care centers. Women were told that these would be made available as soon as the higher priority goals had been achieved.

In practice, this has meant that more than 50 years after the revolution there is much housework that needs to be done in the Soviet Union, most of it by women. To the extent that official notice is taken of this at all, the proposed solution still is that with growing affluence the state is offering more of the promised facilities and will continue to do so. Sharing of household responsibilities between men and women has never been part of the Marxist ideology espoused by the regime.

The results of this mixed situation are, inevitably, also mixed. Not only is the status of women clearly better than it was in prerevolutionary Russia, but in some respects it compares favorably with that in other advanced, industrialized countries. Labor force participation in the USSR for women of prime working ages, between 20 and 49, has for some time been close to 90 percent. The proportion of those with secondary education changed from 8.5 percent for women and 11.6 percent for men, a ratio of .73, in 1939, to 49.4 percent for women and 56.6, for men, a ratio of .87, in 1977. The comparable figures for higher education changed from 0.5 percent for women and 1.1 percent for men, a ratio of .45, in 1939, to 5.3 percent and 6.5 percent, a ratio of .82 in 1977. The proportion of women in the most heavily male sectors of the economy is 24 percent in transportation, 29 percent in construction, and 44 percent in socialized agriculture. Not only are 7 out of 10 physicians women, but also 4 out of 10 engineers. The former occupation is not very well paid, the latter is.

This is, however, only one side of the story. In the Union of Soviet Socialist Republics, as in the United States, there is a noticeable tendency for women to be heavily represented in the low-paying occupations. There is ample evidence that they also tend to be concentrated at the lower levels of occupational hierarchies. They do the least sophisticated and least mechanized work in agriculture, which also brings the lowest rewards. In the health professions, virtually all nurses are women, as are 90 percent of pediatricians. On the other hand, only 6 percent of surgeons, and 50 percent of all chief physicians

---

[21]This was particularly true during the Stalinist period when, for instance, abortions were made illegal.

and executives of medical institutions, are women. Last, but not least, there have been virtually no women in the top echelons of the powerful government hierarchy.

No official data are available from the USSR on men's and women's earnings. The only Soviet-bloc country that provides such information is Czechoslovakia where the ratio of women's to men's earnings in 1972 was 67.5, well within the range of figures for the Western advanced industrialized countries. One estimate of the earnings ratio for the USSR is that it has been 70.0 between 1960 and 1980.[22] A survey conducted in Soviet Armenia in 1963, for the purpose of carrying out a methodological study on estimating family income distributions, provided, as a by-product, data on earnings of all family members. A careful analysis of these data suggests that at that time women brought home about 65 percent as much as men.[23] This is interpreted to be largely the result of the greater amounts of time and energy women, as compared to men, spent on housework, a situation which, as we have seen, continued into a later period.

Life would, no doubt, improve for women in the USSR if they were relieved of more family work. This would not, however, resolve all of what is generally referred to as "the woman question" there. Such tasks as food preparation, laundry, and child care tend to be low status and poorly paid when they are done outside the home, and they are almost exclusively performed by women. Also, not all housework can be "socialized." Thus, the Marxist solution, even in principle, leaves something to be desired. For an approach that endeavors to get to the heart of the problem of stereotypical gender roles we must look not to the Soviet Union but to Sweden.[24]

SWEDEN:
IDEOLOGY VS. TRADITION[25]

In the late 1960s, the Swedish government officially accepted the view that a policy that attempts to give women an equal place with men in economic life while at the same time confirming woman's traditional responsiblity for care

[22]Mincer, "Inter-Country Comparisons of Labor Force Trends."

[23]Michael Swafford, "Sex Differences in Soviet Earnings," *American Sociological Review* 43, no. 5 (October 1978): 657–73.

[24]Though a good deal has been written about the development of women in China since the revolution the information offered tends to be based on necessarily selective personal observations, since virtually no data are available. See, for instance, Elisabeth Croll, *Feminism and Socialism in China* (London: Routledge and Kegan Paul, 1978) and Phyllis Andors, *The Unfinished Liberation of Chinese Women, 1949–1982* (Bloomington, IN: Indiana University Press, 1983). It is nonetheless clear that here, as in the USSR, women have made considerable progress since the days when their feet were bound, and Confucian ideology consigned them to an entirely subservient position but have failed to achieve full equality either in the household or in the public sphere.

[25]Much of the information in this section is derived from Siv Gustafsson and Roger

of the home and children has no prospect of fulfilling the first of these aims. It was the first country to put such emphasis on the achievement of equality of men and women in the household, as well as in the labor market. The stage was set for a struggle between a profound commitment to this egalitarian ideology and a deeply rooted traditional paternalism.

The government has pursued a consistent campaign to change the institution of the family ever since. Considerable efforts have been made to discourage gender-based stereotypes at all levels of the education system. Legislation was introduced to make marriage an equal partnership, including abolishing the right of the wife to be supported. All sex differences in public aid were removed. The joint income tax for spouses was eliminated (except for nonwage income) and replaced with a system of individual taxation.[26] Generous arrangements for parental leave, which may be taken by fathers or mothers, were provided. Such benefits are allotted in proportion to foregone earnings, so that there are strong incentives for women to have a job before the birth of the first child and again before the second child is born. Heavily subsidized day-care is available for almost one-third of preschool children. Low as this ratio is, it compares very favorably with most other countries.

Women's education has been increasing more rapidly than men's, gradually narrowing the difference between the two, even though sex segregation by field continues in higher education. Hence, women were in a good position to take advantage of the removal of barriers to entry into the labor market, in general, and into nontraditional jobs, in particular. At the same time, all low wage earners benefitted from the concerted efforts of the powerful, centralized union movement in Sweden to reduce inequalities between classes of workers.

All this adds up to an impressive set of favorable circumstances for women to make progress toward the professed goals of an egalitarian family and equality in the labor market. The stress up to 1980 was, however, almost entirely on social policy rather than on any antidiscrimination legislation. While in 1980 the Act on Equality between men and women was passed, it will be some time before its effects can be felt and before the data necessary for evaluating them become available. Thus, it is not surprising that the record, as of the early 1980s, was somewhat mixed.

In 1982, labor force participation of all women aged 20–59 was 83.7 percent and of married women in that age group 83.5. Further, it was 83.0 percent for women between age 20 and 29 and, even higher, 85.7 percent for women 30

Jacobson, "Trends in Female Labor Force Participation in Sweden," eds. Layard and Mincer, *Growth of Women's Labor Force Participation;* Siv Gustafsson, "Equal Opportunity Policies in Sweden,"eds. Gunther Schmid and Renate Weitzel, *Sex Discrimination and Equal Opportunity,* (Aldershot, England: Gower Publishing Company Limited, 1984), pp. 132–54.

[26]The importance of this must not be underestimated. When the income tax is highly progressive, as it is in Sweden, the applicable rate for the wife is much lower when she is taxed as an individual rather than a second earner. Further, any amount she earns by entering the labor market leaves them more disposable income than the same amount of *additional* earnings he may be able to make by working harder, longer hours, or whatever. The effect of the tax structure on labor force participation in the United States was discussed in Chapter 4.

to 39. It would, however, be a mistake to conclude homemaking no longer interferes with women's labor market activity. It must be noted that 53.3 percent of the female workers were in the labor market only part-time (compared to 28 percent in the United States) and that women constituted only 31.2 percent of the full-time labor force, even though they comprised 44.6 percent of the total labor force. Further, about one-fifth, 20.5 percent, of female workers were absent for the whole week during which the data were collected, most of them on parental leave. This is easier to understand when we learn that the demand for child care far exceeds supply at existing prices and that women continue to do the bulk of housework. It appears that here, as elsewhere, changes in women's labor force participation tend to be far more rapid than changes in men's share of household responsibilities. While fathers are equally eligible for parental leaves, it is still very unusual for them to avail themselves of the opportunity.

As was mentioned previously, occupational segregation in Sweden continues to be high, with women particularly disproportionately represented in clerical and other white-collar jobs. The quadrupling of women in the government sector during the last two decades, while remaining almost constant in the private sector, has no doubt been one of the factors inhibiting any significant decrease in sex segregation. Thus, it would appear that, in spite of all the efforts, men have not been fully integrated in the household nor women in the labor market.

Americans who have analyzed the position of women in Sweden, not infrequently, tend to end on this negative note. This does not do justice to the very real achievements. It must not be dismissed as a technicality that women in the United States often quit their job when they have a child, while women in Sweden tend to take paid leave. Not only are the latter receiving payments while they are at home, but they are guaranteed the right to return to their job and without loss of seniority. Similarly, working part-time may be less disruptive to maintaining and accumulating market skills than dropping out entirely. Nor should one dismiss the importance of providing, in principle, parental leaves to both men and women, even when few men take them or providing government supported day-care, even when its supply is inadequate. Both at least provide an official stamp of approval for new and different arrangements and should serve to reduce the qualms of young people who may wish to use them.

Last, but certainly not least, Sweden is foremost among the countries that have succeeded in rapidly reducing the earnings gap between men and women. It is true, as has been pointed out, that it is only hourly wages of women in industry that are as high as 90 percent of those of men and that this must, in part, be credited to the impact of unions in narrowing earnings differentials. But the ratio of the annual earnings of all full-time, year-round female to male workers, for which data have only been available since 1973, increased from 71.5 during that year to 81.2 in 1980. This compares very favorably with the situation in the United States, where the comparable figure was 64 percent as recently as 1983.

Clearly, no amount of effort and good will can fundamentally change a society overnight, especially one which in many ways had been more traditional in its gender roles than the United States ever was. But reason dictates that we recognize that moving toward a goal, albeit slowly and at times uncertainly, is better than standing still because utopia cannot be achieved quickly.

CONCLUSION

Our survey of several indicators of the economic status of women showed that there are great differences with respect to all except the division of housework. It is likely that if we could get data on other factors, which influence the extent to which men and women are unequal, such as polygamy, seclusion, legal rights, etc., we would find even greater variation between different economies and cultures. These cannot readily be explained without taking into account factors other than merely varying economic conditions. We, therefore, conclude that there is a possibility for discretionary changes, though it may be neither easy nor painless to make them.

While cross-country comparisons also show that progress toward equality in one respect is no guarantee of progress in all other respects, they provide no evidence of negative relationships. Increasing women's labor force participation does not appear to increase occupational segregation or depress their wages as compared to those of men. Thus, based on this data, there appears to be no cause to worry about negative feedback. There is also evidence both in the Union of Soviet Socialist Republics and in Sweden that the government has played a significant role. In previous chapters of this book, we have considered existing and possible future policies that might be used in the United States to reduce inequality between men and women in opportunities and economic outcomes. Our review of the experience of other countries leads us to be reasonably optimistic about the potential role of government intervention in this area.

SUGGESTED READINGS

BENERIA, LOURDES, ed. *Women and Development. The Sexual Division of Labor in Rural Societies.* NY: Praeger, 1980.

BOSERUP, ESTER, *Women's Role in Economic Development.* New York: St. Martin's Press, 1970.

LAPIDUS, GAIL WARSHAFSKY, *Women in Soviet Society.* Berkeley, CA: University of California Press, 1978.

LAYARD, RICHARD AND JACOB MINCER, eds. *Growth of Women's Labor*

Force: Causes and Consequences. Chicago: University of Chicago Press, 1985.
ROOS, PATRICIA,   *Gender and Work: A Comparative Analysis of Industrial Societies.* Albany, NY: SUNY Press, 1985.
SCOTT, HILDA, *Does Socialism Liberate Women? Experiences from Eastern Europe:* Boston. Beacon Press, 1974.
UNITED NATIONS,   *The Economic Role of Women in the ECE Region.* New York, 1980.
YOUSSEF, NADJA,   *Women and Work in Developing Societies.* Berkeley: University of California Press, 1974.

EPILOGUE

We have seen throughout this book that women's role in the economy has been changing rapidly in recent decades. We also learned that many policies affecting women have been changing, albeit often slowly, in ways that have tended to enhance their status as compared to men. At the same time, however, we showed that we are far from having achieved equality between the sexes. What does all this portend for the future?

On the basis of the low birthrate, the continuing tendency of young women to get more, and more job-oriented, education, the growing recognition that husbands and wives do not always live together happily forever after, and the increasing acceptance of the two-earner family, we would expect the labor force participation of women to continue to increase, though not necessarily as rapidly as in the 1970s. If new technology should greatly reduce the demand for clerical workers—still by far the largest single source of employment for women—or if the general unemployment level should continue to remain high, women's labor force participation rate may rise relatively slowly for some time. But virtually no reasonably foreseeable conditions are expected to cause an actual downturn.

As the labor force participation of women remains high and is likely to continue to increase, young women will be even more likely to invest in their human capital in preparation for market work and to continue moving into less traditional occupations. Both these trends should continue to reduce the male-female earnings gap, most likely at a faster pace than in the past. To the extent that existing laws and regulations are enforced, labor market discrimination should be reduced. This, too, would be expected to directly contribute to a narrowing of the pay gap and also to encourage women to further broaden their horizons.

At the same time, increased experience with women workers should reduce statistical discrimination and prejudice to the extent that these are based on stereotypical ideas of women as unsuited for nontraditional jobs, while women's growing attachment to the labor force should help to counter the view that they are unstable workers. Finally, as women stay in the labor market more consistently and for longer periods of time, and as those few who have been successful help to open the doors and smooth the path for others, women may be expected not only to move into a greater variety of occupations but also to rise to higher levels within them. All of this does not mean that occupational segregation or the earnings gap are likely to disappear overnight. It is possible that they will never disappear entirely. This does not detract from the importance of any substantial move in that direction. The experience of other countries, like Sweden, suggests that substantial increases in economic equality between men and women are certainly feasible, given appropriate government policies.

Next to occupational segregation and the earnings gap, the disparity between men and women that has for a long time proved most resistant to change has been in the amount of time devoted to housework. The amount of market work done by women has been increasing rapidly, but, until recently, there has been little evidence of men doing more work in the household. To the extent that the "housework gap" diminished in the seventies, this was because of a decline in time devoted to housekeeping by women, both full-time homemakers and participants in the labor force. Smaller families, the availability of attractive market substitutes for home-produced goods and services, and possibly tolerance of less exacting standards of housekeeping most likely contributed to this trend. In the 1980s, there was also some evidence of growing participation of husbands in housework. Because the increase was largest among younger men, there is good reason to expect this trend to continue. Thus, men and women in the "liberated" family of the future may share household tasks and also find ways of reducing the work that needs to be done.

Lest this concluding section sound too much like a prediction of utopia, it should be noted that not all market work is fun, challenging, and highly paid. There are dangerous jobs in mines, boring jobs on assembly lines, jobs with low pay and low prestige in laundries. Similarly, it would be unrealistic to assume that housework can be reduced to a well-scheduled and minimal routine, so that it will never interfere with a career. Appliances break down, family members become ill, children expect parents to be present at school events at unpredictable times. As long as work is often a chore, and as long as job and household responsibilities tend to come into conflict, there will be problems in allocating responsibilities in the two spheres among spouses. There will also be people who will look back with nostalgia to the days when such problems did not exist, because men and women each knew their place.

Nonetheless, more and more couples continue to opt for two jobs and two paychecks. While men have clearly not been as eager to participate in housework as women have been to take on market work, they appear to be increasingly willing to make some compromises to accommodate the two-earner lifestyle. Virtually all signs point toward a continuation of these trends. The only real question is at what rate further changes are likely to take place.

Author Index

Weinberg, C. B., 129n
Weir, T., 133n
Weiss, J., 315n
Weiss, Y., 261n
Weitzman, L. J., 197n, 198n
Welter, B., 30n
Wertheimer, B. M., 274n
White, L., 125n
Wilson, E. O., 18n
Withey, S. B., 133n
Wolcott, C., 16n
Woodrow, K., 123n

Woods, M. E., 126n
Wright, J. D., 133n

Y

Youssef, N., 306n, 333n

Z

Zabalzo, A., 325n
Zellner, H., 185n

Subject Index

351